VOTES FOR WOMEN

The women's suffrage movement is central to any study of gender and political history. *Votes for Women* provides an innovative and unrivalled re-examination of the movement, presenting new perspectives and dimensions which challenge existing literature on this subject.

This fascinating book charts the history of the movement in Britain from the nineteenth century to the postwar period, assessing important figures such as Emmeline Pankhurst and the militant wing and Millicent Garrett Fawcett, leader of the constitutional wing. The stories of forgotten women, such as Lily Maxwell and Lady Constance Lytton are told as well as Jennie Baines's link with international suffrage movements. In addition, there are reappraisals of the ideas of British suffragism; of campaigns of women teachers; of the neglected Women's Freedom League; of interwar activity, and of life away from the metropolis. An illuminating first chapter, which reviews the way that suffrage accounts have been written, illustrates how women's history remains contested ground. *Votes for Women* examines the importance of the suffrage movement to women's general emancipation in the twentieth century, and discusses its role as catalyst to women's social and political equality.

June Purvis is Professor of Women's and Gender History at the University of Portsmouth and **Sandra Stanley Holton** is Senior Australian Research Fellow in History at the University of Adelaide, Australia

Women's and Gender History

General Editor
June Purvis
Professor of Women's and Gender History, University of Portsmouth

Published
Lynn Abrams and Elizabeth Harvey
Gender relations in German history: power, agency and experience from the sixteenth to the twentieth century

Elizabeth Crawford
The Women's Suffrage Movement: a reference guide 1866–1928

Shani D'Cruze
Crimes of outrage: sex, violence and Victorian working women

Carol Dyhouse
No distinction of sex? Women in British universities, 1870–1939

Bridget Hill
Women, work and sexual politics in eighteenth-century England

Linda Mahood
Policing gender, class and family: Britain, 1850–1940

June Purvis (editor)
Women's history: Britain, 1850–1945

Gillian Scott
Feminism and the politics of working women: the Women's Co-operative Guild, 1880s to the Second World War

Wendy Webster
Imagining home: gender, 'race' and national identity, 1945–64

Barbara Winslow
Sylvia Pankhurst: sexual politics and political activism

Jane McDermid and Anna Hillyar
Midwives of the revolution: female Bolsheviks and women workers in 1917

VOTES FOR WOMEN

Edited by June Purvis and
Sandra Stanley Holton

London and New York

First published in 2000
by Routledge
2 Park Square, Milton Park, Abingdon, Oxon, OX14 4RN

and

Simultaneously published in the USA and Canada
by Routledge
270 Madison Ave, New York NY 10016

Routledge is an imprint of the Taylor & Francis Group

Transferred to Digital Printing 2009

© 2000 Edited by June Purvis and Sandra Stanley Holton

Typeset in Times by
J&L Composition Ltd, Filey, North Yorkshire

British Library Cataloguing in Publication Data
A catalogue record for this book is available from the British Library

Library of Congress Cataloging in Publication Data
A catalog record for this book has been requested

ISBN 0–415–21458–0
ISBN 0–415–21459–9

Publisher's Note
The publisher has gone to great lengths to ensure
the quality of this reprint but points out that some
imperfections in the original may be apparent.

This book is dedicated with deep affection to OLIVE BANKS, Emeritus Professor of Sociology at Leicester University. She was appointed as Professor in 1973, the first woman professor at Leicester. Olive has published a number of books on feminism including (with J. A. Banks) Feminism and family planning in Victorian England (Liverpool University Press, 1965), Faces of feminism (Martin Robertson, 1981), The biographical dictionary of British feminists, Vols 1 and 2 (Harvester Wheatsheaf, 1985 and New York University Press, 1990), and The politics of British feminism, 1918–1970 (Edward Elgar, 1993).

CONTENTS

CONTENTS

LIST OF CONTRIBUTORS

Johanna Alberti teaches for the Open University. She is the author of
Beyond suffrage: feminists in war and peace, 1914–1928 (Macmillan,
1989) and Eleanor Rathbone (Sage, 1996), as well as articles and chapters on British feminism in the interwar period.

Christine Bolt is Professor of American History at the University of Kent at
Canterbury. Her publications include The anti-slavery movement and
reconstruction (Oxford University Press and Institute of Race Relations,
1969); Victorian attitudes to race (Routledge, 1971); A history of the USA
(Macmillan, 1974); Power and protest in American life (co-author with A.
T. Barbrook, Martin Robertson and St Martin's Press, 1980); Anti-
slavery, religion and reform (co-editor with Seymour Drescher, Dawson
and Archon, 1980); American indian policy and American reform (Unwin
Hyman, 1987); The women's movements in the United States and Britain
(Harvester Wheatsheaf and University of Massachusetts Press, 1993);
Feminist ferment (UCL Press, 1995).

Hilary Frances teaches in a secondary school. Since completing a PhD in
women's history at the University of York in 1996, she has written several
articles, including entries for the New dictionary of national biography,
about the lives of Edwardian suffragists who continued to be active feminists concerned with issues of sexual politics during the interwar years.

June Hannam is a Principal Lecturer in History in the Humanities Faculty,
University of the West of England, Bristol. She is the author of Isabella
Ford, 1855–1924 (Blackwell, 1987) as well as numerous articles on
women and politics in the nineteenth and early twentieth centuries. She is
currently writing a book with Dr Karen Hunt on socialist women,
1880–1920s.

Sandra Stanley Holton is a Senior Research Fellow in the Department of
History in the University of Adelaide, South Australia. She is the author
of Feminism and democracy: women's suffrage and reform politics in
Britain 1908–1918 (Cambridge University Press, 1986) and Suffrage

days: stories from the women's suffrage movement (Routledge, 1996), as well as numerous articles and chapters on women's suffrage. She is currently researching the life of the Quaker and suffragist, Alice Clark.

Janet Howarth is a Fellow and Tutor in Modern History at St Hilda's College, Oxford and a member of the inter-faculty committee that runs the Oxford Masters course in Women's Studies. Her publications include an edition of Emily Davies's The higher education of women, articles on the history of women's education and contributions to the History of the university of Oxford.

Marie Mulvey-Roberts is a Senior Lecturer in English at the University of the West of England, Bristol. The author of British poets and secret societies (Croom Helm, 1989) and Gothic immortals: the fiction of the Brotherhood of the Rosy Cross (Routledge, 1992), she has edited over forty books including Sources, perspectives and controversies in the history of British feminism (1993–1995). Currently she is the co-editor of the journal Women's Writing.

Alison Oram is Reader in Women's Studies at Nene University College Northampton and author of Women teachers and feminist politics 1900–1939 (Manchester University Press, 1996). She has also published a number of articles on her two main research interests, twentieth-century British feminism, and lesbian history. She is co-editor of a forthcoming source book on nineteenth- and twentieth-century British lesbian history, to be published by Routledge.

June Purvis is Professor of Women's and Gender History at the University of Portsmouth. She has published widely on women's education in nineteenth-century England and is the Founding and Managing Editor of the journal Women's History Review. Her publications include Researching women's lives from a feminist perspective (co-editor with Mary Maynard, Taylor & Francis, 1994); Women's history: Britain, 1850–1945 (editor, UCL Press, 1995); and The women's suffrage movement, new feminist perspectives (co-editor with Maroula Joannou, Manchester University Press, 1998). She is also the Editor for the Women's and Gender History Series with UCL Press, and is currently working on a book about Emmeline and Christabel Pankhurst.

Jane Rendall is a Senior Lecturer and Co-director of the Centre for Eighteenth-Century Studies, University of York. Her publications include The origins of modern feminism: women in Britain, France, and the United States, 1780–1860 (Macmillan, 1985), Women in an industrializing society: England 1780–1880 (Basil Blackwell, 1990), and, with Catherine Hall and Keith McClelland, Defining the nation (forthcoming, Cambridge University Press, 1999).

Judith Smart is a Senior Lecturer in History in the Department of Communication Studies, Royal Melbourne Institute of Technology, Australia. She has published works on working-class women and political protest during the First World War, on feminist Christian citizenship and the Housewives Associations in the first half of this century, and on feminist responses to venereal diseases legislation, 1915–1920. She is currently the editor of Australian Historical Studies and is working on a book on Melbourne during the Great War of 1914–1918.

ACKNOWLEDGEMENTS

Chapter 6, 'Deeds, not words: daily life in the Women's Social and Political Union in Edwardian Britain', by June Purvis, is reprinted in a slightly revised form from the article 'Deeds, not words', Women's Studies International Forum, Vol. 18, 1995, pp. 91–101, with permission from Elsevier Science.

Figures 1, 2 and 3 appear by kind permission of Manchester Central Library, Local Studies Unit.

The print in Figure 4 was supplied by the J. B. Morrell Library, University of York.

Figures 5, 6 and 7 are from the Private Suffrage Collection of June Purvis.

ILLUSTRATIONS

INTRODUCTION

The campaigns for votes for women

June Purvis and Sandra Stanley Holton

The campaigns for the parliamentary vote for women in Britain and Ireland, as well as biographical accounts of some of the figures involved in such activities, have been the subject of extensive research.[1] As Jane Lewis notes, the agitation for women's suffrage is usually dated from John Stuart Mill's 1865 campaign to be elected to parliament, although the subject had been discussed much earlier.[2] Votes for women was part of Mill's election address and, unusually for the time, three middle-class pioneers of the early women's movement, namely Barbara Bodichon, Emily Davies and Bessie Parkes, campaigned on his behalf. The following year, in the context of the debates about the Second Reform Bill which was imminent in parliament, Bodichon asked Mill if he would present a petition in favour of women's suffrage. Mill agreed, advising that anything less than one hundred signatures of support would probably do 'more harm than good'.[3] Bodichon then called together Emily Davies, Jessie Boucherett, Rosamond Hill and Elizabeth Garrett and formed the first Women's Suffrage Committee which worked hard for a fort-night to collect 1,500 'distinguished and respectable signatures'.[4] Although the petition was not successful, other suffrage committees were soon estab-lished with some of the activists, such as Lydia Becker and Millicent Garrett Fawcett, becoming central figures in the Victorian women's movement. Becker and Fawcett were what we may term 'constitutional suffragists' who advocated legal means of campaigning such as parliamentary lobbying. There were, however, 'divided counsels' within the movement,[5] especially over whether the demand for the parliamentary vote should include married women who, under the common law doctrine of coverture, were subsumed in the legal personhood of their husband and thus held no property or wealth in their own right, as well as single women. To demand the vote for married women was more problematic than seeking it for spinsters and widows since the franchise at this time was based upon the ownership or occupation of property; not all men, of course, were enfranchised under these terms either. Matters came to a head in 1874 when Becker, reluctantly, supported a proposed suffrage Bill that would specifically exclude married women, since she believed this would give the Bill greater support. Such actions alienated many of her more radical suffrage friends, such as Elizabeth Wolstenholme Elmy, Richard Pankhurst and Ursula and Jacob Bright, who, together with Emmeline Pankhurst, subsequently became active in the Women's Franchise League, established in 1889, and which included married women in its suffrage demand.[6] At the heart of these tensions, of course, were differing conceptions of women's citizenship and of the strategies to achieve it.[7]

When Lydia Becker died in 1890, Millicent Garrett Fawcett became the key figure in the Victorian women's suffrage movement, especially from 1897 when her hope of bringing about closer union and co-operation between the various societies was realised through the formation of the National Union of Women's Suffrage Societies (NUWSS). At its inception, the NUWSS was headed by an executive committee composed of representatives from the member societies. The executive committee had little power and few funds, functioning like a 'liaison' body between the member societies and parliament'.[8] Although Fawcett was the acknowledged leader of the NUWSS, it was not until 1907, when the NUWSS adopted a new constitution that provided for the election of officers, that she was elected President, a position she held until 1919.[9] The aim of the NUWSS was to obtain the parliamentary vote for women 'on the same terms as it is, or may be granted to men', a goal that was also adopted by the Women's Social and Political Union (WSPU), founded in 1903 by Emmeline Pankhurst and her eldest daughter, Christabel, together with some local women socialist suffragists.[10] Thus both societies upheld this limited claim for women's enfranchisement, seeing the key to the parliamentary franchise as being the breaking down of the sex barrier rather than pressing for the vote for all adults. Although the terms 'constitutional' and 'militant' are usually applied to the tactics of the NUWSS and WSPU, respectively, such a hard and fast distinction has been questioned in recent years. Holton, for example, argues that if 'militancy' involved a willingness to take the issue into the public realm of the street or if it indicated labour and socialist affiliations, then many 'constitutionalists' were also 'militant'; furthermore, if 'militancy' involved a preparedness to resort to extreme forms of violence, then few 'militants' were 'militant', and then only from 1912 onwards.[11] She also emphasises that neither the militant nor the constitutional wing of the movement was as unchanging or as coherent as these categories suggest since both wings experienced internal tensions and sometimes divisions.[12] Nevertheless, Holton and others also acknowledge that there were differences in policies and tactics between the NUWSS and WSPU which cannot be ignored.[13]

Emmeline Pankhurst's decision to found the WSPU was linked to a number of factors including her dissatisfaction with the way women's suffrage had been marginalised within the policies of the Independent Labour Party (ILP), of which she was a member, as well as her concern about the ineffectiveness of the tactics adopted by the NUWSS. In its early years the WSPU engaged in peaceful campaigning, but the limitations of such an approach were soon realised by both Emmeline and Christabel Pankhurst. On 12 May 1905, when a Women's Enfranchisement Bill was talked out of the House of Commons, Emmeline Pankhurst was amongst the crowd of nearly 300 women who heard the disappointing news as they waited in the Strangers' Lobby. Instantly she called upon the women to follow her in a protest against the government, in a way that 'no old-fashioned suffragist had ever attempted'.[14] Those who followed her condemned the government's action in allowing a small minority to talk out the Bill; the incident went relatively unnoticed, the police being content just to take the names of the 'offenders'.[15] Although Emmeline Pankhurst claimed in her ghost-written autobiography, *My own story*, that this was the first 'militant' act of the WSPU, the beginnings of militancy are commonly associated with a protest that took place at the Free Trade Hall, Manchester, some five months later.[16] Christabel Pankhurst, the Chief Organiser and strategist of the WSPU, in consultation with her mother and Annie Kenney, a recent working-class recruit to the WSPU, decided that this more confrontational approach was necessary since it would bring publicity to the women's cause. Thus, on 13 October 1905, Christabel and Annie heckled a leading Liberal politician with the question 'Will the Liberal Government, if returned, give votes to women?', creating a disturbance for which both young women were roughly ejected from the hall. Once outside, Christabel deliberately committed the technical offence of spitting at a policeman in order to court arrest. Charged with disorderly conduct, both women chose, as intended, short prison sentences rather than pay a fine.[17] Such 'militant' action had the desired effect in that women's suffrage suddenly became newsworthy, in a way it had never been before. Furthermore, heckling of parliamentary candidates became a common tactic as well as marches and demonstrations to parliament, to demand the vote. The aim of this strategy was to pressurise the government to bring in a women's suffrage measure, but as the government failed to do so, a second stage of militancy erupted, especially from 1912, when the 'suffragettes', as WSPU members became known, engaged in a range of terrorist acts against property, such as mass window-breaking, setting fire to empty buildings and post boxes, pouring acid on golf courses and cutting telephone and telegraph wires.

How effective militant tactics were in winning the parliamentary vote for women has been a matter of debate amongst historians with a number of influential writers asserting that the more extreme forms of militancy were counter-productive.[18] Nevertheless, the sex barrier against women exercising the parliamentary vote was broken in 1918 and a partial victory won when, under the Representation of the People Act, women over the age of 30 were allowed to vote if they were householders, the wives of householders, occupiers of property with an annual rent of £5 or more, or graduates of British universities.[19] The campaigners for women's suffrage knew that full parliamentary voting rights for women could not be indefinitely delayed, and this was attained ten years later, on 2 July 1928, when women and men who had reached the age of 21 could vote on equal terms.[20]

The essays in this Volume reflect many of the new directions taken by historians of the women's suffrage movement in recent years. Fresh appraisals of the nature and achievements of the campaigns for the parliamentary vote for women follow from these new directions, as this collection sets out to demonstrate. The great complexity of ideas and values that generated and were generated by women's claim to enfranchisement, from the nineteenth century to 1928, for example, is now a subject of extensive analysis.[21] Similarly, there is a greater readiness to recognise how rhetorical strategies may have inflected shifts in the argument and the new forms of actions that were introduced into the twentieth-century campaigns. Christine Bolt's chapter on 'The ideas of British suffragism' explores some of these issues. As she notes, '[T]here is no satisfactory simple explanation of the complex course of suffragist arguments: of why women from frequently similar backgrounds favoured differing intellectual emphases; of why some activists neglected and others concerned themselves with ideology; and of why some individuals developed their thinking about the vote over time, while others did not'.[22] Other chapters in this Volume, such as that by June Purvis on Emmeline Pankhurst, the most in/famous of all the suffrage leaders, looks at how such ideas and values interacted with a particular life. Similarly, Janet Howarth's chapter traces how the trauma of early widowhood informed the views and actions of another of the major figures in the leadership of the movement, Millicent Garrett Fawcett. Marie Mulvey-Roberts, in her account of the militant suffragette Lady Constance Lytton, analyses her involvement in terms of the shape her life had taken prior to the suffrage campaigns, and the meaning of the hunger-strike within that specific context.

The recovery of lost or excluded stories remains an important task for historians of women, for stories like those of Jennie Baines and Lily Maxwell, as told in the chapters by Judith Smart and Jane Rendall respectively, often serve to throw into question established frameworks. Thus, in recent years, as discussed earlier, historians have come to question earlier interpretations which took as self-evident the meaning of terms such as 'militant'. Smart adds to this reappraisal by showing us how the life of Jennie Baines had 'a continuity in militant activism across decades and hemispheres. It was a life driven by a practical working-class feminist consciousness and experience.'[23] In her new home of Australia, Baines became one of the founding members of the anti-war Women's Peace Army, formed in July 1915. She and another ex-suffragette, Adela Pankhurst, youngest daughter of Emmeline Pankhurst, were active during 1917 in organising demonstrations in support of free speech where they drew upon the militancy of their suffrage days.

Similarly, there is also now an increasing readiness among historians to acknowledge that the ideology of the suffrage movement was never fixed or monolithic. It was, indeed, often internally contradictory, a contradiction that is intrinsic to the feminist project. As Nancy Cott argues, 'Feminism is nothing if not paradoxical. It aims for individual freedoms by mobilizing sex solidarity. It acknowledges diversity among women while positing that women recognize their unity. It requires gender consciousness for its basis, yet calls for the elimination of prescribed gender roles.'[24] Moreover, a number of the chapters in this Volume, such as those by Alison Oram on women teachers and suffrage, Johanna Alberti on the women's movement 1918 to 1928, Hilary Frances on the Women's Freedom League (WFL) and June Purvis on the WSPU, illustrate that ideas about sexual equality might take on varying meanings in particular contexts. Oram, for example, illustrates how women teachers, at the height of the suffrage movement from 1908 to 1914, made their arguments for the parliamentary vote on the basis of equal rights with men, stressing their 'professional sameness' with men teachers and the human responsibilities of citizenship rather than emphasising women's gender 'difference' in comparison with men.[25] On the other hand, Purvis's chapter on the daily lives of women in the WSPU reveals that a constant theme in WSPU rhetoric was women's 'difference' from men and the common bonds of sisterhood that united all women irrespective of social class, age or political affiliation.

Several of the chapters in this Volume also emphasise the importance of both the local political context and wider debates within radicalism for the dynamics of suffrage campaigning. Thus the case of Lily Maxwell, examined here by Jane Rendall, takes on a fresh significance. Her name appeared on a Manchester electoral roll in 1867 and reflected a degree of support for women's rights among radical opinion within that city. With the encouragement of local suffragists, she cast a vote on behalf of the Radical-Liberal Jacob Bright who was to prove a long-time friend to the cause in parliament. This apparent breakthrough led the national suffrage movement to shift its focus from parliament to the courts for a period thereafter, and no Bill went before parliament until it had been decided by the courts that women had no right to vote. The picture drawn from the metropolitan focus of earlier suffrage histories is also challenged further by June Hannam's analysis of suffrage campaigns in other regions. As she emphasises, 'it is difficult to understand the growth of the suffrage campaign into a mass movement in the Edwardian period without recognising how much of this was due to the liveliness, enthusiasm and sheer hard work of the provincial branches'.[26] Local branches could initiate new developments, as well as carry out directives from the centre. Hannam further points out that a study of women's involvement in the suffrage movement at the local level is critical for understanding the process by which women became politicised, especially through friendship networks that could help to sustain political activity in often hostile environments. Membership of the NUWSS, she finds, was drawn from well-educated, wealthy, middle-class women who, in many cases, were often seen as closely allied to the Liberal Party. Contrary to the assumption made in most mainstream texts, it appears that working-class women were more likely to be involved in suffrage campaigns in the regions as members of the WSPU, rather than the NUWSS.

Of course, new feminine identities emerged alongside the campaigns for women's rights as various chapters in this Volume illustrate: the 'independent woman', such as Lily Maxwell, who rested her claim to vote on her capacities as property holder and working woman (Rendall); or the 'militant suffragette/suffragist' who engaged in political activism in the public sphere of men (Purvis, Mulvey-Roberts and Frances); or the 'professional woman' to be found within the relatively new occupation for women of state school teacher, one where claims to citizenship meshed also with claims to proper remuneration and recognition of women's equal roles and responsibilities as the educators of future citizens (Oram); or the 'charismatic, militant, woman leader' explored in Purvis's study of Emmeline Pankhurst, or the 'statutory woman' whose emergence in the inter-war period is discussed by Johanna Alberti.

The creation of such new 'types' of womanhood entailed a simultaneous and related challenge to prevailing notions of how political life and the public sphere were constituted. For these ways of conceptualising set up a dichotomy between the domestic sphere of women and the public world of men, one on which the case for women's exclusion from the parliamentary franchise was frequently based. It was a dichotomy that ignored the actuality of most women having to work for a living; of women's role, even within the domestic ideology, as the nurturers and educators of male voters. In the course of the suffrage campaigns, then, advocates of 'the cause' established new conceptions of citizenship, and modified the classic Liberal understanding of the public sphere, and of what might constitute the 'independence' on which radical claims to citizenship had long rested.

Alongside the ideological and activist aspects of the campaigns for the vote, there is now also a greater readiness to acknowledge the *cultural* significance of the suffrage movement.[27] It was not the simple, single-issue demand as it has so often been represented. In identifying and articulating women's claims to enfranchisement, suffragists contested the very gender order itself, most especially in an insistence on the embodied nature of citizenship. Hence the demand for the vote, of necessity, went beyond issues of formal politics to contest, for example, the sexual subjection of women that followed from the legal doctrine of coverture, from low wages, from state regulation of prostitution. This is vividly illustrated in the chapter by Hilary Frances on the WFL and in the chapters by Purvis on Emmeline Pankhurst and on the WSPU.

The suffrage legacy for the interwar period is also re-evaluated here in the work by Johanna Alberti and Hilary Frances. Rather than seeing it as a period of decline or fragmentation, such studies seek to establish this as a period of diversification for the women's movement, and specialisation within it. They also identify clear continuities rather than rupture between the suffrage movement and the interwar women's movement. While social and political diversity always characterised the suffrage movement and its inheritors, the capacity to generate notable degrees of solidarity also needs to be recognised. More particularly, historians of the present day estimate the capacity to build a new woman-centred political culture and agenda as one of the most important achievements of the campaigns for the vote.[28]

All this is not to say that a single, uniform account of the suffrage movement in Britain is to be found within this Volume. Its history remains contested ground, and ground upon which a range of established perspectives have to be engaged with and re-evaluated. This issue is the concern of Sandra Holton's analysis of the making of suffrage history, which forms the following chapter.

NOTES

1 See, for example, Roger Fulford, *Votes for women: the story of a struggle* (London, Faber & Faber, 1957); Josephine Kamm, *Rapiers and battleaxes: the women's movement and its aftermath* (London, Allen & Unwin, 1966); David Mitchell, *The fighting Pankhursts: a study in tenacity* (London, Jonathan Cape, 1967); Marian Ramelson, *The petticoat rebellion: a century of struggle for women's rights* (London, Lawrence & Wishart, 1967); Constance Rover, *Women's suffrage and party politics in Britain 1866–1914* (London, Routledge & Kegan Paul, 1967); R. S. Neale, Working-class women and women's suffrage, in his *Class and ideology in the nineteenth century* (London, Routledge & Kegan Paul, 1972); Antonia Raeburn, *The militant suffragettes* (London, Michael Joseph, 1973); Andrew Rosen, *Rise up women! the militant campaign of the Women's Social and Political Union 1903–1914* (London, Routledge & Kegan Paul, 1974); Martin Pugh, Politicians and the women's vote, *History*, 59, 1974, pp. 358–374; David Morgan, *Suffragists and liberals: the politics of woman suffrage in England* (Oxford, Basil Blackwell, 1975); Midge Mackenzie, *Shoulder to shoulder, a documentary* (London, Allen Lane, 1975); Antonia Raeburn, *The suffragette view* (Newton Abbot, David & Charles, 1976); Richard J. Evans, *The feminists: women's emancipation movements in Europe, America and Australasia 1840–1920* (London, Croom Helm, 1977); David Mitchell, *Queen Christabel, a biography of Christabel Pankhurst* (London, MacDonald and Jane's, 1977); Jill Liddington and Jill Norris, *One hand tied behind us: the rise of the women's suffrage movement* (London, Virago, 1978); Jane Marcus, Transatlantic sisterhood: labor and suffrage links in the letters of Elizabeth Robins and Emmeline Pankhurst, *Signs*, 3, 1978, pp. 744 -755; Martin Pugh, *Electoral reform in war and peace 1906–18* (London, Routledge & Kegan Paul, 1978); Brian Harrison, *Separate spheres: the opposition to women's suffrage in Britain* (London, Croom Helm, 1978); Martin Pugh, *Women's suffrage in Britain 1867–1928* (London, the Historical Association, 1980); Julie Holledge, *Innocent flowers: women in the Edwardian theatre* (London, Virago, 1981); Olive Banks, *Faces of feminism: a study of feminism as a social movement* (Oxford, Martin Robertson, 1981);

Caroline Morrell, *'Black Friday': violence against women in the suffragette movement* (London, Women's Research and Resources Centre, 1981); Linda Edmondson, Sylvia Pankhurst: suffragist, feminist or socialist? in Jane Slaughter and Robert Kern (eds), *European women on the left: socialism, feminism, and the problems faced by political women, 1880 to the present* (Westport, Greenwood Press, 1981), pp. 76–100; Brian Harrison, The act of militancy: violence and the suffragettes, 1904–1914, in his *Peaceable kingdom: stability and change in modern Britain* (Oxford, Oxford University Press, 1982), pp. 26–81; Leslie Parker Hume, *The National Union of Women's Suffrage Societies 1897–1914* (New York and London, Garland Publishing, 1982); *The life and writings of Ada Nield Chew*, remembered and collected by Doris Nield Chew (London, Virago, 1982); Brian Harrison, Women's suffrage at Westminster, in Michael Bentley and John Stevenson (eds), *High and low politics in Modern Britain* (Oxford, Oxford University Press, 1983), pp. 80–122; Elizabeth Sarah, Christabel Pankhurst: reclaiming her power (1880–1958), in D. Spender (ed.), *Feminist theorists: three centuries of women's intellectual traditions* (London, Women's Press, 1983), pp. 256–284; Lindy Moore, The woman's suffrage campaign in the 1908 Aberdeen by-election, *Northern Scotland*, 5, pp. 155–178; Les Garner, *Stepping stones to women's liberty* (London, Heinemann Educational Books, 1984); Rosemary Cullen Owens, *Smashing times: a history of the Irish women's suffrage movement 1889–1922* (Dublin, Attic Press, 1984); Jill Liddington, *The life and times of a respectable rebel, Selina Cooper (1864–1946)* (London, Virago, 1984); Sybil Oldfield, *Spinsters of this parish: the life and times of F. M. Mayor and Mary Sheepshanks* (London, Virago, 1984); Martha Vicinus, Male space and women's bodies: the suffragette movement, in her *Independent women: work and community for single women 1850–1920* (London, Virago, 1985); Elspeth King, *The Scottish women's suffrage movement* (Glasgow, People's Palace Museum, 1985); Dale Spender and Carole Hayman (eds), *How the Vote was Won and other suffragette plays* (London, Methuen, 1985); Sandra Stanley Holton, *Feminism and democracy: women's suffrage and reform politics in Britain 1900–1918* (Cambridge, Cambridge University Press, 1986); Olive Banks, *Becoming a feminist: the social origins of 'first wave' feminism* (Brighton, Wheatsheaf, 1986); David Rubinstein, *Before the suffragettes: women's emancipation in the 1890s* (Hemel Hempstead, Harvester, 1986); Lisa Tickner, *The spectacle of women: imagery of the suffrage campaign 1907–1914* (London, Chatto & Windus, 1987); Brian Harrison, *Prudent revolutionaries: portraits of British feminists between the wars* (Oxford, Oxford University Press, 1987); Susan Kingsley Kent, *Sex and suffrage in Britain 1860–1914* (Princeton, Princeton University Press, 1987); Barbara Castle, *Sylvia and Christabel Pankhurst* (Harmondsworth, Penguin Books, 1987); Jane Lewis (ed.), *Before the vote was won: arguments for and against women's suffrage 1864–1896* (London, Routledge & Kegan Paul, 1987); Philippa Levine, *Victorian feminism 1850–1900* (London, Hutchinson, 1987); Tierl Thompson (ed.), *Dear girl: the diaries and letters of two working women 1897–1917* (London, Women's Press, 1987); Patricia W. Romero, *E. Sylvia Pankhurst, portrait of a radical* (New Haven and London, Yale University Press, 1987); Jane Marcus (ed.), *Suffrage and the Pankhursts* (London, Routledge & Kegan Paul, 1987); Lisa Tickner, Suffrage campaigns, in *The Edwardian era*, ed. Jane Becker and Deborah Cherry (London, Phaidon Press and Barbican Art Gallery, 1987), pp. 100–116; Ann Morley with Liz Stanley, *The life and death of Emily Wilding Davison* (London, Women's Press, 1988); Diane Atkinson, *Votes for women* (Cambridge, Cambridge University Press, 1988); Jihang Park, The British suffrage activists of 1913: an analysis, *Past and Present*, 120, August 1998, pp. 147–162; Iris Dove, *Yours in the cause: suffragettes in Lewisham, Greenwich and Woolwich* (London,

Lewisham Library Services and Greenwich Libraries, 1988); Cliona Murphy, *The women's suffrage movement and Irish society in the early twentieth century* (Hemel Hempstead, Harvester, 1989); Hilda Kean, *Deeds not words: the lives of suffragette teachers* (London, Pluto Press, 1990); Philippa Levine, *Feminist lives in Victorian England: private roles and public commitment* (Oxford, Basil Blackwell, 1990); Lis Whitelaw, *The life and rebellious times of Cicely Hamilton, actress, writer, suffragist* (London, Women's Press, 1990); Les Garner, *A brave and beautiful spirit: Dora Marsden 1882–1960* (Aldershot, Avebury, 1990); Sandra Stanley Holton, 'In sorrowful wrath': suffrage militancy and the romantic feminism of Emmeline Pankhurst, in Harold L. Smith (ed.), *British feminism in the twentieth century* (Aldershot, Edward Elgar, 1990), pp. 7–24; Leah Leneman, *A guid cause: the women's suffrage movement in Scotland* (Aberdeen, Aberdeen University Press, 1991); Kay Cook and Neil Evans, 'The petty antics of the bell-ringing boisterous band?' The women's suffrage movement in Wales, in Angela V. John (ed.), *Our mothers' land: chapters in Welsh women's history 1830–1939* (Cardiff, University of Wales Press, 1991), pp. 159–188; Ellen Carol Dubois, Woman suffrage and the left: an international socialist-feminist perspective, *New Left Review*, 186, March/April 1991, pp. 20–45; Rowena Fowler, Why did suffragettes attack works of art?, *Journal of Women's History*, 2, Winter 1991, pp. 109–125; David Rubinstein, *A different world for women: the life of Millicent Garrett Fawcett* (Hemel Hempstead, Harvester Wheatsheaf, 1991); Elspeth King, The Scottish women's suffrage movement, in Esther Breitenbach and Eleanor Gordon (eds) *Out of bounds: women in Scottish society 1800–1945* (Edinburgh, Edinburgh University Press, 1992), pp. 121–150; Martin Pugh, *Women and the women's movement in Britain 1914–1959* (Basingstoke, Macmillan, 1992); Diane Atkinson, *The purple, white and green: suffragettes in London 1906–14* (London, Museum of London, 1992); Marj van Helmond, *Votes for women: the events on Merseyside 1870–1928* (Great Britain, National Museums & Galleries on Merseyside, 1992); Ian Bullock and Richard Pankhurst (eds), *Sylvia Pankhurst, from artist to anti-fascist* (Basingstoke, Macmillan, 1992); Sheila Stowell, *A stage of their own: feminist playwrights of the suffrage era* (Manchester, Manchester University Press, 1992); Barbara Caine, *Victorian feminists* (Oxford, Oxford University Press, 1992); Christine Bolt, *The women's movements in the United States and Britain from the 1790s to the 1920s* (Hemel Hempstead, Harvester Wheatsheaf, 1993); Leah Leneman, *Martyrs in our midst: Dundee, Perth and the forcible feeding of suffragettes* (Dundee, Abertay Historical Society, 1993); Gillian Hawtin, *Votes for Wimbledon women* (no publisher and place given, 1993); Kathryn Dodd (ed.), *A Sylvia Pankhurst reader* (Manchester, Manchester University Press, 1993); Jo Vellacott, *From liberal to labour with women's suffrage, the story of Catherine Marshall* (Montreal and Kingston, McGill-Queen's University Press, 1993); Jane Rendall, Citizenship, culture and civilisation: the languages of British suffragism, 1866–1894 and Sandra Stanley Holton, From anti-slavery to suffrage militancy: the Bright circle, Elizabeth Cady Stanton and the British women's movement, both in Caroline Daley and Melanie Nolan (eds), *Suffrage and beyond: international feminist perspectives* (Auckland, Auckland University Press, 1994), pp. 127–150 and pp. 213–233, respectively; the John Innes Society, *Dorset Hall 1906–1935: a house, a family, a cause, votes for women!* (Merton, John Innes Society, 1994); Jane Eldridge Miller, Suffragette stories, Chapter 4 of her *Rebel women: feminism, modernism and the Edwardian novel* (London, Virago, 1994); Sandra Stanley Holton, 'To educate women into rebellion': Elizabeth Cady Stanton and the creation of a transatlantic network of radical suffragists, *The American Historical Review*, 99, 4, 1994, pp. 1112–1136; Jacqueline de Vries, Gendering patriotism: Emmeline and Christabel Pankhurst and World War One, in Sybil Oldfield (ed.) *This working-day world, women's lives and culture(s) in Britain 1914–1945* (London, Taylor & Francis, 1994), pp. 75–88; June Purvis, A lost dimension? The political education of women in the suffragette movement in Edwardian Britain, *Gender and Education*, 6, 1994, pp. 319–327; Glenda Norquay (ed.), *Voices and votes: a literary anthology of the women's suffrage campaign* (Manchester, Manchester University Press, 1995); June Purvis, 'Deeds, not words': the daily lives of militant suffragettes in Edwardian Britain, *Women's Studies International Forum*, 18, 1995, pp. 91–111; June Purvis, The prison experiences of the suffragettes in Edwardian Britain, *Women's History Review*, 4, 1995, pp. 103–133; Maroula Joannou, 'She who would be politically free herself must strike the blow': suffragette autobiography and suffragette militancy, in Julia Swindells (ed.), *The uses of autobiography*, London, Taylor & Francis, 1995), pp. 31–44; George J. Barnsby, *Votes for women: the struggle for the vote in the Black Country 1900–1918* (Wolverhampton, Integrated Publishing Services Company, 1995); Sandra Stanley Holton, Women and the vote, in June Purvis (ed.) *Women's history: Britain, 1850–1945* (London, UCL Press, 1995), pp. 277–305; Christine Bolt, *Feminist ferment: 'the woman question' in the USA and England, 1870–1940* (London, UCL Press, 1995); Angela V. John, *Elizabeth Robins: staging a life* (London and New York, Routledge, 1995); Louise Ryan, *Irish feminism and the vote: an anthology of the Irish Citizen newspaper 1912–1920* (Dublin, Folens, 1996); Verna Coleman, *Adela Pankhurst, the wayward suffragette 1885–1961* (Melbourne, Melbourne University Press, 1996); Karen Hunt, *Equivocal feminists: the Social Democratic Federation and the woman question 1884–1911* (Cambridge, Cambridge University Press, 1996); June Purvis, A 'pair of . . . infernal queens'? A reassessment of the dominant representations of Emmeline and Christabel Pankhurst, first wave feminists in Edwardian Britain, *Women's History Review*, 5, 1996, pp. 259–280; Sandra Stanley Holton, *Suffrage days: stories from the women's suffrage movement* (London, Routledge, 1996); Barbara Winslow, *Sylvia Pankhurst: sexual politics and political activism* (London, UCL Press, 1996); Ian Christopher Fletcher, 'A star chamber of the twentieth century': suffragettes, Liberals, and the 1908 'Rush the Commons' case, *Journal of British Studies*, 35, 1996, pp. 504–530; Caroline J. Howlett, Writing on the body? Representation and resistance in the British suffragette accounts of forcible feeding, *Genders*, 23, 1996, pp. 3–41; Cheryl Law, *Suffrage and power, the women's movement 1918–1928* (London and New York, I. B. Tauris, 1997); Angela V. John and Claire Eustance (eds), *The men's share? Masculinities, male support and women's suffrage in Britain, 1890–1920* (London and New York, Routledge, 1997); Barbara Caine, *English feminism 1780–1980* (Oxford, Oxford University Press, 1997); Barbara Green, *Spectacular confessions: autobiography, performative activism, and the sites of suffrage 1905–1938* (Basingstoke, Macmillan, 1997); Sandra Stanley Holton, British freewomen: national identity, constitutionalism and languages of race in early suffragist histories, in *Radical femininity: women's self-representation in the public sphere* (Manchester, Manchester University Press, 1998), pp. 149–171; Cheryl R. Jorgensen-Earp, *'The transfiguring sword', the just war of the Women's Social and Political Union* (Tuscaloosa and London, University of Alabama Press, 1997); Maroula Joannou and June Purvis (eds), *The women's suffrage movement, new feminist perspectives* (Manchester, Manchester University Press, 1998); Harold L. Smith, *The British women's suffrage campaign 1866–1928* (Harlow, Addison Wesley Longman, 1998); Claire Eustance, Joan Ryan and Laura Ugolini (eds), *Themes and directions in British suffrage history, a reader* (London, Cassell Academic, 1999); June Purvis, Emmeline Pankhurst (1858–1928): suffragette, militant feminist and champion of womanhood, in *Representing lives: women and autobiography*, eds Alison Donnell and Pauline Polkey (Basingstoke, Macmillan, 1999).

2 Lewis (ed.), *Before the vote was won*, p. 1.

3 Ray Strachey, *'The cause': a short history of the women's movement in Great Britain* (London, G. Bell & Sons, 1928), p. 104.

4 Ibid., p. 105.

5 Helen Blackburn, *Women's suffrage: a record of the women's suffrage movement in the British Isles with biographical sketches of Miss Becker* (London, Williams & Norgate, 1902), p. 181.

6 Sandra Stanley Holton, Now you see it, now you don't: the Women's Franchise League and its place in contending narratives of the women's suffrage movement, in Joannou and Purvis (eds), *The women's suffrage movement*, p. 20, notes that the League was founded by Elizabeth Wolstenholme Elmy, Harriet McIlquham and Alice Scatcherd. The Married Women's Property Acts of 1870 and 1872, consolidated and advanced in 1882, did give a certain number of married women the necessary property qualification for the parliamentary vote. On these latter campaigns see especially Lee Holcombe, *Wives and property: reform of the Married Women's Property Law in nineteenth-century England* (Oxford, Martin Robertson, 1983); Mary Lyndon Shanley, *Feminism, marriage, and the law in Victorian England, 1850–1895* (Princeton, Princeton University Press, 1989).

7 Holton, *Suffrage days*, p. 40.

8 Hume, *The National Union of Women's Suffrage Societies*, p. 7. Lydia Becker had been the editor of the *Women's Suffrage Journal*, the first periodical devoted exclusively to women's suffrage. On her death, the journal ceased to exist.

9 See Rubinstein, *A different world for women*, p. 154 and p. 252. For a fuller comparison of militants and constitutionalists see Holton, *Feminism and Democracy*, pp. 29–52.

10 Hume, *The National Union of Women's Suffrage Societies*, pp. 6–7; Rosen, *Rise up women!*, Chapter 3; Dame Christabel Pankhurst, *Unshackled: the story of how we won the vote* (London, Hutchinson, 1959), p. 44.

11 Holton, *Feminism and democracy*, p. 4.

12 Holton, Women and the vote, p. 290.

13 See Holton, *Feminism and democracy*; Morley with Stanley, *The life and death of Emily Wilding Davison*; Holton, 'In sorrowful wrath'; Krista Cowman, 'A party between revolution and peaceful persuasion': a fresh look at the United Suffragists, in Joannou and Purvis (eds), *The women's suffrage movement*, p. 78.

14 Emmeline Pankhurst, *My own story* (London, Eveleigh Nash, 1914), p. 43.

15 Ibid., p. 43. See also Rosen, *Rise up women!*, pp. 38–39.

16 Pankhurst, *My own story*, p. 43.

17 See Pankhurst, *Unshackled*, pp. 48–52.

18 See, for example, Harrison, *Separate spheres*, pp. 196–197; Arthur Marwick, *Women at war 1914–1918* (London, Fontana, 1977), pp. 25–26; Harrison, The act of militancy, p. 48 and p. 75; Morgan, *Suffragists and liberals*, p. 160, and Rosen, *Rise up women!*, pp. 243–245.

19 Rosen, *Rise up women!*, p. 266. See also Pugh, *Electoral reform in war and peace 1906–18*, Chapter 10.

20 See Law, *Suffrage and power*.

21 See Holton, *Feminism and democracy*, Chapter 1; Caine, *English feminism 1780–1980*.

22 Christine Bolt, The ideas of British suffragism, p. 34 in this Volume.

23 Judith Smart, Jennie Baines: suffrage and an Australian connection, p. 246 in this Volume.

24 Nancy F. Cott, Feminist theory and feminist movements: the past before us, in Juliet Mitchell and Ann Oakley (eds), *What is feminism?* (Oxford, Basil Blackwell, 1986).

25 Alison Oram, Women teachers and the suffrage campaign: arguments for professional equality, p. 214 in this Volume.

26 June Hannam, 'I had not been to London': women's suffrage – a view from the regions, p. 226 in this Volume.

27 See Tickner, Suffrage campaigns, and also her magnificent *The spectacle of women*; Stowell, *A stage of their own*; Miller, Suffragette stories, as well as the following chapters in Joannou and Purvis (eds), *The women's suffrage movement: new feminist perspectives*: Maroula Joannou, Suffragette fiction and the fictions of suffrage, pp. 101–116; Deborah Tyler-Bennett, Suffrage and poetry: radical women's voices, pp. 117–126; and Claire M. Tylee, 'A better world for both': men, cultural transformation and the suffragettes, pp. 140–156.

28 See, for example, Vicinus, Male space and women's bodies: the suffragette movement; Levine, *Feminist lives in Victorian England*; Purvis, A 'pair of . . . infernal queens'?

1

THE MAKING OF
SUFFRAGE HISTORY

Sandra Stanley Holton

INTRODUCTION

This chapter analyses early models of suffrage history, so as to explore the legacy within and against which the current generations of suffrage historians have defined their agendas for research.[1] I argue that two distinct founding schools of suffrage history, both feminist in perspective, were evident by 1914. These I categorise as the 'constitutionalist' and the 'militant' schools. Two main inheritors of these schools are distinguished, and termed the 'new-feminist' and 'masculinist' schools, within each of which I will identify several varieties, owing differing debts to the two founding schools.[2] Gendered perspectives characterise each of these schools, and by pursuing such a categorisation I seek an alternative way of thinking about suffrage history so as to incorporate gender and cultural contestation *within* that process, to look at the political-cultural formation of suffrage history, rather than the particular formal-political cast of any one school of interpretation.[3]

In distinguishing 'masculinist' from 'feminist' histories I do not intend, then, merely to be derogatory toward the former, though clearly such terms have rhetorical content that reflects my own political beliefs and social values. My principal aim, however, is to suggest an analytical framework for understanding some of the main differences in the varying schools of interpretation now to be encountered in suffrage history, to indicate some of the continuities and disjunctures in the historiography of this field, and to question any claims to greater rationality and objectivity presumed by many of the masculinist school.

THE CONSTITUTIONALIST SCHOOL OF
SUFFRAGE HISTORY

Constitutionalist histories were produced from within the movement from the early 1880s, and drew on a heritage of radical understandings of the libertarian origins of the British constitution in the social, political and legal organisation of Ancient British and Anglo-Saxon societies.[4] They tended to gloss over dissent and division because they were primarily polemical in intent. They adopted a measured tone of quiet confidence that the women's suffrage demand was part of the progressive movement of history. They also increasingly adapted their constitutionalist rhetoric to the new languages of race, and laid claim to, or assumed, the place of female Britons as the natural leaders of the international movement.[5] This was an essentially Whiggish and Anglocentric interpretation in which women of white, Anglo-Saxon descent were to lead the march, onward and ever upward, toward 'civilisation' and away from 'barbarism'.

Until very recently these 'official' histories have remained almost entirely ignored by the current generation of women's historians, largely, no doubt, because they make exceedingly dry reading, and are written from a stance with which few today might sympathise. Their writers took a long view of the past with regard to the position of women, sometimes going as far back as the Ancient Britons. Through such perspectives on the national past they sought to legitimate the demand for women's suffrage in terms of the cultural and political heritage of the 'freeborn Briton'.[6] They argued that women had earlier been included within the unwritten British constitution, most especially in terms of their position under Saxon law and governance. They provided evidence that British women, or at least women among past elites, had, in earlier ages, engaged in battle, held property in their own right, and voted for and participated in parliament. The last remnant of the earlier political recognition of women was the right of female succession to the British throne. Their demand was couched, then, in terms of the *restitution of the lost rights* of 'British freewomen'.

Such appeals to the ancient origins of the British constitution were a long-standing part of the rhetoric of British radicalism. Earlier radical movements had emphasised the Norman conquest and the imposition of 'the Norman yoke' (in the form of feudalism) as the key event in undermining the Saxon foundations of the British polity. Suffragists, however, offered a different perspective on such radical constitutionalism. Charlotte Carmichael Stopes's *British freewomen*, for example, adopted a different periodisation and chronology with regard to women's history. The feudal system was seen as not entirely destructive of the pre-existing constitutional rights of women, which lived on to some extent in 'church and cloister'. It was the gradual erosion of the feudal system and the enunciation in the seventeenth century by Sir William Blackstone of the legal doctrine of coverture that began, Charlotte Carmichael Stopes argued, 'the Long Ebb' in the position of women. Such decline was finally completed, by such accounts, in the 1830s, with women's express exclusion for the first time from the franchise in the 1832 Reform Act, an exclusion compounded by the voting provisions of the Municipal Corporations Act of 1834, and the ending of dower rights in this same period. From this vantage point on British history, suffragists were able to argue that women's enfranchisement also promised a return to the true basis of British democracy.

In consequence of this reading of British history, it was not uncommon for the constitutionalist history-writing of suffragists completely to ignore the ideas of the Enlightenment or of the French Revolution in explaining the origins of their movement. Mary Wollstonecraft rarely received acknowledgement in such accounts until the early twentieth century, as we shall see. In part this reflected a tendency for British radicals to distance themselves from Jacobinism, especially after the Terror, so that figures like Mary Wollstonecraft might come to stand for an un-British form of political extremism. Equally, her unconventional private life also made Mary Wollstonecraft an unlikely icon for a movement still bent on establishing the respectability and reasonableness of its demand. This is not to say that her work went unread by nineteenth-century suffragists. For many, especially among the Radical–Liberal suffragists who continually challenged for the leadership of the movement from its beginnings, her ideas remained a source of inspiration and hope. None the less, in their history-writing suffragists were more likely to identify their cause with earlier British movements of middle-class and popular radicalism: the Anti-Corn Law League, the anti-slavery movement and Chartism, for example.

Constitutionalist suffrage histories also inflected their sense of national identity with the language of racial superiority and imperial destiny. 'Freeborn Britons' were bearers of a particular legal and cultural contribution to the historical process, in a constitutional form of government based on a parliament which was, at least in part, elected by 'the people'. By the end of the nineteenth century suffragist historians had also begun to incorporate into their work the new 'scientific' discourses of racial difference, discourses that allowed them to place the 'English' (together with the United States movement, as each of 'Anglo-Saxon' origin) at the head of an 'ethnological' ordering of national movements for women's rights.[7] Some such sense also informed the 'imperial feminism' of this time, most especially on behalf of the women of peoples under British rule.[8]

Such a view of British history, and of its radical heritage, also shaped the forms of suffrage agitation. The petition to parliament was central to this, especially once recourse to the courts had proved a failure. Aimed initially at collecting evidence of opinion among women from influential social and political elites, this method was gradually adapted to the changing nature of British political life. As increasing numbers of working-class men were enfranchised under the 1867 and 1884 Reform Acts, the collection of petitions was also expanded so as to demonstrate more extensive, popular support. Similarly, that other long-established 'constitutionalist' practice, of holding major public meetings at key points in parliamentary politics, increasingly sought to attract working-class audiences. Leaders of the suffrage movement also began to seek out speakers who knew something of working-class life and politics. Equally, by the late 1870s, the suffrage meeting was beginning to move out of the middle-class drawing room and the town hall, to the village green and the town square. None the less, suffrage agitation remained essentially orderly and reasonable, still intended largely to educate public opinion, and to demonstrate to members of parliament a growing body of support at constituency level.

The National Union of Women's Suffrage Societies (henceforth, National Union), which was formed in 1897 by a reunification of long-established suffrage societies, carried the constitutionalist perspective into the twentieth-century agitation, while among its members were a number who were to continue to write suffrage history from the constitutionalist perspective. The suffrage movement had never been politically homogeneous, however. From the beginning of the campaigns in the mid-1860s there were continual tensions between Radical–Liberal suffragists and more moderate bodies of opinion, tensions that eventually led to organisational division. The first book-length history of the suffrage movement, Helen Blackburn's *Women's Suffrage* of 1902, was written from the perspective of the moderates. Starting out from the same perspective on British history presented some years before by Charlotte Carmichael Stopes, Helen Blackburn restated the case for women's suffrage in terms of a restitution to women of the place held by women within the ancient origins of the British constitution. She celebrated the dogged patience and trust in the methods of pressure-group politics on the part of suffragists, recounting the history of the movement in terms of its societies, committees, petitions and public meetings. Helen Blackburn also made central to her story the career of Lydia Becker (1827–1890), before her death the editor of the *Women's Suffrage Journal* and parliamentary secretary of the original National Society for Women's Suffrage. In consequence, her narrative is one that entirely 'writes out' the perspective and the campaigns of the Radical–Liberal suffragists, among whom Lydia Becker might originally have been counted, but from whom she had become alienated in her last years. Hence, Helen Blackburn downplays, where she does not completely ignore, the role of Radical suffragists like Clementia Taylor and Elizabeth Wolstenholme in helping to found the movement. Similarly, the suffragist origins of the campaign for repeal of the Contagious Diseases Acts in 1870 is also ignored, alongside the connections which Radical suffragists saw between the two issues. Division between moderates and Radical–Liberals over the exclusion of married women in the demand is also completely ignored, though it was one of the main issues that eventually fragmented the movement in the late 1880s.[9]

In turn, Helen Blackburn's history was reticent about the relation between the suffrage movement and party politics – the campaigns appear to have happened in a sphere quite divorced from the wider political arena. Yet they were, of course, necessarily shaped to some extent by the fortunes of Radical politics more generally. The demonised figure of William Ewart Gladstone, the Liberal leader for almost the whole of the nineteenth-century campaigns, is used to displace the need to recognise the extensive and increasingly bitter divisions within British radicalism in these decades, from which members of the suffrage leadership were unable to remain aloof. While Gladstone's opposition did considerable damage to the cause of women's suffrage at a number of key points, such a simplistic explanation prevented discussion of the relationship, for example, between the fortunes of the suffrage cause and that of Irish home rule, or the impact of the growing socialist movement of the 1890s on Radical suffragist opinion.[10]

There was no sustained counter to this constitutionalist perspective, or to the accounts of the moderate faction, until the advent of a 'militant' approach to suffrage campaigning in the early twentieth century. By that time some significant changes had already begun to occur within constitutionalist histories, perhaps most notably in W. Lyon Blease's *The emancipation of English women* (1910). Though this work also looked some centuries backward for the origins of the women's movement, it placed particular importance on the ideas of Mary Wollstonecraft. Also, it viewed women's suffrage as a natural progression in the development of English political institutions by reference to the liberal legacy of the Enlightenment, rather than by reference to the ancient origins of the British constitution. Like Millicent Garrett Fawcett in her subsequent histories and her current statements to the press, W. Lyon Blease acknowledged the importance of the advent of militant methods to the advance of the cause. He also, like her, explained militancy as a consequence of the failings of the Liberal government in its apparent 'ignorance of the meaning of liberty' and of 'the first principles of statesmanship'.[11]

Such perspectives were also to colour Ray Strachey's classic, *The cause* (1928), the last major history written from the constitutionalist perspective by a participant in the movement. *The cause* bore many of the marks of the constitutionalist view of history: it was fundamentally Whiggish, for example, in presenting the women's movement as part and parcel of the social and political progress of the nineteenth century.[12] But Ray Strachey also insisted that the main impetus for the women's movement came from the ideas of the French Revolution. She emphasised the importance of Mary Wollstonecraft's *Vindication of the rights of woman* as a work in which 'the whole extent of the feminist ideal is set out'. She also established the links between the suffrage movement and other radical movements, including Chartism, the Anti-Corn Law League and the anti-slavery campaigns. Unlike Helen Blackburn's history, she acknowledged the role of the middle-class Radical–Liberal circles of the 1860s in raising issues of women's rights, in social reform and in the new field of 'social science'. *The cause* placed considerable emphasis on the legal disabilities of women, especially of wives under coverture. It also reflected the influence of some of the new economic and social history that had begun to appear in the early twentieth century, much

17

of it by women historians. Hence, Ray Strachey emphasised the importance of the changes that accompanied the Industrial Revolution to the formation of a women's movement.[13]

But *The cause* also shows some evidence of the influence of the militant interpretations that had begun to appear prior to the First World War, and that had continued on in the form of memoirs. Ray Strachey's chapters on the twentieth-century campaigns provided, in consequence, an account that acknowledged both the constitutionalist and the militant contributions, though her references to the WSPU and its supporters were often far from complimentary or sympathetic. She wrote, for example: 'Its leaders did not scruple to brush aside the ordinary niceties of procedure, and they did not care who they shocked or antagonised . . . What they believed in was moral violence.' None the less, she also wrote: 'The affairs of the National Union during these astonishing years are not now of much moment', and so she gave somewhat greater coverage to the activities of the militants in these chapters, if often in derogatory terms. And consistently, she presented the differing methods of the two wings as mutually supportive. It was their combined efforts that 'made it impossible for anyone in the country to be unaware of the existence of the demand'.[14]

Ray Strachey vacillated, too, on the importance of militancy, especially after 1912. On the one hand, recording the split between the Pankhursts and the Pethick Lawrences at the end of 1912, she claimed: 'In sober fact . . . the militant movement was now at the end of its importance.' On the other hand she presented the funeral of Emily Wilding Davison the following year as a turning point in public opinion, when there was finally a general recognition that 'It was time that the struggle ended'. This ambivalence undoubtedly reflected some of the difficult inner struggles that Ray Strachey had herself undergone in deciding whether to go with the militants or stay with the constitutionalists.[15] And it has to be said that the treatment of the constitutionalists in the main militant histories was at least as ungracious as, and even more dismissive than, Ray Strachey's account of WSPU efforts. Finally, while both Helen Blackburn and Ray Strachey used biographical portraits in constructing their narratives, the lives reported in their works provided exemplars only – they did not carry the same burden, as makers of history, placed on individual actors in militant histories of the suffrage movement.[16]

THE MILITANT SCHOOL OF SUFFRAGE HISTORY

Militant histories were written from the perspective of the more assertive current that emerged in the early twentieth-century movement with the advent of the Women's Social and Political Union (henceforth, WSPU), founded by Emmeline Pankhurst in 1903.[17] It was the early militant histories, such as Sylvia Pankhurst's *The suffragette* (1911), that established a plot organised around the dichotomous categorisation of suffragists: as radicals or conservatives, as militants or non-militants, as populists or elitists. This was a plot in which clear continuities between nineteenth- and twentieth-century campaigns became almost invisible. Militancy was presented as an unequivocal break with the past, in its readiness to engage in 'the politics of disruption'. Equally, militant histories emphasised the role of heroic individuals in major processes of social change, not the gradual and progressive evolution of a society through its own organic capacity for development and growth.[18] Militant practices were also represented in terms of new, gendered forms of political protest, replacing the real violence of earlier male-led social movements, with feminised, 'symbolic' and non-personal kinds of violence.[19]

Like the early constitutionalist studies, the first militant histories were a form of campaign literature, and as such they also glossed over dissent and division within their own ranks. The focus was very much on the activities of the central leadership, and more especially Emmeline Pankhurst and her daughters, Christabel, Sylvia and, to a much lesser extent, Adela. Hence, a dissident militant, such as Dora Montefiore who helped form the early WSPU branches in London but was subsequently frozen out by its national leadership, also found herself excluded from the first book-length study of the militant campaigns, Sylvia Pankhurst's *The suffragette* of 1911.[20] The socialist suffragists Teresa Billington-Greig and Charlotte Despard, who were similarly ousted in 1907, and subsequently formed the Women's Freedom League, also received very short shrift in this account. These exclusions were compounded in Emmeline Pankhurst's *My own story*, published three years later. Moreover, some who figure prominently in *The suffragette,* but who subsequently left the WSPU, become excised from the militant narrative of *My own story*, including one of its earliest paid organisers and a former member of its national executive, Mary Gawthorpe.[21] Similarly, the significant split with Emmeline and Frederick Pethick Lawrence is quickly passed over here with the explanation: 'personal dissensions have never been dwelt upon in the W. S. P. U.'.[22] Possibly the manuscript for this book was completed too soon to offer any account of the split with Sylvia Pankhurst early in 1914, though there are some references to the overall situation at this time that would suggest otherwise.

Many of these omissions and deflections were more adequately addressed in Sylvia Pankhurst's *The suffragette movement*, published in 1931: Dora Montefiore's part in the formation of the early London WSPU, and in some of the earliest militant demonstrations, is recorded, albeit sometimes with details that serve to undermine any claim to her being a stalwart militant.[23] Similarly, Mary Gawthorpe, as a longstanding member of the WSPU's executive, retains a place in this chronicle, though her brilliance as a speaker and organiser is not recognised in the generous and warm terms to be found in Sylvia Pankhurst's earlier account. Mary Gawthorpe herself was evidently hurt by such dismissiveness, and it seems was spurred to begin her own memoirs in the years following the publication of *The suffragette movement*.[24] This later work also reflects to some degree on the splits of 1907 and 1912 and on Sylvia Pankhurst's own departure from the WSPU in 1914. Her analysis explains these events in terms of the lack of internal democracy within the WSPU, and, in the first two instances, the inflexibility of the main actors. With regard to her own separation from the WSPU, this is presented as no wish of hers, but as forced upon her by her older sister. Christabel Pankhurst is recorded as wishing for this because of the links Sylvia Pankhurst continued to maintain with parts of the socialist movement, the emphasis she put on working-class support and the democratic basis of her East London Federation of suffragettes, as well as the competition it represented for funds. In contrast, Christabel Pankhurst's *Unshackled* ignores the East London Federation altogether, and makes no mention of the split.[25]

Similarly, militant histories largely dismissed from consideration the earlier campaigns for the vote, and the continuing constitutionalist efforts on behalf of the cause. *The suffragette movement* is typical as a militant account in its minimal reporting of the nineteenth-century origins of the suffrage campaigns, and in its adoption of a negative vocabulary that designates constitutionalists merely as 'non-militants'. But it was also the first history to suggest the legacy of the Radical–Liberal suffragist current within the nineteenth-century campaigns. Here we find the first unambiguous reference in suffrage histories to the Women's Franchise League, formed in 1889 in opposition to the moderate leadership of the movement. Sylvia Pankhurst's account of this organisation is somewhat distorted by the partiality of family memory. It is important, none the less, for recognising, albeit to a severely limited degree, certain significant continuities between twentieth-century militancy and the nineteenth-century Radical–Liberal current, of which Richard Pankhurst was a founding member, and in which Emmeline Pankhurst served her apprenticeship as a suffrage campaigner.[26]

The diverging relationship of the two older Pankhurst sisters to socialism was further evident in the way each chose to recount the history of suffrage militancy, and the life of their mother Emmeline Pankhurst. By the 1930s, for example, Sylvia Pankhurst was identifying her mother's links with exiled Russian revolutionaries as 'the final spur which drove her to suffragette militancy'.[27] Similarly, she situated the beginnings of militancy quite clearly within the labour movement, especially socialist women's circles, both in *The suffragette movement*, and even more starkly in her life of her mother.[28] Christabel Pankhurst in *Unshackled* (1959) acknowledged how her mother 'turned to the Labour elements' in the 1890s out of her concern with 'the grim problem of poverty', and also records the founding of the WSPU among working-class socialist women. But she emphasised, too, how later Emmeline Pankhurst abandoned any faith in the labour movement, concluding that what was needed was the women's vote, which required 'starting an independent women's movement'. Similarly, Emmeline Pankhurst's identification with the Conservative Party shortly before her death is linked to her concern at this time with the 'constructive' use of the vote: 'To strengthen the British Empire and draw closer together its lands and peoples was a cause especially dear to her.'[29] Sylvia Pankhurst, in contrast, insisted that to the end 'some sort of socialism' was always at the back of her mother's political values.[30]

Hence, contrasting positions *within* the militant school of suffrage history were firmly established by the late 1950s. The diverging accounts of the WSPU and of the life of Emmeline Pankhurst provided by Sylvia and Christabel Pankhurst subsequently provided many of the elements in the quite distinct socialist-feminist and radical-feminist accounts that began to appear from the late 1960s, to which I will return. What characterised militant histories in general, however, was a celebration of the politics of disruption, a focus on the immediate context of the early twentieth-century campaigns, and a refusal to search back into the mists of time in order to establish women's place within the foundations of the British constitution. Equally, in *The suffragette movement* there is only a brief acknowledgement of the ideas of Mary Wollstonecraft and Mary Astell. Far more emphasis is placed on the social origins of Emmeline and Richard Pankhurst in 'the democratic traditions' of Manchester, in their links with popular radical movements of the nineteenth century, such as Chartism, secularism and republicanism, even communism 'in a broad sense'.[31]

Of still greater significance in the formation of a distinct militant school of suffrage history was the influence of Romanticism on historical interpretation, most especially in terms of the burden placed upon the actions of heroic individuals in securing social change. Central to the plot of militant histories, then, are not the considered deliberations of committees and the staged set-pieces of the public hall meeting. Instead, the story revolves around the wilful acts of heroic individuals bent on making themselves forces of change. Here, history is not the steady, organic process celebrated by the constitutionalists. Rather history is made when change is wrested from the established order by its overthrow. Such change has to be willed by, and requires sacrifice from, those individuals heroic enough to resist tyranny and in this way render themselves forces of history.[32] Militant histories differ also in their frame of vision. The action tends not to occur in the committee room, the drawing room or the town hall, but on the street corner, at the hustings, and, above all, in the prison cell. The narrative is organised far less than in constitutionalist histories in terms of events within the House of Commons. The ceaseless rush from one demonstration, court appearance, gaol sentence, or hunger-strike to the next determines the pace and the structure of the narrative.

This underlying theory of history helps to explain in large part why the militant histories of the suffrage movement all took the form of biography or autobiography.[33] Such a tendency was further encouraged from the early 1930s when militants began to feel that their version of their movement's history was increasingly being undermined or subverted, as the first of what I shall term the 'masculinist' accounts began to appear. The Suffragette Fellowship was formed with the clear intention of keeping alive both the spirit and the historical claims of the militant suffragists. It proceeded to gather in as many memoirs as it could, especially from those who had gone to prison, and undergone the hunger-strike and forcible feeding. By these means, it insisted upon 'the agency and comradeship' of women in winning the enfranchisement of their sex.[34]

THE MASCULINIST SCHOOL OF SUFFRAGE HISTORY

George Dangerfield's *The strange death of Liberal England*, first published in 1935, was among the first and most influential of the masculinist histories written in the English language.[35] Unlike the earlier feminist school, it spoke from outside the movement and adopted the stance of a sardonic, disenchanted Olympian to whom the suffrage campaigns of the early twentieth century appeared as a symptom of both social and individual pathology. This was to be only the first of several varieties of masculinist histories of the suffrage movement, and will be identified here as the 'sardonic-masculinist' perspective. It evidenced some of what were to become the distinguishing features of masculinist histories: the viewing of a political movement among women as by definition a deviant, marginal and even dangerous aberration from the established, essentially androcentric narratives concerned with the history of male elites; the gendered assumptions about what properly constitutes 'political' activity; the narrow interpretation of the meaning of the suffrage demand for women; the mocking and marginalisation of suffragists by the deployment of sexist stereotypes; the celebration of exclusionary male political subcultures; the tendency to 'blame the victim' for the failings of successive Liberal governments, acting against their own basic principles, and resorting to censorship of and brutality toward their female opponents.

George Dangerfield's study was brilliantly written and contained many insights on the nature of Edwardian politics. Its rhetorical strategies were so powerful that, as Jane Marcus has remarked, it established a plot from which few subsequent narratives have been able entirely to break free.[36] In one important respect, however, it is a derivative work. It accepts the main lines of analysis put forward in *The suffragette movement*, for example, in its focus on the Pankhurst leadership; in assuming a major disjuncture in suffrage history occasioned by the advent of the WSPU; in identifying 'militancy' as the defining contribution of the British suffrage movement to women's political practice. But it also overdraws those lines, like the caricaturist working from a likeness, to ridicule by its distortion of particular features. George Dangerfield's method is to suggest the false-heroic and, hence, the comic dimensions of the suffrage campaigns. This is black comedy, however, not merely the hackneyed misogyny of anti-suffrage propaganda cartoons and postcards, one which presents the movement as the symptom of a social pathology within Britain, and a psychological pathology among individual women activists. Ironically, it may be through this re-drawing of her portrait of the movement that Sylvia Pankhurst's original interpretation has had some of its greatest influence.

In his analysis of the women's suffrage movement George Dangerfield adopted some of the fashionable language and concepts from the comparatively new field of psychoanalysis. Hence, the militant suffrage movement, like the Tory rebellion over Ireland, and the widespread labour unrest, was described as a symptom of a 'neurosis' that in turn reflected the death of any respect for 'the processes of democratic government'. He looked for the cause within the 'irrational and unconscious element' of 'the human soul', an element he identified especially with the emergence of women as a force in political life. He read the suffrage movement as a moment when woman had become 'suddenly aware of her long-neglected masculinity'. He linked militancy with the emergence in 1912 of what he termed the 'homosexual movement'. This 'pre-war lesbianism' George Dangerfield characterised as 'more sensitive than sensual', reflecting woman's decision to depart from the company of men so as to 'go out into the wilderness' and 'be alone with herself and her sisters'.[37]

Here was some high-flown name-calling which set the tone for a descent into a demeaning ridicule of the militant wing of the suffrage movement, in references, for example, to 'eldritch screams' and the 'effeminate men' who offered their support to these demented women. Hiding beneath the 'scientific' language of psychoanalysis, then, was an androcentric view of history: one that worked with a sense of the otherness of the female, and that associated women with the unconscious, irrational wellsprings of the uncontrolled and undisciplined in human nature. Civilisation, most especially in terms of liberal parliamentary democracy, depended on women's happy acquiescence in the security of a properly 'masculine' control over such forces. While men's failure to exercise this control was represented as a major factor in the pathology of Edwardian Britain, women's militancy became a symptom of that failure. The militant campaigns were viewed in consequence as a 'brutal comedy' of 'ludicrous appearance'. Any proper assessment of the deliberate mistreatment of militants by the authorities, in line with government directives, was neatly avoided by reference to the 'unhealthy pleasures' that the suffragette martyrs derived from their suffering. Emily Wilding Davison was described as 'a very unbalanced girl', 'so implosive, so capricious, and so hysterical'. In fact, she was at this time a woman in her late twenties, who left, for those who chose to look, ample evidence of a highly developed moral sense, and of the thoughtful deliberations that preceded her actions. Similarly, Christabel Pankhurst was defined as 'a ruthless and intractable spirit', and her actions described in terms of her 'fastidiousness and snobbery', her 'delusions of grandeur'. After all this, there is a hollowness to George Dangerfield's call to his readers to 'honour' the militants for doing what had to be done.[38]

Militant suffragists were consistently diminished in this account, not only by its lofty satire, but also in being made merely the vehicle of a historical process or victims of their own individual pathology, not activists seeking with a clear degree of deliberation to revolutionise sexual relations. It is also the case, of course, that the nature of the continuing constitutionalist campaigns provided evidence quite counter to George Dangerfield's thesis. It is noteworthy that his bibliography included only the accounts of leading figures from the militant wing, and quite ignored those written from a constitutionalist perspective, including the relevant section of Ray Strachey's major work, *The cause*. George Dangerfield's account was so powerfully written and argued, however, that it continued to inform masculinist histories well into the 1970s, for example, in the varieties of social and individual pathology that provide the interpretative framework for Andrew Rosen's *Rise up women!* or David Mitchell's vituperative *Queen Christabel*.[39] All these writers appear to be progressive in their political values, yet this is consistently undermined by a masculinism that emphasised the otherness, the strangeness, the difference, and ultimately the ridiculousness of women in pursuit of their own political and personal ends.

Not all masculinist history, of course, has been written in the sardonic mode. Brian Harrison is never less than considered in his analysis of aspects of the suffrage movement.[40] He dismisses, for example, interpretations that present militancy as 'reflecting the instability of the female temperament' or explain it in terms of 'group psychologism'. Instead, he insists that militancy stemmed from 'temporary tactical necessities', and as such had an immediate rationale. He interprets suffrage militancy, then, as a kind of political pragmatism, albeit one that brought a 'paralysis of intellectual responsibility' and eventually a total loss of political judgement, so that it 'often led nowhere'.[41] Here, then, is a fresh variety of suffrage history which may best be termed 'liberal-masculinist', on the one hand rejecting the sardonic mode of George Dangerfield and those he has influenced, and sympathetic to the ultimate goal of the campaigns, but on the other unable entirely to break away from gendered perspectives on political practice, most notably in analyses of women's militancy.

Brian Harrison is far more positive about the constitutionalists, and those he dubs 'the prudent revolutionaries' in the interwar period. He credits this section of the suffrage movement, and its successors, with working solidly and tenaciously to educate public opinion, and to establish their tactics, strategies and policies on a sound understanding of the processes of British parliamentary politics. Where George Dangerfield took his lead entirely from militant histories, Brian Harrison largely shares the constitutionalist perspective on the women's suffrage movement, and provides some insightful comparison between the histories produced by each wing.[42] There is also evident a degree of vacillation about militancy which recalls aspects of Ray Strachey's work.

Brian Harrison is impressed, for example, with the argument of Harold Laski, reflecting on his own past as a WSPU sympathiser, that appeals to reason will never be sufficient where fundamental social change is the object sought. An element of the irrational, the spontaneous, the passionate is also essential. Brian Harrison is positive, therefore, about some aspects of early militancy, but he sees the clandestine and escalating violence of militancy between 1912 and 1914 as responsible for the failure of a Liberal government to enfranchise women. It was mistaken, by this estimation, because it was tactically inept, politically wrong-headed. At one point, for example, he suggests that the aims of militancy became transformed through its practice – from the pursuit of the vote 'towards repudiating women's subservience to man'. However, this insight is quickly abandoned when he none the less insists on measuring its success in terms of the extent to which it was 'counter-productive for winning the vote'.[43]

By such lines of interpretation the male electorate and male politicians are let off the hook. Late militancy is blamed for undermining completely the achievements of the constitutionalists in educating public opinion for such change, and in adopting politically adept strategies. Militant women defeated the women's cause, not the prejudices of Prime Minister Herbert Asquith, or the cynical wheeler-dealing of Chancellor of the Exchequer David Lloyd George, or the evident lack of any sustained political will to broker a solution acceptable to the majority of suffragists and of the government.[44] Yet the feasibility of such an outcome was proven by the government's successful moves in July 1914 to reach some such agreement, moves that would have ensured the enfranchisement of women by any subsequent Liberal government if the domestic political scene had not been disrupted by the outbreak of war.

In his early work Martin Pugh goes still further to argue that the women's movement had little to do with the eventual enfranchisement of women in 1918. He ignores the widespread sympathy among women suffragists for a universal suffrage so as to present the 1918 Representation of People Act, with its adult-male suffrage provisions, as something suffragists 'reluctantly had to swallow'. He also interprets the co-operation between constitutionalists and the Labour Party from 1912 to the outbreak of war as a symptom of fragmentation and disintegration, apparently ignorant of the consultations between women suffragists and members of the Speaker's conference on franchise reform in 1916. Martin Pugh has moderated these claims somewhat in his more recent studies, presumably in the light of more recent feminist scholarship. Subsequently, he has acknowledged the effectiveness of the National Union's pre-war political strategy, and how suffragists succeeded in keeping their 'machine ticking over' despite the disruptions of war.[45]

As with the ridicule of the sardonic-masculinist interpretations and the more measured criticisms of liberal-masculinist accounts, some socialist historians have also proceeded by assessing the women's suffrage movement by criteria external to its own goals. This socialist-masculinist variety of suffrage history rehearses arguments that were put forward by Marxist and socialist critics of the women's movement in the late nineteenth and early twentieth centuries. It serves to subsume the power relations of the gender order within society under those between economic classes. Accordingly, the women's movement appears, from such a perspective, as a dangerous, bourgeois diversion from the class struggle.[46] In an early essay, for example, Bridget Hill dismisses the suffrage movement as an agent of women's emancipation because it was founded on a middle-class individualism that 'completely obscured the class basis of women's oppression'. R. S. Neale more fully acknowledged the presence of working-class suffragists, but lighted on the memoirs of Annie Kenney to establish that they were no more than the dupes, the tools of middle-class women bent on using such support to their own interests. He insisted, for example, that the women's suffrage campaigns were 'never part of the class war', and that the suffragist leadership quickly forgot the needs of those working-class women it was able to recruit. He argued that the militants defined their goals too narrowly, and that working-class support for the suffrage movement represented 'misdirected energy'. By these lines of argument, he concluded that the suffrage movement 'divided women from women and women from men'.[47]

CONTEMPORARY FEMINIST SCHOOLS OF SUFFRAGE HISTORY

Elsewhere, I have written at length on the re-writing of suffrage history by a 'new-feminist' school of suffrage history, one that has itself produced two distinct varieties of suffrage history, in the differing perspectives of radical and of socialist feminists, since the late 1960s.[48] All I have space to do here is to indicate some of the characteristics of each, and their relation to the original feminist varieties of constitutionalist and militant interpretations of that history.

The radical-feminist historians of the present day share some significant aspects of the militant school of suffrage history. They celebrate, for example, the separate and autonomous political organisation of women, and women's courage, daring and ingenuity in the face of male power. There is, however, far less emphasis on the role of heroic individuals in radical-feminist interpretation. Liz Stanley, for example, traces instead the webs of love and friendship among women as sources of empowerment, and the shared moral and political values on which such relationships might be based.[49] Radical-feminist accounts also realise more fully than the earlier militant historiography the potential for a narrative organised in terms of a sex war, one for which there is indeed no shortage of evidence. Hence, radical-feminist historians reflect many of the concerns voiced by Christabel Pankhurst, often adopting methods of discourse analysis to explore sexual politics that underpinned the demand for the vote, especially in terms of critiques of marriage, of male sexual norms and mores, and of the conspiracy of silence around venereal disease that was broken during the militant campaigns.[50]

Though Sylvia Pankhurst retained the main plot of militant histories in *The suffragette movement*, she also suggested some of the later directions pursued subsequently by a new socialist-feminist history, especially in terms of her recognition of the role of socialist women in the movement, and of some parts of the labour movement. If present-day socialist-feminist historians may have found a lead in aspects of Sylvia Pankhurst's writing, over time they have also increasingly incorporated aspects of the constitutionalist contribution to suffrage history. As such, socialist-feminist suffrage history is something of a hybrid, drawing on both the militant and the constitutionalist historical legacy to construct a further fresh narrative. This situates women's suffrage as part of the long class struggle for more fully democratic forms of government in Britain, and recognises a social movement rather than heroic individuals as the motor for change.

Marian Ramelson provided the first full interpretation on these lines in her *Petticoat rebellion*. Here she regrets the 'political short-sightedness' of the WSPU's resistance to the adult suffrage demand, but also insists that the removal of the sex disqualification in the franchise is of equal significance to political advance, and emphasises the importance of working-class women to the revival of the suffrage cause. Similarly, Sheila Rowbotham, in her founding text for feminist history in Britain, *Hidden from history*, questions the working-class/middle-class dichotomy that informed those I have termed socialist-masculinist accounts, recognising the possibility for a degree of sexual solidarity among women of different classes, and the shared wrongs on which that might be based. Subsequently, the groundbreaking study by Jill Liddington and Jill Norris, *One hand tied behind us*, has demonstrated the particular contribution of working-class women to the early twentieth-century campaigns in the Manchester region. Similarly, my own earlier work focused on the relations between the suffragist and labour and socialist movements so as to argue the importance of a 'democratic suffragist' current that crossed the constitutionalist-militant organisational divide.[51] More recently still, new-feminist studies of the suffrage movement have incorporated the perspectives of cultural history and postcolonial studies. What all varieties of new-feminist scholarship share is an appreciation of the suffrage campaigns as a site of gender contestation, where stereotypes of conventional femininity were challenged and overturned, and feminised conceptions of political life and radical protest were promoted.

CONCLUSION

The history of the suffrage movement, like all history, is contested ground, and remains always a provisional and partial form of knowledge. The position from which historians write will necessarily be reflected in their interpretations. Suffrage history became one of the fields in which, unusually, women historians early on established two of the major frameworks for interpretation. These frameworks were shortly adapted, however, to the masculinist perspectives of a profession which remained, until this present generation, almost entirely male, and which has tended to diminish, if not to deny, the achievements of the suffrage movement.

Such a viewpoint reflects something of a lofty knowingness about the realities of political life and social structure which suffragists are supposed to have misjudged and misunderstood: suffragists are alternately blamed for attempting to deny the differences among women, and then put down because of the evidence of an inability to maintain complete unanimity on issues and policies – an inability reflecting the very diversity among women. Arguments such as these have been based on some gross over-simplifications – it proves possible for suffragists to have a clear sense, for example, of the variety among themselves, whilst also at points recognising where the wrongs of their sex crossed class, national and political boundaries.

One of the principal weaknesses of masculinist accounts has been a too narrow understanding of the cultural significance of women's militancy. Even those who find many of the later actions of militants ethically doubtful and politically inept cannot deny the importance of militancy as a feminist 'discourse of interruption', one that gave to women a political voice even while they remained formally outside the constitution.[52] Nor ought the radical new feminine 'type' or identity that was created in the figure of the suffragette be so readily dismissed in assessing the achievements of the suffrage movement.[53]

There is equally a contradiction in the way masculinist history criticises the suffrage movement for being one-dimensional in its pursuit of a single issue, while dismissing concerns with the sexual exploitation of women as pathological. The suffrage movement can be interpreted as narrow or disordered in approach only by an almost wanton blindness to the sexual politics intrinsic to the suffrage campaigns. Masculinist histories also consistently underrate the symbolic and cultural force, both of the winning of the vote, and of women's militancy. Similarly, it is difficult to understand why the political achievements of the suffrage movement are either denied or diminished in masculinist accounts – Asquith and Lloyd George evidently found it necessary to treat seriously with suffragists in the month or so before the outbreak of war, and the Speaker's conference adopted a formula for women's suffrage which had been worked out as an acceptable compromise by significant sections of the prewar movement. All this would, quite properly, count as a considerable achievement if it were evident in a political movement among men, and analysing that achievement and placing it on record remain central to the project of feminist history.

NOTES

1 In some quarters within the new feminist scholarship, of course, there was a turning away from any interest in 'pioneers' or in political women activists as atypical. See, for example, an early manifesto for feminist history, C. S. Rosenberg, The new woman and the new history, *Feminist Studies*, 3, 1975, pp. 185–198, esp. pp. 186, 188. J. Scott, Women's history, in her *Gender and the politics of history* (New York, Columbia University Press, 1988), pp. 15–27, offers a revaluation of what she terms the 'her-story approach', acknowledging its many achievements, but insisting also on the importance of studies which had, by adopting a broader definition of 'politics', helped to break down the public–private dichotomy that organised the agendas of 'her-story'. I examine some aspects of this question in S. S. Holton, The suffragist and the 'average' woman, in *Women's History Review*, 1, 1992, pp. 9–24.
2 In this paper I adapt the usage of M. Lake, Historical reconsiderations IV. The politics of respectability: identifying the masculinist context, *Historical Studies*, 22, 1986, pp. 116–131, esp. p. 127, which categorises as 'masculinist' certain responses to the women's movement in Australia, where 'Feminists were mocked, abused and insulted' by the press of the day, and argues that such responses were culturally reproduced in the accounts of the building of the nation by subsequent generations of male historians. On the necessity of scepticism toward dominant views for 'a democratic practice of history', and the way largely masculine perspectives have shaped history-writing until very recently, see J. Appleby, L. Hunt and M. Jacob, *Telling the truth about history* (New York, W. W. Norton, 1994), esp. pp. 11, 7.
3 An alternative categorisation of suffrage history in terms of diverging 'liberal', 'socialist' and 'radical-feminist' perspectives is argued in J. Purvis, A 'pair . . . of infernal queens'? A reassessment of the dominant representations of Emmeline and Christabel Pankhurst, first-wave feminists in Edwardian Britain, *Women's History Review*, 5, 1996, pp. 259–280. My intention here is not to question the validity of that categorisation, indeed I will use some of these terms here in a similar way. Nor do I mean to suggest that only women may write 'feminist' history, or only men write 'masculinist' history. I seek, rather, to offer an additional way of thinking about suffrage history through examining the gender politics of its writing.
4 Most notably in C. C. Stopes, *British freewomen: their historical privilege* (London, Swan Sonnenschein, 1909, 4th edn [1894]). Also among these constitutional histories I would include, in chronological order, M. G. Fawcett, England, in

T. Stanton (ed.), *The woman question in Europe* (New York, G. P. Putnam & Sons, 1884), pp. 1–29; C. A. Biggs, Great Britain, in E. C. Stanton, S. B. Anthony and J. Gage (eds), *History of woman suffrage* (New York, Source Books, 1970 reprint, 6 vols [1881–1922]), III, pp. 834–894; H. Blackburn, *Women's suffrage: a record of the women's suffrage movement* (London, Williams & Norgate, 1902); H. Blackburn, Great Britain: efforts for the parliamentary franchise, in S. B. Anthony and I. Harper (eds), *History of woman suffrage*, Vol. IV, pp. 1012–1025; W. Lyon Blease, *The emancipation of English women* (London, Constable, 1910); B. Mason, *History of women's suffrage* (London, Sherratt & Hughes, 1912); M. G. Fawcett, *Women's suffrage: A short history of a great movement* (London, T. C. Jack, 1912); R. Strachey, *'The cause': A short history of the women's movement in Great Britain* (London, Virago, 1978 reprint [1928]). For the place of 'constitutionalism' in British radical thought, see J. A. Epstein, *Radical expression. Political language, ritual and symbol in England, 1790–1850* (Oxford, Oxford University Press, 1994), esp. Ch. 1.

5 For a fuller discussion of feminist usage of languages of race, see J. Rendall, Citizenship, culture and civilisation: the languages of British suffragists, 1866–74, in C. Daley and M. Nolan (eds), *Suffrage and beyond: international perspectives on women's suffrage* (Auckland, University of Auckland Press, 1994), pp. 127–150.

6 The discussion that follows draws on S. S. Holton, British freewomen: national identity, constitutionalism, and languages of race in early suffragist histories, in E. J. Yeo (ed.), *Radical femininity: women's self-representation in nineteenth- and twentieth-century social movements* (Manchester, Manchester University Press, 1998), pp. 149–171.

7 T. Stanton, Editor's preface, in Stanton (ed.), *The woman question*, p. vi.

8 See, for example, the special issue, Feminism, imperialism and race. A dialogue between India and Britain, *Women's History Review*, 3, 1994; A. Burton, *Burdens of history: British feminists, Indian women and imperial culture, 1865–1915* (Chapel Hill, University of North Carolina Press, 1994); Vron Ware, *Beyond the pale. White women, racism and history* (London, Verso Press, 1992).

9 Blackburn also downplays Lydia Becker's own radical origins, for which see A. Kelly, *Lydia Becker and the cause* (Lancaster, Centre for North-West Regional Studies, University of Lancaster, 1997), esp. p. 3. B. Mason, *Women's suffrage* is more even-handed in its recognition of some among the Radical–Liberal suffragist leadership, but even so, like Blackburn's history, it was essentially a piece of campaign literature, and so downplayed, where it did not ignore, division and dissent within the movement. Compare with S. S. Holton, *Suffrage days: stories from the women's suffrage movement* (London: Routledge, 1996), Chs 1–4.

10 The relation between women's suffrage and party politics first received more detailed analysis in C. Rover, *Women's suffrage and party politics* (London, Routledge & Kegan Paul, 1967). See also D. Morgan, *Suffragists and Liberals: the politics of woman suffrage in England* (Oxford, Basil Blackwell, 1975); L. P. Hume, *The National Union of Women's Suffrage Societies, 1897–1914* (New York, Garland Publishing, 1982); S. S. Holton, *Feminism and democracy: women's suffrage and reform politics, 1900–1918* (Cambridge, Cambridge University Press, 1986); Holton, *Suffrage days*.

11 Blease, *Emancipation of English women*, pp. 73–95, 249–269, esp. p. 269.

12 See also the stimulating analysis in K. Dodd, Cultural politics and women's historical writing. The case of Ray Strachey's *The Cause*, *Women's Studies International Forum*, 13, 1990, pp. 127–137.

13 Strachey, *The cause*, pp. 5, 30f., 64–69, 77f., 15, and pp. 12, 52, 231, and see her bibliography.

14 Strachey, *The cause*, pp. 12 and 309–310, and p. 302. It is in exploring some of these ambivalences that my assessment departs somewhat from that offered in Dodd, Cultural politics, though I agree overall with her argument.

15 Strachey, *The cause*, pp. 327, 332, and see the testimony of her daughter, Barbara Strachey, in her Introduction to ibid., p. 3.

16 See K. Dodd, Introduction. The politics of form in Sylvia Pankhurst's writing, in K. Dodd (ed.), *A Sylvia Pankhurst reader* (Manchester, Manchester University Press, 1993), pp. 1–30, esp. pp. 21–25, which discusses Sylvia Pankhurst's choice of the autobiographical form to counter Strachey's history.

17 I take the key works of militant history to be, in chronological order, E. S. Pankhurst, *The suffragette* (London, Emmeline Pankhurst, 1911); E. Pankhurst, *My own story* (London, Eveleigh Nash, 1914); A. E. Metcalfe, *Woman's effort, 1865–1914* (Oxford, Blackwell, 1917); E. S. Pankhurst, *The suffragette movement: an intimate account of persons and ideals* (London, Virago, 1977 reprint [1931]); E. S. Pankhurst, *Life of Emmeline Pankhurst* (New York: Kraus, 1969 reprint [1934]); C. Pankhurst, *Unshackled: the story of how we won the vote* (London, Cresset Women's Voices, 1987 reprint [1959]). Here, I have found especially helpful Dodd, Introduction, on the need to acknowledge form, rhetoric and historical context in analyses of the writing of Sylvia Pankhurst, but depart from her analysis in so far as I argue for the existence of a distinct militant school of suffrage history *prior* to any clearly articulated socialist-feminist account. My argument diverges from Purvis, 'Infernal queens', in the same respect.

18 J. Marcus, Introduction, in J. Marcus (ed.), *Women's suffrage and the Pankhursts* (London, Routledge & Kegan Paul, 1987), p. 17; Dodd, Politics of form, p. 16.Yet such methods had long been part of the existing Radical–Liberal suffragist repertoire for confronting and resisting a perceived tyranny; for example, in campaigning for repeal of the Contagious Diseases Acts in the 1870s and 1880s. J. Walkowitz, *Prostitution and Victorian society. Women, class and the state* (Cambridge, Cambridge University Press, 1980) argues that these campaigns prefigure suffrage militancy.

19 See S. S. Holton, 'In sorrowful wrath'. The Romantic feminism of Emmeline Pankhurst and suffrage militancy, in H. A. L. Smith (ed.), *British feminism in the twentieth century* (Aldershot, Edward Elgar, 1990), pp. 7–24, and S. S. Holton, Manliness and militancy: the gendering of the 'suffragette' identity, in A. V. John and C. Eustance (eds), The *men's share? Masculinities, male support and women's suffrage in Britain, 1890–1920* (London, Routledge, 1997), pp. 110–134.

20 D. Montefiore, *From a Victorian to a modern* (London, Edward Archer, 1927), p. 51.

21 For example, compare the two accounts with regard to Mary Gawthorpe's part in a Welsh by-election campaign in 1906, in E. S. Pankhurst, *The suffragette*, p. 98, and E. Pankhurst, *My own story*, p. 74.

22 E. Pankhurst, *My own story*, p. 261; see also the cursory treatment in C. Pankhurst, *Unshackled*, p. 226, while pp. 82–83 provided a short account of the split that resulted in the formation of the WFL and simply concluded: 'thus there were two militant organisations instead of one, and all ended happily'.

23 E. S. Pankhurst, *Suffragette movement*, esp. pp. 178, 237, and see also pp. 184, 192, 214, 228.

24 Holton, *Suffrage days*, p. 239–240. See also the passing references in C. Pankhurst, *Unshackled*, pp. 71, 92, which give no indication that Mary Gawthorpe was for some years a member of the WSPU's executive committee.

25 E. S. Pankhurst, *Suffragette movement*, pp. 265, 413, 517; E. S. Pankhurst, *Emmeline Pankhurst*, pp. 70, 110–115, 141.

26 See the discussion in S. S. Holton, Now you see it, now you don't: the Women's Franchise League and its place in contending narratives of the women's suffrage movement, in M. Joannou and J. Purvis (eds), *The women's suffrage movement, new feminist perspectives* (Manchester, Manchester University Press, 1998), pp. 15–36.

27 E. S. Pankhurst, *Emmeline Pankhurst*, p. 160. See also, Holton, 'Now you see it'.

28 The chapter 'The suffragette movement' in E. S. Pankhurst, *Emmeline Pankhurst*, pp. 46–67, links the commencement of militancy to the decision in 1899 to run Labour parliamentary candidates under the auspices of the Labour Representation Committee, the precursor to the Labour Party.

29 C. Pankhurst, *Unshackled*, pp. 34, 43, 297.

30 E. S. Pankhurst, *Emmeline Pankhurst*, p. 165, and compare with her mother's declaration of her support in 1927 for the 'Constitutionalists' and her opposition to the 'Revolutionaries', quoted in Dodd, Politics of form, p. 27.

31 E. S. Pankhurst, *Emmeline Pankhurst*, pp. 7–10, 27–30 and *Suffragette movement*, pp. 6, 17–21, 53-54, 89–97; C. Pankhurst, *Unshackled*, pp. 15, 29–30.

32 For a more extended discussion see Holton, Sorrowful wrath, pp. 11–16.

33 Dodd, Politics of form, pp. 19–21; and see also the discussion in H. Kean, Searching for the past in present defeat: the construction of historical and political identity in British feminism in the 1920s and 1930s, *Women's History Review*, 3, 1994, pp. 57–80.

34 For a more extended discussion, see L. E. N. Mayhall, Creating the 'suffragette spirit': British feminism and the historical imagination, *Women's History Review*, 4, 1995, pp. 319–344.

35 G. Dangerfield, *The strange death of liberal England* (London, Paladin, 1970 reprint [1935]). But see also, E. Halevy, *The rule of democracy, 1905–14* (London, Ernest Benn, 1961 reprint [first published 1932 in the French edn, and 1934 in the English edn]), pp. 490–527.

36 Marcus, *Suffrage and the Pankhursts*, p. 3, and for an example of her point, see R. C. K. Ensor, *England 1870–1914* (Oxford, Clarendon Press, 1936), pp. 397–399, 459–461, while for evidence of the longevity of this perspective, see N. F. Cantor, *The age of protest* (London, Allen & Unwin, 1970), pp. 3–23. Its influence is also evident in R. Fulford, *Votes for women: the story of a struggle* (London, Faber & Faber, 1957), a study that is otherwise the first example of the liberal-masculinist variety of suffrage history to be discussed below.

37 Dangerfield, *Strange death*, pp. 132, 133, 139, 140.

38 ibid., pp. 145, 155, 156, 157, 158, 146. Contrast with the interpretation in A. Stanley and L. Morley, *The life and death of Emily Wilding Davison* (London, Women's Press, 1988).

39 A. Rosen, *Rise up women! The militant campaigns of the Women's Social and Political Union* (London, Routledge & Kegan Paul, 1974), p. 196, explains late militancy as a kind of millenarianism, and p. 200 interprets the actions of Emily Wilding Davison in terms of a 'quasi-sexual fulfilment'. D. Mitchell, *Queen Christabel* (London, Macdonald & Jane, 1977), emphasises the lesbian circles in which Christabel Pankhurst moved, to establish his interpretation of her as a psychological and social deviant. For more extensive critiques of his account, see E. Sarah, Christabel Pankhurst: reclaiming her power, in D. Spender (ed.), *Feminist theorists: three centuries of women's intellectual traditions* (London, Women's Press, 1983); Purvis, 'Infernal queens'.

40 B. Harrison, *Separate spheres: the opposition to women's suffrage in Britain* (London, Croom Helm, 1978); Harrison, The act of militancy: violence and the suffragettes, 1904–14, in his *Peaceable kingdom: stability and change in modern Britain* (Oxford, Clarendon Press, 1982), pp. 226–281; Harrison, Women's suf-

frage at Westminster, in M. Bentley and J. Stevenson (eds), *High and low politics in modern Britain* (Oxford, Clarendon Press, 1983), pp. 80–122; Harrison, *Prudent revolutionaries: Portraits of British feminists between the wars* (Oxford, Clarendon Press, 1987).

41 Harrison, Act of militancy, pp. 28, 29, 30, 43, 72.

42 Ibid., pp. 77–80, and 72–73.

43 Ibid., p. 48, and *Separate spheres,* pp. 196–197. Similarly, Brian Harrison blames the slow advance of women's issues in the interwar period on the suffrage movement. He argues that its vision was too narrow, that it placed too much emphasis on a single issue, that it mistakenly believed the vote could alter the sexual order, that it sowed the seed of division and conflict among women; *Separate spheres,* p. 238.

44 Harrison, *Separate spheres* p. 91, even denies the misogyny of the male leadership of the Anti-Suffrage League, apparently on the grounds that they loved their mothers and/or wives, though on p. 98 he retracts so far as to admit there was sometimes 'what might be described as an intermittent or localised misogyny'.

45 M. Pugh, Politicians and the women's vote, *History,* 59, 1974, pp. 358–374, esp. pp. 358, 360, and compare M. Pugh, *Women's suffrage in Britain, 1867–1928* (London, Historical Association, 1980), esp. pp. 21, 33, 25, and *Women and the women's movement in Britain, 1914–1956* (London, Macmillan, 1992), esp. pp. 5, 12, 36. Contrast with Holton, *Feminism and democracy,* pp. 129–150.

46 For a thoughtful and subtle analysis of the position of the Social Democratic Federation on the women's question in this period, see K. Hunt, *Equivocal feminists: the Social Democratic Federation and the Woman Question, 1884–1911* (Cambridge, Cambridge University Press, 1996).

47 B. Hill, The emancipation of women, *Marxist Quarterly,* January 1956, pp. 40–57; R. S. Neale, Working-class women and women's suffrage, in his *Class and ideology in the nineteenth century* (London, Routledge & Kegan Paul, 1972), pp. 143–195, esp. pp. 165, 167, 144.

48 I look at present-day 'new-feminist' accounts in S. S. Holton, Contemporary feminisms and the rewriting of suffrage history, in Claire Eustance, Joan Ryan and Laura Ugolini (eds), *Themes and directions in British suffrage history: a reader* (London, Cassell Academic, 1999 forthcoming).

49 For example, Sarah, Christabel Pankhurst; Stanley and Morley, *Emily Wilding Davison.*

50 S. Jeffreys, *The spinster and her enemies* (London, Pandora, 1985); S. K. Kent, *Sex and suffrage in Britain, 1860–1914* (Princeton, Princeton University Press, 1987).

51 M. Ramelson, *The petticoat rebellion: a century of struggle for women's rights* (London, Lawrence & Wishart, 1967); S. Rowbotham, *Hidden from history* (London, Pluto Press, 1973), pp. 77–89, esp. p. 79; J. Liddington and J. Norris, *One hand tied behind us: the rise of the women's suffrage movement* (London, Virago, 1978; Holton, *Feminism and democracy.*

52 Marcus, *Suffrage and the Pankhursts,* p. 9.

53 This issue is beautifully explored in L. Tickner, *The spectacle of women: imagery of the suffrage campaigns* (London, Chatto & Windus, 1987).

2

THE IDEAS OF BRITISH SUFFRAGISM

Christine Bolt

INTRODUCTION

> To say that a woman is unfit to vote in a land where a woman rules, is like saying that to pull an oar requires more intelligence than to steer.[1]

This suggestion was made by a contributor to a collection of *Opinions of women on women's suffrage* published by the National Society for Women's Suffrage in 1879. But in Britain as in other comparable countries, securing the vote proved to be the hardest task of the women's movement. The edge Queen Victoria gave British feminists was a limited one, for all their stress upon her combination of private and public virtues. While her eminence as a monarch in her own right was gratifying, it was an accidental eminence. If Victoria privately lamented the burden of frequent pregnancies, publicly, as Linda Colley has argued with reference to earlier royal women, she 'dignified by example the mundane private life of many ordinary female Britons'. The queen's reliance on male political advisers – including Prince Albert – was marked, and she was known to regard the women's rights agitation as a 'mad, wicked folly'. It is small wonder that the forthright American suffragist Elizabeth Cady Stanton was irritated by the tributes to Victoria she heard at the meetings of British activists, since the queen 'has never done anything to merit the approbation of the advocates of suffrage for women'.[2] Stanton had little time for the diplomatic style that was a feature of Victorian feminism and did so much to remind the British and Americans of their national differences.

When the demand for women's suffrage was first seriously but unsuccessfully broached in parliament during the 1860s, in the context of pressure for the Second Reform Act, it did well enough to fill some suffragists with 'bright hopefulness' about speedy success.[3] Like the members of all social movements, however, they needed powerful arguments to persuade the ignorant and the hostile, and to rebut the damaging objections to female voting that might deter the waverers and the faint-hearted. As they fashioned their case, they would be able to demonstrate women's intellectual ability and rationality, thereby increasing their own confidence. And their ideas were bound to be varied, since suffragism, as part of feminism, reflected the diverse personnel, broad aims and eclectic ideology of the larger movement. Its adherents were also obliged to consolidate and add to their ideas once opposition views had been elaborated, time had passed, and emphases that had suited one era and set of leaders would no longer suffice. Because it was difficult to gauge which arguments were most effective, and many suffragists remained part of the campaign for decades, familiar points were not discarded when new ones were devised or new recruits appeared. Most ominously, it was not clear whether the demand for the vote could be formulated on terms that would accommodate moderates willing to seek the suffrage 'for women who could satisfy the same property qualifications required of male voters', without alienating radicals opposed to all limited claims for female enfranchisement.[4]

Suffrage ideas were, of course, adapted by the movement's leaders to the key moments they encountered and the major constituencies they targeted during a long campaign. But there is no satisfactory simple explanation of the complex course of suffragist arguments: of why women from frequently similar backgrounds favoured differing intellectual emphases; of why some activists neglected and others concerned themselves with ideology; and of why some individuals developed their thinking about the vote over time, while others did not. Although it was stated in 1884 that women's suffrage had been claimed in England 'on the ground of expediency' rather than 'abstract and inalienable right', such claims were probably designed to reassure conservatives, ever fearful that what they thought of as the American clamour for equal rights had crossed the Atlantic. In fact, justice and expediency arguments were both used from the beginning to the end of the British suffrage movement, and its ideas remain difficult to characterise, being at once lighthearted and profound, democratic and elitist, constant and protean.[5]

Yet two things are apparent. First, arguments urged by moderates and radical suffragists alike failed to secure the parliamentary franchise. And secondly, it became very evident by the late nineteenth century, when a large number of MPs in the two major parties were ostensibly sympathetic and women were still voteless, that the suffrage was not going to be won principally by debate. Tactics had to be reinvigorated over the years, political circumstances had to change, and the personal qualities of the suffragists had to count for more. Accordingly the militants of the Women's Social and Political Union (WSPU, founded in 1903) adopted as their motto 'Deeds Not Words', and strove to demonstrate their zealous and selfless devotion to the cause. Unfortunately, as Les Garner has pointed out,[6] historians have tended to pay undue attention to these shifting suffrage tactics. The result has been to confirm the stereotyped image of women as doers rather than thinkers. Even the feminist philosopher John Stuart Mill, when considering *The subjection of women* (1869), asserted that:

> looking at women as they are known in experience, it may be said of them, with more truth than belongs to most other generalizations on the subject, that the general bent of their talents is towards the practical. This statement is conformable to all the public history of women, in the present and the past. It is no less borne out by common and daily experience.[7]

There are, none the less, several extremely useful introductions to the suffragist case for the vote. Thus, for instance, Constance Rover devotes two chapters of her pioneering account of women's suffrage and party politics to the arguments used 'throughout the whole period' of struggle. Garner's study demonstrates how the principal strands of feminist thinking shaped the suffrage movement in the vital years from 1900 to 1918. Susan Kingsley Kent establishes how suffragists sought to 'redefine and recreate, by political means, the sexual culture of Britain'. And Sandra Stanley Holton's books assess the debate between supporters of adult and women's suffrage; reappraise the Radical–Liberal strain in British suffragism; and trace the thinking as well as the actions of several of the movement's lesser-known individuals. These and other works have influenced this chapter, and particularly its attempt to show that suffragist ideas were impressively varied, as well as seeking women's emancipation in the very broadest sense.[8]

THE POLITICAL CASE

The ideas used by suffragists fell into three broad categories: political and explanatory; socially reassuring; and generally threatening or dismissive. As one might expect, the explanatory political arguments were the most important and the most persistent. Moving in Liberal and Radical political circles, it came naturally to early feminists such as the purity crusader Josephine Butler and the writer and Liberal MP's wife Millicent Fawcett to argue for the vote by appealing to the varied tenets of liberalism. Giving expression to the eighteenth-century Enlightenment's endorsement of individual human rationality and rights, of equality before the law, economic freedom and government based on consent, liberalism was an undeniably progressive creed and sustained a reforming tradition. And by the 1860s, as Jane Rendall has reminded us, that creed had begun to focus on social altruism and moral character in a way that is often overlooked and was helpful to feminists, who claimed women had both. When during his brief period as an MP, Mill introduced a women's suffrage amendment to the 1867 Reform Bill, he was acting on his belief that 'the course of history, and the tendencies of progressive human society', afforded 'no presumption in favour' of the prevailing 'system of inequality of rights' between men and women 'but a strong one against it'. Indeed, the denial of women's rights stood out as 'an isolated fact in modern social institutions; a solitary breach of what has become their fundamental law'. Female suffragists similarly pressed for women's rights, presenting the suffrage as a right from which they were kept only by male might; one which would bring with it political enlightenment, and would complement the gains women had been making in other fields.[9]

Mill none the less found it advisable, when addressing the House of Commons, to refer to expediency as well as justice; and to stress that 'justice, though it does not necessarily demand that we should bestow political rights on every one, does demand that we should not capriciously and without cause give those rights to one, and withhold them from another'.[10] His caution alerts us to the difficulties feminists encountered when they attempted to adapt any existing ideology to their needs. Classic liberalism had never challenged the association of women with duties rather than rights; with the subordination of self rather than competitive individualism. Its ideologues were men writing with men in mind. They constructed a masculine political culture, albeit not a static one, and the social contract offered to women was very different from that offered to men with the state and over women: 'Women refrained, at least in theory, from invading the public sphere, the realm of action, on the understanding that their moral influence would be respected and recognised.'[11]

Mary Shanley has shown that in the campaign which began during the 1850s to reform the marriage laws, men were willing to give women legal protection, not equality. But both she and Philippa Levine have established that feminists worked to challenge the liberal respect for the separation of the sexes by illustrating in a novel way the intersection of the public and private spheres, and hence the appropriateness of raising ostensibly private issues in the public arena. Moreover, a number of scholars have recently demonstrated that this strategy emboldened women to question the sexual aspects of male power, and to mount a determined campaign against the double moral standard. In the process, Lucy Bland has stressed, the diverse women campaigners managed to bring about a new sexual politics. And it was one which, by focusing on female self-ownership, demanded a further consideration of the meaning of citizenship: debated with growing vigour from the end of the eighteenth century, as part of the process of defining and building the nation, and traditionally associated with *independence*. It would be the work of suffragists of various dispositions to try and enlarge the definition of that term.[12]

However, British suffragists were in time obliged to accept that they faced a formidable range of obstacles to change. On the one hand, political revolution and economic change might have combined to produce a more democratic polity, greater literacy, more varied economic, urban and reform opportunities, and stronger 'pressures from without' on parliament. On the other hand, the first half of the nineteenth century saw the strengthening of Britain's emphatically masculine empire, trading network and metropolitan establishment; the self-conscious defence of class divisions; and renewed efforts to keep aspiring women in their place.[13] Under these circumstances, suffragists constructed their case with prudence as well as boldness. They accepted Mill as their intellectual figurehead – despite his trying ego and undue focus on the marriage question and the middle class – because of his political prominence and the worldwide impact of his writing, unequalled by any woman exponent of feminism in the nineteenth century.[14] In addition, when analysing the concept of citizenship, suffragists maintained that at least some women had been deemed fit to vote in the distant past and were fit to do so in the present.

The Radical MP's daughter Barbara Leigh-Smith Bodichon, though a woman of wide sympathies and unconventional views, was prepared in 1866 to single out female freeholders and householders as being fit for the vote:[15] a direct acknowledgement of the fact that the franchise in Britain since 1832 had been based on national residence and property qualifications, and had been extended to include male members of the middle class. The largely middle-class female suffragists repeatedly complained that it was both unjust and illogical to disfranchise women who were holders of property and payers of rates and taxes, and were incensed when only male ratepayers, house owners and lodgers were enfranchised in the towns in 1867. They pushed their point to the end, protesting taxation without representation in the twentieth century through the Women's Freedom League (founded in 1907) and the Women's Tax Resistance League (formed in 1910).[16] The injustice was particularly keenly felt because before 1832, suffragists proclaimed, some women had been able to vote 'in those cases where they were entitled as landowners or as freewomen of certain towns to do so'.[17] Despite their ingenuity, women's efforts to get history effectively on their side – as most sensible reformers try to do – came to nothing in this instance. The suffragists' attempt to enfranchise themselves by claiming that they were not legally excluded from doing so by the language of nineteenth-century legislation concerning the vote likewise led nowhere: the Court of Common Pleas ruled against them in a test case decided in 1868 and involving the 1867 Reform Act.[18] But historical arguments were not abandoned and the decision to seek the franchise on 'the same terms as it is or may be granted to men' was a matter of lasting contention.

This is not surprising, since the formulation was, in fact, a compromise between two groups of suffragists. On the one hand were those who were ready to confine voting to property-owning widows and spinsters, excluding married women who did not control their own property because they were affected by the common law doctrine of coverture: the doctrine that the 'legal existence of a woman is suspended during marriage, or at least incorporated and consolidated into that of the husband, under whose wing, protection and coverage she performs everything'. On the other hand were suffragists who were unwilling to countenance the acceptance of coverture. The two groups competed for control of suffragism throughout its complex course.[19] But when the demand for the vote on the same terms as men was first made, the trouble that would be caused by it could not have been predicted. No party favoured universal suffrage, all feared a large increase of the electorate, women voters were an unknown quantity, and greedy demands do not become a fledgling movement. The enfranchising of a minority of women might persuade sceptical politicians that they could risk extending the vote to the rest of the female sex, and it would certainly give hope to the suffrage campaigners. Yet notwithstanding the suffragists' reminder that the women they said were fit to vote were useful and accomplished, and that it was women with 'well-feathered nests' who opposed enfranchisement, their enemies used the suffragists' compromise claim to associate the cause with prosperous and self-interested women, and to point up the differences between women in a movement predicated on the universality of sisterhood.[20]

Although the exclusion of married women was not explicitly conceded when suffragists first sought the vote in the 1860s, practicality and precedent inclined moderates towards it. The campaign to secure for married women control over their property and earnings did achieve important victories in 1870 and 1882; but it was hard fought, and while some married women were voting in local elections even before the landmark 1894 Local Government Act, with regard to property rights, full equality between married and single women was achieved only in 1935. Until a breakthrough was made, it might seem practical to seek the parliamentary vote for spinsters and widows who met the prevailing property requirements. Women, after all, had been granted municipal suffrage on this basis. Of course the strategy, if successful, would have resulted in the enfranchisement of very limited numbers of women: perhaps 300,000 or 400,000 in the 1860s and some 1.25 million in 1909, in a country where women were the majority of the population.[21] But Britain in 1908 gave the vote to a mere 16.5 per cent of the total population 'compared with 27.9 per cent in France, 21.2 per cent in Germany and Bulgaria and 19.0 per cent in Portugal',[22] and eventually conceded women's suffrage in two stages (1918 and 1928). A modest gain, albeit one that sacrificed the principle of sexual equality, was once more regarded by some suffragists as the only gain sensibly to be hoped for.

Because we now know that modesty was welcomed without concession by politicians, it is easy to condemn the moderate suffragists' judgement. However, we also need to remember that Victorian feminism was concerned with both married and unmarried women, married women's interests being addressed in the debates over divorce and separation arrangements, child custody, men's physical abuse of their wives, prostitution and the married women's property laws. And its advocates frequently preferred to keep controversial matters like suffrage and coverture apart, to minimise opposition.[23] After the passage of the 1882 Married Women's Property Act, debate on the matter unfortunately could not be stifled, though in the interest of the campaigners' public image, Lydia Becker, the unmarried industrialist's daughter and cautious national leader of British suffragism from the 1860s, was adept in talking down splits.[24]

Radical women such as Ursula Bright protested when the 1884 Reform Act was in the offing that suffragists, hoping to benefit, could not ignore qualified married women 'without making ourselves & our cause ridiculous';[25] and the British anti-suffragist and political commentator James Bryce irritatingly reported that whereas the attempt to do so had caused 'much controversy' in Britain, in the United States 'No one dreams of drawing any distinction between the claims of the single and the married, or of making marriage entail disfranchisement. To do so would be alien to the whole spirit of American legislation, and would indeed involve a much grosser anomaly or injustice than the exclusion of all women alike from political functions.'[26] When she was visiting her daughter Harriot in Britain during the late nineteenth century, Elizabeth Cady Stanton confirmed that this was the American view, commenting testily (and inaccurately) that the spinsters' attitude in the British dispute demonstrated that, if enfranchised, they 'were not to be trusted' to urge the vote for their married sisters.[27] She was therefore glad to be involved with a network of like-minded British feminists centred round the Bright women – part of the famous Quaker reforming family.

The activities of the group's members have been illuminated by Sandra Stanley Holton, who has looked again at the work of their Women's Franchise League (founded in 1889) and shown how strongly they adhered to the belief that the 'position of the married woman provided . . . the fullest measure of women's subordination': the most complete and unacceptable denial of their right to 'autonomous self-development'. Hence they campaigned – unsuccessfully – for propertied married women qualified under the reformed married women's property laws to be enfranchised. The circle produced its own divisions, ultimately parting company with Elizabeth Wolstenholme Elmy, whose unconventionality began with her personal life and extended into her activities for social purity, marriage reform and the suffrage. Yet it provided an invaluable counter-balance to the narrower suffragists, being impatient, in Alice Scatcherd's words, with 'a little bit, a little shred, a little fragment of freedom'. For these women, representing a long established Radical–Liberal current in British politics and British suffragism, it was vital to fight for equality on all fronts, to acknowledge the importance of every kind of female work, and to reach out for contacts with working-class women and the international arm of feminism.[28]

40

If suffragists sought the vote as a right, and to achieve political equality between qualified male and female citizens, they also used functional or expediency arguments for their enfranchisement. Political emancipation, they urged, would educate women 'as only political responsibility can educate', and prevent them as a class from being 'either politically ignorant and indifferent, or disaffected'. Although women were already flattered by the accolade that they were morally superior to men, exercising the vote would, it was suggested, reduce their still common concern with 'narrow private ends' and generally raise the position of their sex. If men ultimately had to be relied upon to uphold the law by force, it was stressed that women's moral and mental force would be valuable in politics and that force was less important in civilised society than it had been in primitive times. Suffragists asserted that the vote would allow women to protect themselves against neglect or oppression by politicians, and in particular would prevent obstacles being thrown up in the way of their obtaining a fair day's wage for a fair day's work. They added that since our 'legislation is becoming so increasingly domestic in its character, and deals so largely now with the *home life* of the people', excluding women from the franchise was an old-fashioned and inappropriate prohibition, denying any national political outlet for women's special qualities and valuable experience as mothers and social reformers.[29]

This functional approach may at first sight seem more conservative than an appeal based on justice, because it was grounded on assumptions about the difference between men and women: a difference enthusiastically expounded by anti-suffragists. However, suffrage claims acknowledging sexual differences had been made by the advocates of female enfranchisement who appeared periodically in the half-century before the establishment of an organised women's movement, and it would have been wise for later suffragists to continue to utilise such popular assumptions even if they had dissented from them. But on the whole, regardless of class and especially in the nineteenth century, they were favoured by female and male suffragists alike. And so activists acknowledged the deficiencies and vulnerability of women confined to a separate sphere, while trying to turn the veneration of that sphere to their advantage. The danger remained that expediency arguments encouraged politicians to fall back on them too, and find it expedient to delay meeting the suffragists' demand well after accepting it in principle.[30]

The need of poorer women for protection against exploitation was recognised by middle-class suffragists long before the advocates of a class-based socialism were practically able to do anything about it, and after the collapse of utopian socialism had revealed the obstacles facing any attempt to create a 'new moral world' which included sexual equality.[31] Suffragists quite took the point made by the Labour MP, Keir Hardie, in a 1902 speech, that 'without the active support and co-operation of working women they will have no chance whatever of being successful'.[32] After 1912, the leaders of the National Union of Women's Suffrage Societies (NUWSS, formed in 1897) increasingly looked to a pact with the Labour Party, which was by then pledged to seek female suffrage as part of its campaign for adult suffrage. These suffragists hoped to shake up the recalcitrant Liberals, on whom they had formerly placed great reliance, but they also recognised the need to rally more working-class sympathy, members and speakers.[33] They were happy to petition politicians jointly with working-class women, emphasising that 'the women of the professional and working classes contribute by their work to the wealth of the community'.[34] And they were not alone, for Jill Liddington and Jill Norris have shown that the radical working-class suffragists of Lancashire determinedly pursued their case through Labour and cross-class organisations, rejecting a legalistic emphasis on women's rights and linking the suffrage to ambitious objectives such as equal pay and family allowances; while Sandra Stanley Holton has traced the activities of working-class activists and democratic suffragists who strove, across class and party lines, to link the call for women's suffrage to 'a more general democratisation of British society'.[35]

The emphasis on women's distinct qualities and needs had the advantage of disarming those who complained that women's enfranchisement would simply duplicate existing votes without bringing anything new to parliament. It demolished whatever remained of the pre-1832 doctrine of virtual representation: the notion that MPs represented various interests, so that there was no need for each one or each individual to be directly represented. For suffragists, it was plain that representative government must reflect the wishes of the people, and that no man could speak for women as effectively as a woman could.[36] The stress on women's need for the protection of the vote was more troublesome, since politicians and labour leaders proved considerably keener to offer women (sometimes welcomed) protective industrial legislation, which could easily be used to restrict the work they did, than to offer them the protection of the vote or the protection of equality in the labour movement. Nor did it prove possible to marry the feminist and socialist ideologies, despite the links between some of their supporters in the early twentieth century, and their shared condemnation of the prevailing power structure and women's exploitation, notably in the family. If suffragists, like other feminists and reformers, were adjusting their view of the government's proper role by the late nineteenth century, and saw the need for female involvement in social production, they certainly did not share socialists' commitment to the assumption of household duties by the state. Some of them, and most famously the suffragist historian of the women's movement, Ray Strachey, remained wedded to a liberalism which offered 'patronage to the lower classes'.[37]

An equally troublesome claim, in the long run, was that women brought something distinctive to politics because they were 'more free from party politics and party bias than men are, and, consequently, more likely to take measures on their own merits'.[38] Branch secretaries of the NUWSS were instructed that they must 'put the interests of suffrage before party consider-ations', and the arguments used by suffragists were not determined by their party leanings, with the exception of the case for adult suffrage advanced by Labour women.[39] The suffragists' approach had some merits. After all, none of the political parties wished to move independently on women's suffrage, the Conciliation Bills of 1910–1912 were designed to produce a women's franchise measure that suffragists of all parties would accept, and women received the first stage of enfranchisement in 1918 from a coalition govern-ment. But the Conciliation Bills failed and not just because of suffragette impatience with them. What is more, they would, if successful, have enfran-chised fewer women than gained the vote in 1918. Opposing political parti-sanship also threatened to set suffragists swimming against the tide. As Brian Harrison has pointed out, the parties exercised growing power in the British political system by the last stages of suffragism, and their successful bid from the 1880s for unpaid female labour to take on constituency chores has been interestingly investigated. At the very least, the suffragists' non-partisanship failed to prepare them for the intense party political competition of the interwar years of the twentieth century, and underlined an unappealing difference between men and women in the eyes of professional politicians.[40]

REASSURANCES

All the expediency arguments noted above were intended to be reassuring as well as convincing, and their emollient effect was increased by several sub-ordinate and summarising claims. The most important of these was that votes for women and feminism generally would benefit the whole community. According to Mrs Fawcett, 'this is what we meant when we called our paper the *Common Cause*. [Suffrage] was the cause of men, women, and children. We believe that men cannot be truly free so long as women are held in polit-ical subjection.'[41] By this line of attack, she hoped to demolish the charge that votes for women was merely the concern of a selfish and unrepresenta-tive minority of women. Contrary to anti-suffragist fears, said suffragists, there was no obvious evidence from British women's local government fran-chises, or from the parts of the world where women voted, that bad women flocked to the polls; that election days were disrupted; that women became obsessed with their vote at the expense of their families, or unduly influenced by others in its use. On the contrary, it was contended, women had responded well to enfranchisement; and Patricia Hollis has told the gripping story of English suffragists' efforts to ensure that women exercised their local votes, served on school and poor law boards, and acted as local councillors. Their creditable performance was then used by suffragists to argue that women were equally fit for the parliamentary franchise, although reassurances drawn from women's local government experience could quite easily become threats, in the opinion of anti-suffragists. The demands of Conservative and Liberal suffragists were very different: they offered no threat to the existing class system, and such suffragists inclined to the view of the feminist educator Emily Davies that there would be 'no very marked immediate effect on legislation from the concession. But the moral effect would . . . be deep and far-reaching.' It was anticipated that most women would not want to become political agitators or candidates for parliament. And neither were they driven by dislike of men. Millicent Fawcett, the devoted wife and gallant widow, put the point well:[42]

> I never believe in the possibility of a sex war. Nature has seen after that: as long as mothers have sons & fathers daughters there can never be a sex war. What draws men and women together is stronger than the brutality & tyranny which drives them apart.

Was this reassuring line of appeal a wise one? The answer must be yes and no. Suffragists were right in their grumbles that anti-suffragists were frequently emotional rather than rational, and feared the social consequences of votes for women as much as the political. They were right to confront fears that voting women would destroy the home as haven; right to address themselves to the men who preferred male company outside the home, or saw no reason why women should encroach on the masculine sphere when they had a respected one of their own, unchallenged by men. Furthermore, the female vote may have been secured in the end because many men had accepted the suggestion that its impact would be either conservative or slight, or both. On the other hand, opinions buttressed by sentiment and custom are seldom shaken by polite reassurances, notwithstanding the suffragists' conviction that their emphases would persuade anti-suffragists repelled by the militancy of the WSPU. Mrs Fawcett's amiable view of the male sex was also directly at odds with the denunciation by WSPU leaders Mrs Emmeline Pankhurst and her daughter Christabel of men's reduction of women to sex objects; and with their emphasis on the venereal disease that followed from men's sexual immorality.[43]

THREATS

More assertive general arguments have often been associated with the WSPU, and linked with its self-consciously militant tactics. It is now clear that the Union's suffragettes did not hold a monopoly on militancy, entertained varied views, developed them over time, were not simply in thrall to their glorified leaders, and used many of the arguments for the vote favoured by the other suffrage societies. Like the moderates, for example, they sought enfranchisement on the same terms as men, thereby drawing upon themselves the complaint of radicals such as Julia Dawson that WSPU banners demanding *Votes for Women* really meant 'votes for *some* women. Not for me, certainly; and not for you, perhaps, my gentle reader, but for some other women who have qualifications which we have not.' Nevertheless, militancy produced some distinctive emphases. In particular, we should note the militants' adoption of the language of warfare in their campaign literature, a device favoured by American reformers too.[44] Also striking was the presentation of militancy as a kind of religious indignation, and as a willingness to risk all in the face of male intransigence: women were, Christabel Pankhurst proclaimed, 'fighting against the Government for the good of our own souls, and for the improvement of the souls of men'. This approach was just as well, in view of suffragettes' abandonment of women's proud boast that they relied only on moral force. Alternatively, militancy could be seen as an unavoidable adaptation of the masculine justification of force – including violence – to advance a stalled political cause. Hence the women's way would be to justify a vigorous response to violence, but not (for the most part) to excuse initiating it. In the process, militants disposed of anti-suffragist claims that women were incapable of deploying physical force, and sought to put their commitment to it into an international context and a revolutionary tradition. The Irish example was a special inspiration to the Pankhursts; and yet a supporter who eventually broke with the WSPU, Teresa Billington-Greig, offered a telling critique of the suffragette stance, which encouraged law-breaking and then unreasonably condemned the authorities for seeking to repress it: which encouraged, in other words, a 'double shuffle between revolution and injured innocence'.[45] And Mrs Fawcett was similarly accurate in pointing out that the militants had no leverage comparable with the Irish dissidents' ability to 'disrupt political authority in Ireland', and so influence parliament in London.[46]

The historian George Dangerfield may have admired the suffragettes' bid to get beyond respectability and acquire an abstract goal in life,[47] but the attention of contemporaries was more commonly focused on militant *methods*, as when a reporter in the *Jewish Chronicle* in 1913, covering a militant protest at a West End synagogue, dwelt almost exclusively on the tactics of 'these quasi-demented creatures'. The *Chronicle* concluded that 'wise men' objected to 'making a concession to crime, outrage, blasphemy – and bad conduct'. To some extent militancy encouraged this focus, and the Pankhursts certainly came to display a dispiriting intolerance towards arguments they found challenging or unconvincing. Yet militancy was plainly associated with an intellectual stance: namely with the repudiation of submissiveness and the double moral standard; with the belief that women's special qualities and concerns entitled them to citizenship, which would in turn benefit men, women and the state; with a conviction that economic and political enfranchisement went hand in hand; and with a general 'love of freedom'.[48]

Somewhat less alarming than militancy, but intended to jolt the complacency of proud patriots, was the claim that suffragism was an international cause in which other countries and even the British colonies were shamingly showing the way to their mother country. New Zealand, for example, instead of becoming 'a dreadful object lesson' to the rest of the British Empire following the adoption of women's suffrage in 1893, had flourished: 'prosperous and happy and loyal to the throne and race to which she owes her origin'.[49] In similar vein, women resorted to ridicule of those who resisted their campaign, pointing out that history was on their side. Not only had some women been eligible to vote in the past and not only were some bold countries permitting them to vote in the present; by the end of the nineteenth century they had also demonstrated their abilities and made remarkable gains in public service, education and the workforce. Ancient arguments about female physical weakness and mental incapacity had thereby been undermined, if not destroyed. In the context of these developments, women's suffrage had to be seen as overdue in a progressive country, and its opponents as poorly informed, prejudiced and reactionary. Moreover, the denial of the vote could be presented as the symbol of women's oppression in Britain, which claimed to be one of the world's great civilised powers, accepted women's civilising mission, and pronounced the position of women to be the test of how civilised any nation was. The emphasis here on women's oppression had its risks. As the American suffragist and historian Mary Beard complained, it presented a picture of women as victims not actors, as weak not forceful, and in so doing drifted towards the judgement of anti-feminists. But for a group which is all too often seen as upholding the class system, the argument that removing female disfranchisement removed a cornerstone of privilege was a refreshingly bold one.[50]

ENGLAND DID NOT STAND ALONE

Historians of feminism have rightly been criticised for dwelling too much upon the activities of English women. This situation is now being remedied, and very helpfully so in the case of the vote, because the suffrage movement was manifestly British in scope and enfranchised British women at its close. Since suffrage legislation had to be secured from the parliament based in London, a thorough scrutiny of the crucial political activities in the metropolis is necessary. But until recently it has led to neglect of regional as well as non-English campaigns for the vote,[51] and does less than justice to the suffragists' awareness of the need for getting their message across throughout Britain. This proved to be no easy task, because local traditions and circumstances determined both what could be done and what could, most effectively, be said. When English suffragists tried to show that their dissent in no way detracted from their national pride, they might even encourage awkward nationalist assertiveness among Irish, Scottish and Welsh activists. Attention to political *context* here was unusually important, and suffrage leaders in the metropolis had to accept that ideas would circulate that were beyond their control.

Just as non-western women have denied that feminism, as it developed in their countries, relied on the inspiration of western intellectuals and activists, so suffragists in Wales, Scotland and Ireland wished to put their own stamp on suffragism. The desire for autonomy was most marked among the Irish activists, whose story has been told by Cliona Murphy, Rosemary Owens and Margaret Ward. Like their English counterparts, they produced a range of suffrage associations with a range of opinions; and it was the nationalist Irish Women's Franchise League (IWFL, established in 1908) that found greatest fault with the assumptions of the NUWSS and WSPU. Christabel Pankhurst attempted to smooth over differences by arguing that:

> there ought not to be a distinction between the English and Irish Movement. . . . It is not as though English interests were not at stake in Ireland. They are. Indeed, it may almost be said that the Nationalist Members hold the fate of the suffrage cause for the whole kingdom in their hands . . . it is not nationality but personality that counts . . . the Suffrage Movement has united women of differ-ent races. We are all one in the Woman's Suffrage faith.[52]

On a number of counts, Pankhurst was mistaken. While the personalities of reformers were invariably important and attacked, English women, including suffragists, who participated actively in the affairs of their country and took a keen interest in empire, wanted the vote because it recognised them as full members of the nation. And it seems indisputable that their determination to help Indian women struggling to improve the educational, welfare, organisational and political rights of their sex was driven by assumptions about white superiority and white women's moral mission abroad that could impede racial unity, even as it resulted in valued practical help.[53] Nor could their joint interest in the behaviour of the Irish Nationalist MPs do much to unify the cause of Irish and English suffragists, because the MPs failed to help the activists of either country. Their preoccupation with their own interests left them no time for women's suffrage. The IWFL leader Hanna Sheehy Skeffington reflected the nationalist sentiment of her group of suffragists when she argued that 'The suffrage movement in Ireland is one of native growth, managed and controlled within Ireland, and wholly indepen-dent of inspiration from outside.' Irish women took an interest in suffrage efforts in different parts of the world, and were especially warmly inclined towards the United States, appreciating its interest in the Home Rule strug-gle. Skeffington complained that though English suffragists were 'with us in our sex's war for freedom, yet in our national struggle they are with the men of England and against us'. This might have been true of some of the English women, but it was not true of all of them; and the Irish suffragists were to find, as women did in nationalist contests throughout the world, that their support for male nationalists was accepted dismissively by men who expected them to subordinate feminism to nationalism, arguing that they would automatically be emancipated with the triumph of the latter, not the former. Irish suffragists, like English liberal suffragists faced with the rise of socialism, were unable to weave two conflicting ideologies together into a new synthesis helpful to women.[54]

In Wales, where political nationalism was less disturbing, nationalist forces none the less had an impact on the presentation of suffragism. Accordingly, one Welsh reformer found it agreeable to suggest that 'the Saxon has not the courtesy of the Celt to women': a sentiment echoed in Ireland. After all, gaoled Irish suffragettes were not treated with the brutality meted out to their incarcerated English sisters, and the operation of the WSPU in Wales, though it brought hostile crowd and press reaction, provoked nothing like the repression campaigners encountered in England.[55] Despite being inhibited by women's low involvement in paid work in Wales, which reduced the relevance of some functional arguments for the vote, Welsh suffragists resembled Irish activists in liking to deploy the symbols of local pride and culture. Under these circumstances, WSPU attacks on the dominant political party in Wales and on its hero, Lloyd George, were distinctly maladroit.[56]

In Scotland, similar manifestations of independence were to be expected. It was recognised that 'Scottish people hang together',[57] and, shaped by their different legal system and the economic and cultural power of their great cities, reformers had long shown themselves able to sustain a confident Scottish presence in British reform movements like anti-slavery and temperance. When suffragism emerged, Scottish advocates on the whole chose the expediency arguments that they thought suited their circumstances, and, though they were willing to accept the intervention of English organisers and 'proud to be British', Leah Leneman has stressed that they 'were also proud to be Scottish and resented their national sensitivities being ignored'. Echoing the Irish and Welsh suffragists, they were dismayed at the authorities' harsh treatment of suffragettes, for '"It had been fondly believed that this brutality was to be left in England"'.[58] And they asserted their autonomy as far as possible, not least by utilising the Scottish thistle as a distinguishing feature in the visual imagery in which suffragism of all kinds excelled, and which was designed, Tickner has vividly revealed, to construct an alternative iconography of woman to the one created by mainstream artists.[59]

CONCLUSION

Several general criticisms of the ideology of suffragism recur. A movement which campaigned for so long, and introduced most of its arguments early in the struggle, tended to subordinate them to tactical manoeuvres in the critical last stage of the campaign. Drawing in diverse women by using diverse claims gave suffragism the supporters it needed but left them disunited once the vote had been won.[60] Even while the campaign endured, most Britons were exposed to suffrage arguments in speeches that were easily forgotten or in pamphlets which specialised in necessary but unexciting lists of points in favour of enfranchisement. As a result, one of the most engaging features of the women's message – humour – tends to get lost. The woman reformer, especially if single, was invariably seen as a dour and humourless individual: self-important, concerned with procedure and protocol, and definitely opposed to the pleasure principle. But actually Mrs Fawcett was lively as well as proper; Mrs Pankhurst was mischievous as well as brave; heckling was relished as an opportunity for wit, not as a threat; and many suffragists were prepared to agree with the message of George Eliot's Mrs Poyser: 'I'm not denyin' the women are foolish. The Almighty made 'em to match the men.'[61]

The anti-suffragists had an elaborate case against female voting, as Brian Harrison has shown.[62] Women, argued 'antis', lacked the physical, mental and property qualifications for the vote; and enfranchised women would allegedly become masculine and selfish, destroy chivalry, present problems for all the political parties, send a dangerous message to restless colonies, and end up being manipulated by male politicians. Suffragists had to spend an unfortunate amount of time on refuting these views. It was unfortunate because so much opposition to change is based on unprovable assertions about the present and unprovable predictions about the future. All too often, it seemed, women's reassuring pronouncements did not appease men, and women's assertive opinions – and behaviour – only served to confirm anti-suffragists' conviction that women out of their sphere and men's control were irrational, combative, hysterical and undeserving. The word propaganda has innumerable meanings and is mostly applied in a pejorative sense. The doctrines and practice that the suffragettes sought to propagate inclined their critics to see them as agents of emotion rather than the creators of democratic opinion. Such critics did not acknowledge that new approaches were long overdue when the WSPU made its appearance, or highlight the fact that militancy was abandoned during the First World War. Nor did they admit that radical and democratic suffragism were important features of the campaign.

Yet it was never going to be easy to tackle the anti-suffrage opinions that were spread throughout the British establishment and entrenched in publications of every kind. If women finally secured the vote, it proved impossible to destroy the association of their political emancipation with danger to the family and social stability; and with the disparagement of a domestic order said to be prudently upheld by most of their sex. Even a sympathiser like the novelist Thomas Hardy envisaged women's suffrage bringing about 'the probable break-up of the present marriage system, the present social rules of other sorts, religious codes, legal arrangements on property, etc. (through men's self protective countermoves)'.[63] It proved hard to shake the conviction of 'antis', such as the successful writer Eliza Lynn Linton, that women already had enough to do; and that if they wanted reform, they could try and do it better instead of abandoning duty, innocence and the shield of men's chivalry.[64] Male opponents of enfranchisement, in particular, while they did not continue to campaign against female voting once it had been conceded, clearly did not abandon a view of women and men's contract with them that had ancient sanction, conformed with Social Darwinism's emphasis upon progressive specialisation, and made men feel good about themselves.[65]

Finally, were British women's arguments for the vote distinctive? There are many obvious similarities between suffragists in western countries. Functional and justice arguments were used in all of them. They all experienced differences between liberal and socialist feminists, and their feminists commonly associated women with the forces of nationalism and race pride in a way that we now find problematical. Feminists at home and abroad encountered fierce opposition and were consequently inclined to exaggerate the benefits that would come from the vote (just as the 'antis' exaggerated the drawbacks). British, American and continental European activists all involved themselves in internationalising suffragism from the 1880s, for it was helpful to claim that their case had a universal validity, and to put their own activities into perspective. And suffragists in and beyond Britain were both undermined and empowered by the First World War, which allowed them to perform patriotic war work and benefit from exceptional socio-political conditions even as it distracted some from suffragism, undermined the confidence of pre-war suffragist internationalism, and challenged women's assertion that their maternal duties and personal sensitivity made them regard war differently from men.

On the other hand, national circumstances always shape reform movements in important ways. British women often looked towards the empire for transnational inspiration, and were certainly slower in pursuing and attending international women's gatherings than their American sisters, many of whom had the money to travel, the desire to avoid intellectual insularity, and a vision of the exceptional role the United States was destined to play in the world. From the outset, campaigners in Britain realised responses to their arguments were adversely affected by the knowledge that, with a democratic franchise, women voters would be in a majority. They were similarly aware of framing their case in a class-conscious country with a powerful establishment and strong political parties that set out to engage women's loyalties in a way that loosely organised political parties in the United States did not. Whereas anti-suffragists commonly held up the American example as one to avoid, British suffragists – with the exception of certain Irish activists – valued their transatlantic links but prided themselves on accommodating British prejudices and preferences.[66] In practice this meant claiming the vote with reference to a judicious blend of duties and rights, and collaborating with men without ever yielding their right to direct the long drive for women's suffrage.[67] Although avoiding the trap of seeking for women 'a position apart, a sort of sentimental priesthood',[68] British suffragists of a liberal and conservative persuasion did not mount a case for the vote which substantially challenged the power structure of British society. Those with socialist convictions may have protested women's sexual and economic oppression more trenchantly, but their limited numbers and alarming message ensured them a still smaller impact.[69]

NOTES

I should like to thank the editors for their extremely helpful comments on the draft version of this chapter.

1 *Opinions of women on women's suffrage* (London, Central Committee of the National Society for Women's Suffrage, 1879), p. 18; see also p. 20.
2 L. Colley, *Britons: forging the nation, 1707–1837* (London, Pimlico, 1994, originally published 1992), pp. 272–273; Queen Victoria quoted in C. Rover, *Suffrage and party politics in Britain, 1866–1914* (London and Toronto, Routledge & Kegan Paul and University of Toronto Press, 1967), p. 34; M. Fawcett, *Life of her majesty Queen Victoria* (London, W. H. Allen, 1895); E. C. Stanton, *Eighty years and more: reminiscences, 1815–1897* (New York, Schocken Books, 1971, originally published 1898), p. 354.
3 H. Blackburn, *Women's suffrage: a record of the women's suffrage movement in the British Isles* (London and Oxford, Williams & Norgate, 1902), quotation from p. 169; R. Strachey, *'The cause': a short history of the women's movement in Great Britain* (London, Virago, 1978, first published 1928), p. 109.
4 S. S. Holton, *Suffrage days: stories from the women's suffrage movement* (London and New York, Routledge, 1996), p. 20.
5 *The woman question in Europe: a series of original essays*, ed. T. Stanton (New York, G. P. Putnam's Sons, 1884), pp. 4–5; American historians *have* detected a shift of emphasis in the American suffrage movement from justice to expediency arguments: see, for example, W. O'Neill, *Everyone was brave: a history of feminism in America* (New York, Quadrangle, 1969); A. Kraditor, *The ideas of the woman suffrage movement, 1890–1920* (New York, W. W. Norton, 1981); and S. M. Buechler, *The transformation of the woman suffrage movement: the case of Illinois, 1850–1920* (New Brunswick, NJ, Rutgers University Press, 1990), who offers a new gloss on the work of O'Neill and Kraditor.
6 L. Garner, *Stepping stones to women's liberty: feminist ideas in the women's suffrage movement, 1900–1918* (London, Heinemann Educational Books, 1984), p. vii.
7 *The subjection of women*, in *John Stuart Mill and Harriet Taylor Mill: essays on*

sex equality, ed. A. S. Rossi (Chicago and London, University of Chicago Press, 1970), Chapter 3; S. Strauss, *'Traitors to the masculine cause': the men's campaigns for women's rights* (Westport, Greenwood Press, 1982), pp. 28–36.

8 Rover, *Suffrage and party politics in Britain*, Chapters 4 and 5; Garner, *Stepping stones to women's liberty*; S. S. Kent, *Sex and suffrage in Britain, 1860–1914* (London, Routledge, 1995, originally published 1987), p. 3; Holton, *Suffrage days*; and S. S. Holton, *Feminism and democracy: women's suffrage and reform politics in Britain, 1900–1918* (Cambridge, Cambridge University Press, 1986).

9 *The subjection of women*, pp. 142, 146; *Opinions of women on women's suffrage*, pp. 25, 27, 31, 33; J. Rendall, Citizenship, culture and civilization: the language of British suffragists, 1866–1874, in *Suffrage and beyond: international feminist perspectives*, ed. M. Nolan and C. Daley (Auckland, Auckland University Press, 1994), pp. 127–150.

10 Quoted in Rover, *Suffrage and party politics in Britain*, p. 30.

11 Colley, *Britons*, quotation from p. 263; B. Caine, *Victorian feminists* (Oxford, Oxford University Press, 1992), pp. 32–42; Z. Eisenstein, *The radical future of liberal feminism* (New York, Longman, 1981); C. Pateman, *The sexual contract* (Oxford, Polity Press, 1988).

12 L. Bland, *Banishing the beast: English feminism and sexual morality, 1885–1914* (Harmondsworth, Penguin Books, 1995), Introduction and *passim*; Kent, *Sex and suffrage in Britain*; M. Jackson, *The real facts of life: feminism and the politics of sexuality, c.1850–1940* (London, Taylor & Francis, 1994); Holton, *Suffrage days*, pp. 27, 40–41 and 80–82; M. L. Shanley, *Feminism, marriage and the law in Victorian England, 1850–1895* (Princeton, Princeton University Press, 1989); P. Levine, *Feminist lives in Victorian England: private roles and public commitment* (Oxford, Blackwell, 1990); see also M. E. Doggett, *Marriage, wife-beating and the law in Victorian England* (Columbia, University of South Carolina Press, 1993); and J. Rendall's important essay, Nineteenth-century feminism and the separation of spheres: reflections on the public/private dichotomy, in *Moving on: new perspectives on the women's movement*, ed. T. Andreasen *et al.* (Aarhus, Aarhus University Press), 1991, pp. 17–37.

13 Colley, *Britons*, Chapter 6 and *passim*; L. Davidoff and C. Hall, *Family fortunes: men and women of the English middle class* (Chicago and London, Chicago University Press, 1987); C. Hall, The early formation of Victorian domestic ideology, in *Fit work for women*, ed. S. Burman (London, Croom Helm, 1978), pp. 21f.; R. Hyam, *Britain's imperial century, 1815–1914: a study of empire and expansion* (Basingstoke and London, Macmillan, 1993); P. Hollis (ed.), *Pressure from without in early Victorian England* (London, Edward Arnold, 1974); B. Harrison, A genealogy of reform in modern Britain, in *Anti-slavery, religion, and reform: essays in memory of Roger Anstey*, ed. C. Bolt and S. Drescher (Folkestone, Dawson, 1980 and Hamden, Archon, 1980), pp. 119–148.

14 Caine, *Victorian feminists*, pp. 33–36; B. Caine, John Stuart Mill and the English women's movement, *Historical Studies*, 18, 1978, pp. 119–148; G. Tulloch, *Mill and sexual equality* (Brighton, Harvester, 1984).

15 B. Bodichon, *Reasons for the enfranchisement of women* (National Association for the Promotion of Social Science, 1866), p. 12.

16 *Opinions of women on women's suffrage*, pp. 9, 14, 20–22, 24, 33, 46, 48–50, 55, 57; L. L. Shiman, *Women and leadership in nineteenth-century England* (Basingstoke and London, Macmillan, 1992), pp. 121–122; Rover, *Suffrage and party politics in Britain*, p. 31.

17 M. G. Fawcett, *Women's suffrage: a short history of a great movement* (London, T. C. and E. C. Jack, 1912), pp. 8–9; and see Charlotte Carmichael Stopes'

impressive analysis of women's historic rights, *British freewomen: their histori-cal privileges* (London, Swan Sonneschein, 1894).

18 Fawcett, *Women's suffrage*, pp. 9–11.

19 Holton, *Suffrage days*, Chapter 1 and *passim*; J. Perkin, *Women and marriage in nineteenth-century England* (London, Routledge, 1989), Introduction and Chapter 1.

20 Frances Power Cobbe's view in *Opinions of women on women's suffrage*, p. 17; B. Harrison, Women's suffrage at Westminster, 1866–1928, in *High and low pol-itics in modern Britain: ten studies*, ed. M. Bentley and J. Stevenson (Oxford, Clarendon, 1983), pp. 80–122; Rendall, Citizenship, culture and civilisation, pp. 132–133; J. Lewis, *Women in England, 1870–1950* (Brighton, Wheatsheaf, 1984), p. 78.

21 Rover, *Suffrage and party politics in Britain*, Chapter 3.

22 M. Ramelson, *The petticoat rebellion: a century of struggle for women's rights* (London, Lawrence & Wishart, 1967), p. 77.

23 See, for instance, Blackburn, *Women's suffrage*, pp. 120–121.

24 Ibid., pp. 175–177; Becker herself only agreed – from 1874, for tactical reasons – to tolerate the exclusion of married women from the vote, following the elec-tion of a Conservative government: see Holton, *Suffrage days*, pp. 39–40.

25 Ursula M. Bright to Mr Henry Fawcett, 8 February 1884, Autograph Letter Collection, Fawcett Library, London.

26 J. Bryce, *The American commonwealth* (London, Macmillan, 1889, 2 vols), II, p. 557.

27 Stanton, *Eighty years and more*, pp. 368–369; in fact, married and single women were to be found on both sides of the debate about the exclusion of married women from the vote.

28 S. S. Holton, 'To educate women into rebellion': Elizabeth Cady Stanton and the creation of a transatlantic network of radical suffragists, *The American Historical Review*, 99, 1994, pp. 1112–1136, quotation from p. 1130; and Holton, *Suffrage days*.

29 *Opinions of women on women's suffrage*, pp. 11, 17, 21, 28–29, 32, 35, 39, 42, 49, 53; Bodichon, *Reasons for the enfranchisement of women*, p. 37; *The English Woman's Review*, I, October 1866, pp. 31, 34; A. John, *Elizabeth Robins: staging a life, 1862–1952* (London, Routledge, 1995), p. 157.

30 See, for instance, B. Parkes, *Essays on women's work* (London, Alexander Strahan, 1865), pp. 221–222; and article in *The Woman Citizen*, 50, June 1918–May 1919, p. 1020, on the four arguments historically made for the suffrage, and arguing that practicality, justice and right are easily established, leaving expediency to be urged; also Strauss, *'Traitors to the masculine cause'*, *passim*.

31 B. Taylor, *Eve and the New Jerusalem: socialism and feminism in the nineteenth century* (London, Virago, 1984, originally published 1983).

32 Mr Keir Hardie, MP, speech of 18 February 1902 on women's suffrage, Autograph Letter Collection, Fawcett Library.

33 L. Hume, *The National Union of Women's Suffrage Societies, 1897–1914* (New York, Garland Publishing, 1982); Holton, *Feminism and democracy*.

34 *Jus Suffragii*, No. 7, 15 March 1907, petition for the suffrage sent to Sir Henry Campbell-Bannerman from Eva McLaren, Louise M. Knightly, Isabella O. Ford, Millicent Garrett Fawcett and Selina Cooper. This journal is located at the Fawcett Library.

35 Holton, *Feminism and democracy*; Holton, *Suffrage days*, especially Chapters 2 and 5 on Jessie Craigen and Hannah Mitchell; J. Liddington and J. Norris, *One hand tied behind us: the rise of the women's suffrage movement* (London, Virago Press, 1978).

36 Fawcett, *Women's suffrage*, p. 57; D. Rubinstein, *Before the suffragettes: women's emancipation in the 1890s* (Brighton, Harvester, 1986), p. 171.

37 K. Dodd, Cultural politics and women's historical writing: the case of Ray Strachey's *The cause, Women's Studies International Forum*, 13, Nos. 1/2, 1990, p. 136. See also S. Alexander (ed.), *Women's Fabian tracts* (London, Routledge, 1988), and C. Dyhouse, *Feminism and the family in England, 1880–1939* (Oxford, Blackwell, 1989).

38 *Opinions of women on women's suffrage*, pp. 10, 17.

39 Marion Phillips, secretary NUWSS, to branch secretaries, 24 January 1910, Autograph Letter Collection, Fawcett Library.

40 B. Harrison, *Prudent revolutionaries: portraits of British feminists between the wars* (Oxford, Oxford University Press, 1987); Rubinstein, *Before the suffragettes*; L. Walker, Party political women: a comparative study of the Liberal women and the Primrose League, 1890–1914, in *Equal or different: women's politics, 1800–1914*, ed. J. Rendall (Oxford, Blackwell, 1987), pp. 165–191; M. Pugh, *Women and the women's movement in Britain, 1914–1959* (London, Macmillan, 1992).

41 M.G. Fawcett, *The women's victory – and after: personal reminiscences, 1911–1918* (London, Sidgwick & Jackson, 1920), p. 157.

42 *Opinions of women on women's suffrage*, pp. 9, 34, 40–41; Mrs Fawcett to Lady Frances Balfour, 5 March 1910, Autograph Letter Collection, Fawcett Library; Fawcett, *Women's suffrage*, p. 40; S. Pankhurst, *The suffragette movement* (London, Virago, 1984, originally published 1931), p. 608; Hume, *The National Union of Women's Suffrage Societies*, p. 15; P. Hollis, *Ladies elect: women in English local government, 1865–1914* (Oxford, Oxford University Press, 1987); and Hollis, Women in council: separate spheres, public space, in *Equal or different?*, ed. Rendall, pp. 192–213.

43 R. J. Evans, *The feminists: women's emancipation movements in Europe, America and Australasia, 1840–1920* (London, Croom Helm, 1977), p. 235, on the importance to victory of moving away from individualistic liberal demands for the vote; R. G. Paulson, *Women's suffrage and prohibition: a comparative study of equality and social control* (Glenview and Brighton, Scott, Foresman, 1973), p. 184 and *passim* on the granting of suffrage to secure social cohesion; J. Marcus (ed.), *Suffrage and the Pankhursts* (London, Routledge & Kegan Paul, 1987); Bland, *Banishing the beast*, pp. 245–247.

44 Liddington and Norris, *One hand tied behind us*, p. 204; S. Holton, 'In sorrowful wrath': suffrage militancy and the Romantic feminism of Emmeline Pankhurst, in *British feminism in the twentieth century*, ed. H. L. Smith (Aldershot, Edward Elgar, 1990), pp. 7–24; S. D. Hoffert, *When hens crow: the woman's rights movement in antebellum America* (Bloomington and Indianapolis, Indiana University Press, 1990), pp. 60f.

45 John, *Elizabeth Robins*, pp. 159, 162; Marcus (ed.), *Suffrage and the Pankhursts*, p. 42; T. Billington-Greig, *The militant suffrage movement* (London, Frank Palmer, 1911), p. 24; *Opinions of women on women's suffrage*, p. 45; B. Harrison's assessment of Billington-Greig in his *Prudent revolutionaries*, Chapter 2; C. McPhee and A. Fitzgerald, *The non-violent militant: selected writings of Teresa Billington Greig* (London, Routledge & Kegan Paul, 1987); Strauss, *'Traitors to the masculine cause'*, Chapter 7.

46 Hume, *The National Union of Women's Suffrage Societies*, p. 51.

47 G. Dangerfield, *The strange death of Liberal England* (New York, Capricorn Books, 1961).

48 *Jewish Chronicle*, 17 October 1913, quoted in D. Englander (ed.), *A documentary history of Jewish immigrants in Britain, 1840–1920* (Leicester and New York,

Leicester University Press and St Martin's Press, 1994), pp. 177–178; A. Morley and L. Stanley, *The life and death of Emily Wilding Davison* (London, Women's Press, 1988), Chapter 5; Marcus (ed.), *Suffrage and the Pankhursts*, pp. 156, 276 and *passim*.

49 Fawcett, *Women's suffrage*, p. 39; Marcus (ed.), *Suffrage and the Pankhursts*, pp. 148–149.

50 D. Morgan, *Suffragists and Liberals: the politics of woman suffrage in Britain* (Oxford, Blackwell, 1975), pp. 18–22; A. Rosen, *Rise up women! The militant campaign of the Women's Social and Political Union, 1903–1914* (London, Routledge & Kegan Paul, 1974), p. 77; John, *Elizabeth Robins*, p. 93; *Opinions of women on women's suffrage*, p. 43; M. Beard, *Woman as force in history: a study in traditions and realities* (New York, Macmillan, 1946).

51 The neglect of the north of England suffragists is remedied in, for example, S. Holton's *Suffrage days*, Chapter 5, especially; J. Liddington's *The life and times of a respectable rebel: Selina Cooper, 1864–1946* (London, Virago, 1984); J. Hannam's 'In the comradeship of the sexes lies the hope of progress and social regeneration': women in the West Riding ILP, in *Equal or different?*, ed. Rendall, pp. 214–238; Liddington and Norris, *One hand tied behind us*; L. Leneman, A truly national movement: the view from outside London, in M. Joannou and J. Purvis (eds), *The women's suffrage movement: new feminist perspectives* (Manchester, Manchester University Press, 1998); and June Hannam's chapter in this Volume.

52 C. Murphy, *The women's suffrage movement and Irish society in the early twentieth century* (New York and Hemel Hempstead, Harvester Wheatsheaf, 1989), pp. 75, 77 (source of Pankhurst quotation), 200; R. C. Owens, *Smashing times: a history of the Irish women's suffrage movement, 1889–1922* (Dublin, Attic Publishing, 1984); M. Ward, *Hanna Sheehy Skeffington: a life* (Dublin, Attic Press, 1997).

53 See, for instance, A. Burton, *British feminists, Indian women and imperial culture: 1865–1915* (Chapel Hill, University of North Carolina Press, 1994); B. Ramusack, Cultural missionaries, maternal imperialists, feminist allies: British women activists in India, 1865–1945, *Women's Studies International Forum*, 13, Nos. 1/2, 1990, pp. 309–321.

54 Murphy, *The women's suffrage movement and Irish society*, pp. 43, 45, 61, 64, 71, 74, 76, 80–81, 164f., 200; L. Levenson and J. H. Natterstad, *Hanna Sheehy-Skeffington, Irish feminist* (Syracuse, Syracuse University Press, 1986).

55 K. Cook and N. Evans, 'The petty antics of the bell-ringing boisterous band?' The women's suffrage movement in Wales, 1914–1917, in *Our mothers' land: chapters in Welsh women's history, 1830–1939*, ed. A. V. John (Cardiff, University of Wales Press, 1991), pp. 165, 170, 174–175; Murphy, *The women's suffrage movement and Irish society*, pp. 89, 92, 106, for similar sentiments in Ireland.

56 Cook and Evans, The petty antics, in *Our mothers' land*, ed. John, pp. 181, 184.

57 Elsie Inglis to Ray Strachey, 10 August 1913, from the Scottish Federation of Women's Suffrage Societies, Autograph Letter Collection, Fawcett Library.

58 L. Leneman, *A guid cause: the women's suffrage movement in Scotland* (Aberdeen, Aberdeen University Press, 1991), pp. 71–72, 178, 196; E. King, The Scottish women's suffrage movement, in *Out of bounds: women in Scottish society, 1800–1945*, ed. E. Breitenbach and E. Gordon (Edinburgh, Edinburgh University Press, 1992), pp. 141–143.

59 King, The Scottish women's suffrage movement, p. 140; see also L. Tickner, *Spectacle of women: imagery of the suffrage campaign 1907–14* (London, Chatto & Windus, 1989), p. 10 and *passim*.

60 Garner, *Stepping stones to women's liberty*; Buechler, *The transformation of the woman suffrage movement*, pp. 178–179.

61 Mrs Poyser featured on a popular women's suffrage postcard.

62 B. Harrison, *Separate spheres: the opposition to women's suffrage in Britain* (London, Croom Helm, 1978).

63 Thomas Hardy to Miss Helen Ward, 22 December 1908, Autograph Letter Collection, Fawcett Library.

64 See N. F. Anderson, *Women against women in Victorian England: a life of Eliza Lynn Linton* (Bloomington and Indianapolis, University of Indiana Press, 1987). On a still more famous female anti-suffragist, see J. Sutherland, *Mrs Humphry Ward: eminent Victorian, pre-eminent Edwardian* (Oxford, Oxford University Press, 1990).

65 Harrison, *Separate spheres*, especially Chapters 4 and 11: Afterwards; Sir A. E. Wright, *The unexpurgated case against women's suffrage* (London, Constable, 1913).

66 C. Bolt, *The women's movements in the United States and Britain from the 1790s to the 1920s* (Hemel Hempstead, Harvester Wheatsheaf, 1993 and Amherst, University of Massachusetts Press, 1993); C. Bolt, *Feminist ferment: 'the woman question' in the USA and England, 1870–1940* (London, UCL Press, 1995).

67 Strauss, *'Traitors to the masculine cause'*, Chapters 6 and 7; O. Banks, *Becoming a feminist* (Brighton, Wheatsheaf, 1986), Chapter 6; D. J. Morgan, *Discovering men* (London, Routledge, 1992), Chapters 1 and 7.

68 H. T. Mill, The enfranchisement of women, in *John Stuart Mill and Harriet Taylor Mill*, p. 120.

69 Garner, *Stepping stones to women's liberty*.

3

WHO WAS LILY MAXWELL?

Women's suffrage and Manchester politics, 1866–1867

Jane Rendall

Lilia Jacobensis [Jacob's Lily]

But wonder! a woman – a voter appears
Who bears of this shy tender floweret the name,
And this 'person' – disguising her feminine fears
Runs for Jacob all risks of derision and shame.

Then hail to the Lily! Let voters subdue
Their 'favours' inflaming and put in their coats
Mrs Maxwell's sweet namesake, and vow that its hue
Shall not be more modest and pure than their votes.

(Free-Lance, 7 December 1867)

INTRODUCTION

On 26 November 1867, five months after the passing of the second Reform Act a woman called Lily Maxwell cast a parliamentary vote on the hustings in a by-election held in Manchester. Who was Lily Maxwell? To the *Englishwoman's Review*, she was 'an intelligent person of respectable appearance . . . [who] keeps a small shop for the sale of crockery ware', 'a woman of strong political opinions . . . delighted to have a chance of expressing them', in voting for Jacob Bright, the Liberal candidate and the brother of the better-known Liberal politician, John Bright.[1] Lily Maxwell's vote, cast in a by-election in the immediate aftermath of the Reform Act of 1867, was the result of a fortuitous clerical error, enthusiastically exploited by the suffragist Lydia Becker and by Jacob Bright. By October 1868 the Manchester branch of the National Society for Women's Suffrage could describe this vote as the event which 'removed women's suffrage from the region of theoretical possibilities to that of actual occurrences'.[2]

Much analysis of the complex history of these earliest years in the campaign for women's suffrage has focused on the difficulties of the London committee. Little attention has, however, been given to the immediate political circumstances in which a strongly based Manchester organisation appeared, and in which Lily Maxwell cast her vote. Yet the particular character of Manchester politics in the 1860s can help to explain the circumstances of Lily Maxwell's vote, and the significance it assumed. For women's political history needs also to be integrated within an understanding of local and national contexts. Lily Maxwell's vote, cast in an election marked by particular conflicts of identity and interest, can be placed in the aftermath of the Reform Act for England and Wales of 1867, and for a candidate who represented a particular moment of connection between radical Liberals, with roots in the Anti-Corn Law League and militant Dissent, and the survivors of successive campaigns for manhood suffrage.

PARLIAMENTARY REFORM AND THE EMERGENCE OF THE WOMEN'S SUFFRAGE MOVEMENT

The demand for votes for women was not new. In Britain in the first half of the nineteenth century, it had been voiced particularly within radical Unitarian circles, and among some Owenites and Chartists.[3] In 1851 Harriet Taylor Mill, from those radical Unitarian groups, published 'The enfranchisement of women' in the *Westminster Review*. Though there was no immediate response to her challenge in Britain, her opinions and those of John Stuart Mill, her husband, were nevertheless widely known and discussed.[4] From 1858 the group of women around Bessie Parkes and Barbara Leigh Smith Bodichon, the founders of the *English Woman's Journal*, had campaigned for improvements in women's education and employment prospects.[5] Yet the editor of the *Journal*, Bessie Parkes, was initially very cautious of such divisive issues as 'divorce & the suffrage'.[6]

Fifteen years later, however, the appearance of feminists like Bessie Parkes and Barbara Bodichon in John Stuart Mill's successful election campaign in Westminster in 1865, and a political climate much more receptive to the reform of the House of Commons, signalled new possibilities. Mill was returned to the House of Commons with other members of the Victorian intelligentsia believed to be sympathetic to the cause.[7] In November 1865 five women, including Barbara Bodichon and Mill's stepdaughter, Helen Taylor, wrote papers on women's suffrage for the Kensington Ladies Debating Society. As Emily Davies wrote on 10 November, 'some people are inclined to begin a subdued kind of agitation for the franchise'.[8]

In early 1866 Lord Russell's government was in the process of preparing a Liberal Reform Bill, their task complicated by the absence of any reliable survey of the electorate itself, and the desire to preserve adequate safeguards against the dangers, as they saw it, of universal male suffrage. The problem was exacerbated by the complexities and local variations in the system of registration for the suffrage, which in many areas excluded householders who 'compounded' for payment of their rates. John Lambert, an official of the Poor Law Board, when asked to make an estimate of the numbers of working men to be enfranchised by a £6 rating qualification, reported in March 1866 on the difficulties of accurate calculation given the large numbers of tenants compounding, and of female occupiers in this category.[9]

On 9 May Bodichon sought the guidance of Mill and Helen Taylor on the most suitable date for the presentation of a petition on the extension of the suffrage to women while the Bill was under discussion. Even the drafting of the petition raised an important issue of principle, in the situation of married women, whose legal existence was under English common law subsumed into that of their husbands; the husband assumed legal rights either as owner or as guardian of his wife's property. In such a situation a married woman could not legally qualify for a vote. The final petition modestly asked that the House 'consider the expediency of providing for all householders, without distinction of sex, who possess such property or rental qualification as your Honourable House may determine'. That wording reflected not the desire to enfranchise only propertied women but the debates within the House of Commons as to the right level of enfranchisement for all householders, including tenants. It was phrased so that it did not specifically exclude married women, although that would inevitably be the result.[10]

Bodichon, Taylor, Emily Davies and Kensington Society activists circulated and gained 1,521 signatures for the petition, mainly through the energy of individual canvassers.[11] Mill presented the petition on 7 June, and on 17 July asked for a return of the number of women householders who would qualify if not excluded by sex. He spoke briefly and cautiously, and was heard with respect.[12] As Ann Robson has argued, he had succeeded in this session in getting women's suffrage on to the parliamentary agenda and had avoided undue ridicule.[13] But the Liberal government had fallen, and women's suffrage had to await new developments.

The next twelve months, between August 1866 and the passing of the Conservative Reform Bill, saw the emergence of an organised women's suffrage movement in Britain. It also saw the emergence of differences of personality and principle among the women and men involved. Already from the summer of 1866 differences between those women active in the Kensington Society and Langham Place and those in the circle around John Stuart Mill were becoming evident. Davies and Bodichon thought that the most practical way forward was to demand the vote for single and widowed women who qualified, though Mill and Taylor were increasingly unprepared to accept any explicit exclusions. Taylor believed that a women-only committee should be set up, but Davies and Bodichon preferred a mixed general committee. On 20 October 1866 a committee of women active in the Society and Langham Place was formed for 'obtaining the abolition of the legal disabilities which at present unqualifies [*sic*] women from voting for members of Parliament'. Its affairs for the next nine months were troubled and unsatisfactory, with Davies as a reluctant leader and the majority of the committee unsympathetic to political radicalism. Mill and Helen Taylor remained critical and hostile.[14] Interest was not, however, limited to London. In the summer of 1866 Bodichon gave a paper to the Social Science Association meeting at Manchester, subsequently published as *Reasons for the Enfranchisement of Women.*[15] That paper was heard with interest by a Manchester woman, Lydia Becker, and marked the beginning of Becker's lifelong activism.

In late 1866 and early 1867, the proposals for reform to be made by the new Conservative ministry under Benjamin Disraeli were eagerly awaited. The claim to national leadership of the London women's suffrage committee was to be challenged by the Manchester women's suffrage committee. Accounts differ as to the date of its foundation; Elizabeth Wolstenholme claimed that it existed as early as October 1865, and certainly Manchester women contributed to the 1866 petition.[16] However, the first historian of the movement, Helen Blackburn, recorded the first meeting of the committee as on 11 January 1867, with six members. At that meeting Jacob Bright took the chair, with Elizabeth Wolstenholme and Elizabeth Gloyne, both already actively involved in women's suffrage and education campaigns, Max Kyllmann, a friend of John Stuart Mill, and the local Unitarian minister, Saul Alfred Steinthal, at the home of a Dr Louis Borchardt.[17] Lydia Becker of Manchester, who was to be the major force behind the women's suffrage movement nationally for the next few years, was already in correspondence with Emily Davies in London about the plans for a further petitioning campaign, and in February she was appointed secretary of an expanded Manchester committee.[18] In the same month Benjamin Disraeli presented the Conservative Reform Bill to the House of Commons.

Davies suggested to Becker that she might like to answer an attack on women's suffrage in the columns of the *Spectator*; in doing so, Becker was to stake the claims of Manchester working women:

> Among the occupations exercised by Manchester women, we find those of schoolmistresses, manufacturing chemists, ironfounders, silversmiths, cotton spinners, brewers, joiners, builders, and shop-keepers of every grade. Each one who pursues her calling successfully must be to some extent a 'thinking and experienced woman' though her attention may not happen to have been turned in the direction in which she is expressly and legally excluded from action.

Why should it be assumed as a sort of axiom that only highly culti-
vated and intelligent women are fit to have votes?[19]

She also put the same points directly to Benjamin Disraeli.[20] At the same
time the Manchester committee was working together with the London committee in canvassing signatures for petitions. On 28 March a general petition
with 3,559 signatures was presented to the House of Commons by Henry
Austin Bruce, South Wales industrialist and landowner, and on 5 April one
with 3,161 signatures from Manchester was presented by Mill. Three days
later Russell Gurney presented one from 1,605 women qualified to vote.
More followed, though at no stage did the size or scale of petitions reach
very large numbers, and Emily Davies of the London committee was blamed
by some for this.[21]

The Conservative Reform Bill for England and Wales provided for household suffrage in the boroughs, with safeguards which were gradually
amended or discarded in the Commons. Most notably, on 17 May Grosvenor
Hodgkinson's amendment abolishing the practice of compounding for rates
was passed. Few understood the potential radicalism of this measure at the
time. Its implied consequence for women householders who were tenants
was the abolition of what was to them a convenient method of incorporating
the payment of rates into the rent, without any corresponding benefits and a
potential extra cost.[22]

John Stuart Mill's amendment to the Reform Bill, to substitute 'person'
for 'man' in clause 4, which dealt with the occupation qualification for
voters in the counties, was introduced on 20 May. In a powerful speech, he
limited himself to the concerns of women householders, though, looking to
the future, he did not rule out a far wider enfranchisement.[23] Mill's amendment attracted 73 votes (81 including pairs and tellers) against an opposition of 196 (or 204 as above). Among his supporters was Sir Thomas
Bazley, Liberal MP for Manchester; the other member for Manchester, the
moderate Liberal Edward James, paired in its favour also.[24] In spite of the
failure of the amendment, it was pointed out in subsequent debates that in
this area as in very many others, the Bill had been drafted so hastily that
the legal implications were unclear, and it could be argued that the Act
already included women. An Act of 1850 (Romilly's Act), which clarified
the terms to be used in parliamentary legislation, had very specifically prescribed that the term 'man' should also incorporate women, and that 'male
person' should be used in all legislation where the intention was gender-
specific. That requirement was ignored, and the term 'man' used almost
throughout.[25]

To MPs who sat for the larger urban constituencies of England and Wales,
the Reform Act passed into law in August 1867 meant the prospect of a considerably expanded electorate, even a 'borough revolution', though the
boundaries of that electorate were in 1867 by no means clearcut, given the

complexities of rating legislation.[26] To those active within the women's suffrage movement, it presented a new point of departure.

By that point, however, the dissolution of the original London committee had been brought about by the divisions within it. Mill's fine speech on 20 May had strengthened the position of Helen Taylor, and on 17 June the first women's suffrage committee had resolved on dissolution. The new London committee which was subsequently formed did not draw upon the former Langham Place activists. This schism had a lasting effect on the movement, in that it left an executive that was subject to weak and often absent leadership, with many formerly active women channelling their energies elsewhere. It allowed the more dynamic, though politically less radical, Lydia Becker to play the major organisational role in the first years of the women's suffrage movement, a role which also allowed her to appeal to the radical and Liberal networks of the major industrial cities.[27]

MANCHESTER POLITICS AND THE ELECTION OF NOVEMBER 1867

The Manchester suffrage movement built upon the energies of an active group of women, including Josephine Butler and Elizabeth Wolstenholme, who were also to play a leading role in the North of England Council for promoting the Higher Education of Women, founded in autumn 1867, in the formation of the Married Women's Property Committee in April 1868, and from 1869 in the campaign against the Contagious Diseases Acts.[28] However, the support given to the movement for women's political activism in Manchester also had a longer history. Manchester liberalism had in the past drawn upon that wider involvement of women in different forms of pressure group politics, first and most clearly identified with the anti-slavery movement.[29] In the 1840s George Wilson and Richard Cobden, the political organisers of the Anti-Corn Law League, had chosen to use the organisational power and influence of women. That mobilisation can be attributed to the legitimating power of the sentimental concept of 'woman's mission'. But it can also be interpreted as a recognition of the capacities of women to understand and participate in the arguments of political economy. Women petitioned and organised, as well as being involved in extensive fund-raising, on behalf of the League.[30] Many of those later to be active in the women's suffrage movement had sympathised with its populist, anti-aristocratic politics. Elizabeth Wolstenholme and Bessie Parkes had both identified with the cause of the League.[31]

Cobdenite radicals maintained a powerful political and electoral machine long after the repeal of the Corn Laws, dominating Manchester politics and those of a number of neighbouring towns, for the next twenty years. The League had been run from 'Newall's Buildings' in the 1840s, and though the buildings were demolished in 1867, the 'Newall's Buildings clique' remained a useful term of abuse in the elections of the 1860s.[32] This political leadership was strongly linked to local dissenting communities, including key Unitarian and Independent chapels, and to Quakerism. Their power also rested on an electorate which had steadily expanded; by 1860 Manchester was benefiting from a relatively efficient and automatic system of voter registration.[33] Leaders of the Manchester school continued to pursue their earlier commitments to peace, retrenchment and reform throughout the 1850s and early 1860s, though these goals were also linked to support for European nationalisms, to moderate extension of the franchise, and to the politics of temperance. In the 1860s Cobdenism was still at the heart of polit-ical events in Manchester, backed by the *Manchester Examiner and Times*, which expressed a lively Liberal populism with a wide-ranging appeal to reformers and radicals.

Two organisations which united important elements of liberal opinion in the early 1860s were created through the initiatives of Manchester Cobdenites. One was the Union and Emancipation Society, founded in 1863, which united many shades of opinion on behalf of the North in the American Civil War, including local ex-Chartists. Its most prominent officers included Thomas Bayley Potter, MP for Rochdale, and Jacob Bright, the brother of John Bright.[34] The other was the National Reform Union, which in the spring of 1864 attempted to bring together, under Cobdenite leadership, existing middle-class reform organisations and former Chartists and local manhood suffrage campaigners in Lancashire and the north.[35]

For there were continuities with Chartism, the widespread working-class movement of the 1830s and 1840s which had as a part of its aims the achievement of manhood suffrage. These continuities were, however, less powerful in Manchester than elsewhere. In the 1850s the survivors of Manchester Chartism were gradually taking up other causes, like temper-ance. Some, like Abel Heywood and Edward Hoosen, divided their interests between the movement for co-operation and continuing the struggle for man-hood suffrage. Liberal strength brought a diffusion of energies and by 1858, many former Chartists and Cobdenites were working closely together. In 1861, one of the outstanding ex-Chartist leaders, the barrister Ernest Jones, moved to Manchester having married a Manchester schoolteacher. In 1862, Jones did his best to revitalise the Manchester Manhood Suffrage Association, rallying many former supporters, and new recruits from the co-operation movement.[36] The Reform Union founded in 1864 sought to attract manhood suffragists to give support to a more limited enfranchise-ment, their programme of household suffrage. Jones initially rejected such efforts, and in the general election of 1865 energetically supported Abel Heywood as a manhood suffrage candidate.

Though Cobdenite Liberals had in 1865 hoped to present a united front with radicals, and considered Abel Heywood as a potential joint candidate, he was finally dropped in favour of Jacob Bright, a resolute defender of household suffrage. Bright was an attractive figure to represent such an alliance, having worked with Chartists in Rochdale in the 1840s, and given robust support to the rights of Irish tenants in the 1860s. In 1865, however, Bright was defeated, as the Liberal vote was eroded, both by Heywood, and by the successful conservative Liberal, Edward James. Bright was nevertheless clearly identified as the hope of a future 'progressive' alliance; his interest in women's suffrage was seen by many of his associates as potentially damaging to this hope.[37] By 1866 Ernest Jones, recognising as did others the strength of Manchester Liberalism, had come to work with radical Liberals. In the course of 1866 he found common cause with Jacob Bright on a number of issues, especially those relating to Ireland, and came to know Dr Richard Pankhurst, already a member of the National Reform Union.

In March 1867 Lydia Becker wrote publicly to three local MPs to ask for their support on the grounds of the self-reliance and industry shown by Manchester women, in the terms of her *Spectator* article. Thomas Bazley and Edward James of Manchester and John Cheetham of Salford gave support in principle, though they were wary of diverting the issue from the immediate one of a reform bill.[38] In April Ernest Jones's young son, Llewellyn Atherley-Jones, who later remembered Lydia Becker as a family friend, defended the cause of women's suffrage in the *Preston Chronicle*.[39] And at some point in the spring of 1867, the names of the Manchester Women's Suffrage committee came to include the Rochdale MP, the radical Liberal Thomas Bayley Potter, the ex-Chartists Ernest Jones and Edward Hoosen, the ex-Owenite Robert Cooper and the co-operator E. O. Greening. Apart from Potter and Jones, it is not known how active a part they played. But the alliance brought together by the National Reform Union, represented by Jacob Bright, was clearly one in which much sympathy for the women's cause was to be found. R. D. Rusden, the treasurer of the National Reform Union, was a constant source of support to Lydia Becker.[40] In April the committee member Mary Hume-Rothery called for universal adult suffrage in the pages of the *Manchester Examiner and Times*.[41]

In spite of the failure of Mill's amendment to the Conservative Reform Bill, the appeal of the women's suffrage movement increased in the aftermath of the Reform Act. In August 1867 the Manchester Committee adopted its formal constitution. Throughout the autumn of 1867 the desirability of continuing the petitioning campaign was assumed. Lydia Becker wrote to Helen Taylor on 27 September that a paid canvasser, a Miss Knott, 'an intelligent superior person of her class', was having great success in Liverpool securing about sixty names a day to the petition. But the next immediate consequence of the Reform Act was the revision of the electoral register according to the complex new criteria. This suggested an alternative strategy. Lydia Becker suggested that, given the technical weaknesses in the Act, instead of petitioning, women who would qualify as householders should be encouraged to put forward their claims to a vote, in the approved way, before the overseers and revising barristers. By October, it had become evident that there would be an inconsistency between petitioning to change the law, and the argument that women were already entitled to the vote. Steinthal and others in the Manchester group were strongly of the view that the petitioning campaign should be abandoned.[42] Throughout November these alternatives were debated, but the issue was to be determined by a remarkably opportune event in the by-election held in November 1867 in Manchester.

In this by-election, caused by the death of Edward James, Jacob Bright stood against two candidates, one an independent Liberal, the other a Liberal Conservative, as the candidate of the United Liberal Party in a 'progressive' alliance between the Manchester leaders of the National Reform Union, and campaigners for manhood suffrage. This was the first Manchester election since the Reform Act, though fought on the old franchise.[43] Although all the candidates claimed some Liberal credentials, it was contested with unusual warmth, as Jacob Bright was labelled by the Conservative *Manchester Courier* 'the apostle of democracy in its most violent form'.[44] In this election the politics of identity and interest emerged particularly sharply, as the Irish and Jewish communities of Manchester looked for support to their representatives, and the representatives of trade unionism, temperance and the brewery interest scrutinised the record of the candidates. Jacob Bright came under particular attack for his refusal to declare his commitment to any religious denomination.[45]

From 28 October to 13 November Manchester newspapers had been dominated by reports of the trial of members of the Irish Republican Brotherhood for the killing of a policeman in Manchester, as two prisoners were rescued from a prison van. The electoral campaign took place against urgent appeals for mercy for the three Irish Fenians condemned to death, who were executed on 23 November, just two days before the poll opened. The radical Liberals of Manchester opposed the executions and the anti-Catholic, ultra-Protestant demagoguery which had been sweeping Lancashire, and called for mercy.[46] Jacob Bright had a good record of support on Irish issues in the past, and was the candidate endorsed by the Irish Electors Association.[47] Nevertheless the strength of a virulently anti-Catholic Protestant Electoral Union in Lancashire created serious tensions only too evident at electoral meetings.

The Jewish community had an important presence within Manchester and normally saw Cobdenite Liberalism as the party of tolerance. However, an incautious and anti-Semitic remark which Bright had made about Disraeli alienated many members of the Manchester Jewish community, and was rapidly picked up by his opponents. Bright, constantly pressed, had to strive to restore his credibility and mobilise his Jewish supporters. He acknowledged his fault, in a comment made in the heat of events following the Reform Bill, and disavowed any 'prejudice of race or religion'.[48] The rabbi

Dr Gottheil was at his side on the platform at the crowded meeting at the Town Hall on 20 November.[49]

Bright's manifesto, unlike that of the other two candidates, had called for much closer supervision of the licensing of beerhouses and pubs, and indicated that he would accept a future Bill which allowed ratepayers a veto; he was endorsed by a conference of temperance reformers, while his most conservative opponent, Alderman Bennett, was supported by the Manchester Wine and Beer Sellers Association.[50] The Manchester Trades Council too delivered their support, to the candidate most identified with their aims.[51] The Bright manifesto, unlike that of the other candidates, had also attacked the abolition of compounding, as imposing increased charges on many of the poor, who were coming to bear the extra costs of the rates. The consequences of this ill-thought-out policy were already being felt among local householders.[52]

The question of women's suffrage was not a major issue in the campaign, but, with those outlined above, it clearly figured at electoral meetings. Both by letter and in person, the members of the Manchester Committee for the Promotion of Women's Suffrage asked all three candidates to state their views. An independent Liberal, Mitchell Henry, refused to answer a question from a male member of the Manchester committee.[53] When three days later an unnamed woman put the question at a crowded meeting at Chorlton Town Hall, he played it for laughs:

> An intrepid female wanted to know if he would support woman suffrage. Mr Henry did not answer the question directly; she repeated her question, telling him to answer 'yes' or 'no' (Cheers and laughter). Mr Henry said it was unusual for a lady to ask a direct question, but he should be delighted if that lady had the franchise. (A Voice: 'Say "no" right out.' Laughter).[54]

On 15 November Professor Greenbank, of the women's suffrage committee, asked Alderman Bennett whether he supported women's enfranchisement 'amidst uproarious laughter'. The ambiguous response was: 'If I had been in Parliament last session, I am too gallant a man to have voted against Stuart Mill.' In their published replies to Lydia Becker, Henry replied that he saw no reason why women with property 'should be excluded from the franchise solely on account of sex', and Bennett declared himself 'in favour of giving the franchise to those unmarried women whether widows or spinsters, who are householders and ratepayers'.[55]

Jacob Bright proclaimed at his meeting of 19 November in the Town Hall, in answer to a letter from Lydia Becker, that women's suffrage 'would only be consistent with almost everything, I believe, that takes place in the old parochial matters of the county'. His commitment was unequivocal, and associated with his membership of the Reform Union:

I have long been a member of a political organisation in this town, in favour of household suffrage, I don't know how that association exactly interprets the matter, but when I speak of household suffrage, I mean household suffrage. (Hear [*sic*])...if it happens that some houses – unfortunately, as I believe it generally would be – had no male head but only a woman as householder and ratepayer, I can see no reason for making those houses any exception with respect to the vote. (Applause)[56]

The Manchester electorate had expanded rapidly even before the Reform Act, as it adopted a system of automatic and relatively efficient registration, which included tenants who compounded for their rents, after 1860. A minor amendment to the Reform Act had strengthened the provisions against the payment of canvassers; and in this election Bright's backers, the National Reform Union, called for all its members and friends to take an active part in ward canvassing since 'under the new Act, any elector receiving payment for canvassing would render his vote invalid'.[57] The degree of canvassing at ward level was clearly very high, and was acknowledged to be so by Bright's opponents.[58] The turnout of electors was exceptional, Bright achieving more personal votes than any previous candidate in Manchester except for one.[59]

It was under these circumstances, in an election of particular interest after Bright's earlier defeat, as votes were heavily canvassed, that, on 26 November 1867, Lily Maxwell cast her vote on the hustings in Manchester. Recollecting this, Lydia Becker wrote to Mary Smith of Carlisle that this was not a claim to vote, but a mistake:

Her name got on the register by mistake. It is spelt Lilly – and the overseer must have thought it was a masculine name. But *being* on the register – her vote could not be refused. The fact that a woman was registered as a voter was discovered by Mr Bright's committee in the course of their canvass – they first wrote to me – and I called on her & took her to the poll. She was rather timid at first – and I believe I should never have got her to come, only that she was so strongly in favour of Mr Bright.[60]

Yet in the printed versions of the electoral register for Manchester, for 1866–1867 and 1867–1868, Lily Maxwell's name is spelt with one 'l', though both spellings do occur elsewhere.[61] Manchester street directories for 1865 and 1868 indicate that she kept a chandler's shop at 25 Ludlow Street, Chorlton-upon-Medlock, between these years.[62]

A surviving portrait of Lily Maxwell in Manchester Central Library suggests that she had been an old family servant in the home of Sir Thomas Bosdin Leech, Manchester businessman, Mayor of Manchester and pioneer

Borough of Manchester. 1866-7

Booth No. 40

TOWNSHIP OF CHORLTON-UPON-MEDLOCK.—ALL SAINTS' WARD.—H 12033 to M inclusiv[e].

Prog. No.	Christian Name and Surname of each Person at full length.	Place of Abode.	Nature of Qualification.	Street, Lane, or other place in this Township, and Number of House (if any), where the property is situated.
12324	Mattinson James	Oxford street	house and shop	5, Oxford street
12325	Mawdesley Thomas	Park street	house	27, Park street
12326	Maxwell Lily	Ludlow street	house	25, Ludlow street
12327	McAllister John	Union street	house	34, Union street
12328	McBriar Charles	Bond street	beerhouse	1, Bond street
12329	McClean Thomas	Higher Cambridge street	house	118, Higher Cambridge street
12330	McConnell William	Bridge street west	house	57, Bridge street west
12331	McCready James	Union street	house	32, Union street
12332	McCready John	20, Irwell street, Strangeways	building	York street
12333	McDonald William	Coupland street	house	57, Coupland street
12334	McFarlane John	Lloyd street	house	155, Lloyd street
12335	McFarlane William Alexander	Eagle street	house	33, Eagle street
12336	McGann John	Stockton street	house	22, Stockton street
12337	McGregor Peter	Lime grove	house	2, Lyme grove
12338	McGregor William	Chatsworth street	house	27, Chatsworth street
12339	McKay John	Booth street west	house	77, Booth street west
12340	McKeand Joseph	Oxford street	house	170, Oxford street
12341	McKerrow John Begg	Cecil street	house	55, Cecil street
12342	McKillum Robert	Pigot street	house	52, Pigot street

Figure 1 This copy of the electoral register for Manchester in 1866–1867 was marked by the returning officer with the pledges and votes given, and here with a comment on Lily Maxwell's vote: 'Woman!!!' in the margin.

Figure 2 Lily Maxwell: this sepia photograph, marked on the back 'Lily – an old servant of the family', was presented to Manchester Central Library by a
member of the Bosdin Leech family.

of the Manchester Ship Canal.[63] Her past is confirmed in the correspondence
of Lydia Becker, who later wrote of her as a widow, and as:

> a Scotchwoman who has lived for many years in domestic service in
> Manchester. As years advanced and activity diminished she set up a
> small shop.[64]

Lily Maxwell must have moved to this address sometime between 1861 and
1865. Ludlow Street, once part of the pleasant suburb of Greenheys, was a

Figure 3 Ludlow Street, Chorlton-upon-Medlock: a photograph acquired by
Manchester Central Library in 1964

street of terraced houses, numbered up to 82, in the area between Boundary
Lane, Coupland Street and Cambridge Street, now occupied by the Dental
Hospital. In 1867 seventy-four households in Ludlow Street were assessed
for payment of the poor rates; twenty-one of these were households headed
by women.[65] It was a mixed street of houses occupied by tenants, mainly
artisans and shopkeepers. There were only two owner-occupiers: Mary Fox
at number 40, whose house had a rateable value of £10 5s 0d, and the
wealthier beer retailer Richard Crozier, occupying the beerhouse at number
20, and the landlord of four other houses in the street.

Lily Maxwell paid a weekly rent of 6s 2d for her house and shop, which
had a rateable value of £11 5s 0d; this placed her in that 38 per cent (28) of
the moderately better-off households in the street rated at between £10 and
£12. Of the seventy-four households, thirty-five had a clear rateable value of
£10 or above, and were therefore eligible for a vote under the pre-1867 franchise. The majority of the householders of Ludlow Street, (47) 64 per cent,
were still compounding for their rates, which were paid by their landlords.
But Lily Maxwell paid hers directly, and promptly.

The occupations of the male householders of Ludlow Street included joiners, mechanics, bootmakers, warehousemen, and a watchmaker, book-keeper and hairdresser, and also butchers and provision dealers.[66] The women who headed households assessed at over £10 are described in the Manchester street directories either as householders or, like Lily Maxwell, as keeping some kind of small business, as did her neighbour Ann Bains at number 23, a provision dealer, or Ann Furniss, who occupied a beerhouse at number 44. Among the slightly less well-off women householders were the nurse, Maria Daniels, at number 81, the dressmaker Mary Ann Powers at number 64, and the milliners Hannah and Martha Critchlow at number 60.

The marked electoral roll for Manchester for the election of December 1867 survives, indicating both the candidates to whom electors pledged their vote in advance, and the candidates for whom they voted.[67] Thirty-four householders from Ludlow Street, including Lily Maxwell, appear on the electoral roll, and twenty-three actually cast their votes. Of these, the majority, fifteen, both pledged their votes in advance to Jacob Bright and voted for him; two simply cast their votes for him. Six voted for the Liberal Conservative, Alderman Bennett. Bright's 'progressive' candidature and extensive canvassing clearly won a substantial degree of support from Ludlow Street, a street in which the transition to household suffrage would shortly see a significant increase in the electorate, though one which would still exclude female-headed households.

Lydia Becker lived only a few streets away in Carter Street, which ran between Boundary Lane and Denmark Road. The house in which she lived in 1867, 85 Carter Street, Greenheys, had a rateable value of £15 15s 0d, and was one of five houses, numbers 81–89, owned by a female landlord, Elizabeth Holroyd; numbers 83 and 85 were both occupied by women tenants, Margaret Platt and Eliza Glover.[68] A recent historian has described this area as:

> a dense mass of common brick houses, intersected by narrow streets, which by the 1860s, were overwhelming the detached subur-ban villas of the 1820s.[69]

A local observer wrote of the same area as containing 'as complete a combi-nation of wealth and poverty...as could well be got together in a single suburb'.[70] Lydia Becker lived in relatively close proximity to the different kinds of housing, the terraces and villas, inhabited by tradesmen, artisans and labourers, as by the professional and middle classes. She would also have been personally familiar with the reality of the lives of women house-holders, as tenants, owners and landladies at different social levels.

Lily Maxwell's vote was known only on the day that the results were announced. The most detailed contemporary account is in the *Manchester Guardian*, which described her casting her vote for Jacob Bright, in public, at Chorlton Town Hall, accompanied by ladies, to a round of applause.[71] We do not know when the ironical entry 'Woman !!!' was made in the electoral register, though the clerk may have recorded the event in this way. In his speech from the steps of the Town Hall, made just after the result was declared, Bright generously gave prominence to Maxwell's vote, rapidly turning laughter into applause as he proclaimed two reasons for celebration. The first was that Manchester was won again to the cause of 'peace retrenchment and reform', the other that, for the first time, to his knowledge since 1832, a woman had voted:

> This woman is a hardworking honest person, who pays her rates as you do...if any woman should possess a vote, it is precisely such a one as she.[72]

THE USES OF LILY MAXWELL'S VOTE

The immediate responses to the news of this vote were, predictably, varied. *The Times* took immediate note, in a hostile editorial which identified Jacob Bright's words very closely with the wider arguments for enfranchisement heard in the reform agitation of 1866–1867:

> '...such a one as she'. What more need be said? This was the simple theme, which, with a hundred variations, was so successful before, and why should it not be successful again, especially as it would in this case be supported by so pleasant an influence, and no hard words could be uttered anywhere as to the personal qualifications of these new candidates for the suffrage?[73]

Lydia Becker responded to this editorial in its own terms. For to Becker the publicity given to Lily Maxwell could be utilised to suggest those qualities of citizenship which women might demonstrate, qualities which had much in common with those of the 'independent' artisan: independence, respectability and political commitment. Her letter to *The Times* declared:

> Lily Maxwell is a widow, who keeps a small shop in a quiet street in Manchester. She supports herself and pays her own rates and taxes out of her own earnings. She has no man to influence or be influenced by, and she has very decided political principles, which determined her vote for Mr Jacob Bright at the recent election.[74]

The readers of the *Englishwoman's Review* were given a more detailed report of the circumstances. Neither Lydia Becker nor Lily Maxwell had been aware until a day or so before the election that her name was on the list. Once informed. she declared herself a keen admirer of Jacob Bright, 'declar-

" LILY MAXWELL TRIUMPHANT."

OR, THE FIRST PERSON SINGULAR.

" In the course of the polling, a lady, duly entered on the register as LILY MAXWELL, appeared to record her vote for MR. JACOB BRIGHT : as the name was found on the register, the vote was duly recorded."—*Manchester Papers.*

HUZZAH for the great Female Movement's
　　Pioneer in the Manchester school,
That still leads the race of improvements,
　　Whose " exceptions " ere long " prove the rule ! "
To the fair LILY MAXWELL a bumper,
　　Who in petticoats rushed to the poll,
And for JACOB BRIGHT entered her plumper,
　　MILL'S first " person," singular, sole !

As in old times, by heralds dwelt much on,
　　For heroes who great deeds would dare,
The Sovereign bestowed, in their scutcheon,
　　Arms of honour, appropriate, to wear,
So now in LA MAXWELL'S coat-armour—
　　Or petticoat—*Punch* would propound,
This device,—which he's certain will charm her—
　　" Argent, wavy,* a Bright Lily crowned ! "

And when in the course of the ages,
　　Which in good time all good measures bring,
Our *femmes soles*, like birds out of cages
　　Released, on the register sing,
To the poll, as on steel-stiffened pinions,
　　Once doves, henceforth eagles, they press,
Let a Bright Lily badge deck their chignons,
　　And be clan-Maxwell tartan their dress.

As the name seems to show that North Britain
　　Gave her blood to their fair pioneer,
A tribute to Scotland might fit in
　　With a change whose convenience is clear.
As long clothes ill fit crush and quarrel,
　　And male roughs are hard to control,
To the work, ladies, cut your apparel,
　　And in kilts make your rush to the poll !

* If this be bad heraldry, the " blazon " must yield to the verse.

Figure 4 A verse from *Punch,* 7 December 1867

ing that if she had twenty votes she would give them all to him', belying any suggestion that working-class women had no political views:

> Accordingly on the following day she went to Mr Bright's commit-
> tee room, accompanied by Miss Becker, the zealous and able secre-
> tary of the Manchester Suffrage Society, and by another lady, also a
> member of the committee. From thence the ladies were escorted by
> several gentlemen to the polling place...

There they had attracted cheers but no inconvenience.[75] The vote also attracted, of course, several satirical responses, from the Manchester paper *The Free-Lance*, as from *Punch*, who responded on 7 December with:

> Huzzah for the great Female Movement's
> Pioneer in the Manchester school...[76]

However, the future for Lily Maxwell herself was not so promising. We may gain a little insight into this from the correspondence between Susan B. Anthony, pioneering women's suffrage campaigner in the United States, who had written to enquire about the circumstances surrounding her vote, and Lydia Becker. In October 1868, Becker, who had become Maxwell's channel of communication 'as the poor old lady is no scribe', reported that illness last spring had 'rendered her incapable of active exertion' and that

> she is now living in a little house near here – where I hope she may
> find peace and some degree of comfort at the close of her simple and
> useful and unpretending career.

Maxwell's name is present in the 1869 street directory but she was not assessed for rates in that year, either in Ludlow Street or at 17 Cowgill Street, to which she had moved.[77] She had little chance of comfort in retirement, as a later letter from Becker reported:

> you will be sorry to hear she is in trouble – she is very poor, and
> pecuniary and entirely unmerited misfortune has overtaken her – but
> as it does not need much to set her straight, I hope we will manage
> to help her in her need.[78]

Becker's stalwart and determined defence of the respectability and industry of likely women voters was clearly undertaken in full knowledge of their vulnerability to illness and financial disaster in nineteenth-century Manchester.

One month after Lily Maxwell's vote, another woman, Jesse Godber, also cast a vote, this time in a municipal by-election in the Oxford ward of the city. Although the local press immediately recalled Lily Maxwell in their comments, the response of women's suffrage campaigners was very different. The *Englishwoman's Review* briefly reported that a Jessie Goodwin had cast her vote.[79] Manchester papers variously referred to Jessie Goodwin, Jessie Godwin and Jessie Godber.[80] In fact, it was as Jesse Godber, of a 'house and shop' in 22 London Road, that this voter appeared in the municipal electoral rolls for 1866 and 1867, and *also* in the parliamentary electoral rolls for the same years.[81] She too was escorted by two women, a Mrs Shepherd and a Mrs Royse, to the poll.[82] The relative indifference of the women's suffrage movement to this particular woman voter may have related to the way in which she cast her vote, for the successful candidate, Mr Ingham, who was opposed by a good friend to women's suffrage, the treasurer to the National Reform Union, R. D. Rusden.

Ingham had proclaimed himself also a Liberal; but Rusden was accused of being imposed upon the ward by the Liberal political machine running Manchester. The other major issue was that of temperance. Ingham, who kept a pub, complained that 'the waterdrinkers...had been pressed into the service against him'.[83] Jesse Godber was resident only for a short time at 22 London Road. In 1865, this address was occupied by Samuel Turner, a beer retailer, and in 1868 by Samuel M. South, also a beer retailer. It would seem not impossible that she either had connections with, or that her vote was mobilised by, the brewery interest. And she had clearly not been identified as a potential parliamentary voter by the zealous canvassing committees of Jacob Bright.

Lily Maxwell's vote, however, had offered a providential opportunity for Lydia Becker to pursue a policy which rested on claiming the vote for women directly. By the end of 1867 she had already begun to try to convince the Overseer and Town Clerk of Manchester to put qualified women on the register.[84] Although Maxwell's vote was strictly irrelevant, the reaction from the canvasser employed by the Manchester women's suffrage committee to gather signatures for petitions was immediate, according to Becker:

> She immediately began to feel that she must wait for instructions, lest it should not be right to go on collecting signatures, and she said people refused to sign because they said women could vote now.

Thomas Hare, the friend of John Stuart Mill, acting as a friendly adviser in this context, drafted a new petition form, asking for a declaratory act to clarify the state of the law on women's suffrage.[85] Three months after the by-election, a meeting of the National Reform Union gave an extremely sympathetic hearing to a call for the vote for all qualified women by committee members Alice Wilson and Jacob Bright, though the Chair ruled that the rules of the association could not be altered without notice. Jacob Bright believed that a more forceful response might have succeeded in winning the Union over.[86]

The contradictions at the heart of the radical Liberal position, within the 'progressive' alliance between adult suffrage and household suffrage, became more evident in the accelerating campaign for women's suffrage in 1868. In May 1868 Becker wrote to Richard Pankhurst of the desirability of universal adult suffrage, as 'the ultimate end to which all efforts at partial enfranchisement are subsidiary'.[87] Yet her desire to demonstrate that women *could* vote entrenched the single woman householder at the heart of her politics. Throughout 1868, Becker worked to register qualified women, identifying up to 13,000 potential voters. She sought, with her supporters, to persuade overseers to register them, occasionally with success. Where overseers refused, qualified women had to be persuaded to stake a claim. In September 1868, appeals by claimants who had been refused were heard by revising barristers in registration courts across Britain, though the most active debates were heard in Lancashire. There the case for 5,750 claimants was put forward by counsel instructed by the Liberals and opposed by the representative of the Conservative Association. Similar battles took place throughout England and Scotland, though much further research is needed here.[88]

Throughout that year she received continuing support from the 'United Liberal' alliance. The first annual meeting of the Manchester society was held in October 1868 in the mayor's parlour of Manchester Town Hall. Those who spoke exemplified her support: Lydia Becker herself, Jacob Bright, Ernest Jones and Richard Pankhurst.[89] In the general election of 1868, nine out of thirteen women voters who remained on the register cast their votes, eight of them for the Liberal Party, with the help of Lydia Becker who escorted them to the poll. Their background was later described as ranging 'in social grade from the rank of well-to-do shopkeepers down to that of the very poorest labourer', and, in an echo of Lily Maxwell, they were said to have displayed genuine political feeling, intelligence and interest, 'a fair sample, it was suggested, of the 10,000 eligible women ratepayers of Manchester'.[90]

Of the three Liberal candidates in Manchester in 1868, allied as United Liberals, Sir Thomas Bazley, Jacob Bright and Ernest Jones were all supporters of women's suffrage in different degrees; so too, however, was the popular local employer, the Conservative Hugh Birley, who defeated Ernest Jones.[91] In their disappointment at Jones's defeat, the United Liberals organised a test secret ballot for their supporters to determine who should be the Liberal candidate if Birley's election were judged void. In this interesting experiment, they made particular provision for women still on the electoral register to participate.[92]

CONCLUSION

Of course, the campaign was to take much longer than Becker expected. Lily Maxwell's fortuitous vote had provided a signal of what was possible, a chance to be exploited in the interests of a Liberal vision of the woman voter. It was a vision increasingly shaped partly by a tactical commitment to household suffrage, partly by an immediate sense of the possibilities of more rapid progress for women householders following the debates of the Reform Bill. Her policy did not derive from any desire to enfranchise simply wealthy or propertied women. It addressed itself rather to those classes whose potential voting power remained undetermined in the immediate wake of 1867. The single or widowed woman householder, who could be a tenant as well as an owner, was as likely to be a small shopkeeper or a dressmaker, as an independent woman of wealth. The enfranchisement of the highly mobile urban population of male tenants, so nervously debated in the House of Commons, was gradually and uncertainly to follow the Reform Act of 1867. The compounding of rates was restored in 1869, when women householders, like others, no longer had to bear excess costs for which they received no benefits. Also in 1869 women householders – women like Lily Maxwell and Jesse Godber – were granted the municipal franchise without significant opposition in the House of Commons, on the grounds that such a provision was in tune with ancient and constitutional practice.[93]

The after-effects of Lily Maxwell's vote are not easy to gauge. The apparently easy successes of the next two years, when in 1869 the municipal franchise was won, and in 1870 the second reading of Jacob Bright's Women's Disabilities Bill was passed by 33 votes, were won at a price. And the price was the legacy of the acceptable woman voter, the single and industrious householder, indebted to no man. It was an image which was far removed from the reality of Lily Maxwell's world, in which female-headed households were indeed common, but so too were the labour of domestic service and the patronage of the better-off, under the continuing threat of illness and financial misfortune. Lydia Becker continued to work with her radical Liberal colleagues to introduce women's suffrage Bills which did not explicitly exclude married women, until in 1874 she pragmatically accepted their explicit exclusion in a Bill introduced by a Conservative MP, as more likely to succeed with a Conservative ministry. The battle to include married women divided the movement in 1874 and again in 1889, as that for adult suffrage was later to do.[94] The Manchester committee had already even in 1867 reflected such tensions, as when in April Mary Hume-Rothery had noted the importance of principles which would not only 'serve the passing hour' but give greater vitality to a growing movement, recognising the equality and independence of mind of married as of unmarried women. Lily Maxwell's vote sadly represented the alternative – and the immediately attractive – path.

NOTES

I would like to thank the British Academy for their financial support, the staff of the Local Studies Unit and the Archives Department of Manchester Central Library for their unfailing, cheerful and expert assistance, and the editors of this volume for their suggestions.

1 *Englishwoman's Review (EWR)*, VI, January 1868, pp. 359–369. Jacob Bright, (1821–1899) was the younger brother of John Bright, one of the leading politicians of mid-Victorian Britain, and became an outstanding parliamentary spokesman for the women's movement. From a Quaker background, he spent much of his early life in the family business and local politics in Rochdale; his career has had little notice, but see *Dictionary of British radicals*, ed. J. O. Baylen and N. J. Gossmann, 4 vols, (Brighton, Harvester, 1984), Vol. 3, pp. 126–128; obituary in the *Manchester Guardian (MG)*, 9 November 1899.

2 *First annual report of the executive committee of the Manchester National Society for Women's Suffrage* (Manchester, Alexander Ireland, 1868), pp. 4–5.

3 For general discussions of claims for women's suffrage before 1866, see: H. Blackburn, *Women's suffrage: a record of the women's suffrage movement in the British Isles* (1902, reprinted New York, Source Book Press, 1970); K. Gleadle, *The early feminists: radical Unitarians and the emergence of the women's rights movement, 1831–1851* (Basingstoke, Macmillan, 1995), Ch. 3; J. Rendall, The citizenship of women and the Reform Act of 1867, in C. Hall *et al.*, *Defining the Victorian nation* (forthcoming, Cambridge, Cambridge University Press, 2000).

4 H. T. Mill, Enfranchisement of women, *Westminster Review*, 55, July 1851, pp. 289–311, reprinted in J. S. Mill, *Essays on equality, law and education*, ed. S. Collini, in *Collected works of John Stuart Mill (CW)*, ed. J. M. Robson (Toronto, University of Toronto Press, 1972–) , Vol. XXI, pp. 393–415.

5 On this group see J. Rendall, 'A moral engine'? Feminism, liberalism and the *English Woman's Journal*, in J. Rendall (ed.), *Equal or different: women's politics 1800–1914* (Oxford, Basil Blackwell, 1987).

6 B. R. Parkes to B. Bodichon, 21 August n.y., Parkes Papers, Girton College, Vol. V, f. 86.

7 B. L. Kinzer *et al.*, *A moralist in and out of parliament: John Stuart Mill at Westminster, 1865–1868* (Toronto, University of Toronto Press, 1992), pp. 113 and 270–271; F. B. Smith, *The making of the second Reform Bill* (Cambridge, Cambridge University Press, 1966), p. 54.

8 E. Davies to Mr Tomkinson, 10 November 1865, Family Chronicle, Davies Papers, Girton College, f. 439.

9 The Reform Acts of 1832 had broadly established a £10 occupier franchise in the boroughs of England, Scotland and Wales, based on a ratepaying qualification, as well as stipulating that the voter had to be male. All qualified voters in both counties and boroughs had to be entered on the register of electors, revised annually, in order to cast a vote; in the boroughs this was done automatically, though in the counties electors had to claim their votes. The tenants of £10 occupancies who were 'compounders' paid their rates and other taxes with their rent to their landlord who then paid the rates. Legally, such tenants were entitled to claim a vote, but the difficulties were considerable, and the numbers voting depended on local efficiency and the interest of local political parties, who put forward the claims of some voters and objected to others. See Smith, *Making of the second Reform Bill*, pp. 18–19, and 64–65.

10 Draft letter of H. Taylor to B. Bodichon, 9 May 1866, and E. Davies to H. Taylor, 6 August 1866, Mill–Taylor papers (MT), London School of Economics, Vol. XIII, ff. 107–110, 183; Petition for extension of the electoral franchise to all householders, without distinction of sex...(7 June 1866, No. 8501), *Reports of the Select Committee of the House of Commons on Public Petitions, Session 1866*, Appendix, p. 305. See also A. P. Robson, The founding of the National Society for Women's Suffrage 1866–1867, *The Canadian Journal of History*, 8, 1973, pp. 1–22.

11 Correspondence between Bodichon and Taylor, May 1866, MT, Vol. XII, ff. 105–114. For a detailed analysis of the petition and its signatories, see A. Dingsdale, 'Generous and lofty sympathies': the Kensington Society, the 1866 women's suffrage petition, and the development of mid-Victorian feminism, DPhil, University of Greenwich, 1995.

12 *Public and parliamentary speeches by John Stuart Mill*, ed. J. M. Robson, in *CW*, Vol. XXVIII, pp. 91–93.

13 The account given above is drawn from A. Robson, No laughing matter: John Stuart Mill's establishment of women's suffrage as a parliamentary question, *Utilitas*, ii, 1990, pp. 88–101; Kinzer *et al.*, *A moralist in and out of Parliament*, Ch. 4. The return of female householders was apparently never made, though it was eagerly awaited. E. Davies to H. Taylor, 18 July and 26 November 1866, MT, Vol. XIII, ff. 181 and 189.

14 Davies to L. Becker, 28 February 1867 and Harriet Cook to Lydia Becker, 8 April 1867, M50/1/2/13 and 18, Manchester Central Library (MCL); the story of these conflicts is clearly told in Robson, Founding of the National Society, pp. 11–22, and A. Rosen, Emily Davies and the women's movement, *The Journal of British Studies*, 19, 1979, pp. 111–121.

15 *Reasons for the enfranchisement of women* (London, J. Bale, 1866); see S. Herstein, *A mid-Victorian feminist, Barbara Leigh Smith Bodichon* (New Haven and London, Yale University Press, 1985), pp. 157–161.

16 For discussion of these different views of the foundation of the Manchester society, see Sandra Holton, *Suffrage days: stories from the women's suffrage movement* (London, Routledge, 1996), pp. 21–22, and 254, note 25; see also Sylvia Pankhurst, *The suffragette movement: an intimate account of persons and ideals* (1931, reprinted London, Virago, 1977), pp. 30–31.

17 Blackburn, *Women's suffrage*, p. 59; M. L. Shanley, *Feminism, marriage and the law in Victorian England, 1850–1895* (Princeton, NJ, Princeton University Press, 1989), pp. 50–52; Max Kyllmann, a German native, was a friend and correspondent of Mill, an active supporter of the North in the American Civil War, and interested in co-operation, Mill, *The Later Letters of John Stuart Mill, 1849–1873*, ed. F. E. Mineka and D. N. Lindley, in *CW*, Vol. 15, p. 810.

18 On Becker, see A. Kelly, *Lydia Becker and the cause* (Centre for North-West Regional Studies, University of Lancaster, 1992); Blackburn, *Women's suffrage*, pp. 59–60.

19 *The Spectator*, 23 February 1867; the debate between S.D.C. and L.E.B. can be followed in the issues of 2 and 23 February, 2 and 23 March; Davies to Becker, 19 January, 16 and 22 February 1867, M50/1/2/5 and 10–11, MCL. See also Becker's article, Female suffrage, *Contemporary Review*, 4, March 1867, pp. 307–316.

20 Lydia Becker to Benjamin Disraeli, 2 March 1867, Hughenden Papers, Box 40/1, ff. 115–116, Bodleian Library.

21 Rosen, Emily Davies and the women's movement, pp. 118–119; J. Boucherett to H. Taylor, 30 April 1867, MT, Vol. XII, ff. 149–153; *EWR*, III, April 1867, 197–198.

22 See n. 9 above; Smith, *Making of the second Reform Bill*, pp. 196–203; B. Keith Lucas, *The English local government franchise: a short history* (Oxford, Basil Blackwell, 1952), p. 73.

23 The admission of women to the electoral franchise, 20 May 1867, *Public and parliamentary speeches, CW*, Vol. XXVIII, pp. 151–162.

24 *EWR*, IV, July 1867, p. 199.

25 *Hansard*, Vol. 187, cols 833–835, 29 May 1867.

26 J. Parry, *The rise and fall of Liberal government in Victorian Britain* (New Haven and London, Yale University Press, 1993), p. 221.

27 Robson, Founding of the National Society, pp. 17–22; Rosen, Emily Davies and the women's movement, pp. 120–121.

28 Shanley, *Feminism, marriage and the law*, pp. 52–53; Blackburn, *Women's suffrage*, pp. 58–60; Davies to Becker, January–March 1867, M50/1/2, ff. 1–17, MCL.

29 See the authoritative discussion of the relationship between anti-slavery and abolitionist movements, and the women's movement, in C. Midgley, *Women against slavery: the British campaigns, 1780–1870* (London and New York, Routledge, 1992), Chs 8–9, and Anti-slavery and feminism in Britain, *Gender & History*, 5, 1993, pp. 343–362.

30 A. Tyrrell, 'Woman's mission' and pressure group politics (1825–1860), *Bulletin of the John Rylands Library*, 1980, 194–230; *Anti-Corn Law Circular*, 11 February 1841, cited in S. Morgan, Beyond 'woman's mission': women and the Anti-Corn Law League, unpublished paper, to whose work on the League I am indebted here.

31 Holton, *Suffrage days*, p. 11; B. Parkes to M. Swainson, 5 June 1851, Parkes Papers, Vol. 3, f. 23.

32 'Newall's Buildings, Manchester', *Manchester Faces and Places*, V, 1893–1894, pp. 83–86.

33 This interpretation of Manchester politics is greatly indebted to an unpublished thesis, A. D. Taylor, Modes of political expression and working-class radicalism 1848–1874: the London and Manchester examples, 2 vols, PhD, Manchester, 1992; see also H. J. Hanham, *Elections and party management: politics in the time of Disraeli and Gladstone*, 2nd edn, (Hassocks, Sx, Harvester, 1978), pp. 308–312.

34 Taylor, Modes of political expression, Vol. 1, p. 357; on Potter, a Unitarian and member of a leading Manchester family, formerly an activist of the Anti-Corn Law League and Complete Suffrage Union, see *Dictionary of British radicals*, ed. Baylen and Gossmann, Vol. 2, pp. 418–422.

35 Taylor, Modes of political expression, Vol. 2, pp. 490–504; F. E. Gillespie, *Labor and politics in England 1850–1867* (1927, repr. New York, Octagon, 1966), pp. 243–257.

36 On Jones, Heywood and Hoosen, see A. D. Taylor, Ernest Jones: his later career and the structure of Manchester politics 1861–1869, MA thesis, University of Birmingham, 1984, pp. 9-11; see also *Dictionary of labour biography*, ed. J. E. Bellamy and J. Saville (London, Macmillan, 1972–) .

37 Becker to S. B. Anthony, 13 October 1868, M50/1/3, ff. 397–402, MCL.

38 *Manchester Examiner and Times* (*ME*), 9 March 1867.

39 Taylor, Ernest Jones, p. 49; L. A. Atherley-Jones, *Looking back: reminiscences of a political career* (London, Witherby, 1925), pp. 10–11; *Preston Chronicle*, 20 April 1867, in M50/1/9/1, MCL.

40 Manchester Committee for the Enfranchisement of Women [Manchester, 1867], and list of supporters headed Enfranchisement of Women, M50/1/9/1, MCL; this early list of Manchester committee members can be dated by its commitment to

prepare the two petitions presented in April 1867. On Cooper and Greening, see *Biographical dictionary of British radicals*, ed. Baylen and Gossmann; *Dictionary of labour biography*, ed. Bellamy and Saville; Taylor, Ernest Jones, pp. 9–11. On Rusden, see Becker to Taylor, 8 January 1868, MT Vol. XII, ff. 80–83.

41 *ME*, 2 and 20 April 1867.

42 Correspondence between Lydia Becker and Helen Taylor, August–November 1867, MT, Vol. XII, ff. 43–63.

43 For the background to this election see Hanham, *Elections and party manage-ment*, pp. 310–311; Taylor, Modes of political expression, Vol. 2, pp. 417–424 and 490–504.

44 *Manchester Courier (MC)*, 26 November 1867.

45 *ME*, 22, 23 and 25 November 1867.

46 Neville Kirk, *The growth of working class reformism in mid-Victorian England* (London and Sydney, Croom Helm, 1985), pp. 323–324; Patrick Quinlivan and Paul Rose, *The Fenians in England 1865–1872: a sense of insecurity* (London, John Calder, 1982), pp. 56–67; Hanham, *Elections and party management*, p. 421.

47 *ME*, 12 November 1867. It was however also true that Bright, like many sympa-thisers with Garibaldi and Italian unification, felt little empathy for the position of a Catholic Church identified as reactionary and unprogressive, and was attacked by some Irish electors in 1867 for his support of Garibaldi. 'An Irish elector', *To the Catholics of Manchester* [1867], Broadsides Collection, MCL.

48 *ME*, 13, 15, 20 and 23 November 1867; Bill Williams, *The making of Manchester Jewry, 1740–1875* (1976, repr. Manchester, Manchester University Press, 1985), p. 335; *Jewish Chronicle*, 29 November, 6 and 20 December, 10 January 1867.

49 *ME*, 20 November 1867.

50 *Ibid.*, 18 and 20 November 1867.

51 'A member of the Manchester and Salford Trades Council Executive', Manchester election. To the members of trade societies, n.p. [1867], Broadsides Collection, MCL.

52 For the effect of the ratepaying clauses on poor Manchester householders, women as well as men, see *MC*, 30 October, 5 and 9 November 1867.

53 *ME*, 15 November 1867.

54 *MC*, 18 November 1867.

55 *ME*, 16 and 21 November 1867.

56 Ibid., 20 November 1867.

57 Taylor, Modes of political expression, Vol. 2, pp. 101–103; on this clause, see *MC*, 3 July 1867; *ME*, 13 November 1867.

58 See the comments of 'An elector', *MC*, 3 December 1867.

59 *ME*, 27 November 1867.

60 Lydia Becker to Mary Smith of Carlisle, 20 May 1868, M50/1/3, ff. 138–139, MCL.

61 *The register of persons entitled to vote in the election of members for the borough of Manchester, 1866–7...* (Manchester, Arthur H. Burgess, 1866); *The register of persons entitled to vote in the election of members for the borough of Manchester, 1867–8...* (Manchester, Arthur H. Burgess, 1867).

62 Microfilmed Manchester Street Directory for 1865; *The business directory of Manchester, 1868–1869* (London, J. S. C. Morris, 1868); both are in the Local Studies Unit, MCL.

63 Information with portrait, and from librarian, Local Studies Unit, MCL; for Leech (1836–1912), see *Dictionary of national biography*.

64 Becker to *The Times*, 2 December 1867, and to S. B. Anthony, 13 October 1868, M50/1/3, ff. 397–402, MCL.

65 The information in the next two paragraphs is taken from the ratebooks of the township of Chorlton-upon-Medlock, All Saints' Ward, 1867, M10/9/5/65, MCL.

66 Microfilmed Manchester Street Directory for 1865; *The business directory of Manchester, 1868–1869.*

67 *The register of persons entitled to vote in the election of members for the borough of Manchester, 1867–1868* . . .; the marked version is in series F352 042 M45, MCL.

68 Ratebooks of the township of Chorlton-upon-Medlock, All Saints' Ward, 1867, M10/9/5/65, MCL.

69 M. Hewitt, *The emergence of stability in the industrial city: Manchester 1832–1867* (Aldershot, Scolar Press, 1996), p. 56.

70 *Manchester City News (MCN)*, 18 November 1871, quoted in Hewitt, *Emergence of stability*, p. 62.

71 *MG*, 27 November 1867.

72 Lydia Becker to Susan B. Anthony, 13 October 1868, M50/1/3, ff. 397–402, MCL; *ME*, 27 November 1867.

73 *The Times*, 29 November 1867.

74 *The Times*, 2 December 1867, reprinted in *MC*, 4 December 1867.

75 *EWR*, VI, January 1868, pp. 359–362.

76 *Punch*, 7 December 1867.

77 Becker to Anthony, 13 October 1868, M50/1/3, ff. 397–402 (Becker gives Maxwell's address as 17 Cowgill Street, a small street just off Ludlow Street); *Slater's general and classified directory and street registry of Manchester and Salford* . . . (Manchester, Isaac Slater, 1869); *Slater's general and classified directory and street register of Manchester and Salford* . . . (Manchester, Isaac Slater, 1871–1872).

78 Becker to Anthony, 13 November 1868, M50/1/3, ff. 464–466, MCL.

79 *EWR*, VI, January 1868, pp. 393–394.

80 She was 'Jessie Goodwin' in *ME*, 'Jessie Godwin' in *MG*, 'Jessie Godber' in *MC*, all on 27 December 1868.

81 Microfilms, *Citizens roll of the City of Manchester in the township of Manchester, 1866–1867* [Manchester, 1866]; *Citizens roll of the township of Manchester in the City of Manchester, 1867–1868* [Manchester, 1867]; *Register of persons entitled to vote in the election of members for the borough of Manchester, 1866–1867*; *Register of persons entitled to vote in the election of members for the borough of Manchester, 1867–1868.*

82 *MC*, 27 December 1868.

83 *MC*, 27 December 1867.

84 *EWR*, VI, January 1868, pp. 393–394; Becker to Taylor, 27 December [1867], MT, Vol. XII, ff. 75–79.

85 Becker to Helen Taylor, 5 December [1867], MT, Vol. XII, ff. 66–73; Katharine Hare to Helen Taylor, 14 January [1868], MT, Vol. XIII, f. 206.

86 *ME*, 12 February 1868, and other unidentified cuttings in M50/1/9/1, MCL; Lydia Becker to Helen Taylor, 12 February [1868], MT, 12, ff. 11–12; Lydia Becker to Jessie Boucherett, 1 April 1868, M50/1/3, ff. 40–41, MCL.

87 Becker to Pankhurst, 24 May 1868, M50/1/3, f. 161, MCL; for Pankhurst's similar view, see his The right of women to vote under the Reform Act, 1867, *Fortnightly Review*, 10 o.s., 4 n.s., September 1868, pp. 250–254.

88 M50 1/9/1–2 contains numerous cuttings on the progress of this campaign. See also Blackburn, *Women's suffrage*, 74–88; *EWR*, IX, October 1869, pp. 57–64; *First annual report of* . . . *the Manchester NSWS*, pp. 7–13; Rendall, The citizenship of women and the Reform Act of 1867.

89 *Second annual report of the executive committee of the Manchester National*

Society for Women's Suffrage...Manchester, Alexander Ireland, 1869; *ME*, 31 October 1868 and 16 December 1869.

90 *Second annual report of...the Manchester NSWS*, pp. 6–7; *EWR*, X, January 1869, pp. 137–140.

91 Birley voted for Jacob Bright's Women's Disabilities Bill in 1870.

92 *Second annual report of the...Manchester NSWS*, p. 7.

93 *Hansard*, o.s.196, 1 n.s. Appendix, 7 June 1869, cols 1973–1976; *EWR*, XII, July 1869, pp. 275–279.

94 Holton, *Suffrage days*, pp. 39–40, 76–82.

4

MRS HENRY FAWCETT (1847–1929)

The widow as a problem in feminist biography

Janet Howarth

INTRODUCTION

Shortly before the First World War, as part of its drive to distance 'law-abiding' suffragists from the violent tactics of the WSPU, the National Union of Women's Suffrage Societies (NUWSS) issued biographical sketches of a number of its activists. First in the series was 'Mrs Henry Fawcett', the 'veteran leader of British women suffragists': she had been active in the movement since 1867, a key figure in the formation of the NUWSS in 1897 and its president since the onset of the climactic phase of agitation in 1907.[1] The sketch places her in a reassuring context of family life and the continuities of British politics. Reference is made to Mrs Fawcett's 'equally famous sister, Dr. Garrett Anderson', to her democratic and statesmanlike style of leadership and commitment to the values of liberal constitutionalism. For her, women's claim to vote was based on the commonplaces of a mid-Victorian political tradition, essentially 'English' and associated with her husband's mentor, John Stuart Mill. In her own words, quoted in the sketch: 'I cannot say I *became* a suffragist. I always was one, from the time I was old enough to think at all about the principles of Representative Government.' But the intimate touch in this portrait of a well-known public figure is the claim that 'those who know her best think of her above all as the devoted wife of a blind scholar, and as the ideal mother . . . The picture of her on the platform addressing meetings fades before another picture of her knitting stockings by her own fireside, while her daughter reads aloud to her.'

The image was well chosen to support the claim that she was 'as far from the popular picture of a "suffragette" as could well be'. But there is no doubt that Millicent Garrett Fawcett (to give her the name by which she is generally known) concurred in this representation of herself as 'above all' wife and mother. The compatibility of women's rights with 'womanly' roles and qualities was a point of conviction for her and the section of the Edwardian women's movement that she led. She maintained that she got no pleasure from public speaking and would much prefer to be at home with her books.[2] To feminists of more radical persuasions, then as now, this construction of a suffrage leader as Everywoman might seem less than appealing but it was at least authentic – consistent with what she told others of her inner sense of self. The intriguing feature of this cameo is however the reference to her married life. She is named as wife, not widow, but Henry Fawcett (1833–1884), the blind Cambridge Professor of Political Economy and Radical MP, Postmaster General in Gladstone's second ministry, had been dead for thirty years. The fact was too well known, of course, to need stating, and the image of the Fawcetts as man and wife would still have been familiar to many readers. The NUWSS journal *Common Cause* had recently featured a photograph of the National Portrait Gallery's picture of them, painted in 1872 by Ford Madox Brown (better known as the artist who created another classic representation of Victorian values, *Work*).[3] It shows the husband, seated in the foreground in academic dress, expounding to the young wife, as she perches on the arm of his chair, on a letter held before his sightless eyes: her gaze is fixed on him and, pen in hand, her arm rests protectively upon his shoulder. This was the portrait Fawcett herself used as the frontispiece for her memoirs, *What I remember* (1924). More recently it was the jacket illustration for Lawrence Goldman's volume of essays on Henry Fawcett.[4] But it is not an image that Mrs Fawcett's biographers have chosen to reproduce.

This is, in one sense, unsurprising. Dame Millicent (as she became in 1925) is above all known as a suffragist – the woman who, according to her memorial inscription in Westminster Abbey, 'won citizenship for women'. If we are interested in her formation as a suffragist, this portrait could be seen as positively misleading in the relationship it suggests between dominant husband and attentive wife. Although Millicent Garrett was only nineteen when she married Henry Fawcett in 1867 and he was fourteen years her senior, her values as a feminist were formed in her family of birth. Six of the ten surviving children of the self-made Suffolk businessman Newson Garrett were active in the Victorian women's movement, as was their cousin Rhoda Garrett.[5] Tradition has it that Millicent was marked out when still a teenager as a future suffrage leader, by Emily Davies, close friend and ally of her elder sister Elizabeth (the future Dr Garrett Anderson) in the Langham Place circle, originators of the women's movement of the 1860s. We know, moreover, that when she met her future husband he was already in search of a feminist wife: Henry Fawcett had made unsuccessful marriage proposals to both her sister Elizabeth and Bessie Rayner Parkes. In Millicent he found a partner who shared also his Radical politics and admiration for John Stuart Mill. He wrote of the 'perfect intellectual sympathy' between them at the outset of the marriage.[6] Five years later, in the same year as their portrait was

Emery Walker photographer

HENRY FAWCETT F.R.S., M.P. AND MRS. FAWCETT.
FROM THE PICTURE IN THE NATIONAL PORTRAIT GALLERY BY FORD MADOX BROWN

Figure 5 Henry Fawcett, FRS, MP, and Mrs Fawcett; postcard of the picture in the
National Portrait Gallery by Ford Madox Brown

painted, the Fawcetts published jointly a collection of *Essays and lectures on
social and political subjects*. This volume suggested to Henry's biographer,
Leslie Stephen, that 'their alliance implied the agreement of independent
minds, not the relation of teacher and disciple', and that has been the verdict,
too, of Millicent's biographers.[7]

For the greater part of a public career that lasted over sixty years, moreover, Millicent Fawcett was a widow – and the tendency has been to treat her
early bereavement as something of a 'release'. The marriage launched her as
a public figure and writer, but Henry's death left her free, it seems, to

develop a more independent role. Fawcett's memoirs, which focus mainly on her work as a suffragist, can be read as confirmation of this view of her widowhood as enabling. She tells us that it was only from the 1890s that platform-speaking for women's suffrage became her 'chief occupation'; before that 'my work with my husband prevented me from giving as much time to speaking as I did later'.[8] Yet as a widow her political activities, at least before the Edwardian era, were by no means confined to suffrage work. Modern assessments of her dwell particularly on her involvement in national party politics as a Unionist and in the purity movement. And she continued to hold views, shared with Henry in his lifetime, that could prove divisive within the women's movement – the fierce patriotism that distressed some feminist colleagues during the Boer War and First World War, the commitment to individualist political economy that distanced her from twentieth-century social feminism. Can we, perhaps, make more sense of this record by reconsidering the place of widowhood in her life and the lingering presence in her identity of the 'devoted wife of a blind scholar'?

THE PLACE OF WIDOWHOOD IN MILLICENT GARRETT FAWCETT'S LIFE: SOME QUESTIONS

Our knowledge of Fawcett's life has increased significantly in recent years. In the half-century after the publication of her official biography by a friend and colleague, Ray Strachey, historians of the suffrage movement tended to show more interest in the Pankhursts.[9] A new generation rediscovered her in the 1980s. Biographical essays by Ann Oakley and Barbara Caine reassessed her from a feminist standpoint.[10] Brian Harrison portrayed her with Emmeline Pankhurst as 'two models of feminist leadership'.[11] Recent work in suffrage studies has, on the whole, enhanced Fawcett's reputation as leader in the Edwardian agitation, endorsing the wisdom of her constitutional strategy but also revealing her as bolder and more sympathetic in her reactions to militancy than she appeared in Strachey's portrait.[12] But other features of her career attract less favourable comment. Her writings as a political economist, culminating in the breach with Eleanor Rathbone over Family Allowances in the 1920s, were critically assessed by Michele Pujol.[13] Fawcett figures, equally problematically, in (for example) Lucy Bland's studies of feminism and sexual morality, Antoinette Burton's work on imperialist feminism and Jo Vellacott's on feminist pacifism.[14] David Rubinstein's sympathetic and thoroughly researched full-length biography, *A different world for women* (1991), takes up the challenge of re-evaluating a life about which more is now known than Strachey (or Fawcett herself, when she wrote her memoirs) felt able to reveal.

The episodes in her life that have come to seem most in need of explanation belong chiefly to the years after Henry Fawcett's death. In the wake of

W. T. Stead's exposure of child prostitution in 1885 she became involved, as chair of the preventive sub-committee of the National Vigilance Association, in the more authoritarian activities of the purity movement. She also broke with the Gladstonian Liberal Party, in which Henry had made his political career, as MP for Brighton (1865–1874) and later Hackney (1874–1884), and became a prominent Unionist campaigner against Home Rule for Ireland. At times she appeared less committed to the suffrage cause than to these ventures into sexual politics and Unionism – and also more emotionally driven and 'intemperate' (the term is Rubinstein's) in her language than can easily be reconciled with the rational, self-controlled style she adopted as a suffrage leader.[15]

There is general agreement with Oakley's estimate of Fawcett as a woman whose values cannot be subsumed into a straightforward category of 'feminism'. As a suffragist she drew on liberal individualism; her values on sexual morality are much less accessible; her patriotic and liberal imperialist creed was shared by many other suffragists, and certainly by the Garrett family and by Henry Fawcett (an admirer of Palmerston and 'as thoroughly hearty an Englishman as any Conservative').[16] More open to question is Oakley's suggestion that Fawcett's outlook remained constant throughout her life and did not change or develop over time.[17] Both Caine and Rubinstein discern significant changes in the years after Fawcett's bereavement, although they interpret them differently. Caine distinguishes between her commitment to Unionism, which was apparently in line with views held by Henry Fawcett in his lifetime, and her campaigns for sexual purity, which Caine is convinced that Henry would have 'strongly discouraged'.[18] Caine's belief that liberalism cannot provide an ideological framework for feminism encourages her to suggest that in these campaigns Fawcett expressed a more distinctively feminist understanding of women's oppression. Rubinstein, on the other hand, interprets her activities at this period of her life as a shift to the right and as a symptom of erratic judgement in 'the absence of [Henry's] influence': 'her views and behaviour on a range of questions became increasingly dogmatic, intolerant, and for a prolonged period, Conservative'.[19]

These differences of opinion raise questions about Fawcett's experience of widowhood. Can we do more to understand the impact on her of Henry Fawcett's death, and the identity she created, or was encouraged to create, for herself as a political widow? This cannot be a straightforward exercise. All writers on Fawcett note the shortage of surviving material on her personal life and intimate relationships. She made a habit of reserve about personal feelings. As Patricia Jalland has shown, the generation to which she belonged was much less inclined to articulate feelings about death and bereavement than its evangelical forebears.[20] Even within that generation she appeared, as Strachey describes her, to be 'exceedingly afraid of showing emotion, and almost passionately reticent'.[21] Yet there are resources that biographers have not so far exploited. One is the modern literature on bereavement.[22] Another is Fawcett's own writings, from which more can be learned if we set aside the mistrust of Victorian sentimentalism that tends to inhibit twentieth-century biographers.

My own interest in Millicent Garrett Fawcett's widowhood stems from one of those coincidences that can create intertextualities between the lives of biographer and subject. Like her, I became a widow at the age of thirty-seven after seventeen years of married life. I realized that we had this experience in common only after working for some time on a revised entry on her for the *New dictionary of national biography* – at a moment, to be precise, when I began to ask myself why I felt that the recent literature had not altogether done her justice. Was the answer, perhaps, that there were unexplored issues about her identity as a widow?

There is, in fact, a fair measure of agreement on the positive features of her widowhood, for her own career and ultimately for the suffrage movement. The image with which we began, of the woman who 'looked nice, dressed becomingly, was married to a heroic blind politician and was to him the perfect wife', remained with her and fellow suffragists agreed that it was empowering.[23] In Strachey's words, 'The tall blind man and his gentle wife were romantic figures in the public mind, and on his death the romance stayed and clung to his widow.'[24] As Brian Harrison points out, she inherited a position that was both financially and politically much more secure than that of Emmeline Pankhurst, whose husband Richard died in 1898 after a relatively unsuccessful political career.[25] Fawcett's interventions in public life, for whatever cause, gained weight from her status as wife and widow of a minister. Mary Stocks attributed the 'tradition of political expertise' in the British suffrage movement largely to Fawcett's experience of 'the inner ring of parliamentary activity'.[26]

More elusive are questions about Fawcett's experience of bereavement. Recent writers have not been inclined to probe its inwardness. Oakley notes that it 'released' her 'for a wider public role'.[27] Caine, emphasising the supportive role played by her family of origin, also conveys an impression of 'release' by the way she interprets Fawcett's new commitment to sexual politics.[28] Rubinstein acknowledges the impact on Millicent of Henry's death – a 'catastrophe', a 'crushing blow from which she did not soon recover' – but the focus quickly shifts to its place in the contours of her career. 'It enabled her to develop the independent public life begun in her dazzling youth and somewhat overshadowed subsequently by her role as academic and political wife. As her sister's biographer comments, his death was for her both an end and a beginning.'[29] Largely missing here is any treatment of mourning as a process or of the transition from wifehood to widowhood. Strachey, who knew Fawcett personally, though only in later life, dealt at more length with her emotions on bereavement and conveys rather more of the conscious effort needed to recover a sense of identity and purpose.

Three years after Henry's death Millicent Fawcett wrote in a letter of condolence: 'I do not think constancy and fidelity to dead friends consists in any strain to keep up the great pain of the time when you first know you have lost them . . . but rather in trying to be and to do what they wished and what they thought you capable of doing and being.'[30] How is a feminist biographer, interested in her subject's experience of a woman's life-cycle, to read this statement?[31] If we admit, as I think we must, that it is more than a sentimental formula and reflects honest introspection, an attempt on Fawcett's part to describe the way she herself was resolving the process of grieving, then it points up the risk of oversimplification if we focus simply on the liberating features of her widowhood. The self that is being refashioned is not autonomous but a projection of Henry's wishes for her; and though these were enabling in one sense – he had always encouraged her public and writing career – we should not underestimate the stress involved in this style of 'being' and 'doing'. Strachey recalls that it was not until the last years of her life that Fawcett had fully come to terms with Henry's death: 'even twenty and thirty years later her friends could detect the desperate and rigid self-control with which she met any sudden mention of her husband's name'.[32]

Strachey's mode of writing about Fawcett's intimate life has been described as 'cloying'.[33] Her problem was perhaps one that still confronts us, that it is easier to put on record evidence of these powerful emotions than to evaluate it.

THE WIDOW AS A PROBLEM IN FEMINIST BIOGRAPHY

Feminist writing on widowhood is sparse. It is not hard to understand why. The modern taboo on death, associated with increased life expectancy, and the disappearance in Western societies of mourning dress – the 'widow's weeds' – have tended to make widows vanish from sight as a social category.[34] In a survey of current work on widows in the United States and Britain, Carol Barrett found that they were themselves parties to this process. 'Most widows hate the word "widow"', she wrote. Widows were perceived as 'carriers and transmitters of the reality of death'.[35] Equally unattractive are some age-old associations. The 'widow' is identified in relation to her husband and the term embodies cultural assumptions that deny her personal identity. The feminist dictionary *Womanwords* notes that the word is derived from an Indo-European root (*widh-* or *wiedh-*) meaning to be empty, citing one earlier dictionary gloss: 'Since marriage has made two of one, a widow is a woman that has been emptied of herself'.[36] Widowhood is, in short, an offputting subject. It is also an elusive concept, as Helena Znaniecka Lopata points out, in the sense that modern Western societies recognise widowhood largely as a transitory role, associated with a woman's 'exit from the role of wife' – a role that has meaning in the context of the funeral and its immediate aftermath and in commemoration of the husband. But the widow's role has no definite ending, while the personal effects of bereavement may in practice be profound and long-lasting.[37] We need more information about a condition that is part of the life cycle for so many women. Equally, feminist biographers need historical perspectives on widowhood in order to contextualise the ways in which women experienced it in past societies.

Patricia Jalland has shown the way forward in her pioneering study of *Death in the Victorian family*. Here widows are treated within a wide-ranging survey of death and bereavement in the upper and middle classes.[38] Drawing on the archives of over fifty families, Jalland challenges preconceptions about the Victorian culture of mourning and shows how insights can be derived from modern studies of bereavement. A major conclusion is her claim that by the 1880s the experience of family bereavement was much closer than has sometimes been suggested to patterns of behaviour associated with the twentieth century. The elaborate mourning rituals of the mid-Victorian era, like the evangelical obsession with the deathbed, were already going out of fashion. Even before that, Queen Victoria's extreme and prolonged reaction to widowhood was, like modern instances of chronic grief and depression, the exception rather than the norm. Then as now, bereavement was a gendered experience, commonly (though not invariably) bringing more insecurity and disruption in the lives of widows than of widowers. Widows were less likely to remarry or to have interests or occupations to sustain and distract them. But there are also, intriguingly, signs that Victorian widows were more repressed in the mourning process than their modern counterparts. Jalland's subjects were much less apt to express the anger and guilt that are now regarded as a normal response to the loss of a partner, and especially common, according to some studies, in cases of sudden death.[39]

The modern literature on bereavement in adult life helps us to treat widowhood in perspective and detach it from misogynistic traditions. It does, however, confirm that the loss of a spouse is (like the loss of a child) an acutely stressful and disruptive event, whether for husbands or for wives. The intensity of grief is a function not so much of the loving nature of the relationship as of the depth of involvement in it. 'Normal' experiences of grief following a partner's death contain much the same elements for both sexes. They travel through stages: an initial reaction of shock, disbelief or denial followed by a period of one or two years in which there is an 'intense emotional, physical and cognitive reaction to the loss', often involving preoccupation with the dead person and feelings of anger and guilt. (Millicent Fawcett put it succinctly: 'One can't feel anything at first but a sort of numbness and then pain.')[40] This may be followed by – or alternate with – a third stage marked by periods of apathy, fatigue and despair. A common experience is the loss of a sense of identity. The more the roles and interactions of married life have formed each person's sense of self, the greater the threat to personal identity when a partner dies. In 'normal' cases this is resolved with the passage of time, but 'reconstructing the self-concept' is recognised as a necessary part of the processes of grieving.[41]

Widowhood, however hard we may find it to discuss without embarrassment, or from a feminist standpoint, must be taken seriously as a life-shaping event. What follows is an attempt to reposition this experience in the life of Millicent Fawcett. The first step must be to summarise what is known – and this is largely uncontroversial – of the Fawcett marriage.

THE FAWCETT PARTNERSHIP: AN EXEMPLARY MARRIAGE

Rubinstein's account of the marriage between Henry and Millicent Garrett Fawcett shows that it was both exceptionally close and rooted in mutual interdependence and, for her, a crucially formative experience. Henry's blindness, the result of a shooting accident, made him physically dependent on her as 'eyes and hands', guide, and for many years secretary. Millicent's close involvement in his academic and political work brought, on the other hand, unique opportunities for an ambitious young wife. It was with Henry's encouragement, and to some extent as a 'spin-off' from his activities as a Cambridge professor and Radical MP, that she made her name both as an economist and within the women's movement. After helping to revise her husband's *Manual of political economy* she went on to publish (with his publishers, Macmillan) a popular school textbook, *Political economy for beginners* (1870), which ran into ten editions and was translated into many languages; following it with a volume of *Tales in political economy* (1874) modelled on the writings of the pioneering feminist populariser of economics, Harriet Martineau. As an academic wife, Millicent was naturally drawn into moves to introduce women's higher education in Cambridge. Henry Sidgwick's scheme of lectures for women was launched at a meeting in the Fawcetts' drawing room in 1869, leading to the foundation of Newnham Hall (later College), of whose council she became a prominent member. As for national politics, her long connection with suffrage work began at the age of twenty, months after her marriage, when she joined, in July 1867, the executive committee of the London National Society for Woman (later Women's) Suffrage. She made an impact as a suffrage speaker and, although others were more active on suffrage platforms in these years, it was she who contributed the essay on suffragism in England to the volume of essays on the women's movement in Europe, edited by Theodore Stanton in 1884.[42] At the same time the Fawcetts operated as a partnership in Westminster politics. Millicent became one of the few women members of the Radical Club, founded by Henry Fawcett and others to promote Mill's political agenda, which placed 'women's rights' in a context of liberal utilitarian arguments for free trade, equal opportunities and fair representation of all interests in parliament.[43] As political economists they thought alike on what was needed to promote self-reliance amongst the working classes – for the most part, *laissez-faire* policies, but education should be compulsory (though not free) and trade unionism should be encouraged. Millicent identified, too, with the causes Henry championed as an independent Radical backbencher. These included the removal of religious restrictions in Irish universities – an issue on which he secured the defeat of Gladstone's first government in 1874 – the agitation against atrocities committed by the Turkish troops in Bulgaria in 1877, and his campaign against wasteful expenditure of the taxpayer's money by the British government in India.[44]

As Henry Fawcett's biographers have noted, he was an ambitious politician who contrived to turn his blindness to advantage.[45] The most eloquent testimony for the gospel of self-help he preached as an economist to the workers was his own triumph over that disability. His marriage to Millicent won yet more sympathy for the husband who could not see his 'bonnie' young wife, petite, graceful, with a mass of light brown hair.[46] She, meanwhile, played her part in extracting advantage from a relationship in which she acted a highly visible role as helpmate while gaining freedom to act independently, but also with Henry's authority. This can be seen above all from Rubinstein's analysis of the way she established herself as a suffrage speaker, at a time when it was controversial for women to speak in public. Her debut as platform speaker was made, with perfect propriety, when she read a paper of Henry's to the Social Science Association in October 1868: from this she progressed to her first suffrage speech in July 1869 at London's first women's suffrage meeting, then a public lecture on the same subject in March 1870 to a packed audience of Henry's constituents in Brighton Town Hall. The following year she went on a speaking tour in the West of England, accompanied by Lilias Ashworth but not this time by Henry. Audiences cheered him, however, for 'his unselfish kindness in sparing his wife – on whom he was so specially dependent – to go forth and plead for this new gospel'.[47] This was a feminist marriage, but it took its special characteristics from the habit of life acted out as public example that marked Henry Fawcett's career. It was fashioned as an exemplary marriage to promote their shared goals.

A daughter, Philippa, was born in 1868 and she remained an only child. This was wholly consistent with the Fawcetts' views on the duty of parents (and not only in the working classes) to have no more children than were wanted and could be afforded. There was gossip, evidently unfounded, that Millicent neglected her as a baby. But in due course Philippa too became part of the family project for women's advancement, groomed from an early age as a mathematician by Cambridge tutors (though she also attended school and Bedford and University Colleges in London before winning a scholarship at Newnham in 1887).

For all the calculation that went into shaping the marriage, it was a relationship based on love and also one in which Millicent retained a distinct identity of her own. For her, at least, loveless marriage was a sin: in later life she described it as 'on a par with what goes on between twelve and two every morning in the Haymarket and Piccadilly Circus'.[48] The daughter of an evangelical mother, she never followed Henry in his indifference to religion, uncertain as her own beliefs became; and there was a vein of sentimentality in her that Henry altogether lacked. Seen by his friends as a typical Cambridge man, he was a mathematician by training, committed to the scientific approach, uninterested in philosophy or culture, and (although he did not publicise the fact) an agnostic.[49] He said of himself that he had no imagination.[50] The unsystematic literary education that Millicent received as a girl, at home and for four years at the Blackheath boarding school kept by the Misses Browning (step-aunts of Robert Browning), together with her thorough grounding in the Bible, gave her a quite different range of reference. As an economist and a speaker and writer on public matters, she learned to deploy the Cambridge academic style to her own purposes, always publishing during Henry's lifetime under the name Millicent Garrett Fawcett. But an early novel, *Janet Doncaster* (1874), contrives to affirm the continuing influence on her both of her literary upbringing and of her love for Henry. The heroine – a thinly disguised autobiographical figure – is tricked into a loveless marriage with a weak aristocrat with whom she has nothing in common, punished by her discovery that he is an alcoholic, but released by his death to find true love and happiness with a Cambridge tutor who shares in her ideals.

Was there a dominant partner in this marriage? The only point of difference between them mentioned in Millicent's memoirs is Henry's love of fishing, which she – finding blood sports distasteful – 'could never endure'.[51] They resolved it by taking their holidays apart, his autumn fishing expeditions coinciding with Millicent's travels on the continent with family or friends. As for public matters, Henry once described her as 'a helpmate whose political judgment was much less frequently at fault than his own'.[52] It has been suggested that Millicent was guided by Henry in standing aside in the 1870s from Josephine Butler's campaign against the Contagious Diseases Acts, in deference to Mill's view that it would damage the suffrage agitation if the two issues were linked.[53] The evidence is, however, far from conclusive and Rubinstein is inclined to accept the version of events given by Strachey, in which Millicent herself, despite her sympathy with the abolitionist campaign, decided for opportunistic reasons to take no part in it.[54] Her own family was divided on the CD Acts, which Elizabeth Garrett Anderson supported on public health grounds, while a younger sister, Agnes, and their cousin Rhoda Garrett took part in the campaign against them. We know, too, that Millicent shrank personally from public discussion of sexual issues – witness the language of her refusal to support Charles Bradlaugh and Annie Besant, charged in 1877 with obscenity for publishing a birth-control tract. She wrote of her 'extreme pain' at the prospect of giving evidence; and, in associating herself with Henry's 'strongly condemnatory' view of the book, was at pains to make clear that she had not read it.[55]

Henry Fawcett's popular reputation grew in his years as Postmaster General: he created more jobs for women as Post Office clerks, raised wages, introduced paid holidays and incentive schemes for workers, besides bringing in such new ventures as postal orders, cheap telegrams and a parcel post. But he found himself in a ministry with which he and fellow Radicals frequently disagreed. The last public demonstration of Fawcett solidarity came with the Third Reform Bill in 1884. Millicent campaigned for the enfranchisement of women householders. Henry backed the amendment that would have included them in the Bill, proposed in June by William Woodall. When Gladstone made the rejection of Woodall's amendment an issue of confidence, Henry was one of three Radical ministers – the others being Leonard Courtney and Charles Dilke – who defied him by abstaining. A month after Fawcett's death Courtney resigned, when proportional representation, another cause dear to Millite Radicals, was also ruled out by Gladstone. Millicent wrote to him, 'You know, I am sure, you would not have been alone in this action of yours if Harry had been here to join you. He often spoke of this to me.'[56]

BEREAVEMENT

Henry Fawcett died suddenly on 6 November 1884 when a cold, which he had tried to shake off by outdoor exercise, turned to pneumonia. There was a crowded service in Westminster Abbey but the funeral was at the parish church at Trumpington, a village two miles outside Cambridge where he had ridden some days earlier. Business came to a halt in Cambridge. A special train brought mourners from London. The plain oak coffin was hidden under wreaths of white flowers, the bier drawn from Cambridge by bay horses without funeral trappings.[57] Mourners at the church were so numerous – friends, academic and political colleagues, Post Office employees, troops of admirers of this charismatic blind man – that they broke down the churchyard wall.[58] Railway workers in Henry's first constituency, Brighton, sent his widow a tribute offering to petition for a public pension or get up a penny subscription among working people for her and her daughter. True to the Fawcetts' style, her reply was that her husband's 'forethought and prudence' had left them well provided.[59]

Perhaps with the same thought for her financial situation, within weeks of his death she was offered the post of Mistress of Girton College. Her comment, as recorded by Strachey – 'I felt incapable of thinking about any subject but one' – has been taken by some as a reference to women's suffrage.[60] That is plainly not what Strachey's readers were meant to infer, nor is it remotely plausible that a spouse in the early stages of mourning a partner with whom there were such close bonds would have any preoccupation other than that. How to cope with bereavement and widowhood?

The Fawcetts did not believe in an afterlife, nor was Millicent tempted by the vogue for spiritualism. All the more important were what Jalland terms the 'consolations of memory'.[61] The commemoration of Henry Fawcett took many forms, public and private. No less than eight memorials were put up to affirm his place in social memory. They included a monument in Westminster Abbey and a drinking fountain on the Thames Embankment recording his services to women. The biography Millicent commissioned from an old Cambridge colleague, Leslie Stephen, dwelt on his subject's exemplary qualities and it reached a wide audience, going through five editions within a year.[62] Her own memoirs recall the part played by family in these processes of remembrance. A Garrett nephew born the year after Henry died was named after him and she became his godmother.[63] When Philippa gained her distinguished result at Cambridge in 1890, classed 'above the Senior Wrangler' in the Mathematical Tripos, Mrs Fawcett was told that the examiners had recognised in her papers the style of Henry Fawcett. 'Her work was similar to that of her father (but with greater mathematical knowledge), no shots, no sheets of paper wasted, but grasp of question and proper application, the only errors and erasures being unimportant ones of analysis, and these only occasional.'[64]

Millicent Fawcett was in many respects more fortunately placed than most young widows of her class and generation. There was the usual break-up of the family homes – the Fawcetts' houses in Cambridge and Vauxhall were given up – but exceptional support from her family of birth. With Philippa she now joined the household at 2, Gower Street in London which had been shared by a favourite sister, Agnes, with Rhoda Garrett, her partner in a successful house-decorating business, until Rhoda's death in 1882. Sam Garrett, a solicitor and the brother to whom she was closest, lived near by: he became Millicent's business adviser and, as she put it, 'first and foremost among my men friends'.[65] Moreover the social processes that tended to prevent widows from finding distraction in work were in her case altogether absent. The Garretts were activists in the women's movement, there were friends and colleagues of Henry's who welcomed her as an ally in public causes and her income, though adequate, was usefully supplemented by writing. At the same time it was only to be expected that she would look for yet more ways of commemorating Henry.

Mrs Fawcett's first interventions in public life as a widow fell within the period that is now supposed to be overshadowed by the 'normal' process of grieving after the loss of a spouse. The 'Maiden tribute of modern Babylon' articles appeared in the *Pall Mall Gazette* in July 1885; in August she came out in support for Stead and the newly formed National Vigilance Association (NVA).[66] In June 1886 she published extracts from Henry's speeches in a letter to *The Times* to support the claim that he would have opposed Gladstone's Irish Home Rule Bill.[67] It is time to look at the connections between these initiatives and her bereavement.

'MY DEAR HUSBAND'S EXAMPLE'; CONTINUING HARRY'S WORK?

Letters written in 1885 and quoted by Strachey bear witness to Millicent Fawcett's idealisation of her dead husband and emotional dependence on the sense that 'courage and goodness have been made easier by his example'. 'The worst is when it seems as though people forgot him and that his great good influence is gone.' And again: 'I think what we should all feel who have been privileged to live in constant companionship with an exceptionally noble nature from which we are now removed, is not how wretched we are to have lost them, but how blessed we are to have had them to lift up our lives by their beautiful example.'[68] Nothing could be more mistaken than to dismiss sentiments of this kind as mere conventional pieties – above all in a generation for which truth in human love became for some a substitute for religious faith. ('Ah, love, let us be true / To one another . . . ', as Matthew Arnold wrote in the last stanza of 'Dover Beach', his elegy to the ebbing 'Sea of Faith'). Acting on, and perpetuating, Henry's example was a necessary commitment for his widow.

The difficulty, however, was – and remains – to decide how he would have acted, or wished her to act, in circumstances that arose after his death. Would he have broken finally with Gladstone over Home Rule? Would he have discouraged her involvement in the 'moral panic' of the late 1880s? In both cases the answer is much less clear than is Henry's ghostly presence in Millicent's thinking on these issues, together with the sensations – anger, guilt, insecure sense of identity – that normally accompany the loss of a partner.

Modern authorities on Henry Fawcett are not at all certain how he would have reacted when Gladstone suddenly declared his conversion to Home Rule for Ireland in December 1885.[69] Up to that point the maintenance of the Union had been Liberal Party policy, so that speeches Henry made in 1884 and earlier cannot provide conclusive evidence. What made Millicent so sure that he would have become a Unionist? A large majority of university liberals did break with Gladstone over Home Rule.[70] In these circles Gladstone's policy was seen as a betrayal of Liberal values and particularly of England's duty to promote the rule of law – perhaps as the prelude to a wholesale repudiation of imperial responsibilities. Among those who took this line was Leonard Courtney, who had the strongest claim to be seen as Henry's political heir.[71] The Fawcetts' Irish connections, dating from the 1870s, had moreover brought Millicent into touch with the women's movement there, which was before the twentieth century predominantly Protestant and Unionist.[72]

The clinching factor may, however, have been her personal hostility to Gladstone, identified by Rubinstein as a 'dominating passion' in her own work for Unionism.[73]

It is justified at some length in her memoirs. Gladstone's behaviour over Woodall's amendment certainly contributed to it. His pronouncements on women's suffrage before 1884 had been characteristically ambiguous and Mrs Fawcett recalls the 'deep feeling of anger and mistrust' among women suffragists produced by his refusal to proceed with the Reform Bill if the amendment were passed.[74] Her own feelings were influenced also by loyalty to Henry. Whereas Stephen's biography made light of Henry's disputes with Gladstone in his years as Postmaster General, her account dwells on a history of grievances. He was not in the cabinet and on Post Office issues it seemed to her that 'his superiors in the Governmental hierarchy went out of their way to slight him'.[75] She believed that Gladstone had never forgiven Henry's part in the fall of his first government. Yet her lifelong bitterness may well have owed as much to the pathology of mourning as to the vicissitudes of politics. 'A curious little sidelight on Mr. Gladstone's retentive memory in some matters may be inferred', she wrote, 'from the fact that at the time of my husband's death in 1884, though I received hundreds of letters of sympathy and condolence from all sorts and conditions of people, I received not one word from the Prime Minister under whom he had served.'[76] But Gladstone's diary records that he did write to her on the day Henry died. Though no copy of that letter has survived, generous tributes from Gladstone are on record, in a statement in the House of Commons and in a letter to Henry's father (later published).[77] What really happened? We cannot know. But it does seem likely that her feelings towards Gladstone took their cutting edge from the anger that accompanies bereavement. This anger may find its targets erratically.

Not only anger but guilt too found an outlet in her reactions to the Stead case as it unfolded in the second half of 1885. Responding to a plea from Josephine Butler and others to assist the campaign to raise the age of consent from thirteen to sixteen, Stead bought a thirteen-year-old girl from her mother: his sensational account of the transaction achieved its object in forcing parliament to pass the 1885 Criminal Law Amendment Act and mobilising support for vigilance work, but he was left open to prosecution on a technical point and landed up in prison.[78] Millicent became one of Stead's most passionate defenders. What would Henry have felt about that? As in the case of Home Rule, we cannot infer the answer from views he held in earlier years. Contrary to most expectations, Josephine Butler had succeeded where the suffragists had for the time being failed: parliament suspended the Contagious Diseases Acts in 1883 (in 1886 they were finally repealed).[79] Opportunistic arguments for separating suffrage and sexual politics were less persuasive than they had seemed in the 1870s. Child prostitution was, moreover, a particularly shocking subject. At the same time, the 'Maiden tribute' articles did polarise opinion: mass meetings were held in support of Stead but he was denounced for obscenity in the press and parliament.

Millicent Fawcett needed to believe that Henry would have been on the right side. In an eloquent article, 'Speech or silence', she compared Stead's actions with other *causes célèbres* that had divided the nation – Italian unification, the American Civil War, the Bulgarian atrocities.[80] These were all issues on which she and Henry had agreed. The language she now used might almost have been addressed to him, as a man of courage and principle. Silence protected the wicked. Stead had 'not so much told us what we did not know before, as whipped and lashed us to a sense of our dastardly cowardice in knowing these things and making no effort to stop them'. A passage in her memoirs suggests that she felt that Henry might have tried to protect her from courting unpopularity, however just Stead's cause. She referred to an episode in the Bulgarian atrocities agitation when Auberon Herbert, who had been attacked by 'jingo' mobs, had rejected Henry's advice to stay away from further demonstrations. Now, when Herbert urged Millicent to attend a Stead Defence meeting, she replied in the words he had himself used on that earlier occasion: 'if I am alive I shall be there.'[81] The issue was courage versus cowardice. One gesture points to her certainty that Henry would, in the end, have agreed. When Stead was serving his sentence in Holloway prison she sent him her husband's dressing-gown – a 'sort of sacred possession', a gift to him from her sister Agnes. (Stead's biographer, who records the incident, notes primly that 'both Stead and Mrs Stead were delighted with the gift'.)[82] It was a powerful gesture, the more so for its intimacy, at once co-opting Henry's support for the martyred prisoner and asserting that, for her, Stead's 'courage and goodness' would be associated with Henry's example.

Whether or not Caine is right in believing that Henry would 'never have countenanced' his wife's commitment to the purity movement, we can be fairly certain that she herself did not believe it.[83] It is true that her closest allies in this cause were members of the Garrett family. Even Elizabeth Garrett Anderson, who was critical of the NVA, was among the four sisters who signed the women's protest of 1889 against the nomination as LCC alderman of Charles Dilke, after his failure to clear himself of allegations of 'French vice' in the scandalous Crawford divorce case.[84] Their cousin Edmund Garrett became involved in vigilante and 'rescue' work of the kind encouraged by the NVA.[85] A journalist who began his career on the *Pall Mall Gazette*, and a protégé of Stead's, he may have been the author of the profile of Fawcett in *The Review of Reviews* which depicted her as 'vengeful and remorseless' in pursuit of men who did women 'cruel wrong'.[86] This has been treated as an apt description of her campaign in 1894–1895 to discredit the Conservative MP Henry Cust, who had planned to abandon his pregnant mistress and marry another woman.[87] In this campaign, too, she relied on the support of Agnes and Sam Garrett, together with an old Cambridge friend, Kathleen Lyttelton (whose husband was vicar of Eccles in Lancashire, near to a Manchester constituency that adopted Cust as a candidate).[88] Yet at the same time it cannot have been difficult for Fawcett to maintain the emotional association between her moral reform initiatives and Henry's memory. One campaign she led, backed by the NVA, against the employment of children in theatres and pantomime, was wholly in line with their views on the need for compulsory education and an end to child labour.[89] Henry's successor as MP for Hackney, James Stuart – another Cambridge friend – was a long-standing supporter of Josephine Butler; and though Henry had differed from Stuart over the Contagious Diseases Acts, there is no doubt that the mood among university men changed in response to the scandals of the 1880s. Particularly poignant was the case of Dilke: a pupil of Henry's, it was he who had commissioned, and owned till his death, the portrait of the Fawcetts by Ford Madox Brown.[90] In 1888 he was expelled by the Ad Eundem Club, a select dining club of Oxford and Cambridge liberals to which Henry had belonged.[91]

In the final reckoning, however, there are features of Millicent Fawcett's public life in the decade or so after Henry's death that are hard to reconcile with the values he had professed. As a founder member of the Women's Liberal Unionist Association in 1888 and a speaker on Unionist platforms in Britain and Ireland, she could hardly conform to the spirit of Henry's injunction (quoted in her letter to *The Times* in 1886) that the Irish question should be approached 'in a broad and national spirit unprejudiced by party'. Partisan feeling spilled over into suffrage politics too. In the dispute that split the National Society for Women's Suffrage (NSWS) in December 1888, Fawcett took the lead in opposing moves that would have enabled branches of the Gladstonian Women's Liberal Federation to affiliate to the society.[92] As for the NVA's campaigns against 'vice', they used tactics that were clearly at odds with Millite liberalism, including the public shaming of individuals and pressure for police harassment of prostitutes.[93]

IDENTITY AND JUDGEMENT

Millicent Fawcett's early return to public life must have helped her through the processes of grieving. The work she took up, I have argued, did seem to her consistent with the urge to commemorate Henry and live by his example. It gave her an occupation and a focus for the anger and guilt that, according to Jalland, were normally repressed by Victorian widows. Yet decisions taken in the heat of emotion may not be well judged – and indeed there is an inevitable tendency to lean on the judgement of others when bereavement undermines the individual's sense of identity. In retrospect Fawcett dwelt on her dependence on the networks of friendship and kinship that provided her with support. 'Left alone after seventeen years of happy active married life . . . I might have fallen into a lethargic melancholy if it had not been for the help I received from many of my husband's old friends, and also in a very high degree from all the members of my own family.'[94] Biographers have not taken this comment very seriously. Even Strachey wrote briskly, 'Lethargic melancholy could surely never have overcome a nature like Millicent's, even had she stood alone, for she was neither selfish nor weak nor self-absorbed.'[95] This rather misses the point that something more than moral fibre was required in the adjustment to widowed life. How did bereavement affect her sense of self?

One immediate consequence was that she was now normally, though not invariably, and even in her publications, styled 'Mrs Henry Fawcett' rather than 'Millicent Garrett Fawcett'. The significance of this can be understood in various ways, by no means mutually incompatible. It marked a change of status and affirmed a continuing partnership in which Henry's authority re-inforced her own, but it also, perhaps, signalled a loss of touch with the con-fidently autonomous self she had constructed within her marriage. Intriguingly, in an interview she gave in 1888 she described herself as 'not at all educated'. Referring to the family governess 'over whom we tyrannised' and her brief period at school, she made little of the grounding in economics or the political apprenticeship that followed her marriage.[96] Was it hard to recover a self-concept that allowed her to own these important stages in her formation? Some indications that this was the case can be read from a series of biographical sketches she wrote for the *Mothers' Companion* in 1887–1888, reprinted in 1889 as *Some eminent women of our times*. The self-reflexive element in these portraits is clearest in her treatment of Charlotte Brontë, whose last novel *Shirley* was written during her sister Anne's last illness. 'Not one to give way to self-indulgent idleness, even in the hour of darkest despair' (did Strachey unconsciously echo these senti-ments?), Brontë continued the book after her sister's death; 'but those who knew what her private history at the time was, can trace in the pages of the novel what she had gone through. The first chapter she wrote after the death of Anne is called, "The Valley of the Shadow of Death".'[97]

Fawcett's chief message in this series of exemplary lives, mostly of nine-teenth-century Englishwomen, was that women's advances in education and opportunities for achievement had not led them 'to neglect womanly work'. These women are framed in a much more limiting conception of womanli-ness than she embraced at other stages of her life. The tone of her commen-tary would not, one suspects, have appealed to Henry. Elizabeth Barrett Browning's 'sweetness, her purity, and the tender womanliness of her char-acter, made her friends forget her learning and her genius'; and she is applauded for drawing inspiration in her poetry from 'the deep joy of moth-erhood'.[98] Achievement is often presented as a result of (even legitimated by) personal misfortune – the 'whip of poverty' that forced Mary Somerville to write, the blindness of Elizabeth Gilbert which meant that 'the light of her own life was found in working for the welfare of others'.[99] These women are humble about their work and it is carefully noted that most of them owed their formation and encouragement to men – fathers, brothers, husbands (here the Brontë sisters are a rare exception). Particularly striking is the comment attributed to the astronomer and musician Caroline Herschel: 'I am nothing, I have done nothing: all I am, all I know, I owe to my brother. I am only a tool which he shaped to his use.'[100] The dispiriting quality of these sketches surely tells us something about Millicent Fawcett's own frame of mind in her early years of widowhood. She was secure in her own domestic femininity – the 'bliss of motherhood', the 'early training' that had saved her, like Jane Austen, 'from being a literary lady who could not sew'.[101] But was it not much harder to recover the assured public identity that had been 'shaped' in the context of her relationship with Henry?

It would be good to know more about how Fawcett herself looked back on her public role in the early years of her widowhood. Little is said in her memoirs of her work for the Unionists, though one striking passage implies that, whether she remembered it or not, she took no satisfaction from her part in the NSWS split of 1888. Praising the willingness of Irish suffragists to work together, despite their party loyalties as Home Rulers or Unionists, she notes that 'such an amount of good sense and moderation was not to be found in either England or Scotland at the time'.[102] The memoirs do not distance her in the same way from her work on moral issues – and indeed, as Susan Kingsley Kent has pointed out, sexual politics were to become an important dimension of the Edwardian suffrage agitation.[103] But the emphasis is very much on the work of others – Josephine Butler, Stead and the secretary of the NVA, W. A. Coote – for whom she placed on record her admiration.[104] Fawcett's own role in the purity movement derived its significance from who she was, yet she had no distinctive insights to offer on sexual issues. We do know, moreover, that some views she held during her association with the late-Victorian 'repressive purity feminists' were subsequently modified.[105] Her evidence to the Edwardian Royal Commission on Divorce favoured divorce by consent where marriages had broken down.[106] Twenty years earlier she had declared that 'people who . . . think marriages should be dissolvable at will . . . are in effect anarchists'.[107]

MRS HENRY FAWCETT IN LATER LIFE

The liberating effects of widowhood can doubtless be seen more clearly once the turmoil of emotion surrounding bereavement has subsided and the 'self-concept' is re-established. In the nature of things, there can be no specific moment when these processes are completed. In Fawcett's case, as we have seen, her involvement in regular suffrage speaking in the 1890s seemed to her, with hindsight, to mark the end of a phase of life when her chief commitment was to her husband's work. Yet he was to remain an important point of reference in her life. And her biographers are certainly correct, on the other hand, in noting that the initiatives she took in the immediate aftermath of Henry's death, however emotionally driven, played their part in establishing her as a public figure in her own right and in the stature she later achieved as suffrage leader. One significant moment of recognition came in 1899, when her NVA ally James Stuart, as Lord Rector of the University of St Andrews, conferred an honorary degree on her (ostensibly for her services to women's education). In public life and in her publications she was now normally styled 'Mrs Henry Fawcett, LL D'.

At some point she did recover the ability to draw on Henry's political and intellectual legacy, while remaining free to speak confidently in a voice that was more distinctively her own. This is shown in her later biographical writings, which at times adopt the unsentimental, 'manly' Cambridge style and at others reflect the more sentimental aspects of her Garrett upbringing. A life of Sir William Molesworth, published during the Boer War, found antecedents for liberal imperialism in the work of an early-Victorian Radical with whom Henry had identified.[108] But a study of *Five famous Frenchwomen*, published in 1905, took a quite different tack.[109] In contrast to the 'eminent women' of 1889, the medieval and Renaissance figures in this later volume are affirmed as stronger and more creative than the men of their day. Victorian Cambridge would have been especially taken aback by her treatment of Joan of Arc, compared to Socrates and Christ – 'pure white souls' who died by public execution. 'She knew that more than once God's people had been saved by a woman, a Judith, a Deborah, and she remembered that there was a prophecy, which was also a promise, that a woman should bruise the serpent's head.'[110]

Yet the sense of Henry's association with her work never left her, despite the independent achievements of her later career. The biography of Molesworth was completed while she was in South Africa, where she had been sent in an official capacity, as leader of a women's committee of enquiry into conditions in the concentration camps where Boer women and children were interned.[111] In 1904 she broke with the Unionists when the party abandoned the policy of Free Trade, a cardinal point in the Fawcetts' creed. In her years as suffrage leader she publicly recalled Henry's support for the cause and privately found comfort in his example. 'Fawcett, quietly beating one hand against the other, kept repeating in a low voice, as it were to himself, "You must press on and do what's right" . . . ' – it was to this memory of his response to Anglo-Irish problems in the 1880s that she turned in the crises over suffrage militancy two decades later.[112] Later, in the Great War, months after her godson Henry Fawcett Garrett had been killed at Gallipoli, she donated to a British Red Cross Appeal the silver candlesticks and inkstand given her in 'affectionate remembrance' of Henry by his Post Office colleagues, recalling in her memoirs: 'I felt sure that my husband would have approved this disposal of them.'[113]

CONCLUSION

If this chapter has achieved anything, it is by attempting to explore the trauma of widowhood in Millicent Garrett Fawcett's life in the light of modern studies of bereavement and of her own writings. I have argued that this exercise is entirely in the spirit of feminist biography, despite the special problems that arise in writing about widowhood. In Fawcett's case, it has suggested a reading of her life which, while dependent on – and not necessarily at odds with – the work of her biographers, dwells more closely on her widowed identity. Her public activities after Henry's death are interpreted here as conditioned by her bereavement. Her 'exit from the role of wife' was a complex process, marked at first by powerful emotions, and a weakened sense of self, which necessarily affected her judgement and, for all the independent qualities that were revealed in her later career, was in some senses never complete.

All biographical writing is to some extent conjectural and this reading of Fawcett's life is, of course, no exception. Yet by focusing on it as a *widow's* life we can at least recover a dimension that features strongly in her own presentations of self and, at the same time, find new perspectives on episodes that have puzzled or divided her biographers.

NOTES

1 NUWSS Information Bureau Department, Biographical Sketches, Fawcett MSS M50/2/10/20, Manchester Central Library.
2 *Common Cause*, 9 April 1914, p. 6 quoted in B. H. Harrison, *Prudent revolutionaries: portraits of British feminists between the wars* (Oxford, Clarendon Press, 1987), p. 24.
3 *Common Cause*, 25 January 1912, cover.
4 L. Goldman (ed.), *The blind Victorian: Henry Fawcett and British Liberalism* (Cambridge, Cambridge University Press, 1989).
5 D. Rubinstein, *A different world for women: the life of Millicent Garrett Fawcett* (Hemel Hempstead, Harvester Wheatsheaf, 1991), pp. 3–4, 47. Rhoda's half-brother, Edmund, was also 'an ardent advocate of the women's movement'; see E. T. Cook, *Edmund Garrett: a memoir* (London, Edward Arnold, 1909), p. 6.
6 Rubinstein, *A different world for women*, p. 24.
7 L. Stephen, *Life of Henry Fawcett* (London, Smith, Elder, 1885), p. 127.
8 M. G. Fawcett, *What I remember* (London, Fisher Unwin, 1924), p. 124.
9 R. Strachey, *Millicent Garrett Fawcett* (London, John Murray, 1931).
10 A. Oakley, Millicent Garrett Fawcett: duty and determination (1847–1929), in D. Spender (ed.), *Feminist theorists: three centuries of women's intellectual traditions* (London, Women's Press, 1983), pp. 184–212; B. Caine, *Victorian feminists* (Oxford, Oxford University Press, 1992), pp. 196–238.
11 Harrison, *Prudent revolutionaries*, pp. 17–44.
12 See especially S. S. Holton, *Women's suffrage and reform politics in Britain 1900–1918* (Cambridge, Cambridge University Press, 1986); L. Tickner, *The*

spectacle of women: imagery of the suffrage campaign, 1907–14 (London, Chatto & Windus, 1987).

13 M. A. Pujol, *Feminism and anti-feminism in early economic thought* (Aldershot, Edward Elgar, 1992).

14 L. Bland, *Banishing the beast: English feminism and sexual morality, 1885–1914* (Harmondsworth, Penguin Books, 1995); A. Burton, *Burdens of history: British feminists, Indian women and Imperial culture, 1865–1915* (Chapel Hill and London, University of North Carolina Press, 1994); J. Vellacott, Feminist consciousness and the First World War, *History Workshop*, 23, 1987, pp. 81–101.

15 Rubinstein, *A different world for women*, p. 118; and see also pp. 128, 253, for comments on the patriotism – 'narrow to the point of vindictiveness' – that she displayed in wartime.

16 Oakley, Millicent Garrett Fawcett, pp. 190–196; Stephen, *Henry Fawcett*, p. 219.

17 Oakley, Millicent Garrett Fawcett, p. 190.

18 Caine, *Victorian feminists*, pp. 211–212.

19 Rubinstein, *A different world for women*, p. 71.

20 Patricia Jalland, *Death in the Victorian family* (Oxford, Oxford University Press, 1996), p. 5.

21 Strachey, *Millicent Garrett Fawcett*, p. 103.

22 See, for example, J. Littlewood, *Aspects of grief: bereavement in adult life* (London and New York, Tavistock/Routledge, 1992); B. Raphael, *The anatomy of bereavement: a handbook for the caring professions* (London, Routledge, 1984); H. Z. Lopata, *Current widowhood: myths and realities* (Thousand Oaks, CA, Sage Publications, 1996).

23 H. M. Swanwick, *I have been young* (London, Victor Gollancz, 1935), p. 186.

24 Strachey, *Millicent Garrett Fawcett*, p. 147.

25 Harrison, *Prudent revolutionaries*, p. 32.

26 Mary Stocks, *My commonplace book* (London, Peter Davies, 1970), p. 76.

27 Oakley, Millicent Garrett Fawcett, p. 189.

28 Caine, *Victorian feminists*, pp. 209–211.

29 Rubinstein, *A different world for women*, pp. 64, 71, citing J. Manton, *Elizabeth Garrett Anderson* (London, Methuen, 1965).

30 Fawcett to Clotilda Bayne, n.d. 1887, quoted in Strachey, *Millicent Garrett Fawcett*, pp. 103–104.

31 For this approach to feminist biography, see especially B. Caine, Feminist biography and feminist history, *Women's History Review*, 3, 1994, pp. 247–261.

32 Strachey, *Millicent Garrett Fawcett*, p. 103.

33 Rubinstein, *A different world for women*, p. 18.

34 G. van Os, Widows hidden from view, in J. Bremner and L. van den Bosch (eds), *Between poverty and the pyre: moments in the history of widowhood* (London and New York, Routledge, 1995), pp. 230–246.

35 C. J. Barrett, Women in widowhood, *Signs*, 2, 1977, p. 856.

36 J. Mills, *Womanwords: a vocabulary of culture and patriarchal society* (Harlow, Longman, 1989), p. 259.

37 Lopata, *Current widowhood*, pp. 15, 18, 89–94, 221.

38 Jalland, *Death in the Victorian family*, Chapter 7.

39 Lopata, *Current widowhood*, p. 73.

40 Littlewood, *Aspects of grief*, p. 54; Strachey, *Millicent Garrett Fawcett*, p. 104.

41 Littlewood, *Aspects of grief*, p. 41; Raphael, *Anatomy of bereavement*, pp. 177–180; Lopata, *Current widowhood*, pp. 120–124.

42 M. G. Fawcett, England. 1. The women's suffrage movement, in T. Stanton (ed.), *The woman question in Europe: a series of original essays with an introduction by Frances Power Cobbe* (London, Samson Low, 1884). On the limitations of this

account, written from a metropolitan perspective, see S. S. Holton, *Suffrage days: stories from the women's suffrage movement* (London, Routledge, 1996), Chapters 1–3 and pp. 277–278, n. 28.

43 L. Goldman (ed.), *The blind Victorian*, p. 14.

44 Fawcett, *What I remember*, pp. 92–95; M. G. Fawcett, *The martyrs of Turkish misrule* (London, Cassell, Petter & Galpin, 1877).

45 L. Goldman (ed.), *The blind Victorian*, pp. 5–6.

46 Millicent Garrett Fawcett and her daughter, in *The Review of Reviews*, July 1890, p. 20.

47 D. Rubinstein, Victorian feminists: Henry and Millicent Garrett Fawcett, in L. Goldman (ed.), *The blind Victorian*, pp. 82–83.

48 The emancipation of women, in *The Fortnightly Review*, 56, November 1891, p. 679.

49 Stephen, *Henry Fawcett*, pp. 90–97; C. Harvie, Fawcett as a professional politician, in L. Goldman (ed.), *The blind Victorian*, p. 184.

50 *Chambers's Encyclopedia* (London and Edinburgh, W. & R. Chambers, 1889 edn), IV, p. 568.

51 Fawcett, *What I remember*, p. 135. 'Let them leave the slaughter of animals for amusement to those who had been condemned to it by tradition and education', she told students at Bedford College, London; *Women's Suffrage Journal*, 1 November 1886, p. 153. See also H. Kean, *Animal rights: political and social change in Britain since 1800* (London, Reaktion Books, 1998), p. 157.

52 Stephen, *Henry Fawcett*, p. 128.

53 Caine, *Victorian feminists*, pp. 226–227.

54 Rubinstein, *A different world for women*, p. 46.

55 Mrs Fawcett to Bradlaugh, June 1877, in Strachey, *Millicent Garrett Fawcett*, p. 89. See also her later confession to Stead, quoted by Rubinstein, that she had a 'morbid horror of breaking down in public' if she spoke out about child sexual abuse: *A different world for women*, p. 86.

56 Fawcett to Courtney, 2 December 1884, in G. P. Gooch, *Life of Lord Courtney* (London, Macmillan, 1920), pp. 209–210.

57 *The Times*, 11 November 1884, p. 10.

58 Strachey, *Millicent Garrett Fawcett*, p. 102.

59 Stephen, *Henry Fawcett*, p. 467.

60 Strachey, *Millicent Garrett Fawcett*, pp. 106–107; Oakley, Millicent Garrett Fawcett, p. 189; Harrison, *Prudent revolutionaries*, p. 21.

61 Jalland, *Death in the Victorian family*, pp. 284–299.

62 Collini, 'Manly fellows': Fawcett, Stephen and the liberal temper, in L. Goldman (ed.), *The blind Victorian*, p. 42.

63 Fawcett, *What I remember*, p. 136. Henry Fawcett Garrett was one of the ten members of her own immediate family who were killed in the First World War.

64 Ibid., p. 141. Henry Fawcett had been 7th Wrangler in 1856.

65 Ibid., p. 136.

66 Rubinstein, *A different world for women*, pp. 85–86; W. A. Coote (ed.), *A romance of philanthropy* (London, National Vigilance Association, 1916), pp. 7, 16.

67 *The Times*, 7 June 1886, p. 16.

68 Letters from Fawcett to Frances Barton and Clotilda Bayne, n.d. 1885, quoted in Strachey, *Millicent Garrett Fawcett*, pp. 104–105.

69 Goldman (ed.), *The blind Victorian*, pp. 37, 187.

70 C. Harvie, *The lights of Liberalism: university Liberals and the challenge of democracy 1860–1861* (London, Allen Lane, 1976), pp. 218–227; J. Roach,

Liberalism and the Victorian intelligentsia, *Cambridge Historical Journal*, 18, 1957, pp. 58–81.

71 Rubinstein, *A different world for women*, p. 117.

72 Fawcett, *What I remember*, pp. 94–100.

73 Rubinstein, *A different world for women*, p. 61.

74 Fawcett, *What I remember*, p. 113.

75 Ibid., p. 111.

76 Ibid., p. 115.

77 H. C. G. Matthew (ed.), *The Gladstone diaries*, Vol. XI (Oxford, Clarendon Press, 1990), p. 235; *Parl. Deb.*, third series, CCXCIII, 1884, cols 1222–1223; W. Holt, *A beacon for the blind: a life of Henry Fawcett* (London, Constable, 1915), pp. 313, 317–318.

78 For a full account see The maiden tribute of modern Babylon, in J. R. Walkowitz, *City of dreadful delight: narratives of sexual danger in late-Victorian London* (London, Virago, 1992), pp. 81–120.

79 Fawcett, *What I remember*, pp. 127–128.

80 M. G. Fawcett, 'Speech or silence', *Contemporary Review*, 48, September 1885, pp. 326–331.

81 Fawcett, *What I remember*, p. 132.

82 F. Whyte, *The life of W. T. Stead* (London, Jonathan Cape, 1925), Vol. L, p. 159.

83 Caine, *Victorian feminists*, p. 211.

84 *Women's Penny Paper*, 2 February 1889, p. 3.

85 Cook, *Edmund Garrett*, pp. 18–19: he was also involved in the *Pall Mall Gazette*'s campaign against C. S. Parnell at the time of the O'Shea scandal in 1891. Agnes Garrett became Edmund's guardian after his sister Rhoda's death and for a time he lived at 2, Gower Street.

86 'Millicent Garrett Fawcett and her daughter'. The author is described as 'one who knows Mrs Fawcett well' and the article includes some intimate detail on Garrett family life.

87 Rubinstein, *A different world for women*, pp. 87–89. For more sympathetic accounts of this incident, see Caine, *Victorian feminists*, pp. 231–233 and S. K. Kent, *Sex and suffrage in Britain 1860–1914* (Princeton, Princeton University Press, 1987), pp. 152–154.

88 Although the Cust affair brought Fawcett into conflict with her fellow suffragist Lady Frances Balfour, the copious correspondence and notes preserved in the Fawcett Library show that she was not without allies: GB/106M/MGF/90A/ CUST.

89 See especially Mrs Henry Fawcett, *Holes in the education net* (London, NVA, 1887).

90 T. Newman and R. Watkinson, *Ford Madox Brown and the pre-Raphaelite circle* (London, Chatto & Windus, 1991), p. 158; D. Nicholls, *The lost prime minister: a life of Sir Charles Dilke* (London, Hambledon Press, 1995), p. 234.

91 Henry Fawcett's membership of the Ad Eundem Club is referred to in Stephen, *Henry Fawcett*, pp. 79–80. The date of Dilke's expulsion is given in Arthur Sidgwick's journal as 11 February 1888; Bodleian Library, Oxford, MS Eng.misc.e, f. 657. Dilke's recent biographers conclude that he was probably innocent of the charges made against him by Virginia Crawford, but damaging evidence was given against him by his sister-in-law, Mrs Ashton Dilke, who was a prominent suffragist; Nicholls, *The lost prime minister*, pp. 176–211.

92 Rubinstein, *A different world for women*, pp. 132–133; *Women's Penny Paper*, 15 December 1888, pp. 4–5; 22 December 1888, p. 4. For an account of other issues that contributed to the split, see Holton, *Suffrage days*, pp. 71–79.

93 Bland, *Banishing the beast*, pp. 95–123.

94 Fawcett, *What I remember*, p. 135.
95 Strachey, *Millicent Garrett Fawcett*, p. 101.
96 *Women's Penny Paper*, 3 November 1888, pp. 4–5.
97 Mrs Henry Fawcett, *Some eminent women of our times: short biographical sketches* (London, Macmillan, 1889), p. 107. Fawcett was herself to use that title for the chapter in her biography of Queen Victoria that dealt with Albert's death: *Life of Her Majesty Queen Victoria* (London, W. H. Allen, 1895).
98 Fawcett, *Some eminent women*, pp. 114–115.
99 Ibid., pp. 41, 130.
100 Ibid., p. 19.
101 Ibid., p. 139.
102 Fawcett, *What I remember*, p. 191.
103 Kent, *Sex and suffrage, passim*.
104 Fawcett, *What I remember*, pp. 132–133; M. G. Fawcett and E. M. Turner, *Josephine Butler: her work and principles and their meaning for the twentieth century* (London, Association for Moral and Social Hygiene, 1927).
105 The term is used by Lucy Bland; *Banishing the beast*, Chapter 3.
106 Her evidence to the Gorell Commission is recorded in *Parliamentary Papers*, 1912–1913, XIX, pp. 371–379 and summarised in Rubinstein, *A different world for women*, pp. 208–209.
107 Fawcett, The emancipation of women, p. 675, quoted in Bland, *Banishing the beast*, p. 134.
108 *Life of the Right Hon. Sir William Molesworth* (London, Macmillan, 1901).
109 Mrs Henry Fawcett, LL D, *Five famous Frenchwomen* (London, Cassell, 1905).
110 Ibid., pp. 3, 12.
111 Rubinstein, *A different world for women*, p. 123.
112 *The Times*, 11 November 1884, p. 10; M. G. Fawcett, LLD, *Women's suffrage. A short history of a great movement* (London, T. C. & E. C. Jack, 1912), pp. 62–63.
113 Fawcett, *What I remember*, p. 110.

5

EMMELINE PANKHURST (1858–1928) AND VOTES FOR WOMEN[1]

June Purvis

INTRODUCTION

When Emmeline Pankhurst died on 14 June 1928, one month before her seventieth birthday, many tributes were paid to her suffragette days when she had been leader of the Women's Social and Political Union (WSPU), the most notorious of the groupings campaigning in Edwardian Britain for votes for women on equal terms with men. Her one-time rival, Charlotte Despard, leader of the Women's Franchise League (WFL), commented that Emmeline Pankhurst 'was a born fighter. Demanding risks from others, she was ever ready to take risks herself. Nothing in truth, daunted her.'[2] Indeed, Emmeline Pankhurst's life was regarded as so significant by the press that numerous pronouncements were made that she would be assured a place in history.[3] While it is undoubtedly true that in the popular imagination the name 'Pankhurst' is associated with 'votes for women', the majority of historians have presented the leader of the WSPU in a negative manner. Thus Dangerfield ascribes 'motives of self-interest' and 'moments of exhibitionism' to both Emmeline Pankhurst and her eldest daughter, Christabel, also a leader of the WSPU; Mitchell describes Emmeline and her three daughters (Christabel, Sylvia and Adela) as 'wonderful, crazy, intolerant and sometimes intolerable busybodies'; Brendon suggests that Emmeline Pankhurst was a messianic despot who fostered 'a quasi-religious hero-worship of herself' while for Harrison she was a 'subversive firebrand'.[4]

If we turn to historians writing from a socialist perspective, instead of a liberal or conservative persuasion as those quoted above, we find a similar story although Emmeline Pankhurst is now presented primarily as a right-wing, bourgeois autocrat. Thus her socialist daughter, Sylvia, in her monumental work *The suffragette movement*, first published in 1931, presents the leader of the WSPU as a traitor to the socialist cause. Pugh asserts that

Emmeline Pankhurst's by-election policy of campaigning against liberal candidates in order to force the Liberal Government's hand on the women's issue, made the WSPU appear 'as one among a large clutch of Conservative-financed pressure groups' while Rowbotham, and Liddington and Norris, speak of the 'organisational ruthlessness' and 'elitism', respectively, of the Pankhurst leaders as they moved further and further away from the Labour Party.[5]

More sympathetic portrayals of Emmeline Pankhurst are to be found only amongst a minority of historians, including Spender, Marcus, Holton and Purvis.[6] My aim in this chapter is to build upon this minority of accounts by focusing upon a neglected theme, Emmeline Pankhurst's part in the votes for women campaign.

FOUNDATION AND EARLY YEARS OF THE WSPU

During the 1890s, Emmeline Pankhurst and her husband, Richard, a radical lawyer, together with their two eldest daughters, Christabel and Sylvia, were active in socialist politics in their home city of Manchester. Both Emmeline and Richard were members of the newly formed Independent Labour Party (ILP) and their children often accompanied their parents to political and social events that the ILP organised.[7] A popular figure, who campaigned vigorously for the right of free speech in the open space of Boggart Hole Clough, Emmeline was elected to the National Executive Council (NEC) of the ILP in 1897. When her beloved husband died unexpectedly the following year, she temporarily lost an interest in politics and, in her grief, was preoccupied with financial matters. Since Richard's connection with the ILP had lost him many professional clients, he left many debts which had to be paid by his wife who now had to provide for their four surviving children. Robert Blatchford, Editor of the *Clarion*, asked his readers for contributions towards a fund for the family, an offer which Emmeline firmly rejected pointing out that she could not expect working people to contribute towards the cost of her children's schooling when they could not afford to pay for their own; instead she suggested that money be raised to build a hall for socialist meetings, in her husband's memory.[8] The family moved to a humbler house at 62 Nelson Street and Emmeline resigned from her philanthropic work as a Poor Law Guardian and took a salaried post as Registrar of Births and Deaths. In this work she met many despairing working-class women, burdened with over-numerous families; in particular, she was especially moved by the plight of single mothers, some of them as young as thirteen, who, having been seduced by a father or close male relative, came to register the birth of their babies.[9] Her conviction grew that if women were to progress, then they had to lift themselves out of their subordinate position and campaign for the parliamentary vote, a view not always welcomed by some of the key figures

within the ILP. Indeed, Emmeline's disillusionment with the lukewarm attitude (and in some cases, hostility) of socialist men towards women's suffrage deepened when, five years after her husband's death, she heard that the
hall to be opened in his memory would be used as the headquarters of an ILP
branch that would not admit women. Declaring that she had wasted her time
in the ILP, she decided to form a new women's organisation that would run
parallel to it.[10] Thus on 10 October 1903, she called to her home some wives
of ILP men and, with her eldest daughter Christabel, formed the WSPU, an
organisation that was to campaign for the vote for women on the same terms
as it is, or may be, granted to men. The new organisation, whose membership
was to be limited to women only, was to be free from affiliation to any particular social class grouping or to any of the male political parties of the
day.[11] Always a practical politician, Emmeline resolved that the WSPU
should be 'satisfied with nothing but action on our question. Deeds, not
words, was to be our permanent motto.'[12] As was characteristic of her, Sylvia
later recalled, once her mother had re-entered the franchise struggle, it
became for her the only cause in the world.[13] Emmeline's single-mindedness
about votes for women, fuelled by her passion to end the unjust and
oppressed condition of her own sex, was to be severely tested in the years to
come.

During these early years, there were close links between the WSPU and
the socialist movement, Emmeline, her daughters and her only surviving son,
Harry, being members of their local ILP branch, as were many other Union
members. Indeed, Emmeline was popular enough within the ILP to be
elected again as a member of its NEC, at the Easter Conference in Cardiff, in
1904, where her resolution on women's suffrage was carried. However,
although the ILP agreed to sponsor a Women's Franchise Bill, there were
many socialists, such as Philip Snowden, who were hostile to such a measure, believing that the enfranchisement of women on the same property
qualification that applied to men would give the vote only to 'ladies' who
were more likely to vote conservative.[14] Snowden and his supporters
favoured an Adult Suffrage Bill, a move which aroused deep suspicion
amongst many feminists since it was thought to be a mask for manhood
suffrage.[15]

In February 1905, Emmeline travelled to London in an attempt to persuade
a member of parliament to sponsor the proposed Women's Enfranchisement
Bill as a private member's Bill, places for which were drawn by ballot.
Although the well-known Labour MP and Pankhurst family friend, Keir
Hardie, had promised to sponsor the Bill, his name was not drawn and
Bamford Slack, who drew thirteenth place, agreed to undertake the task.
'This being the first suffrage bill in eight years', recalled Emmeline, 'a thrill
of excitement animated not only our ranks but all the old suffrage soci-
eties.'[16] But hopes were soon to be dashed in a way that was to become all
too familiar when, on 12 May, the second reading of the Bill was talked out.

As the news reached the crowd of nearly 300 women suffragists waiting in the Strangers' Lobby, the more placid representatives of the National Union of Women's Suffrage Societies left. Emmeline Pankhurst, on the other hand, instantly decided that the time had come for a demonstration such as 'no old-fashioned suffragist had ever attempted'. Thus she called upon the women to follow her for a protest against the government, a protest that she saw as the first 'militant' act of the WSPU.[17] The aged suffragist Elizabeth Wolstenholme Elmy began to speak and the police rushed into the crowd of women, ordering them to disperse. The WSPU leader, 'with tremulant voice and blazing eyes, passionately feminine, proudly commanding', helped the women to re-group as they demanded government intervention to save the talked-out Bill while the police took the names of the offenders.[18] This protest displayed some of the qualities that were to mark her future leadership of the WSPU, in particular the fact that she could be 'superb in moments of crisis',[19] initiating action and taking command.

The autumn of 1905 brought fresh hope since a general election was to be held in which it was assumed that the Liberals, who were promising a number of reforms, would be returned rather than the Conservative Party that had held office for twenty years. Realising that the old method of seeking pledges of support for women's suffrage from MPs was futile, Christabel, in discussions with her mother and some other trusted WSPU members, decided on a new confrontational policy that she hoped would bring publicity to the women's cause. On 13 October, Christabel and Annie Kenney, a working-class woman who had recently become a Union member, attended a Liberal Party meeting in Manchester where Sir Edward Gray was to outline future liberal policy. 'Will the Liberal Government, if returned, give votes to women?' was the insistent and repeated question they asked, to which they received no reply. This unprecedented interruption of male political discourse, as Jane Marcus so aptly describes it, was greeted with ferocity. The women were roughly handled and dragged outside by stewards where Christabel deliberately committed the technical offence of spitting at a policeman in order to be arrested. In court the next day, Christabel and Annie refused to pay the fines imposed on them and were sentenced to one week and three days imprisonment, respectively.[20] An anxious Emmeline Pankhurst hurried to the room into which the two young women were ushered and pleaded with Christabel, 'You have done everything you could be expected to do in this matter. I think you should let me pay your fines and take you home.' But her daughter was resolute, replying, 'Mother, if you pay my fine I will never go home.'[21] Emmeline did not disagree. Believing that her first-born had the finest political instinct, she 'identified herself' with the new tactics promptly and unreservedly, evidence, claimed Evelyn Sharp, not only of her perception but also of her 'perfect understanding' with Christabel. Indeed, Sylvia Pankhurst asserted that from the day of Christabel's first imprisonment, their mother proudly and openly proclaimed her eldest daughter, her favourite child, to be her leader.[22] Although Christabel herself always repudiated such a claim, she and her mother were regarded as two sides of a coin. Emmeline's faith in Christabel's tactics was justified since the defiant stand of the two protesters became headline news. Although most newspapers condemned their action, many sympathetic letters were sent to the press, new members joined the WSPU and women's suffrage became a live issue in a way that it had never been before.[23] Furthermore, heckling of politicians and a willingness to go to prison became key tactics in the WSPU campaign to force the government to give women the vote.

Emmeline, who was described by the American suffragist Harriot Stanton Blatch as 'a living flame . . . active as a bit of quicksilver, as glistening, as enticing . . . very beautiful', now threw herself with great zeal into the women's cause. She had the gentlest of natures, commented Union member Mary Richardson, coupled with a fiery spirit. Her love of dramatic adventure, noted Sylvia, found full vent in militancy which 'fitted her like a glove'.[24]

Emmeline and Christabel decided that London, the centre of parliament, would be a fertile ground for campaigning and so in January 1906 sent Annie Kenney there, with £2 in her purse. Annie stayed with Sylvia, now at art college, and together they planned a meeting and procession to parliament for 19 February, the day of the King's speech regarding the policies of the new government. Emmeline, travelling from Manchester, spoke on the appointed day. 'With scarcely a gesture', Sylvia recalled, 'phrases of simple eloquence sprang to her lips . . . Her wonderful voice, poignant and mournful, and shot with passion, rose with a new thrill' as her audience of mainly poor women from the East End listened.[25] When news came that women's enfranchisement had not been mentioned in the King's speech, Emmeline announced that they must march to the Commons as a lobbying committee. In the cold rain, the defiant women waited outside the Strangers' Entrance since only twenty at a time were allowed in to petition MPs. Although no MP could be persuaded to support the women's cause, the experience convinced Emmeline that women were now roused into a consciousness about their subordinate position and were prepared to fight for their own human rights.[26] Later that month, on the recommendation of Keir Hardie, who had raised £300 to help the WSPU get started in London, Emmeline Pankhurst asked Emmeline Pethick Lawrence, a social worker, to become treasurer of the WSPU. Together with her husband, Frederick, a lawyer, Emmeline Pethick Lawrence brought necessary administrative skills to the growing organisation, as well as considerable wealth and social contacts, and became an influential member of the newly formed Central London Committee.[27]

At the ILP Easter Conference that year, Emmeline Pankhurst and Isabella Ford were chosen as delegates for the Labour Representation Conference to be held in Belfast the following year. But the difficulty for Emmeline of

Figure 6 Emmeline Pankhurst: a postcard. *c.* 1909

remaining within the ILP was beginning to show since she insisted that for WSPU members the immediate enfranchisement of women 'must take precedence . . . of all other questions'.[28] Convinced that Hardie's resolution in favour of the enfranchisement of women to be presented in the House of Commons on 25 April 1906 would be talked out, she travelled down to London, determined not to let the moment pass without creating a disturbance. When an anti-suffragist MP began to do exactly as Emmeline had predicted, she gave a signal to the small group of suffragettes sitting with her in the Ladies Gallery who cried out 'Divide, divide' and 'We refuse to have our Bill talked out' as they pushed flags through the grille. MPs, including Hardie, were angered by the breach in decorum as the police hastily cleared the gallery. Outside, the WSPU members met a hostile reception from ILP supporters such as Ethel Snowden who believed their militant methods had wrecked the chance of winning the support of the House.[29] Nevertheless, the militants continued to press their claim as they planned for a meeting with the Liberal Prime Minister, Campbell-Bannerman. 'We feel this question so keenly', pleaded Emmeline, 'that we are prepared to sacrifice for it life itself, or what is perhaps even harder, the means by which we live!' The Prime Minister, however, could only preach the virtue of 'patience', while also insisting that he believed in women's enfranchisement.[30]

THE BREAK WITH THE ILP

The relationship between the WSPU and the ILP became further strained during the Cockermouth by-election in August 1906 when Christabel, who had now moved to London and become the WSPU's Chief Organiser, announced a new 'independent' policy, namely opposition to all parliamentary candidates of any political persuasion, a situation that created 'uncomfortable political choices' for many socialist suffragettes such as Mary Gawthorpe who represented the Women's Labour League and was to speak for the Labour candidate, Robert Smillie.[31] When the Conservative candidate was returned with 4,595 votes, Smillie polling only 1,436, the defeat was blamed on the WSPU. Although the Manchester Central Branch of the ILP decided not to expel their two 'recalcitrant' members, Christabel Pankhurst and Teresa Billington, the issue of how women's enfranchisement fitted into a men's political party in which women's issues were only of secondary importance became an increasingly pressing issue for both Emmeline and Christabel. Matters came to a head at the Labour Party Conference in January 1907 when, despite the plea of Hardie to secure women suffrage and then fight for adult suffrage, it was decided to put adult suffrage first. In dejected spirit, Hardie announced that if the resolution that had been carried was intended to limit the action of the Labour Party in the Commons, he would have to seriously consider whether he could remain a member. Emmeline Pankhurst sat silent amongst the stunned delegates, knowing that she could not advise her old friend to leave the Labour Party since it would leave him politically isolated. Faced with the threat of Hardie's resignation, the Party Executive gave its members freedom to choose between women's enfranchisement on existing terms or adult suffrage, a decision which meant that the party itself would take no action at all.[32]

The WSPU advertised a Women's Parliament to be held on 13 February, presided over by Emmeline Pankhurst, to mark the opening of a new parliamentary session the previous day. A resolution was passed expressing indignation over the fact that the King's speech had contained nothing about votes for women and demanding immediate facilities for a women's Bill.

Emmeline's motion that the resolution should be taken to the Prime Minister was carried and a deputation sallied forth under the leadership of Charlotte Despard. The women met with fierce resistance from foot and mounted police, two of Emmeline's daughters – Christabel and Sylvia – being amongst the fifty-four women arrested.[33] The resolve of the Union's leader did not weaken, however; indeed she had renewed hope that the campaigning might soon be over since for the first time ever, the MP who drew first place in the Private Members Ballot, W. H. Dickson, a Liberal, said he would introduce a women's suffrage bill. Emmeline warned that if the government did not give facilities for the Bill, Union members would not 'shrink from death if necessary for the success of the movement. We are not playing at politics in this agitation. If the Government brings out the Horse Guards, and fires on us, we will not flinch.'[34] Hopes were dashed again as a number of professed suffragists in the Commons complained that the Bill was not democratic enough and it was talked out. More brute force was used against and more arrests were made from processions of women who marched from a second Women's Parliament held on 20 March. The English government, complained Emmeline, was sending to prison women whose 'militancy' consisted merely of trying to carry a resolution to the Prime Minister in the House of Commons.[35]

The Union leader now had also to face criticisms of WSPU tactics from suffragists within and outside her own organisation as earlier disagreements surfaced again at the ILP Conference held on 1 and 2 April. On behalf of Charlotte Despard and Annie Cobden Sanderson (and two non-Union members, Ethel Snowden and Isabella Ford), ILP member Margaret McMillan read out a message which repudiated the independent stand of the WSPU at Cockermouth and reaffirmed a pledge never to go down to any constituency or take part in an election unless it was to help the Labour Party. Emmeline disclaimed all connection with the declaration, pointing out that it was only by putting pressure on the present government, by opposing all government nominees, that the vote would be won. 'If you think my conduct inconsistent with my membership', she threatened, 'I will resign.'[36] A few weeks later she and Christabel left the ILP.

THE 1907 SPLIT: 'AUTOCRAT' OF THE WSPU?

Further tensions emerged during the summer months between members of the WSPU Central Committee. It would appear that Teresa Billington-Greig (who had married some months earlier) felt deep resentment when, with the arrival of Christabel in London, she was transferred to the provinces to establish new branches. In favour of greater branch autonomy and democracy, it was rumoured that she and other socialist suffragists, such as Charlotte Despard and Edith How Martyn, intended a coup against the leadership, a move that would be made at the annual conference planned for October. Emmeline, travelling in the provinces, wrote to Sylvia in June, 'As for as the TBG [Teresa Billington-Greig] affair we have just to face her & put her in her place.'[37] When she returned to WSPU headquarters at Clements Inn, at the request of the Pethick Lawrences, Emmeline declared the democratic constitution of the WSPU abolished, the annual conference cancelled, and invited the members who were ready to follow her to still do so.[38] Unable to follow a leader who had 'proclaimed herself as sole dictator of the movement', Billington-Greig and the other disaffected members left the Union, forming a grouping later called the Women's Freedom League while the majority supported Emmeline Pankhurst.[39] Emmeline offered no apology for the autocratic organisational structure of the WSPU since she believed it was the most effective structure for winning the vote. As she later emphasised:

> The W.S.P.U. is not hampered by a complexity of rules. We have no constitution and by-laws; nothing to be amended or tinkered with or quarrelled over at an annual meeting. In fact, we have no annual meeting, no business sessions, no elections of officers. The W.S.P.U. is simply a suffrage army in the field. It is purely a volunteer army, and no one is obliged to remain in it.[40]

As Rebecca West was to comment in an insightful essay in 1933, in the midst of her battle for democracy, Emmeline Pankhurst was obliged, lest that battle should be lost, to become a dictator.[41]

Emmeline Pankhurst's autocratic rule, however, was in theory only since during the years immediately following the 1907 split she did not choose to exercise any direct personal control. Although she was consulted on all major policy issues, she had absolute confidence in Christabel's judgement. The daily executive control of the Union was undertaken by Christabel and the Pethick Lawrences with whom Christabel lived, the three being known as the 'triumvirate'.[42] By now Emmeline was travelling around the country, speaking in endless meetings and leading the by-election campaigning. Earlier in the year she had resigned from her Registrar post and given up her Manchester home,[43] her main source of income now being her £200 fee per annum as a Union speaker. From now until the end of the militant campaign she had no settled home but stayed in a number of rented flats, hotels or homes of friends. When the spur of the cause flagged, her life seemed 'harsh and joyless'; while she might be applauded on a public stage, her private life was often lonely.[44]

Often Emmeline became a target for rough treatment and violence as on 18 January 1908 when the by-election result was announced at Newton Abbot in favour of the Conservative candidate. She and her co-worker, Nellie Martel, were attacked by a group of young male clay-cutters who had supported the ousted Liberal candidate, whom the women had opposed. While

Emmeline was running to the haven of a grocer's shop, a staggering blow fell on the back of her head, rough hands grasped the collar of her coat and she was flung to the muddy ground. Afraid that she might be placed in an empty barrel nearby, she courageously asked, 'Are none of you *men*?' Although the mob fled when the police arrived, it was two hours before it was considered safe for the women to leave.[45] The experience did not deter the intrepid Union leader from rushing to another by-election, this time in Leeds, and then, still lame from the injury to her ankle, returning to London to lead a deputation of women to parliament on 13 February. Charged with obstruction and refusing to be bound over, Emmeline and eight of the twelve women were sentenced to six weeks in the Second Division.

This was Emmeline's first imprisonment, the harshness and indignity of which she never forgot. After two days of solitary confinement, afflicted with migraine, she was sent to the hospital where she was awoken, during the night, by the moaning of a woman in the cell next to her own. She suddenly realised that the woman was in labour. 'I shall never forget that night,' she recollected, 'nor what I suffered with the birth-pangs of that woman, who, I found later, was simply waiting trial on a charge which was found to be baseless.'[46] Released on 19 March, Emmeline could have rested quietly, at home. But ever restless, and with a flair for the dramatic, she made an unexpected entrance at an Albert Hall meeting that night, to mark the end of a Self-Denial Week to raise money for the cause. Like an actress in the wings, she waited till all the others were seated and then walked quietly onto the stage, removed the placard on her seat saying 'Mrs Pankhurst's Chair' and sat down, to great applause. Deeply moved by the love shown her, it was some time before she could speak:

> I for one, friends, looking around on the muddles that men have made, looking round on the sweated and decrepit members of my sex, I say men have had the control of these things long enough, and no woman with any spark of womanliness in her will consent to let this state of things go on any longer.[47]

At Easter 1908, Campbell-Bannerman resigned and was succeeded as Prime Minister by the notorious anti-suffragist, Asquith. Nine by-elections followed in which, Emmeline proudly recalled, the WSPU with its active anti-government stance, succeeded in pulling down the Liberal vote by 6,663.[48] Asquith refused to give the required facilities for the Woman Suffrage Bill of Stanger, an MP, despite the fact that the Bill had passed its second reading, and stated that the government intended to bring in a reform bill that would be worded in such a way as to admit a woman-suffrage amendment, if any member chose to move one, provided the amendment was on democratic lines and had the support of the women of the country, as well as the electorate. The WSPU took up the challenge, planning a great demonstration for 21 June in which members would wear favours in the Union's colours of purple (for dignity), white (for purity) and green (for hope). Emmeline, accompanied by the oldest living suffragist, Elizabeth Wolstenholme Elmy, led the seven processions that converged that day in Hyde Park, attracting crowds of over 300,000.[49] As Holton notes, this colourful, peaceful demonstration was a watershed in the development of militancy for the WSPU since Asquith remained unmoved by the scale of support; from this time, militancy, conceived as the heckling of Liberal MPs, civil disobedience and peaceful demonstrations, was gradually replaced by the organisation of more threatening demonstrations and acts of violence, initially in the form of undirected and uncoordinated individual acts of window-breaking.[50] Emmeline participated readily in these new forms of militancy though whether she was a follower here, 'driven' by Christabel, is a moot point.[51] Nevertheless, through all the following years of militancy, Emmeline came to be seen as the 'embodiment of the nation's motherhood, striving magnificently for citizenship, churlishly thwarted and betrayed'.[52]

'MILD' MILITANCY CONTINUED

After the June demonstration, Emmeline realised that the WSPU had 'exhausted argument'.[53] She held another Women's Parliament on 30 June and then, at half past four, led another deputation to Asquith which was repulsed from the Commons. That evening, in Parliament Square, women were roughly handled by the police as they made speeches, some twenty-five being arrested. Outraged by the police brutality, Mary Leigh and Edith New threw stones at Asquith's official residence at 10 Downing Street, were arrested and sentenced to two months in the Third Division. The two women sent word to the Union leader that, having acted without orders, they would not resent her repudiation of their acts. Far from repudiating them, Emmeline went at once to see them in their cells and 'assured them' of her approval.[54] On 14 October, she stood in the dock at Bow Street, alongside Christabel and Flora Drummond, charged with 'inciting to disorder', based upon a handbill that had been published advocating that the public 'rush' the Commons the day before. The case was recessed until 21 October when the three accused did not employ counsel but conducted their own defence. As she rose to speak, Emmeline assumed an appearance of calm that she did not feel. Then she made a poignant speech, relating her life experiences as a working mother and as a Poor Law Guardian where she had learnt about the unjust marriage and divorce laws that deprived women of maintenance for their children and gave them no legal right of guardianship. She stressed how she and other WSPU members had tried to be patient and 'womanly', using constitutional methods, all to no avail and pleaded:

> We have taken this action, because as women . . . we realise that the condition of our sex is so deplorable that it is our duty to break the law in order to call attention to the reasons why we do so . . . We are here not because we are law-breakers; we are here in our efforts to become law-makers.[55]

Although Christabel's brilliant advocacy earned her the nickname of 'Portia in the dock', it was Emmeline's pleading that moved her listeners to tears. No mercy was shown, however, and all three defendants were sent to prison. Characteristically, at this trial, which had attracted widespread newspaper coverage, Emmeline emphasised that she accepted full responsibility for the present agitation, a theme she often stressed during subsequent years. On 19 December, the day of Christabel's release, Emmeline was discharged from Holloway also, two weeks early. The joyous celebrations included a procession and a special meeting, held early in the New Year, when the beloved Union leader was presented with a chain and pendant of amethysts, pearls and emeralds, wrought in gold, as a symbol of the dignity, purity and hope she had brought into her followers' lives. As one WSPU member recalled, 'while we admired Christabel, we loved Mrs Pankhurst'.[56] Indeed, Emmeline Pankhurst's gift of inspiring love and devotion was legendary. A charismatic person, a leader of 'power and magnetism',[57] she drew people to her. Mary Philipps, a Scottish suffragette, expressed the thoughts of many Union members when she enthused that their leader's splendid courage, and the complete trust she placed in them, gave her 'a place in the hearts of those who knew her best'.[58]

The year 1909 marked another important point in the suffrage struggle. On 24 June Marion Wallace Dunlop, a sculptress, printed on the wall of St Stephen's Hall in the House of Commons an extract from the 1689 Bill of Rights: 'It is the right of the subjects to petition the King, and all committments and prosecutions for such petitioning are illegal.'[59] Five days later, Emmeline led a deputation of eight women who insisted on the right to petition at the door of the Commons. Afraid that two elderly protesters might be jostled by the police, she quickly decided to secure immediate arrest by striking a number of blows at Inspector Jarvis. Soon other small groups of women made dashes to the Commons, with 108 women and 14 men being arrested. Emmeline's case, together with that of the Honourable Evelina Haverfield, was selected as the test case. Although the magistrate agreed that the right of Petition existed, he also ruled that the women were wrong not to obey police instructions to go away. An appeal, heard in December by the Lord Chief Justice, upheld that the conviction in the lower court had been proper and the appeal was dismissed with costs. 'Far from discouraging or disheartening us,' noted the determined Union leader, 'it simply spurred us on to new and more aggressive forms of militancy.'[60]

In particular, Emmeline claimed that between the arrest of Marion Wallace

Dunlop in June and the December ruling, the militant movement was lifted onto 'a new and more heroic plane'.[61] On 5 July the imprisoned Marion Wallace Dunlop, on her own initiative, had begun a hunger-strike in an effort to be granted political offender status and placed in the First Division; after ninety-one hours of fasting, she had been released. Other imprisoned suffragists, hoping for a quick release, had adopted the hunger-strike too but by the end of September the government had responded with forcible feeding. With disbelief, shock and deep anger, Emmeline Pankhurst, Emmeline Pethick Lawrence and Christabel condemned the government for violating the exhausted and starved bodies of women who had been driven to the last extremity of passive resistance.[62] The impassioned and yet compassionate leader, who claimed she could not write, took up her pen and accused the government of torture. 'The spirit which is in woman to-day', she warned, 'cannot be quenched; it is stronger than all earthly potentates and powers . . . than all tyranny, cruelty, and oppression . . . stronger even than death itself.'[63] Private troubles also weighed heavily on her at this time since her son, Harry, who had been a delicate child, had developed inflammation of the spinal cord and was paralysed from the waist down. Needing money for his medical treatment, she felt she could not cancel her already planned North American and Canadian tour and so set sail on 12 October. Wherever she went, enthusiastic crowds came to hear her, especially at New York's Carnegie Hall. When the small, well-dressed leader rose to speak, a hush fell over the audience. But at her first words, spoken in a calm, lady-like voice, 'I am what you call a hooligan', a great wave of sympathetic laughter erupted.[64] She returned to England in December, only to learn the bitter truth from which both Sylvia and Christabel had tried to protect her, namely that Harry would never walk again and that his future was bleak. When he died early in the New Year, Sylvia recollected that her mother was broken as she had never seen her; 'huddled together without a care for her appearance, she seemed an old, plain, cheerless woman'.[65] But her power of detachment, her ability to subordinate private claims to public service, 'always a distinguishing mark of her character', came to the fore.[66]

With a heavy heart and yet characteristic zeal, Emmeline threw herself into by-election work since a general election had been called, campaigning against the Liberal Government in forty constituencies. To what extent the heavy losses sustained by the Liberals were due to WSPU policy is debatable, but they were returned with no overall majority in the Commons polling only 275 seats while the Conservatives held 273, the Irish Nationalists 82 and Labour 40.[67] Realising that the new political situation might be useful to the women's cause, Henry Brailsford, a journalist who had earlier resigned from the *Daily News* in protest against the support of its editor for forcible feeding, set about forming a Conciliation Committee for Women's Suffrage which eventually consisted of fifty-four MPs across the political spectrum. Although initially doubtful about this new venture, the

WSPU leaders offered their support, Christabel explaining that the Conciliation Committee might avert the need for 'stronger militancy' since mild militancy was more or less played out.[68] On 31 January, Emmeline declared that there would be a truce on militancy, only peaceful and constitutional methods being used.

The Conciliation Committee's Women's Franchise Bill was deliberately drafted along narrow lines in order to win the support of the Tories and thus it sought to extend the parliamentary vote to women occupiers but not to wives for the same qualification as their husbands. Since relatively few married women or working-class women would be enfranchised under these terms and women lodgers excluded, many critics voiced their concerns including Emmeline Pankhurst who, wisely, lamented the Bill's narrowness only in private.[69] Although the Bill passed its second reading on 12 July, with a majority of 109, both the Home Secretary, Lloyd George, and the Prime Minister, Asquith, voted against it. The Commons then voted to send the Bill to a committee of the whole House, thereby extinguishing its chances. Emmeline's fears of treachery were confirmed on 23 July when Asquith informed Lord Lytton that the Bill would be granted no further time that session.[70] At an enthusiastic meeting held on 10 November, she warned that a WSPU deputation to be sent in eight days' time would be the last constitutional effort by the Union to secure the passage of the Bill into law. 'If the Bill, in spite of our efforts, is killed by the Government,' she warned, ' then . . . I have to say there is an end to the truce.'[71]

When Parliament reconvened on 18 November, Asquith announced that precedence would be given to government business for the next ten days and made no reference to the Conciliation Bill. The women's deputation that set out, in contingents of twelve, was treated with exceptional brutality by the police who prolonged the struggle by trying to force them back, on what became known as 'Black Friday'; women were thrown from one policeman to another who punched them with fists, striking the women in their faces, breasts and shoulders.[72] Emmeline Pankhurst was not amongst the 115 women and 4 men arrested but saw with horror the treatment meted out to the women who later told her 'We cannot bear this'; indeed, for many women window-breaking, which resulted in immediate arrest, was beginning to seem a 'safer' form of militancy.[73] Four days later, Emmeline was speaking at Caxton Hall when a message reached her that Asquith had stated that after the general election the government would, if still in power, give facilities for a Bill that would be so framed as to admit of free amendment. Immediately she heard the news of such a vague, ambiguous promise, Emmeline declared with that decisiveness and swiftness of impulse that were characteristic of her leadership, 'I am going to Downing Street. Come along, all of you.'[74] They took a new and uncrowded path to Downing Street, and the police had time only to form a single cordon across the narrow street. Unhesitating, Emmeline, who had a 'marvellous way of remaining, in the midst of crowds and struggles, as calm and proudly dignified as a queen', walked straight through their midst, the other women pressing steadily forward.[75] The police line broke. When reinforcements arrived, violent struggles broke out. This time Emmeline was amongst the 156 arrested but since no evidence was offered against her, she was discharged. In her special message to the members of the Black Friday and Downing Street demonstrations, she praised the 'magnificent courage and self-restraint' the women had shown and humbly confessed, 'I feel myself deeply honoured to be your leader.'[76] Two days before Christmas, she presided over the welcome meeting for the released prisoners, including her sister, Mary Clarke, who suddenly died on Christmas Day. As before, Emmeline attempted to cope with another personal tragedy by channelling her efforts into the cause so dear to her heart. Her New Year message was one of hope – 'We who remain, as soldiers in the women's army, must continue the good fight until the victory is won.'[77]

In the January 1911 general election, Asquith was returned to power with the distribution of seats in the Commons being little changed. The WSPU renewed the truce of militancy in the hope that the revised Conciliation Bill (now titled 'A Bill to Confer the Parliamentary Franchise on Women') would win greater support since it included all women householders and, with its broader title, made amendment possible. The Bill, which had gained widespread support throughout the country, resolutions in its favour being passed by eighty-six city, town and urban district councils, passed its second reading on 5 May with a majority of 167.[78] On 29 May Lloyd George told the Commons that although no time could be found for the Conciliation Bill that year, a day would be granted for another second reading in 1912. Asquith further explained, in a letter to Lord Lytton, that although the government was divided on the merits of the Bill, its members were 'unanimous' in the promise in regard to the granting of facilities.[79] On the evening of 17 June, the day of the WSPU-sponsored Women's Coronation Procession, in which twenty-eight other suffrage groupings took part, Emmeline Pankhurst spoke at a joyful meeting at the Albert Hall. 'Here we are to-night . . . with a sure and certain knowledge that victory is near,' she reassured her audience. 'We have proved that we can combine; we have proved that we can put aside all personal beliefs and all personal doubts for a common end.'[80]

ESCALATING DESTRUCTION OF PROPERTY

That autumn, on another lecture tour of the USA and Canada, Emmeline Pankhurst impressed her audience wherever she went. 'The moment she appeared on the platform', commented one American newspaper, 'one realised by what power of personality she has become the best loved and best hated woman in England.'[81] On 7 November she was cabled the devastating news that Asquith had announced that a Manhood Suffrage Bill would be introduced next session which would allow amendment, if the Commons so desired, for the enfranchisement of women. Realising that such an amendment would be doomed, since it was impossible to have manhood suffrage for all men and a property qualification for women, Emmeline cabled 'Protest imperative!' to Christabel who was already organising a deputation for 21 November. As the deputation marched on that day, another, smaller group of women armed with bags of stones and hammers broke windows in businesses and government offices. When three days later Lloyd George announced that the Conciliation Bill had been 'torpedoed', the WSPU truce was finally ended as Christabel defended the broken windows policy. Emmeline's message to Union members, published in early December, urged her followers to engage in a 'civil war', the outcome of which would be the withdrawal of the Manhood Suffrage Bill.[82] On 15 December, Emily Wilding Davison, a well-known militant, came before the magistrate for attempting to set fire to a letter-box, something which she claimed she had already done to two other post-boxes earlier that day, acting entirely on her 'own responsibility'.[83] It was to this state of affairs that Emmeline Pankhurst returned to England on 18 January 1912, with the words 'Sedition!' and 'The Women's Revolution' on her lips.[84]

In mid-February, at a meeting to welcome the released window-breakers, Emmeline announced that the weapon and argument they were going to use at the next demonstration was the stone. 'Why should women go to Parliament Square and be battered about and insulted, and most important of all, produce less effect than when they throw stones?' she indignantly asked. Although Emmeline expected to be arrested for this speech, she was not and shortly afterwards spent some time being taught how to throw stones by Ethel Smyth, the composer and recent Union recruit.[85] Ready for the affray, Emmeline and two other women broke windows at 10 Downing Street on 1 March, while about 150 other suffragettes smashed shop windows in London's West End. This was the first time the WSPU had mounted a militant demonstration without announcement. In court the next day, where she reminded the magistrate that women had failed to gain the vote since they had failed to use the methods of agitation of men, she was sentenced to two months' imprisonment.[86] After two more days of window-smashing, the police swooped on WSPU headquarters with a warrant for the arrest of the Pethick Lawrences, Christabel, Mabel Tuke and Emmeline. The latter two were already in prison and only the Pethick Lawrences were found. Christabel, who was staying in a flat nearby, spent the night in hiding and then escaped to Paris. 'My relief, when I learned of her flight,' recollected her mother, 'was very great because I knew that whatever happened to the Lawrences and myself, the movement would be wisely directed.'[87] In her damp, sunless cell, Emmeline contracted bronchitis; her petition for release on bail, to recover her health, was refused. On 28 March, she was committed for trial, together with Mabel Tuke and the Pethick Lawrences, on the charge of 'conspiracy'. Eleven days later she was released from prison, her sentence for window-breaking having been remitted until after this new trial. Amid widespread public concern for her health and treatment, the Rev. Hugh Chapman warned, 'We constantly kill our prophets and afterwards erect their sepulchres.'[88]

At the conspiracy trial, which began on 15 May, the 54-year-old leader of the WSPU made another poignant speech in which she explained how women had been driven to greater militancy by the stubborn opposition of the government.[89] The defendants were found guilty and, despite the jury's recommendation of leniency, were sentenced to nine months' imprisonment; in addition, Emmeline Pankhurst and Frederick Pethick Lawrence were also ordered to pay the prosecution costs.[90] The Pethick Lawrences and Emmeline Pankhurst threatened to hunger-strike, unless they were treated as political offenders and placed in the First Division, a request that was granted. However, since the same privilege was not extended to other suffrage prisoners, all three joined with other imprisoned suffragists in a mass hunger-strike that began on 19 June. Three days later, forcible feeding began. Holloway became a place of 'horror and torment', recollected Emmeline, as she listened to the cries of women undergoing instrumental invasion of the body. When her own cell door was opened, she picked up a heavy earthenware jug and with an air of authority cried to the doctors and wardresses, 'If any of you dares so much as to take one step inside this cell I shall defend myself.'[91] They all retreated. Two days later, both Emmeline Pankhurst and Emmeline Pethick Lawrence were released, on medical grounds.

Travelling under the name of 'Mrs Richards', Emmeline Pankhurst now made the first of many visits to Christabel in France where she sought to consult with her daughter, take rest and seek cures for her poor health. In early July, Emmeline asked the Pethick Lawrences to Boulogne where differences of view in regard to the future direction of the WSPU were discussed. While Emmeline and Christabel favoured greater militancy, the Pethick Lawrences did not. Shortly after the latter returned in early October from a lecturing tour of Canada, Emmeline told them that she had decided to sever their connection with the WSPU. Shattered by such news, the Pethick Lawrences insisted that Christabel come to London to debate the matter; travelling in disguise, Christabel emphasised that she and her mother were 'absolutely united in this matter'.[92] Most WSPU members seem to have been shocked by this action; while some of Emmeline Pankhurst's followers accepted the situation, agreeing with their leader that it was the cause rather than the individual that was important, the WSPU lost many of its most influential supporters. Jessie Kenney recalled that loyalties were 'even fiercer'.[93]

HONORARY TREASURER OF THE WSPU AND FUGITIVE

Emmeline Pankhurst now became honorary treasurer of the Union, with responsibility for raising finances. Consequently, less time was spent as an itinerant speaker, campaigning around the country. At the Royal Albert Hall meeting on 17 October, she brought the power of her oratory to the full as she outlined the new militant policy which was to include relentless opposition not only to the party in power, the Liberals, but also to the Irish and Labour Parties, and to feature attacks on public and private property but not on human life. She encouraged her audience to 'Be militant each in your own way' and warned, 'And my last word is to the Government: I incite this meeting to rebellion.'[94] The following day a new WSPU newspaper appeared, *The Suffragette*, edited by Christabel from Paris; the Pethick Lawrences kept control of *Votes for Women*.

When Asquith announced to the Commons on 27 January 1913 that the Manhood Suffrage Bill was dropped for that session, Emmeline immediately declared war on the government, saying that suffragettes were 'guerrillists' who would do as much damage to property as they could if that was the necessary means to win the vote.[95] Over the next eighteen months, the WSPU was increasingly driven underground as it engaged in large-scale window-smashing, setting fire to pillar-boxes, false fire alarms, arson and bombing, attacks on art treasures, the cutting of telegraph and telephone wires, and damage to golf courses. The Union leader frequently stressed that she took full responsibility for all acts of militancy, as at a WSPU meeting on 30 January 1913 – 'I want to say that, placed as I am in the responsible position, with others, of guiding the movement, that for all the women have done, and for what all the women are doing, I take full responsibility.'[96] Now regarded as a dangerous subversive, she was watched by the police who appeared in plain clothes at her meetings and transcribed her speeches. On 2 April she was sentenced to three years' penal servitude for committing offences contrary to the Malicious Injuries to Property Act of 1861. However, she served less than six weeks of her sentence between the time of her conviction and the time when militancy was suspended. Using the Prisoners' Temporary Discharge for Ill-health Act, known as the 'Cat and Mouse Act', which allowed prisoners who had damaged their health to be released on a licence in order to recover so that they would be fit enough to be re-admitted, she was repeatedly in and out of prison.[97] Never once did she hesitate to share with her followers that which they too experienced.[98] Sustained by her single-minded devotion to the women's cause, her defiance, determination and courage won admiration, even from many who considered WSPU tactics ill-conceived. Furthermore, Emmeline saw herself in an historic role as an individual who brought about radical change through political action, a view, claims Holton, that was largely derived from the writings of the influential historian Thomas Carlyle.[99] 'O kind fate that cast me for this glorious role in the history of women!' she once wrote when recovering from a hunger-strike in May 1913.[100] In the autumn, while still under sentence, she made another trip to the USA where she was detained at Ellis Island as an undesirable alien, a ruling that was overturned by President Wilson. 'Nothing ever has been got out of the British parliament without something very nearly approaching a revolution,' she told an enthusiastic audience in New York on 21 October. 'Men got the vote because they were and would be violent,' she continued. 'The women did not get it because they were constitutional and law-abiding.'[101] On arrival back in England, she was re-arrested, released after a hunger-strike and then travelled, openly, to Paris where she spent all of January 1914.

Family concerns which had been pressing for some time were now confronted when Emmeline's two younger daughters visited their mother and Christabel in Paris. In mid-January, Sylvia was told by Christabel, with Emmeline's support, that her East London Federation must be separate from the WSPU since it was allied with the Labour Party, contrary to Union policy. On 29 January, Emmeline wrote to Sylvia that she was glad that they had settled as to the separate organisations but unhappy as to the title Sylvia had suggested, 'The East London Federation of the Suffragettes'. '"The WSPU and the Suffragettes" have become interchangeable terms,' Emmeline insisted. 'The use of the word "Suffragette" would prevent the public from realising that your movement in the East End is something distinct and independent.'[102] Adela, who had suffered a breakdown in 1912 and not found a steady job after she had graduated from Studley Horticultural College, was shattered by the news that her mother, to whom she was devoted, considered her a 'failure'; not wishing to clash with her, Adela did not argue against Emmeline's well-meant plan to give her youngest daughter a fresh start in life by giving her the fare to Australia, a letter to Australian suffragist Vida Goldstein and £20.[103] Adela never saw her mother or England again.

Still subject to her three-year sentence, Emmeline managed to evade detectives and travel back to England where her recently formed bodyguard was waiting to protect her from re-arrest. Now like a fugitive, she seldom stayed long in one place but was sheltered by a network of supportive and devoted friends. On 10 February, she spoke from the second-floor window of the private house in which she was staying in Campden Hill Square, challenging the government to re-arrest her and accusing them of cowardice in forcibly feeding suffragettes whom she had incited to militancy while not daring to forcibly feed herself.[104] As she left the house, surrounded by about twenty women, a fierce conflict broke out with the police who arrested a veiled woman in black, only to discover later that she was not Emmeline but a decoy. On 21 February, Emmeline gave another address from a private house, this time from the balcony at Glebe Place, Chelsea. In her speech, she emphasised that the women's campaign was wider than the fight for the vote:

We are fighting for a time when every little girl born into the world will have an equal chance with her brothers, when we shall put an end to foul outrages upon our sex, when our streets shall be safe for the girlhood of our race, when every man shall look upon every other woman as his own sisters.[105]

The following evening another fight took place between women wielding Indian clubs and the police surrounding the house, during which Emmeline escaped into a waiting taxi. 'I have strong hope that I shall get through all my engagements up to Easter unarrested,' she wrote to Ethel Smyth.[106] But it was not to be. Looking pale and fragile, her hair now a silvery white, she appeared on the platform at a meeting in St Andrew's Hall, Glasgow, on 9 March and, after a violent struggle, was arrested again. Sent on a train back to London and imprisonment in Holloway, she was released in a state of utter exhaustion after nearly five days of hunger- and thirst-strike. As Green notes, such wreckage to her body gave Emmeline Pankhurst an 'otherworldly voice' whose power increased as her physical strength failed.[107] The day after the Union leader's arrest, Mary Richardson slashed Velázquez's *Rokeby Venus* in the National Gallery as a protest against the way Emmeline Pankhurst was being 'slowly murdered by a Government of Iscariot politicians'.[108] Suffragettes continued to interrupt church services by saying prayers for the Union leader whom many feared would die.

Some months earlier, Emmeline had written to the King to announce her intention of leading a deputation to Buckingham Palace, the right to petition the reigning monarch being the oldest of all political rights. Although the request was refused, the deputation went ahead as planned on 21 June with the inevitable fracas. Women wielding imitation truncheons and eggshells full of red, yellow and green paint, were roughly handled by the police. Emmeline was amongst those arrested. As Inspector Rolfe lifted her in his arms to a car waiting behind police lines, crushing her ribs, she shouted defiantly, 'That's right! Arrest me at the gates of the Palace. Tell the King!'[109]

Further police raids were now made on WSPU headquarters and private dwellings, in an attempt to crush the movement and the printing and sale of *The Suffragette*. As Honorary Treasurer of the WSPU, Emmeline was actively involved in encouraging subscribers to give to WSPU funds, as on 9 June when she wrote to Mrs Badley, 'They are attempting as they have previously done to terrorise our subscribers by threats of legal action . . . I do hope dear Mrs Badley that you will do all in your power to help me to raise a large sum of money with which to carry on our work to the end of the year.'[110] After the police had vacated WSPU headquarters, Emmeline attempted to resume work there on 8 July but was arrested and sent to prison, her ninth arrest since her sentence in April 1913 to three years' penal servitude. After three days of a hunger- and thirst-strike, she was released in a severely weakened state on a four-day licence in order to prevent her attending a WSPU meeting scheduled for 16 July. Determined to keep her promise to speak at the meeting, she set out on a stretcher from the nursing home, where she was being looked after, was arrested and taken back to jail in an ambulance.[111] Anticipating such a move, she had prepared a defiant message to be read at the meeting. 'There is talk of negotiation and compromise. No negotiations for us. A Government measure giving equal voting rights to women with men is our demand, and we demand it **Now!**'[112] Severely weakened by two arrests in one week, she was released on a temporary discharge to return on 22 July. She managed to evade re-arrest and went to St Malo to recuperate where she was joined by Christabel.

Shortly after the outbreak of the First World War early in August 1914, the government announced that it would remit the sentences of persons now imprisoned for crimes committed in connection with the suffrage agitation. On 12 August, Emmeline Pankhurst sent a letter to all WSPU members announcing 'a temporary suspension of activities'.[113] The militant campaign had ended.

CONCLUSION

I have attempted in this chapter to challenge the negative portrayal offered by so many historians of Emmeline Pankhurst, leader of the WSPU, by reappraising her role in the votes for women campaign. In particular, I would claim that we may see her as a women-identified woman, forerunner of some of the separatist radical feminist ideas articulated in second wave feminism in the USA and Western Europe in the late 1960s and 1970s. As such, she needs to be reclaimed from the denigration of history and represented as she was seen in her time, a 'Champion of Womanhood'.[114]

Charlotte Despard commented, in 1928, that Emmeline Pankhurst's great service to women was that she discovered, stimulated and, through her personal initiative, harnessed for action, a spirit of revolt.[115] Ethel Smyth, onetime close friend of the WSPU leader, similarly claimed:

> The supreme achievement of Mrs Pankhurst was creating in women a new sense of power and responsibility, together with a determination to work out their destiny on other lines than those laid down for them since time immemorial by men.[116]

It is this respect that Emmeline Pankhurst, a strong, charismatic and dignified leader, made her greatest contribution to womankind and to feminism. It is a legacy that still has relevance for today.

NOTES

1 I am grateful to the Master and Fellows of St John's, Oxford, for awarding me a scholarship in 1996 which gave me time to carry out some of the research on which this chapter is based. I would also like to express my deep thanks to Jill Craigie for allowing me to see some of her collection of suffragette material and for the generous way in which she has shared with me her extensive knowledge about Emmeline Pankhurst. My work would be that much poorer without Jill's many kindnesses to me.

2 Mrs Despard, A valiant leader of women, *The Vote,* 22 June 1928.

3 See, for example, the *Manchester Guardian,* 15 June 1928.

4 G. Dangerfield, *The strange death of liberal England* (London, MacGibbon & Kee, 1966, first published 1935), p. 133; D. Mitchell, *Women on the warpath: the story of the women of the First World War* (London, Jonathan Cape, 1966), Preface; P. Brendon, *Eminent Edwardians* (London, Secker & Warburg, 1979), p. 140; B. Harrison, *Prudent revolutionaries: portraits of British feminists between the wars* (Oxford, Oxford University Press, 1987), p. 30.

5 E. Sylvia Pankhurst, *The suffragette movement: an intimate account of persons and ideals* (London, Longman, Green, 1931); M. Pugh, *Women's suffrage in Britain 1867–1928* (London, The Historical Association, 1980); S. Rowbotham, *Hidden from history: 300 years of women's oppression and the fight against it* (London, Pluto Press, 1973), p. 82; J. Liddington and J. Norris, *One hand tied behind us: the rise of the women's suffrage movement* (London, Virago, 1978), pp. 209–210.

6 D. Spender, *Women of ideas and what men have done to them, from Aphra Behn to Adrienne Rich* (London, Routledge & Kegan Paul, 1982), pp. 394–434; J. Marcus, Introduction, re-reading the Pankhursts and women's suffrage, in her edited *Suffrage and the Pankhursts* (London, Routledge & Kegan Paul, 1987), pp. 1–17; S. Stanley Holton, 'In sorrowful wrath': suffrage militancy and the romantic feminism of Emmeline Pankhurst, in H. L. Smith (ed.), *British feminism in the twentieth century* (Aldershot, Edward Elgar, 1990), pp. 7–24; J. Purvis, A 'pair of . . . infernal queens'? A reassessment of the dominant representations of Emmeline and Christabel Pankhurst, first wave feminists in Edwardian Britain, *Women's History Review,* 5, 1996, pp. 259–280.

7 Pankhurst, *The suffragette movement,* pp. 119 and 128.

8 Ibid., p. 153.

9 E. Pankhurst, *My own story* (London, Eveleigh Nash, 1914), p. 32; E. Sylvia Pankhurst, *The life of Emmeline Pankhurst* (London, T. Werner Laurie, 1935), p. 43.

10 Pankhurst, *The life of Emmeline Pankhurst,* pp. 47–48; Pankhurst, *The suffragette movement,* pp. 167–168.

11 See Dame C. Pankhurst, *Unshackled: the story of how we won the vote* (London, Hutchinson, 1959), p. 44 and Pankhurst, *My own story,* p. 38.

12 Pankhurst, *My own story,* p. 38.

13 Pankhurst, *The life of Emmeline Pankhurst,* p. 49.

14 *The Labour Leader,* 16 April 1904, p. 16.

15 For useful discussions on this issue see S. Stanley Holton, *Feminism and democracy: women's suffrage and reform politics in Britain 1900–1918* (Cambridge, Cambridge University Press, 1986), Chapter 3 and K. Hunt, *Equivocal feminists: the Social Democratic Federation and the woman question 1884–1911* (Cambridge, Cambridge University Press, 1996), Chapter 6.

16 Pankhurst, *My own story,* p. 42.

17 Ibid., p. 43. The term 'militant' is somewhat imprecise and in this particular instance could be described as an act of civil disobedience. Holton, *Feminism and democracy*, p. 4 argues, if 'militancy' involved a preparedness to resort to extreme forms of violence then few WSPU members were 'militant' and then only from 1912. However, 'militancy' is usually associated with the actions of WSPU 'suffragettes', as they were called, whether the militant act was heckling or arson. Following Pankhurst, *Unshackled*, p. 153, a distinction is often made between 'mild' militancy, which was more or less played out by 1910, and the later more aggressive forms such as arson, bombing, destruction of property and large-scale window-smashing.

18 Pankhurst, *The life of Emmeline Pankhurst*, p. 51.

19 Letter dated 26 December 1930 from Emmeline Pethick Lawrence to Sylvia Pankhurst, E. Sylvia Pankhurst Archive, Institute for Social History, Amsterdam.

20 Marcus, Introduction, p. 9. Christabel Pankhurst in *Unshackled*, published posthumously in 1959, p. 52 notes, 'It was not a real spit but only, shall we call it, a "pout", a perfectly dry purse of the mouth.' For other versions of this event see Pankhurst, *The suffragette movement*, pp. 189–190 and A. Rosen, *Rise up women! The militant campaign of the Women's Social and Political Union 1903–1914* (London and Boston, Routledge & Kegan Paul, 1974), pp. 49–52.

21 Pankhurst, *My own story*, pp. 48–49.

22 Evelyn Sharp, Emmeline Pankhurst and militant suffrage, *The Nineteenth Century*, April 1930, pp. 518–519. Pankhurst, *The suffragette movement*, p. 192.

23 For discussion of Christabel Pankhurst's role as strategist of the WSPU see J. Purvis, Christabel Pankhurst and the Women's Social and Political Union, in M. Joannou and J. Purvis (eds), *The women's suffrage movement: new feminist perspectives* (Manchester, Manchester University Press, 1998), pp. 157–172.

24 Blatch comment quoted in Pankhurst, *Unshackled*, p. 30; M. Richardson, *Laugh a defiance* (London, Weidenfeld & Nicolson, 1953), pp. 32–33; S. Pankhurst, My mother, rebel to reactionary, *The Star*, 5 March 1930.

25 Pankhurst, *The life of Emmeline Pankhurst*, p. 54. On 10 January 1906 the *Daily Mail* had the headline 'Mr. Balfour and the "suffragettes"', the first time the word 'suffragette' seems to have been used.

26 Pankhurst, *My own story*, p. 56.

27 See J. Balshaw, Sharing the burden: the Pethick Lawrences and women's suffrage, in A. V. John and C. Eustance (eds), *The men's share? Masculinities, male support and women's suffrage in Britain, 1890–1920* (London and New York, Routledge & Kegan Paul, 1997), pp. 135–157.

28 J. Hannam, *Isabella Ford* (Oxford, Basil Blackwell, 1989), p. 116 ; letter from E. Pankhurst, *The Labour Leader,* 6 April 1906.

29 Hannam, *Isabella Ford,* p. 116; Pankhurst, *The life of Emmeline Pankhurst,* p. 59; Rosen, *Rise up women!*, pp. 65–66.

30 Pankhurst, *The life of Emmeline Pankhurst,* p. 60; Rosen, *Rise up women!*, p. 67.

31 S. Stanley Holton, *Suffrage days: stories from the women's suffrage movement* (London and New York, Routledge, 1996), p. 123.

32 Pankhurst, *The life of Emmeline Pankhurst*, pp. 64–65.

33 *Daily Chronicle,* 14 February 1907.

34 *Daily Telegraph,* 18 February 1907.

35 Pankhurst, *My own story*, p. 86.

36 Independent Labour Party, *Report of the Fifteenth Annual Conference, Temperance Hall, Derby, April 1st and 2nd 1907* (London, Independent Labour Party, May 1907), p. 48.

37 Letter dated 22 June 1907 from Emmeline Pankhurst to Sylvia, E. Sylvia Pankhurst Archive, Institute for Social History, Amsterdam.

38 Pankhurst, *The life of Emmeline Pankhurst*, p. 70; letter dated 25 May 1957 from Christabel Pankhurst to Lord Pethick Lawrence, Pethick Lawrence Collection, Trinity College, Cambridge; Pankhurst, *Unshackled*, p. 82. See Emmeline Pethick Lawrence, *My part in a changing world* (London, Victor Gollancz, 1938), p. 176 for a different account where she does not mention that she and her husband urged Emmeline Pankhurst to take such action but suggests, instead, that the Union leader made the decisions on her own.

39 T. Billington-Greig, *The militant suffrage movement: emancipation in a hurry* (London, Frank Palmer, 1911), p. 83. For an account of the Women's Freedom League see C. Eustance, Meanings of militancy: the ideas and practice of political resistance in the Women's Freedom league, 1907–14, in Joannou and Purvis (eds), *The women's suffrage movement*, pp. 51–64.

40 Pankhurst, *My own story*, p. 59. See also M. Vicinus, Male space and women's bodies: the suffragette movement, in her *Independent women: work and community for single women 1850–1920* (London, Virago, 1985), p. 260: 'Joining the WSPU meant joining a spiritual army.'

41 R. West, Mrs Pankhurst, in *The post Victorians* with an Introduction by the Very Reverend W. R. Inge (London, Ivor Nicholson, 1933), p. 500.

42 F. W. Pethick Lawrence, *Fate has been kind* (London, Hutchinson, n.d. [1943]), pp. 75–76. B. Harrison, Two models of feminist leadership: Millicent Fawcett and Emmeline Pankhurst, in his *Prudent revolutionaries*, pp. 32–33 suggests that Emmeline deferred to Christabel on short-term strategy and Christabel to her mother on long-term objectives.

43 In March and April 1907, respectively.

44 Pankhurst, *The life of Emmeline Pankhurst*, p. 72.

45 Pankhurst, *My own story*, pp. 92–93.

46 Ibid., p. 102.

47 *Votes for Women,* April 1908, p. 112.

48 Pankhurst, *My own story*, p. 108.

49 *Daily Chronicle*, 22 June 1908.

50 Holton, *Suffrage days*, p. 134.

51 Those who claim Emmeline Pankhurst was driven by Christabel include E. Sylvia Pankhurst, *The suffragette movement*, pp. 191–192, p. 215; H. Moyes, *A woman in a man's world* (Sydney, Alpha Books, 1971), p. 32; P. Romero, *E. Sylvia Pankhurst, portrait of a radical* (New Haven and London, Yale University Press, 1987), p. 49.

52 Pankhurst, *The life of Emmeline Pankhurst*, p. 81.

53 Pankhurst, *My own story*, p. 116.

54 Ibid., p. 119.

55 *The trial of the suffragette leaders* (London, The Woman's Press, n.d.), p. 21 and p. 24.

56 Z. Proctor, *Life and yesterday* (Kensington, The Favil Press, 1960), p. 95.

57 E. Smyth, *Female pipings in Eden* (London, Peter Davies, 1934), p. 278.

58 *Forward* (Glasgow), 2 January 1909, p. 8.

59 Quoted in Rosen, *Rise up women!*, p. 118.

60 Pankhurst, *My own story*, p. 148.

61 Ibid., p. 149.

62 Letters in the *Daily Mail,* 25 September and in *The Times,* 29 September 1909.

63 *Votes for Women,* 1 October 1909, p. 8.

64 *Votes for Women,* 29 October 1909, p. 76.

65 Pankhurst, *The suffragette movement*, p. 324.

66 Sharp, Emmeline Pankhurst and militant suffrage, p. 516.

67 Rosen, *Rise up women!*, p. 130.

68 Pankhurst, *Unshackled*, p. 153.
69 See Henry Woodd Nevinson Diaries, Bodleian Library, Oxford Mss. Eng. e 618/3, entry for 14 April 1914.
70 Rosen, *Rise up women!*, p. 137.
71 Pankhurst, *My own story*, p. 178.
72 See Pankhurst, *The suffragette movement*, pp. 342–344; Rosen, *Rise up women!*, pp. 138–142; C. Morrell, *'Black Friday': violence against women in the suffragette movement* (London, Women's Research and Resources Centre, 1981).
73 Emmeline Pankhurst speech at the Old Bailey, 21 May 1912 as reported in *Votes for Women*, 24 May 1912, p. 534; Rosen, *Rise up women!*, p. 142.
74 Pankhurst, *My own story*, p. 183.
75 Pankhurst, *Unshackled*, pp. 167–168.
76 Special message from Mrs Pankhurst, *Votes for Women*, 25 November 1910, p. 129.
77 *Votes for Women*, 6 January 1911, p. 228.
78 A. E. Metcalfe, *Woman's effort: a chronicle of British women's fifty years' struggle for citizenship (1865–1914)* (Oxford, Blackwell, 1917), pp. 171–172.
79 Rosen, *Rise up women!*, p. 149.
80 *Votes for Women*, 23 June 1911, p. 630.
81 Quoted in *Votes for Women*, 24 October 1911, p. 196.
82 *Votes for Women*, 8 December 1911, p. 161.
83 *The Standard*, 15 December 1911.
84 Pankhurst, *The life of Emmeline Pankhurst*, p. 103.
85 Pankhurst, *My own story*, p. 212; see also Mrs Pankhurst, The argument of the broken pane, *Votes for Women*, 23 February 1912, p. 319; Smyth, *Female pipings*, p. 208.
86 Rosen, *Rise up women!*, pp. 157–158.
87 Pankhurst, *My own story*, p. 222.
88 *Votes for Women*, 29 March 1912, p. 404.
89 In a letter dated 24 May (postmarked 1912) from Laurence Housman to Sarah Clark he wrote, 'It made my heart ache more than any other speech I have ever read on the suffrage'; quoted in Holton, *Suffrage days*, p. 185.
90 *The Times*, 23 May 1912; Rosen, *Rise up women!*, p. 166.
91 Pankhurst, *My own story*, pp. 252 and 255.
92 Pethick Lawrence, *Fate has been kind*, p. 99. Sylvia in her *The life of Emmeline Pankhurst*, p. 114 notes: 'Though Christabel was no less resolved on it, Mrs Pankhurst took the lead, and drove the matter to its conclusion. As ever, she blossomed to her greatest vigour in turmoil which sapped the strength and crushed the spirit of others.'
93 Jessie Kenney interview with David Mitchell, 24 March 1964, David Mitchell Collection, Museum of London.
94 *The Suffragette*, 25 October 1912, pp. 16–17.
95 Rosen, *Rise up women!*, p. 188.
96 Public Records Office (PRO) HO45/10695/2313666/16, notes on meeting held on 30 January 1913.
97 This Act received the Royal Assent on 25 April 1913.
98 Ann Morley with Liz Stanley, *The life and death of Emily Wilding Davison* (London, The Women's Press, 1988), pp. 176–177, states, 'Mrs Pankhurst was more *removed*, for she was always very much the gracious lady, but she was also more *there*.'
99 Holton, 'In sorrowful wrath', pp. 11–14.
100 Smyth, *Female pipings*, p. 214.

101 *Why we are militant, a speech delivered by Mrs Pankhurst in New York, October 21st, 1913* (London, M. Susman, n.d.), pp. 2–3.
102 Letter dated 29 January 1914 from Emmeline Pankhurst to Sylvia, E. Sylvia Pankhurst Archive, Amsterdam.
103 Verna Coleman, *Adela Pankhurst, the wayward suffragette 1885–1961* (Melbourne, Melbourne University Press, 1996), p. 54. Coleman also suggests that the price of 'any suspected challenge to Christabel was expulsion and rejection'.
104 *The Suffragette*, 13 February 1914, p. 397.
105 *The Suffragette*, 27 February 1914, p. 446.
106 Smyth, *Female pipings*, p. 225.
107 Barbara Green, *Spectacular confessions: autobiography, performative activism, and the sites of suffrage 1905–1938* (London, Macmillan, 1997), p. 141.
108 *The Suffragette*, 13 March 1914, p. 491.
109 *Daily Mirror,* 22 May 1914.
110 Letter dated 9 June 1914 from Emmeline Pankhurst to Mrs Badley, Fawcett Library, Autograph Letter Collection, London Guildhall University.
111 *Morning Post,* 17 July 1914.
112 *The Suffragette*, 24 July 1914, p. 262.
113 Cyclostyled letter dated 12 August 1914 from Emmeline Pankhurst to 'Dear Friend', Suffragette Fellowship Collection, Museum of London.
114 Ethel Hill and Olga Fenton Shafer, *Great suffragists – and why, modern makers of history* (London, Henry J. Drane, 1909), p. 19.
115 Despard, A valiant leader.
116 Smyth, *Female pipings*, p. 280.

6

'DEEDS, NOT WORDS'

Daily life in the Women's Social and Political Union in Edwardian Britain[1]

June Purvis

INTRODUCTION

First-wave feminists who campaigned in Edwardian Britain for the parliamentary vote for women on the same terms as it may, or shall, be granted to men, have attracted the attention of many scholars.[2] In particular, most attention has focused on those women who were members of the Women's Social and Political Union (WSPU), founded on 10 October 1903 by Emmeline Pankhurst and her eldest daughter, Christabel.[3] As members of the Independent Labour Party (ILP), Emmeline and Christabel knew through first-hand experience the problems women faced when asking for women's suffrage to be seriously considered in a male-dominated and male-centred political organisation. In particular, when Emmeline heard that the hall built in memory of her dead husband would be used as the headquarters of a branch of the ILP that would not admit women, she declared that she had wasted her time in the ILP and that a new organisation of women was necessary.[4] 'Women, we must do the work ourselves,' she said on 9 October 1903, when discussing the situation with other socialist women. 'We must have an independent women's movement. Come to my house tomorrow and we will arrange it!'[5] The small group who arrived the next day at the middle-class home at 62 Nelson Street, Manchester, were mostly wives of ILP men. A decision was made to form a women-only, politically active organisation, free from class allegiances, and free from affiliation to any of the male-centred political parties of the day, the motto of the WSPU being 'Deeds, not words'.[6]

From 1905 until the outbreak of the First World War in August 1914, about 1,000 women (and about 40 men) were imprisoned as a result of various 'deeds', the majority of the female prisoners being drawn from the ranks of the WSPU – although some were members of other suffrage groups, such as the Women's Freedom League (WFL).[7] I shall follow conventional practice in referring to WSPU members as 'militants' and 'suffragettes' in contrast to the members of the much larger National Union of Women's Suffrage Societies (NUWSS) who generally engaged in law-abiding, constitutional activity and are usually referred to as 'suffragists'.[8] Such a practice, however, may blur the differentiation within the WSPU which, as Morley and Stanley make clear, was a loose coalition of women whose opinions, analyses and actions differed enormously.[9] In particular, there was a small inner core of militants who were prepared to engage in the more extreme forms of violence, and whose commitment to 'The Cause' seems to have taken a form different from that of the vast bulk of WSPU members. My aim in this chapter is to draw upon this wide range of activity by discussing the 'experience' of the daily life of WSPU suffragettes, both outside and within prison.[10]

FORMS OF ACTIVITY

In its early years the WSPU was centred in the northern town of Manchester and at first there was some compromise about being independent of any political party since Emmeline Pankhurst and her children (Christabel, Sylvia, Adela and Harry) were still members of the ILP as well as very friendly with the well-known Labour MP Keir Hardie; furthermore, as Raeburn notes, the fact that almost every potential Union recruit was also an ILP member made the absolute maintenance of WSPU policy impossible at this stage.[11] Indeed, it was not until the Cockermouth by-election on 3 August 1906 that Christabel reaffirmed the 'independent' political stance of the WSPU when she announced that henceforward the Union would not only oppose all Liberal and Tory parliamentary candidates, but also be independent of Labour men.[12] Such a severance did not mean, however, that the links between the WSPU and socialism were completely severed, especially at the individual level, as Holton has revealed.[13] During these early years, suffragettes engaged in a range of constitutional and peaceful work, such as campaigning at socialist and trade union meetings, as well as in outdoor places such as fairgrounds and parks.[14] Acts of civil disobedience, such as marches and deputations to Parliament, were also common. However, Christabel Pankhurst, strategist of the WSPU, decided that more confrontational methods were necessary in order to make votes for women a national issue and to lift it out of the doldrums where it had lain under the 'ladylike' tactics of the NUWSS. Thus in October 1905, she and Annie Kenney introduced the 'unladylike' tactic of heckling male politicians. Roughly handled and ejected from the Free Trade Hall, Manchester, where Sir Edward Grey was speaking, both women were charged with disorderly behaviour (and Christabel also with the technical offence of spitting at a policeman). However, as planned, both chose imprisonment rather than pay a fine, an action that had the desired effect of making the campaign newsworthy. During the following years, many eye-catching events were staged by the suffragettes in order to bring media attention to their cause, such as posting human letters to the Prime Minister, chaining themselves to railings, or advertising the WSPU from a boat, as well as spectacular demonstrations, complete with banners, brass bands and pageantry, such as the Hyde Park demonstration held on 21 June 1908 and the Women's Coronation Procession of 17 June 1911.[15] But despite many promises to grant facilities for women's suffrage, successive governments, and especially those Liberal governments led by the notorious anti-suffragist Asquith, not only refused to yield but also engaged in repressive treatment of suffragettes. With such provocation, militancy became a *reactive* phenomenon',[16] with more aggressive forms of action being adopted, especially from 1912. Thus in this second stage of militancy, mass window-breaking, especially of well-known shops in London's West End, became common; empty buildings were set on fire; golf courses were burnt with acid; black fluid was poured into letter-boxes to destroy mail; telephone and telegraph wires were cut, and paintings in art galleries attacked. The aim of such 'acts of terrorism',[17] however, was always to damage property, not life. As one aged suffragette recollected in 1965, 'Mrs Pankhurst gave us strict orders about these fires: there was not a cat or a canary to be killed; no life; we were only allowed to give our lives.'[18] Even stones might be wrapped in paper or attached to a string in order to avoid accidental injury to anyone.[19]

These radically new ways in which WSPU members assaulted the male public arena laid bare, as Vicinus comments, prejudices in both sexes, exacerbating the sexual divisions upon which Edwardian society was based; whereas earlier feminists had largely confined themselves to carving out a separate sphere for women or to pressing for legal reforms that specifically affected women and children, the WSPU was 'insisting' upon the prerogative of women to enter the public, male world and to participate as equal citizens.[20] Consequently, the daily experience of life outside prison often involved stigmatisation, various forms of abuse, and violence.

DAILY LIFE OUTSIDE PRISON

The WSPU, like any complex political organisation, had an administrative structure at both national (the headquarters moved from Manchester to London in 1906) and local levels where members, either on a voluntary or paid basis, worked as organisers, typists, secretaries, treasurers, newspaper sellers, sales assistants in WSPU shops, and so forth. Local organisers, who were at the heart of the administrative framework, were paid £2 per week and were mainly young, single women who, in order to parry charges of 'unwomanliness' or 'extreme views', were expected to conform to convention 'in all but militancy'.[21] Their duties included interviewing the Press, contacting local Union women, announcing meetings, selling suffragette newspapers, distributing handbills, addressing meetings, enrolling new members, writing to and interviewing local MPs, organising by-election campaigns, and raising money to cover the cost of their own campaigns as well as a balance to send to the central treasury.[22] The organisers relied upon a large network of women who might be less politically active, but nonetheless make a necessary contribution to Union efficiency and publicity. Harriet Kerr, for example, a red-haired Scotswoman from Aberdeen, who left her secretarial agency in order to become the office manager at the WSPU headquarters in Clement's Inn, London, made it a condition of her employment that her work was entirely administrative and that she was 'not a militant suffragette'.[23] Mary Stocks's Aunt Edith and Cousin Leila, both Union members, carefully restricted their political activity to attending meetings and walking in processions.[24] Pearl Birch, who played no 'active' part in militancy, made valuable contributions to fund-raising by the organisation of social events, such as a week-long fair and fête at Kensington.[25] Yet all WSPU members, irrespective of their form of political activity, ran the risk of being labelled 'wild women'[26] since the wearing of various badges, brooches, scarves, insignia, clothes or sashes in the WSPU colours of purple (for dignity), white (for purity) and green (for hope) was a visible display of membership in an 'unladylike' organisation.

Teresa Billington-Greig, a WSPU member until 1907 when she defected to the WFL, remembered that in her Union days in 1906:

> Every possible device of misrepresentation was employed against us, and personal abuse and scurrility were our daily newspaper fare. Anonymous letters of the vilest descriptions used to reach us. When we travelled about for meetings hotel keepers and landladies were loath to take us in . . . We were faced daily with a hundred petty indignities and insults.[27]

Even when selling on the street the first WSPU newspaper *Votes for Women*, and later its successor *The Suffragette*, the WSPU member had to stand in the gutter or run the risk of being charged by the police with obstruction of the pavement.[28] Some street sellers, such as Kathleen Kelly, who had her pitch at Charing Cross, London, found the men buyers supportive, one even giving her ten shillings as an expression of his 'profound admiration for the pluck and perseverance of the Suffragettes'.[29] But for others, verbal and physical abuse was common. The new recruit Mary Richardson, also living in London, selling the newspaper at the corner of Tottenham Court Road and Oxford Street found the 'sex filth which elderly men in particular seemed determined to inflict' the most hateful part of her job. A 'more friendly bombardment' came from the Crosse & Blackwell's factory women who threw at her whatever rotten fruit and vegetables were in season.[30] Jibes to campaigning suffragettes, such as 'Can any on ye bake a batch o' bread?', 'Han yer mended the stockin's?', 'Go whoam an mind yer babbies', 'Wot ye want is a drop o' gin, old dear' or 'Wot about the old man's kippers?'[31] labelled them as wives and mothers, the traditional roles for women, rather than as politically active feminists. Women who participated in processions and meetings could be roughly handled, knocked down and kicked for daring to interrupt meetings. On 5 December 1908, when a group of Union women shouted, 'Deeds, not words!' at an Albert Hall meeting addressed by Lloyd George, the stewards 'seized them like savage dogs . . . bumped them down the steps of the orchestra . . . dragged them over chairs by the hair'.[32]

Intervention or arrest by the police was no guarantee of personal safety, as was vividly revealed on 18 November 1910, when a deputation of women, some of them over 70 years of age, attempted to reach the Prime Minister, Mr Asquith, in order to protest about his neglect of women suffrage. Hertha Ayrton, a scientist and the first woman to be elected a member of the Institute of Electrical Engineers, was one of the petitioners and recounted:

Before any of us, including Mrs Pankhurst and Mrs Garrett Anderson, could reach the House [of Commons] we had to run the gauntlet of organized gangs of policeman in plain clothes, dressed like roughs, who nearly squeezed the breath out of our bodies, the policemen in official clothes helping them. When Mrs Pankhurst and Mrs Garrett Anderson had got through, it was still worse for the rest of us . . . Women were thrown from policemen in uniform to policemen in plain clothes, literally till they fainted. A lady told me a policeman had told her he would kick her when he got her down – and he did.[33]

The sexual nature of many of the assaults was especially detested. The elderly Mrs Saul Solomon was seized by the breasts and thrown down, while a 'Miss H.' testified how one policeman seized her left breast, nipping it and wringing it very painfully, saying as he did so, 'You have been wanting this for a long time, haven't you.'[34] The police, 'using the most foul language', also deliberately tore Mary Frances Earl's undergarments from her, seized her by the hair and forced her up the steps, on her knees.[35] 'Black Friday', as the day became known, could leave no doubt in the minds of suffragettes about the subordination and brutality that women could suffer at the hands of men when they sought to enter men's public space.

The majority of the suffragettes appear to have been single or widowed rather than married women. In particular, as Rosen notes, between 1906 and 1913, as militancy grew more physically demanding and therefore 'more attractive' to relatively youthful women, the percentage of unmarried subscribers to WSPU funds rose markedly from 45 per cent for the 1906–1907 fiscal year to 65 per cent by 1913–1914.[36] Whether WSPU members who were engaged in the more violent forms of militancy, from 1912, found their tasks 'attractive' or not, is debatable. Many seemed to see their actions as necessary tasks, which had to be undertaken, despite the heartache involved. Maud Kate Smith remembered feeling repelled when setting fire to letter-boxes: '[I]t made me so ill, because I hated doing it. You can imagine. Fancy destroying a private letter of other people! It *rends* your inside. I'd always feel fearfully ill, I didn't know how to walk away from them, but if it's your job it's your job, you see. I never turned back.'[37] Hazel Inglis recalled wandering around in a semi-daze before engaging in breaking windows – '[W]hat's difficult to do is to get through the ten minutes before you do it; that's the awful time. When you have come to do it, it's nothing at all.'[38] Well-known 'freelance militants'[39] included Mary Richardson, Emily Wilding Davison and Charlotte Marsh, all single women, while the husband of another notorious activist, Mary Leigh, seems to 'disappear' although he was present at her trial in 1908 when she was sentenced to two months' imprisonment.[40] Mary Richardson, for example, who engaged in many arson attacks, was undoubtedly not the only militant who realised that she was 'better able to undertake the more difficult tasks in that I had no family to worry about me and no one I needed to worry over'.[41] These guerrilla activists, as Morley and Stanley and Myall have shown, had an extremely difficult relationship with the WSPU leadership.[42] Emily Wilding Davison's habit, for example, of doing what she thought best, without discussion with or the approval of the leaders, was regarded as 'not compatible' with employment by the Union.[43]

For many single women, however, political activity must have intermeshed with home and work lives in complex ways.[44] Daughters living at home, for example, might have to juggle duties to parents, especially if there was strong parental opposition. Annie Elizabeth Bell was forced to leave home by her father, a retired naval officer, after she had been in prison several times. When the father gave up the house, she took him and his solicitor to court since her dead mother had instructed that the house and furniture, which she had owned, should be divided between her two daughters.[45] The widowed mother of Lady Constance Lytton never really came to terms with her daughter's conversion to militancy, although the ties of affection remained strong between them. When on 12 June 1910, Constance was made a paid organiser at £2 per week, she felt 'very much honoured and pleased'.[46] Taking a small flat in London close to WSPU headquarters, she gained more independence than was possible at home where, because of her rheumatic heart, she had a status as an invalid. Constance, of course, did not have to work for a living but single militants who did, such as Sarah Carwin, a hospital nurse, and Florence T. Down, an elementary schoolteacher, both arrested on 29 June 1909 for throwing stones,[47] might find their livelihood was threatened. Elsa Myers, a London County Council teacher somewhere in

North London, arranged to be arrested on the last day of the summer term in order to keep her militant activity 'unknown to the authority'. She spent her summer vacation in jail and was released in time ready for the start of the new term.[48] However, when Jenny Jackson, of the WSPU in Preston, Lancashire, returned to the mill where she worked, after seven days in jail, she was not so fortunate; the weavers conspired against her so that she was forced to find work elsewhere.[49]

Married women may have found it especially hard to engage in militancy since familial ideologies in Edwardian society upheld the idea that a married woman's place was within the private sphere of the home, as a wife and mother, and not in the public arena as a political activist. Suffragette wives, attempting to combine their political life with their domestic responsibilities, may have taken dependent children with them on 'safe' occasions as in the magnificent Hyde Park demonstration, in which some 300,000 women took part on 21 June 1908, where children were carried in mothers' arms or walked holding their hands.[50] The way in which formal politics and domestic life could be interwoven in the life of any one militant wife and mother is vividly illustrated in the cases of Mrs Towler and Mrs Singer. Mrs Towler, of Preston WSPU, was a tackler's wife with four sons. She always kept her house in order and spent a whole week baking for her family, cooking enough to keep them going for a fortnight, in order that she could join protests in London and risk imprisonment.[51] The middle-class Alice Singer combined her selling of *Votes for Women* on the streets, window-smashing, arrest and imprisonment with a busy schedule of running a home, looking after her husband, bringing up their two children, Mary and Emmeline Christabel Kenney, and visiting her friends. Her diary entry for Tuesday 22 December 1908 reads:

> Release of Miss Christabel Pankhurst. Very fine morning; dull later. Mary & I drank to Mrs and Miss Pankhurst at 9.15, stood up at breakfast just as their procession was due to begin breakfast at Inns of Court Hotel.[52]

Mary sometimes accompanied her mother on WSPU business, and on 19 May 1909, when she was nearly eight years old, she presented a bouquet of flowers to Elizabeth Robins, Union member and well-known actress, who opened the WSPU Exhibition. Alice Singer records in her diary that 'Mary's voice was perfectly clear & strong; but from inattention or "stage-fright" she made mistakes in the few words she had learnt to say'. Alice is more reticent, however, regarding her husband's thoughts about her political life but undoubtedly many husbands, of whatever social background, opposed a wife's militancy, carrying as it did the threat of the label 'gaol-bird'.

One evening early in 1912, the middle-class Mr Keller locked his wife, Eva, in the larder in order to prevent her from going on a window-smashing raid. Unknown to Mr Keller, their daughter, Phyllis, went instead, was arrested and sent to Holloway.[53] Similarly, a working-class woman who joined the WSPU in Manchester found that the hostility of husbands limited the range of political involvement:

> Their husbands didn't agree with them, in nine cases out of ten. Well, my - speaking for myself – my husband smashed my – broke my badge, and tore up my card . . . And it took me a long, long time to get him to see my way, and to understand it.[54]

Working-class husbands, as former WSPU activist Hannah Mitchell found out, often became '"anti" if their wives were out too often'.[55] Working men who were socialists, she bitterly complained, were 'still conservative at heart', especially where women were concerned. 'Most of us who were married', she commented, 'found that "Votes for Women" were of less interest to our husbands than their own dinners.'[56] Whereas many middle-class wives and mothers could rely, when absent for militant acts, upon servants to undertake necessary domestic tasks, working-class women like Hannah were dependent upon the goodwill and unpaid labour of neighbours, relatives and husbands. She sadly observed that whereas public disapproval could be faced and borne, 'domestic unhappiness, the price many of us paid for our opinions and activities, was a very bitter thing'.[57] Nevertheless, despite such opposition, Hannah, who left the WSPU and joined the WFL, continued to fight for women's suffrage. Georgiana Solomon, whose brother disowned her and their sister because of their WSPU membership, was of the view that the hostility of their menfolk served only to deepen 'the intensity' of the women's convictions and enthusiasm. 'Opposition, and antagonism, as well as rabid persecution,' she believed, 'truly tend to bring out our grit, & must not therefore be unduly deprecated, however much our hearts may cry out for sympathy.' She had found it 'a glorious time to be outlawed and ostracised', she pronounced.[58]

The differences between the daily lives of WSPU members discussed here, shaped not only by the nature of their political activity but also by their differing marital and social class locations, were not, of course, the only lines along which comparisons may be made.[59] Rich suffragettes would differ from poor, young from old, heterosexual from lesbian, able-bodied from disabled, London-based from provincial, religious from non-religious, and urban from rural.[60] Yet, despite such differentiation, what WSPU members reiterated time and time again was their feeling of comradeship and of sisterhood. For working-class Annie Kenney, who acted as Chief Organiser of the WSPU in 1912 when Emmeline Pankhurst was in prison and Christabel was attempting to direct the movement from Paris, where she lived in exile, the Union was a 'bond of fellowship' which united thousands of women who 'kept in one straight channel and concentrated on one thought . . . "Votes for

Women"'.[61] The wealthy reformer, Emmeline Pethick Lawrence, one of the WSPU leaders and its treasurer until 1912 when she and her husband were ousted by Emmeline and Christabel Pankhurst, also stressed the 'new comradeship with each other' that women in all social classes experienced. Even the disillusioned Hannah Mitchell, who found herself feeling 'very shabby in my old brown costume' in contrast to the 'smart frocks' worn by the London women, recalled that there was 'a unity of purpose' in the suffrage movement which made social distinction seem of little importance. As Evelyn Sharp, a journalist and novelist, commented, the tie with one's fellow suffragettes was 'unbreakable'. You had a different feeling all your life, she believed, about the woman with whom you 'eluded the police sleuth and went forth to break windows in Whitehall, to be mobbed in Parliament Square, or ejected from a Cabinet Minister's meeting'.[62] Beatrice Harraden, a writer, expressed herself more strongly: 'I would prefer to die in the ditch with the militants than be enthroned in heaven with the constitutionals.'[63]

That such solidarity should be expressed should come as no surprise since the cornerstone of WSPU rhetoric and politics was the common bond of womanhood in a 'just' war.[64] The first official newspaper of the WSPU, *Votes for Women*, broadcast this message loud and clear in its first issue in October 1907:

> To women far and wide the trumpet call goes forth, Come fight with us in our battle for freedom ... Come and join us, whatever your age, whatever your class, whatever your political inclination.[65]

The forging of a sense of collectivity was partly welded by the pledge all members had to make, from 1907, to endorse the objects and methods of the Union and to undertake not to support the candidature of any political party at parliamentary elections until women had obtained the parliamentary vote.[66] But, more importantly, it was based on the belief that in a man-made world, all women suffered discrimination because of their sex. 'It is a man-made and man-ruled world,' asserted Emmeline Pethick Lawrence. Its laws were men's laws, she continued, its rules of commerce and everyday business men's rules, its moral standards formed by men. Since women, because of their sex, were barred from voting, they were denied all power in shaping or moulding their own environment or that of their children.[67] Emmeline Pankhurst, the beloved leader of the Union, claimed that men regarded women 'as a servant class', and women would remain as such until they lifted themselves out of it.[68] In a powerful speech given in the Albert Hall on 19 March 1908, she argued forcibly for women's action:

> I for one, friends, looking round on the muddles men have made, looking round on the sweated and decrepit members of my sex, I say men have had the control of these things long enough, and no

woman with any spark of womanliness in her will consent to let this state of things go on any longer. We are tired of it. We want to be of use; we want to have this power in order that we may try to make the world a much better place for men and women than it is to-day . . . They said, 'You will never rouse women.' Well, we have done what they thought and they hoped to be impossible. We women are roused![69]

The feeling of the sisterhood that united all women was the backbone of the strength of the movement. It helped suffragettes to endure the repeated physical attacks and verbal abuse encountered when engaged in political action; it offered a spiritual sustenance to those who went to prison and experienced the pain of hunger-strikes and forcible feeding. As Vicinus perceptively observes, the suffragettes believed that only by giving their bodies – their physical selves – to 'The Cause' would they win that necessary spiritual victory that would enable them to enter the male political world.[70]

PRISON LIFE

As the account presented here reveals, before any suffragette reached the prison gates, she would be clearly aware of the gendered power relations between men and women, and between women and the state.[71] Although prison conditions varied over time and according to local circumstances, the suffragette would find that general prison regulations structured life in a particular way. Maud Joachim in Holloway Gaol in 1908 told a familiar tale:

At about 5.30 a bell rings to warn one that it is time to get up; breakfast comes at 7.15, and before chapel one has to scrub the floor and the boards, fold up the bed-clothes into a roll . . . and stow them away with the mattress and the pillow . . . and, most tiresome of all, polish the bed-room utensils, which are made of tin, with soap and bath-brick.[72]

Inspection, chapel, exercise in a gravelled yard and 'associated labour' such as sewing mailbags, making nightgowns or knitting men's socks were also daily experiences. Although the isolation and restrictions upon one's freedom, letter-writing and visits were especially disliked, frequent mention is also made of monotonous food and dirty bathtubs. Indeed, in some instances, the prisoners had to take their baths 'stepping one after the other into the same water in the company of women with very different standards'.[73]

A key feature of militancy was the struggle to be recognised by the government as political offenders and thus to be placed in the First rather than the Second and Third Divisions.[74] First Division prisoners had certain privileges denied to the other categories of prisoners; for example, they were not searched on admission, could order in their own food, were allowed frequent visits, and could engage in the writing of books and articles. When Marion Wallace Dunlop was sentenced to one month in the Second Division in July 1909, she protested against her non-recognition as a political offender by going on hunger-strike. Her release, after a fast lasting ninety-one hours, was greeted with jubilation, and the political strategy of the hunger-strike was quickly adopted by other imprisoned suffragettes.[75] By the end of September, however, the government had responded to this refusal to take food by intro-ducing forcible feeding, a practice that had traditionally been inflicted on the mentally ill. In the House of Commons on 29 September, Keir Hardie had asked questions about the experiences of the nine women prisoners in Winson Green Gaol, Birmingham, and was told, by a representative of the Home Secretary, that the women were being subjected to 'hospital treat-ment'; the under-secretary admitted that this was a euphemism for adminis-tering food by force, the justification for this action being that women's lives were 'sacred' and 'must be preserved'.[76] From this time until August 1914, when Emmeline Pankhurst called a halt to all militancy, a vicious circle of hunger-strike and forcible feeding was enacted.

The most common method of forcible feeding was by a tube through the nostril, although other methods, such as a tube into the stomach (the most painful method), and feeding by a spoon or cup, were also used. The process was usually accompanied by considerable force and violence. Mary Leigh, a working-class suffragette, the first militant to be force-fed, was pinned down on her bed by wardresses while one doctor stood on a chair and poured a liquid mixture of milk and egg into one end of a tube and another stood behind her, forcing the other end up her nostril and pushing it down some twenty inches. 'The sensation was most painful,' she recalled, 'the drums of the ear seem to be bursting, a horrible pain in the throat and the breast.'[77] When the doctor believed the fluid was not going down sufficiently swiftly, he pinched her nose with the tube in it and her throat, causing even more anguish. She vomited as the tube was withdrawn and also suffered from bad indigestion. The fact that in other cases the liquid was made from fatty meat products or Bovril caused especial revulsion if one was a vegetarian, which many suffragettes were.[78] Requests for a vegetarian liquid were common, even from meat eaters. When the doctor asked Margaret Thompson in Holloway in March 1912 whether she was vegetarian, '*Here* I am,' she wisely replied.[79]

The suspicion that more working-class than middle-class women were harshly treated and forcibly fed was regularly voiced by the militants. *Votes for Women*, for example, commented in 1909: 'It is significant that among the five women arrested at Dundee and released after five days there are no work-ing women, and three at least have very influential family connections.'[80] Lady Constance Lytton determined to expose the disparity. Disguised as a working

Figure 7 Condemnation of the forcible feeding of suffragettes: *The Suffragette*, 6 February 1914

woman named 'Jane Warton', she rejoined the WSPU under her new name. When arrested and later force-fed eight times in Liverpool Gaol, she received no 'class' privileges, which had been evident on a previous occasion when the chaplain had addressed her as 'your ladyship', a term that became her nickname.[81] 'Jane Warton' had neither her heart nor pulse felt before she was force-fed. Indeed, on one occasion after nasal feeding when she vomited over the doctor and wardresses, the doctor struck her on the cheek, 'not violently, but, as it were, to express his contemptuous disapproval'.[82]

The ordeal of forcible feeding was especially cruel and dangerous after the Prisoners' Temporary Discharge for Ill-health Act of April 1913 which allowed a prisoner who had been weakened through hunger-striking to be released on a licence into the community in order to regain her health, only to be re-admitted once she was well enough to continue her sentence. Under the 'Cat and Mouse Act', as it became known, the whole process was prolonged since 'mice' who were often near death (especially after a hunger- and thirst-strike) were released, tried to avoid re-arrest and were then caught (often still in a weakened condition) by the 'cat', as many times as was necessary. There were, of course, many clever plots by which 'mice' hoodwinked the police watching a house where they were staying; Miss Lyness, for example, in order to escape, disguised herself as a schoolgirl complete with gym slip, two long pigtails, spectacles, and a broad hat with a school badge on it.[83] But in other cases, militants were not so fortunate. Mary Leigh recollected seeing some young WSPU women 'on the run with no money, no food, no shelter. I saw two crouching in public phone booths.'[84] One such 'mouse', Lilian Lenton, was re-arrested on 7 October 1913 and remanded on a charge of setting fire to the Kew Gardens tea pavilion in February; the charge against her had never been heard for she 'disappeared' after her release from prison in consequence of a hunger-strike, and when re-arrested on a further charge in June and again released on hunger-striking, she once more escaped, and was missing until re-arrested in October on the charge of burning a house at Hampton the previous week. She now had four offences to her charge, and two sentences to complete of which she as yet had served only twenty-one days.[85] Her fears must have been great since earlier in the year some of the food with which she had been forcibly fed had entered her lungs so that septic pneumonia and pleurisy had developed. Similarly, the double pneumonia that Ethel Moorhead, an artist, developed in Calton Prison, Edinburgh, after her eighth forcible feeding, was attributed to the injection of 'some foreign substance into the lungs'.[86] Mary Richardson fell ill when hunger-striking in the spring of 1914; despite warnings from her medical attendants that if forcible feeding continued there would be grave danger of appendicitis, the authorities persisted until the serious condition of their victim made 'immediate release essential if her life was to be saved'.[87] She was released on a licence for six weeks on 7 April 1914 in order to have an operation for appendicitis. Under such a repressive state policy, many of the prisoners feared not only for their health but also for their mental stability. Kitty Marion, an actress, released on a licence in April 1914, had experienced such excruciating pain during the 232 times that she was forcibly fed that she felt she was going mad and begged the doctor to give her poison. She even considered hanging herself and, in desperation on one occasion, set the bed-clothes on fire.[88] Although her screaming in prison greatly upset the other women, she found it was the only way she could fight against the dreaded tubes and remain sane.[89] Her friends did not recognise her when she was released since she was in a emaciated condition, had lost two stone eight pounds in weight and looked like a seventy-year-old. Rachel Peace, an embroideress, who had already experienced several nervous breakdowns, was not so fortunate. During a period of prolonged hunger-striking and forcible feeding three times a day she wrote, 'I am afraid I shall be mentally affected ... Old distressing symptoms have re-appeared. I have frightful dreams and am struggling with mad people half the night.'[90] Her fears became reality when she lost her reason in prison and spent the rest of her life in and out of asylums, with Constance Lytton maintaining her.[91]

For many of these women, the worst feature of prison life was the 'public' violation of their bodies when being forcibly fed. Helen Gordon Liddle, secretary of the WSPU in Westminster, hated the lack of privacy while Nell Hall spoke of the 'frightful indignity' of it all.[92] The doctor force-feeding Leslie Hall jeered at her that it was 'like stuffing a turkey for Christmas'.[93] For Sylvia Pankhurst, the sense of degradation endured was worse than the pain of sore and bleeding gums, with bits of loose jagged flesh, the agony of coughing up the tube three or four times before it was successfully inserted, the bruising of her shoulders and the aching of her back. Sometimes when the struggle was over, or even in the heat of it, she felt as though she was broken up into many different selves, of which one, aloof and calm, surveyed all the misery, and one, ruthless and unswerving, forced the weak, shrinking body to its ordeal.[94] 'As soon as I could pull myself together after each feeding', she continued, 'I struggled till I had brought up what had been forced into me.'[95] As Maud Ellmann comments, what had been forced into Sylvia (and other imprisoned suffragettes) was not only the food but the ideology and even the identity of the oppressors. 'Under this torture', she suggests, 'starvation rather than ingestion has become the last remaining recipe for authenticity.'[96]

As Tickner notes, the instrumental invasion of the body by force, in a process accompanied by great pain and personal indignity, was felt as a form of rape although the word was not used directly.[97] Instead, we find the words 'violation' or 'outrage'. In a letter of angry and shocked protest, published in *The Times* on 29 September 1909, Emmeline Pankhurst, Emmeline Pethick Lawrence, Mabel Tuke and Christabel spoke of 'the violated bodies of women'. Ethel Moorhead, who wrote a moving account of her prison experiences for *The Suffragette*, noted, 'I was carried back to my cell feeling that

I had been physically and spiritually outraged.'[98] Similarly, Grace Roe insisted that it would be 'morally wrong if we did not struggle against such an outrage'.[99] The feelings of revulsion felt by the women and by the suffragette community were sharpened in 1914 when some prisoners in Scotland were fed by the rectum and, apparently, by the vagina. Frances Gordon, in Perth Prison in July 1914, had tubes forced into her bowels. 'To subject her to it without her consent', thundered Christabel Pankhurst , 'was an act of violence and indecency on the part of the authorities which cannot and will not be tolerated.'[100] 'Janet Arthur', later identified as Fanny Parker, also in Perth prison in 1914, was also fed in gross ways:

> Thursday morning, 16th July . . . the three wardresses appeared again. One of them said that if I did not resist, she would send the others away and do what she had come to do as gently and as decently as possible. I consented. This was another attempt to feed by the rectum, and was done in a cruel way, causing me great pain.
>
> She returned some time later and said she had 'something else' to do. I took it to be another attempt to feed me in the same way, but it proved to be a grosser and more indecent outrage, which could have been done for no other purpose than torture. It was followed by soreness, which lasted for several days.[101]

When she was released, a medical examination revealed swelling and rawness in the genital region.[102] The knowledge that new tubes were not always available and that used tubes may be dirty inside and may have been previously inflicted on diseased persons and the mentally ill, issues that had been openly discussed in the feminist press,[103] undoubtedly added to the feelings of abuse, dirtiness and indecency that the women felt. In a women's political movement where heterosexuality was openly criticised and sexual purity a strong theme, such atrocities were viewed with horror. The fact that the majority of suffragettes were single, some being lesbians and others celibate, must have intensified reactions. Christabel Pankhurst expressed the thoughts of many when she condemned 'this woman-torturing Government composed, not of men but surely of devils!' Forcible feeding, she argued, represented 'all the barbarity, all the blind, brute force upon which the subjection of women depends . . . it *is* the opposition to Votes for Women'.[104]

On 10 August 1914, shortly after the outbreak of the First World War, the government ordered that all persons serving prison sentences for suffrage agitation be released.[105] Three days later, Emmeline Pankhurst called an end to all militancy: 'it has been decided to economise the Union's energies and financial resources by a temporary suspension of activities.'[106] This news must have been greeted with mixed feelings by WSPU militants, glad that their guerrilla activities would end, sad at the prospect of slaughter that war would bring, and disappointed that all their efforts had still not won the parliamentary vote for women. Mary Richardson and other 'battle-worn' suffragettes were delighted to see the last of the policemen and detectives – as the men were delighted to see the last of them.[107] Elsie Bowerman greeted the declaration of war with almost 'a sense of relief . . . as we knew that our militancy, which had reached an acute stage, could cease and we could devote ourselves entirely to the service of our country'.[108] In 1918, under the Representation of the People Act, women over 30 years of age were allowed to vote if they were householders, the wives of householders, occupiers of property with an annual rent of £5 or more, or graduates of British universities.[109] At long last, the sex barrier had been breached and about eight and half million women were eligible to vote. It was not until 1928 that all women over the age of 21 could vote on equal terms with men, the new Bill becoming law on 2 July. Sadly, Emmeline Pankhurst, the much loved leader of the WSPU and a gifted orator, had died some weeks earlier, on 14 June.

CONCLUSION

The militant suffragettes of Edwardian Britain, with their famous slogan 'Deeds, not words', campaigned for the parliamentary vote for women on the same terms as it may, or shall, be granted to men. As the government, despite repeated promises, refused to yield on the issue of women's enfranchisement, they became more daring in their exploits. Developing a critique of male-centred society, they insisted on the unity of theory and practice, since they believed this to be the most effective political strategy to win not just the enfranchisement of women but also an improvement generally in the social position of their own sex. 'We were willing to break laws', explained Emmeline Pankhurst, 'that we might force men to give us the right to make laws.'[110]

The suffragettes, demanding the rights of full citizenship, understood the importance of women working together in a women-only organisation, developing supportive friendship networks, sharing a sense of sisterhood. Indeed, some such as the Viscountess Rhondda claimed the militant fight itself did more to change the status of women – 'because it did more to alter our own opinion of ourselves' – than ever the vote did.[111] Similarly, Alison Neilans, a former WFL member, asserted in 1936 that whatever one may think about militant methods, they affected the majority of women who 'became more independent, more able to stand up for themselves, more self-respecting and respected'.[112] In particular, the insistence of the suffragettes upon the bond of womanhood holds an important message for feminists today. As they knew only too well, for women to emphasise our differences at the expense of our commonalities, is to de-radicalise our politics and to weaken the potential alliances between all women. Their courage, bravery and faith, particularly when enduring repeated imprisonments and the torture of forcible feeding, remain an inspiration to us all.

NOTES

1 This chapter is a slightly revised version of J. Purvis, 'Deeds, not words', the daily life of militant suffragettes in Edwardian Britain, *Women's Studies International Forum*, 18. 2, 1995, pp. 91–101.

2 See, for example, Roger Fulford, *Votes for women: the story of a struggle* (London, Faber & Faber, 1957); David Mitchell, *The fighting Pankhursts: a study in tenacity* (London, Jonathan Cape, 1967); Marian Ramelson, *The petticoat rebellion: a century of struggle for women's rights* (London, Lawrence & Wishart, 1967); Constance Rover, *Women's suffrage and party politics in Britain 1866–1914* (London, Routledge & Kegan Paul, 1967); Antonia Raeburn, *The militant suffragettes* (London, Michael Joseph, 1973); Andrew Rosen, *Rise up women! The militant campaign of the Women's Social and Political Union 1903–1914* (London, Routledge & Kegan Paul, 1974); David Morgan, *Suffragists and liberals: the politics of woman suffrage in England* (Oxford, Basil Blackwell, 1975); Midge Mackenzie, *Shoulder to shoulder, a documentary* (London, Allen Lane, 1975); Antonia Raeburn, *The suffragette view* (Newton Abbot, David & Charles, 1976); Richard J. Evans, *The feminists: women's emancipation movements in Europe, America and Australasia 1840–1920* (London, Croom Helm, 1977); Jill Liddington and Jill Norris, *One hand tied behind us: the rise of the women's suffrage movement* (London, Virago, 1978); Julie Holledge, *Innocent flowers: women in the Edwardian theatre* (London, Virago, 1981); Brian Harrison, The act of militancy: violence and the suffragettes, 1904–1914, in his *Peaceable kingdom: stability and change in modern Britain* (Oxford, Oxford University Press, 1982), pp. 26–81; Leslie Parker Hume, *The National Union of Women's Suffrage Societies 1897–1914* (New York and London, Garland Publishing, 1982); Brian Harrison, Women's suffrage at Westminster, 1866–1928, in Michael Bentley and John Stevenson (eds), *High and low politics in modern Britain* (Oxford, Oxford University Press, 1983), pp. 80–122; Les Garner, *Stepping stones to women's liberty* (London, Heinemann Educational Books, 1984); Rosemary Cullen Owens, *Smashing times: a history of the Irish women's suffrage movement 1889–1922* (Dublin, Attic Press, 1984); Martha Vicinus, Male space and women's bodies: the suffragette movement, in her *Independent women: work and community for single women 1850–1920* (London, Virago, 1985); Sandra Stanley Holton, *Feminism and democracy: women's suffrage and reform politics in Britain 1900–1918* (Cambridge, Cambridge University Press, 1986); Lisa Tickner, *The spectacle of women: imagery of the suffrage campaign 1907–14* (London, Chatto & Windus, 1987); Susan Kingsley Kent, *Sex and suffrage in Britain 1860–1914* (Princeton, Princeton University Press, 1987); Diane Atkinson, *Votes for women* (Cambridge, Cambridge University Press, 1988); Jihang Park, The British suffrage activists of 1913: an analysis, *Past and Present*, 120, August 1988, pp. 147–162; Cliona Murphy, *The women's suffrage movement and Irish society in the early twentieth century* (Hemel Hempstead, Harvester, 1989); Hilda Kean, *Deeds not words: the lives of suffragette teachers* (London, Pluto Press, 1990); Ellen Carol Dubois, Woman suffrage and the left: an international socialist-feminist perspective, *New Left Review*, 186, March/April 1991, pp. 20–45; Leah Leneman, *A guid cause: the women's suffrage movement in Scotland* (Aberdeen, Aberdeen University Press, 1991); Kay Cook and Neil Evans, 'The petty antics

of the bell-ringing boisterous band'? The women's suffrage movement in Wales, in Angela V. John (ed.), *Our mothers' land: chapters in Welsh women's history 1830–1939* (Cardiff, University of Wales Press, 1991), pp. 159–188; Elspeth King, The Scottish women's suffrage movement, in Esther Breitenbach and Eleanor Gordon (eds), *Out of bounds: women in Scottish society 1800–1945* (Edinburgh, Edinburgh University Press, 1992), pp. 121–150; Christine Bolt, *The women's movements in the United States and Britain from the 1790s to the 1920s* (Hemel Hempstead, Harvester Wheatsheaf, 1993); June Purvis, A lost dimension? The political education of women in the suffragette movement in Edwardian Britain, *Gender and Education*, 6, 1994, pp. 319–327; Glenda Norquay (ed.), *Voices and votes: a literary anthology of the women's suffrage campaign* (Manchester, Manchester University Press, 1995); Christine Bolt, *Feminist ferment: 'the woman question' in the USA and England, 1870–1940* (London, UCL Press, 1995); June Purvis, The prison experiences of the suffragettes in Edwardian Britain, *Women's History Review*, 4, 1, 1995, pp. 103–133; Louise Ryan, *Irish feminism and the vote: an anthology of the Irish Citizen newspaper 1912–1920* (Dublin, Folens, 1996); Sandra Stanley Holton, *Suffrage days: stories from the women's suffrage movement* (London, Routledge, 1996); Ian Christopher Fletcher, 'A star chamber of the twentieth century': suffragettes, Liberals, and the 1908 'Rush the Commons' case, *Journal of British Studies*, 35, October 1996, pp. 504–530; Angela V. John and Claire Eustance (eds), *The men's share? Masculinities, male support and women's suffrage in Britain, 1890–1920* (London, Routledge, 1997); Barbara Green, *Spectacular confessions: autobiography, performative activism, and the sites of suffrage 1905–1938* (Basingstoke, Macmillan, 1998); Cheryl R. Jorgensen-Earp, *'The transfiguring sword': the just war of the Women's Social and Political Union* (Tuscaloosa and London, University of Alabama Press, 1997); Maroula Joannou and June Purvis (eds), *The women's suffrage movement: new feminist perspectives* (Manchester, Manchester University Press, 1998); Sandra Stanley Holton, British freewomen: national identity, constitutionalism and languages of race in early suffragist histories, in Eileen Janes Yeo (ed.), *Radical femininity: women's self-representation in the public sphere* (Manchester, Manchester University Press, 1998), pp. 149–171; Claire Eustance, Joan Ryan and Laura Ugolini (eds), *Themes and directions in British suffrage history: a reader* (London, Cassell Academic, 1999, forthcoming).

3 For further discussion of these two key figures see Sandra Stanley Holton, 'In sorrowful wrath': suffrage militancy and the romantic feminism of Emmeline Pankhurst, in Harold L. Smith (ed.), *British feminism in the twentieth century* (Aldershot, Edward Elgar, 1990); June Purvis, Emmeline Pankhurst and votes for women, in this Volume, and June Purvis, Christabel Pankhurst and the Women's Social and Political Union, in Joannou and Purvis (eds), *The women's suffrage movement*.

4 E. Sylvia Pankhurst, *The suffragette movement: an intimate account of persons and ideals* (London, Longman, 1931), pp. 167–168.

5 Dame Christabel Pankhurst, *Unshackled: the story of how we won the vote* (London, Hutchinson, 1959), p. 43.

6 Emmeline Pankhurst, *My own story* (London, Eveleigh Nash, 1914), p. 38.

7 It is impossible to give exact figures here since the records do not exist. These figures are based on the female and male names given in *Roll of honour: suffragette prisoners 1905–1914* (Keighley, The Rydal Press, n.d.) which also lists 49 persons with a surname only and no forename. We must not forget that some of the prisoners were supporters of women's suffrage without being paid-up members of any women's suffrage society. The mother of the Viscountess Rhondda, for example, was not a member of the WSPU but made up her mind that she must go to prison. Knowing she was breaking the law, she held an open-air meeting within a mile of

Westminster and chose prison rather than pay a fine, although the prison sentence was commuted to one day – see Viscountess Rhondda, *This was my world* (London, Macmillan, 1933), pp. 169–170. The Women's Freedom League was formed in November 1907 when a splinter group which was critical of Emmeline Pankhurst's style of leadership left the WSPU – see Claire Eustance, Meanings of militancy: the ideas and practice of political resistance in the Women's Freedom League, 1907–14, in Joannou and Purvis (eds), *The women's suffrage movement*. Rosen, *Rise up women!*, p. 92 suggests that the WFL did not carry more than 20 per cent of the WSPU's membership.

8 See, for example, Vicinus, Male space and women's bodies, p. 352, note 11. The term 'suffragette' was coined by the *Daily Mail* in January 1906.

9 Holton, for example, in *Feminism and democracy*, pp. 4–5 discusses the analytical imprecision of the terms 'militant' and 'constitutional' – 'if "militancy" involved simply a preparedness to resort to extreme forms of violence, few "militants" were "militant" and then only from 1912 onwards . . . [If] militancy connoted among suffragists a willingness to take the issue onto the streets, or if it sometimes indicated labour and socialist affiliations, then . . . many "constitutionalists" were also "militant".' See also Ann Morley with Liz Stanley, *The life and death of Emily Wilding Davison* (London, The Women's Press, 1988), p. xiii. See also Chapter 5 in the latter for a fascinating discussion of the way in which acts of militancy in the WSPU could take place in the context of personal friendship and worries about what was happening to particular feminist women, rather than in relation to the dictates of Christabel or Emmeline Pankhurst. Jorgensen-Earp, '*The transfiguring sword*', p. 15 also states, '[T]he level of WSPU militancy escalated only when new conditions imposed by the suffragettes' opponents threatened to halt Union progress. Militancy under the WSPU, therefore, was not a single tactic but a path forged through new territory whenever more established routes appeared blocked.'

10 For feminists, women's 'experiences' have traditionally formed the bedrock of feminist knowledge and, in particular, their common experiences derived from their subordination under patriarchy. Thus finding women's voices in the past has been regarded as a critical concern for feminist historians who engage in oral history and search for, and quote from, personal texts written by women, such as letters, autobiographical accounts and diaries, as ways of documenting 'experiences'. However, the term 'experience' has recently been subjected to critical enquiry by poststructuralists, especially in the USA. For example, Joan Scott, The evidence of experience, *Critical Inquiry*, 17, Summer 1991, p. 797, points out that the historian cannot capture the lived reality of any one individual, a comment with which many historians would agree. Experience, she suggests, 'is a linguistic event . . . Experience is a subject's history. Language is the site of history's enactment' (p. 793). Yet again, most historians would agree that language is necessary for both the subject of history and for the historian studying that subject to communicate his or her views. However, Scott then goes further in her argument and states that historians 'need to attend to the historical processes that, through discourse, position subjects and produce their experiences' (p. 779). This notion that language/discourses 'produce' experiences and the emphasis generally given by poststructuralists to the study of such phenomena rather than material reality has been strongly criticised by a number of feminists – see, for example, the exchange between Joan Scott and Linda Gordon in *Signs*, 15, 1990, pp. 848–860; Kathleen Canning, Feminist history after the linguistic turn: historicizing discourse and experience, *Signs*, 19, 1994, pp. 368–404, and the critique of poststructuralism offered by Joan Hoff, Gender as a postmodern category of paralysis, *Women's History Review*, 3, 1994, pp. 149–168, and the debate in

Women's History Review, 5, 1996: June Purvis, Women's history and poststructuralism, pp. 5–7; Susan Kingsley Kent, Mistrials and diatribulations: a reply to John Hoff, pp. 9–18; Caroline Ramazanoglu, Unravelling postmodern paralysis: a response to John Hoff, pp. 19–23, and Joan Hoff, A reply to my critics, pp. 25–30. Ruth Roach Pierson, Experience, difference, dominance and voice in the writing of Canadian women's history, in *Writing women's history: international perspectives* (Basingstoke, Macmillan, 1991), pp. 79–106, offers some particularly useful reflections which have influenced my own views on the debate. Thus I argue that a suffragette's 'experience' of life in the WSPU, as evident in the various texts documenting that experience, was not a mere abstraction or a 'discursive' reality; to claim that it was would be to deny that woman a subjectivity from which to speak. Although any one text quoted in this chapter is not that suffragette's experience, it was a lived experience even if mediated through her material, social and interpersonal context – as well as the discourses of the day. Thus any one suffragette's experience would be both 'subject to' and the 'subject of' such phenomena – something about which we cannot draw clear, hard and fast distinctions.

11 Raeburn, *The militant suffragettes*, p. 4.
12 Purvis, Christabel Pankhurst and the Women's Social and Political Union, pp. 158–159. In April 1907, both Christabel and Emmeline Pankhurst resigned their ILP membership.
13 Holton, *Suffrage days*, see especially Chapters 4 and 5 on Hannah Mitchell and Mary Gawthorpe.
14 Pankhurst, *Unshackled*, p. 44.
15 See, for example, Rosen, *Rise up women!*, Chapters 3 and 4 for discussion of some of these issues, as well as Tickner, *Spectacle of women* and Diane Atkinson, *The suffragettes in pictures* (Stroud, Sutton and the Museum of London, 1996).
16 Morley with Stanley, *The life and death of Emily Wilding Davison*, p. 153.
17 Emily Hamer, Suffragette violence against their state, in Alice Myers and Sarah Wight (eds), *No angels: women who commit violence* (London, Pandora, 1996), p. 73.
18 John Gale, 50 years later the suffragettes remember, *The Observer Colour Magazine*, 7 February 1965, p. 9.
19 Rover, *Women's suffrage and party politics in Britain*, p. 81.
20 Vicinus, Male space and women's bodies, p. 264.
21 Pankhurst, *Unshackled*, p. 126.
22 Ibid., p. 126. Paid organisers included such well-known members as Annie Kenney, Mary Gawthorpe, Constance Lytton, Charlotte Marsh and Jennie Baines.
23 Letter dated 27 July 1975 from A. Hessell-Tiltman to David Mitchell, David Mitchell Collection, Museum of London.
24 Mary Stocks, *My commonplace book* (London, Peter Davies, 1970), p. 72.
25 *Calling all women* (newsletter of the Suffragette Fellowship), 1971, p. 20.
26 Ros Billington, Ideology and feminism: why the suffragettes were 'wild women', in *Reassessments of 'first wave' feminism*, ed. Elizabeth Sarah (Oxford, Pergamon Press, 1982), pp. 663–674; Alison Young, 'Wild women': the censure of the suffragette movement, *International Journal of the Sociology of Law*, 16, 1988, pp. 279–293.
27 Teresa Billington-Greig, *The militant suffrage movement: emancipation in a hurry* (London, Frank Palmer, 1911), pp. 66–67.
28 Diane Atkinson, *Suffragettes* (London, Museum of London, 1998), p. 6.
29 *Votes for Women*, 29 October, 1909, p. 66.
30 Mary Richardson, *Laugh a defiance* (London, Weidenfeld & Nicolson, 1953), p. 13.

31 Geoffrey Mitchell (ed.), *The hard way up: the autobiography of Hannah Mitchell, suffragette and rebel* (London, Faber & Faber, 1968), p. 155 and p. 159.

32 Henry W. Nevinson, *More changes, more chances* (London, Nisbet, 1925), p. 323.

33 Evelyn Sharp, *Hertha Ayrton 1854–1923* (London, Edward Arnold, 1926), pp. 221–222.

34 Ibid., p. 221; Caroline Morrell, *'Black Friday': violence against women in the suffragette movement* (London, Women's Research and Resources Centre Publications, 1981), p. 34. This alleged comment said by a policeman should come as no surprise. As late as 1977, the historian David Mitchell in his misogynist book *Queen Christabel: a biography of Christabel Pankhurst* (London, MacDonald & Jane's, 1977) made the following comments about 'Black Friday' – 'Clothes were ripped, hands thrust into upper and middle-class bosoms and up expensive skirts. Hooligans, and occasionally policemen, fell gleefully upon prostrate forms from sheltered backgrounds. Wasn't this they argued, what these women *really* wanted? Perhaps in some cases, and in a deeply unconscious way, it was.'

35 Quoted in Rosen, *Rise up women!*, p. 140.

36 Ibid., pp. 209–210.

37 Quoted in Harrison, The act of militancy, p. 65, from a tape-recorded interview he conducted with Maud Kate Smith, Solihull, 14 January 1975.

38 Quoted in ibid., p. 71, from the author's tape-recorded interview with Miss Hazel Inglis, Coulsden, 16 March 1976.

39 Mitchell, *Queen Christabel*, p. 321.

40 Pankhurst, *The suffragette movement*, p. 286. For Mary Leigh see also Michelle Myall, 'No surrender!': the militancy of Mary Leigh, a working-class suffragette, in Joannou and Purvis (eds), *The women's suffrage movement*, pp. 173–187 and Hilda Kean, Some problems of constructing and reconstructing a suffragette's life: Mary Richardson, suffragette, socialist and fascist, *Women's History Review*, 7, 4, 1998, pp. 475–494.

41 Richardson, *Laugh a defiance*, pp. 53–54. Her pseudonym was 'Polly Dick'.

42 Morley with Stanley, *The life and death of Emily Wilding Davison*; Myall, 'No surrender!'.

43 G. Colmore, *The life of Emily Davison* (London, The Woman's Press, 1913), p. 52.

44 On this point see Sandra Stanley Holton, The suffragist and the 'average woman', *Women's History Review*, 1, 1, 1992, pp. 9–24.

45 *The 'Awakener'*, 31 May 1913, p. 5.

46 Constance Lytton and Jane Warton, Spinster, *Prisons and prisoners, some personal experiences* (London, William Heinemann, 1914), p. 311. See Michelle Myall, 'Only be ye strong and very courageous': the militant suffragism of Lady Constance Lytton, *Women's History Review*, 7, 1, 1998, pp. 61–84 and Marie Mulvey-Roberts, Militancy, masochism or martyrdom? The public and private prisons of Constance Lytton, in this Volume.

47 *Votes for Women*, 2 July, 1909, p. 877.

48 Biographical note dated April 1931 by Rose Lamartine Yates on Elsa Myers, Suffragette Fellowship Collection, Museum of London. See Alison Oram, Women teachers and the suffrage campaign: arguments for professional equality, in this Volume, for discussions about militancy amongst schoolteachers.

49 Phoebe Hesketh, *My aunt Edith* (London, Peter Davies, 1966), p. 52.

50 *Votes for Women*, 25 June 1908, p. 261. For a discussion of this event see Tickner, *Spectacle of women*, pp. 91–100.

51 Hesketh, *My aunt Edith*, p. 52.

52 I am very grateful to Emmeline Christabel Kenney Robinson, nickname 'Kippy', for the loan of her mother's diaries, and for all the help she has given me. Kippy's Christian names, of course, are those of leading suffragettes of her mother's time.

53 This information was kindly given to me by the daughter of Phyllis Murray (née Keller) whom I interviewed on 8 April 1992.

54 Liddington and Norris, *One hand tied behind us*, p. 217.

55 Mitchell, *The hard way up*, p. 130.

56 Ibid., p. 149.

57 Ibid., p. 130.

58 Letter dated 28 January 1914 from Georgiana M. Solomon to Mrs Maude Arncliffe Sennett, Maud Arncliffe Sennett Collection, British Library, C121g1, Vol. 25.

59 Liz Stanley, Recovering *women* in history from feminist deconstructionism, *Women's Studies International Forum*, 13, 1990, pp. 151–157, makes the important point that recognition of the differences between women does not mean that we reject the category 'Women' which some poststructuralists have assumed implies that all women have a unitary experience. As Stanley points out, to say that women share a common material reality because it is one based in a common oppression/exploitation, is to say not that experience is shared equally but that it is fractured along many lines of differences based on such factors as 'race', ethnicity, social class, marital status, sexual orientation, culture, religion, able-bodiedness and age. Similarly, Mary Maynard, Beyond the 'big three': the development of feminist theory into the 1990s, *Women's History Review*, 4, 1995, p. 275 argues that while poststructuralists have sensitised us to the fact that 'woman' is not a unitary category, this means neither that the concept is meaningless nor that it cannot be a unifying term. For further discussion on some of these themes see June Purvis, From 'women worthies' to poststructuralism? Debate and controversy in women's history in Britain, in June Purvis (ed.), *Women's history, Britain, 1850–1945, an introduction* (London, UCL Press, 1995), pp. 1–22.

60 A lack of sources makes it somewhat difficult to research all these themes. For accounts of local involvement see, for example, Leah Leneman, A truly national movement: the view from outside London, in Joannou and Purvis (eds), *The women's suffrage movement*, pp. 37–50 and June Hannam, 'I had not been to London': women's suffrage, a view from the regions, in this Volume. The difficulties of researching 'lesbian' life, however defined, in the WSPU are enormous since few lesbians, in a climate hostile to their sexual orientation, left records of their lives where their lesbianism is made explicit. See Emily Hamer, *Britannia's glory: a history of twentieth-century lesbians* (London, Cassell, 1996), Chapter 2, Lesbians and suffragists. For a discussion of some of the problems faced when researching the suffragette movement generally see June Purvis, Doing feminist women's history: researching the lives of women in the suffragette movement in Edwardian England, in Mary Maynard and June Purvis (eds), *Researching women's lives from a feminist perspective* (London, Taylor & Francis, 1994), pp. 166–189.

61 Annie Kenney, *Memories of a militant* (London, Edward Arnold, 1924), pp. 302–303.

62 Emmeline Pethick Lawrence, *My part in a changing world* (London, Victor Gollancz, 1933), p. 188; Mitchell, *The hard way up*, pp. 149 and 159; Evelyn Sharp, *Unfinished adventure: selected reminiscences from an Englishwoman's life* (London, John Lane, 1933), p. 136.

63 Entry 20 August [1911], Vida Goldstein Papers, Album of her visit to England 1911, Fawcett Library, London Guildhall University.

64 On rhetoric see especially Jorgensen-Earp, *'The transfiguring sword'*.

65 *Votes for Women*, October 1907, p. 6.

66 Ibid., p. 12.

67 Emmeline Pethick Lawrence, *The meaning of the women's movement* [A verbatim report of a Lecture delivered at the Portman Rooms, 3 March 1908] (London, The Woman's Press, n.d. [c. 1908]), pp. 4–5.

68 Pankhurst, *My own story*, p. 35.

69 *Votes for Women*, April 1908, p. 112.

70 Vicinus, Male space and female bodies, p. 268.

71 In this section I shall draw particularly upon Purvis, The prison experiences of the suffragettes in Edwardian Britain, pp. 103–133. See also Leah Leneman, *Martyrs in our midst: Dundee, Perth and the forcible feeding of suffragettes* (Dundee, Abertay Historical Society, 1993) and Caroline J. Howlett, Writing on the body? Representation and resistance in British suffragette accounts of forcible feeding, *Genders*, 23, 1996, pp. 3–41.

72 Maud Joachim, My life in Holloway Gaol, *Votes for Women*, October 1908, p. 4.

73 Aunt Emmeline, *The Times*, 7 July, 1958.

74 A few of the suffragettes were placed in the First Division, especially in the early years. For example, in February 1907, Christabel and Sylvia Pankhurst and Charlotte Despard were First Division prisoners. But this was the exception rather than the general rule.

75 Holton, *Suffrage days*, p. 146 quotes a letter dated 23 September 1909 from Christabel Pankhurst to Jennie Baines, 'Thank goodness for the hunger-strike. But for that the women sentenced at Birmingham would, in view of the long sentences with hard labour, have to undergo a very severe punishment for their brave action.' Holton continues, 'Such equanimity reflected the WSPU's legal advice that any resort of forcible feeding by the prison authorities would be illegal. This advice proved sadly mistaken, as did Christabel Pankhurst's belief that forcible feeding could not be carried out "with any real effect if the prisoners make a resistance".' Jane Marcus, Introduction, in her edited *Suffrage and the Pankhursts* (London and New York, Routledge, 1987), pp. 1–2 interprets the hunger-strike as a 'symbolic refusal of motherhood' since when woman, as the quintessential nurturer, refuses to eat she cannot nurture the nation. Mary Jean Corbett, *Representing femininity: middle-class subjectivity in Victorian and Edwardian women's autobiography* (New York and Oxford, Oxford University Press, 1992), p. 163, argues further that by denying their prescribed reproductive functions, suffragette hunger-strikers were contesting patriarchal definitions of woman-as-mother while also appropriating what had been the political tool of other, mostly male, dissidents to make their own arguments.

76 Mackenzie, *Shoulder to shoulder*, pp. 130–131.

77 *Fed by force: how the government treats political opponents in prison: Statement of Mrs Mary Leigh* (The National Women's Social and Political Union pamphlet, n.d. [c. October 1909]).

78 Joachim, My life in Holloway Gaol, p. 4. Leah Leneman, The awakened instinct: vegetarianism and the women's suffrage movement in Britain, *Women's History Review*, 6, 2, 1997, pp. 271–287.

79 Margaret E. Thompson and Mary D. Thompson, *They couldn't stop us! Experiences of two (usually law-abiding) women in the years 1909–1913* (Ipswich, W. E. Harrison & Sons, 1957), p. 36.

80 *Votes for Women*, 29 October 1909, p. 67.

81 Lytton and Warton, *Prisons and prisoners*, pp. 121–122.

82 Ibid., pp. 269–270.

83 Quoted in Helen Crawfurd, Unpublished autobiography, copy held in William

Gallagher Library, Glasgow, original held in the Marx Memorial Library, London. Judith Smart, Jennie Baines: suffrage and an Australian connection, in this Volume, p. 252, notes that in 1913, Jennie Baines disguised herself as an elderly lady. The Actresses' Franchise League was especially useful in helping people with various disguises – see Holledge, *Innocent flowers*.

84 Mary Leigh interview with David Mitchell, n.d., David Mitchell Collection, Museum of London.
85 *Votes for Women*, 10 October 1913, p. 20.
86 *Votes for Women*, 13 March 1914, p. 498.
87 *Votes for Women*, 10 April 1914, p. 428.
88 *Votes for Women*, 24 April 1914, p. 460.
89 *The Suffragette*, 13 February 1914, p. 392.
90 Quoted in Vicinus, Male space and women's bodies, p. 272, from an undated note by Rachel Peace in Suffragette Fellowship Collection, Museum of London; Raeburn, *The militant suffragettes*, p. 219.
91 Letter dated 13 June 1923 from Emmeline Pethick Lawrence to Mrs Saul Solomon, Autograph Letter Collection, Fawcett Library, London Guildhall University.
92 Helen Gordon [Liddle], *The prisoner, a sketch* (Letchworth, Garden City Press, 1911), p. 58; Nell Hall-Humpherson alias 'Marie Roberts', *Suffragette, a personal experience: the beginnings of women's liberation* (no place of publication given, Fishauf, no page numbers), leaflet in The Fawcett Library, London Guildhall University.
93 Pankhurst, *The suffragette movement*, p. 329.
94 Ibid., p. 444.
95 Ibid., p. 446.
96 Maud Ellmann, *The hunger artists: starving, writing & imprisonment* (London, Virago, 1993) , p. 34.
97 Tickner, *Spectacle of women*, p. 107. Ellmann, *The hunger artists*, p. 33 speaks of 'oral rape'. Howlett, Writing on the body, p. 21 suggests that those who represent themselves as resisting forcible feeding describe the ordeal through the metaphor of rape while those who represent themselves as submitting passively use the metaphor of an operation.
98 *The Suffragette*, 6 March 1914, p. 465.
99 *The Suffragette*, 17 July 1914, p. 243.
100 Ibid., p. 236.
101 Another prison infamy, *Votes for Women*, 7 August 1914, p. 681.
102 Leneman, *Martyrs in our midst*, p. 33; Leneman, *A guid cause*, p. 206.
103 See, for example, *Votes for Women*, 8 October 1909, p. 19.
104 C. Pankhurst, Forcing the pass, *The Suffragette*, 7 August, 1914, p. 300.
105 Rosen, *Rise up women!*, pp. 247–248.
106 Circular letter dated 13 August 1914, written on WSPU official notepaper, signed E. Pankhurst and addressed 'Dear Friend', Suffragette Fellowship Collection, Museum of London.
107 Richardson, *Laugh a defiance*, pp. 189–190.
108 Interview with Elsie Bowerman, 11 October 1964, David Mitchell Collection, Museum of London.
109 Rosen, *Rise up women!*, p. 266.
110 Pankhurst, *My own story*, pp. 187–188.
111 Rhondda, *This was my world*, p. 299.
112 Alison Neilans, Changes in sex morality, in Ray Strachey (ed.), *Our freedom and its results by five women* (London, Hogarth Press, 1936), pp. 220–221.

7

MILITANCY, MASOCHISM OR MARTYRDOM?

The public and private prisons of Constance Lytton

Marie Mulvey-Roberts

INTRODUCTION

Did the extremes of political activism that led suffragettes almost sacrifi-
cially to endanger their lives, contain elements of martyrdom or even
masochism? In spite of revisionist attitudes towards biography, even posing
such a question sounds heretical, in that it challenges the hagiographic
assumptions that still surround so many suffragette heroines. The suggestion
that a campaigner such as Constance Lytton was a martyr or even a
masochist is not intended to collude with the opponents of women's suffrage,
who reduced militancy to such pathologies as 'militant hysteria'.[1] Instead it
seeks to address the contradictions inherent within our understanding of vic-
timhood and its paradoxical relationship to female empowerment, particularly at the point at which militant suffragette hunger-strikers put themselves
in the hands of such agents of oppression as the prison doctor.[2]

There is no better illustration of the way in which punishment and protest
are conflated and the dynamics of male domination and female submission
internalised than the life and writings of Constance Lytton.[3] Her experiences
of imprisonment will be reconstructed here alongside the paradoxes surrounding the costs to her freedom, which endangered and ultimately
destroyed both her health and her life. In a roll call of those who suffered and
died as a result of their harsh prison treatment, Emmeline Pankhurst, in her
autobiography published in the same year as Lytton's *Prisons and prisoners*,
pays special tribute to Constance. She goes on to insist:

> I want to say right here, that those well-meaning friends on the out-
> side who say that we have suffered these horrors of prison, of
> hunger strikes and forcible feeding, because we desired to martyrise

ourselves for the cause, are absolutely and entirely mistaken. We never went to prison in order to be martyrs. We went there in order that we might obtain the rights of citizenship.[4]

Martyrdom as the means and full citizenship as the end are not necessarily incommensurable as Pankhurst implies. Such was Constance Lytton's dedication to the WSPU that an awe-struck relative commented: 'One feels that she would not only go to the stake for her cause but would welcome any pain or any death for it.'[5] The way in which a martyr, especially one as prominent and emotive as Constance Lytton, could galvanise the campaign, may not have been so unwelcome to the militant wing for women's suffrage. Was this the reason why she went beyond the call of duty to greater heights of sacrifice and suffering? Or was it because through her feats of heroism, Lytton was able to act out a catharsis and corollary to the restrictions, lack of control and despair that had circumscribed much of her private life? Another possibility is that she was single-handedly trying to redress the wrongs that her class had inflicted on the poor.

Involvement in the militant suffragette Women's Social and Political Union (WSPU) enabled Lytton to escape from the constraints of the feminine role imposed upon aristocratic women. Towards the end of her life, she resolved to break out of the confines of the domestic sphere into a public life dedicated to the service of others. In both cases Lytton was acting in the full knowledge that she was likely to precipitate her premature death due to a weak heart. Paradoxically, on each occasion, she was under the influence of an authoritarian male physician in direct contravention of the will of her dominant mother. The tensions between mother and daughter became a life-and-death struggle for autonomy and self-determination, which is the unwritten continuation both before and after the events of her autobiographical *Prisons and prisoners* (1914).

Few more compelling or celebrated accounts of suffragette imprisonment, hunger-striking and force-feeding are found than that which is contained in this autobiography. Less well known is Lytton's experience of different forms of incarceration that both pre- and post-dates her custodial sentences. The periods she spent in Walton and Holloway gaols between October 1908 and November 1911 made concrete her sense of imprisonment as a member of the English aristocracy, denied primogeniture on account of her sex, and restricted by her role as a sole spinster daughter, whose duty lay in the care of her mother. Of herself she admitted: 'Without doubt I myself was one of that numerous gang of upper class leisured class spinsters, [who are] unemployed, unpropertied, unendowed, [and] uneducated.' Such women are 'economically dependent entirely upon others' being subject to 'a maiming subserviency' which 'is so conditional to their very existence that it becomes an aim in itself, an ideal. Driven through life with blinkers on, they are unresentful of the bridle.'[6] That the urgency and almost sacrificial nature of

Lytton's attitude towards punishment and imprisonment went beyond the expediencies of suffragette militancy enabled her to satisfy fundamental psychological needs. Through incarceration the image she held of her own imprisoned self could eventually be released.

On the wall of her prison cell, using a slate pencil and soap mixed with dirt from the floor for ink, Lytton wrote 'Under a Government which imprisons any unjustly, the true place for a just man (or woman) is also a prison.'[7] This aphorism is taken from an essay on *Civil disobedience* (1849) by the ex-prisoner Henry Thoreau, who appropriately was another advocate of passive resistance to the injustices perpetrated by governments. Aside from upholding its political injunction, why had Lady Constance located her 'true place' in the austerity of gaol after experiencing, as a child, the opulence of the Indian Empire and then the grandeur of her ancestral home, Knebworth House in Hertfordshire?[8] Just as perplexing is why this daughter of Robert, Earl of Lytton, the Viceroy of India, should have cast her privileges off in Franciscan fashion and temporarily taken the attire of a working-class woman.

The secularised religiosity that pervaded the WSPU, whose messianic leaders were Emmeline and Christabel Pankhurst, filled an emotional void for Constance following an unhappy love affair. John Ponsonby had been a family friend, with whom she had fallen in love. Unable to reciprocate, he became more and more neglectful. Her hopes were dashed when he became involved with someone else. Feelings of abandonment catapulted Constance into a deep depression that made her feel unloved and unlovable. Eventually she transferred her feelings of adulation from Ponsonby to the leadership of the WSPU, and later to the charismatic Homer Lane the physician, who was to become her guru. These mentors opened up alternatives to the 'maiming subserviency' of her life looking after a dominating mother.

While the campaign for women's suffrage provided Lytton with an escape from her domestic role as carer, it also led to more literal forms of incarceration. The most harrowing of her prison sentences was the term spent at Walton Gaol in Liverpool, where she was brutally force-fed following her hunger-strike. Her treatment there precipitated a stroke, which proved to be the harbinger of another kind of imprisonment, this time of one circumscribed by the body. On 5 May 1912 Lytton's visiting cleaning woman found her in bed at her home in London, incapable of movement or speech. Her sister Emily took her to Bloomsbury Square where for several weeks she vacillated between life and death.[9] After the crisis abated, she was left permanently paralysed down her right side and was placed in the care of her mother. For Lytton, the role as an invalid daughter proved to be more confining than the restrictions imposed by her body. Her disabilities compounded her sense of dependency by making it even more difficult to earn a living. It is indeed ironic that her activism had indirectly led to invalidism. What is more disturbing is her realisation that by entering Walton Gaol in January

1910 and leaving her mother's care in March 1923, she was deliberately endangering her own life. She envisioned the Black Maria that carried her to Holloway Prison as a hearse bearing coffins to their graves and transporting her to an underworld. For her to enter the vehicle, which she personified as 'she', was to embark upon 'a sort of living death'.[10] To what extent was this disregard for her safety impelled by a desire to be a martyr for the suffragette cause, a masochistic response to an accumulation of matriarchal restrictions, or a well-earned bid for freedom?

The dialectic between imprisonment and freedom, passivity and active agency was for Lytton sited in her sex, class and body. Her own reconstruction of self is centred upon the episode described in her autobiography, when she disguises herself as a working-class woman, Jane Warton, to ensure that she will be treated equally with other suffragette prisoners. Yet it was precisely because of her family connections that she was able to inspire the suffrage movement by providing women with such a powerful role model of moral courage. Katherine Roberts, a militant suffragette writing of Lytton's bravery, claims:

It has a profound human and moral significance. It is an action that will not be forgotten. Some day, not just now, but before very long, the world will understand it, and then it will be written in letters of gold upon the tablets of human history. In years to come this story of compassion and chivalry will be told in the schools to children yet unborn ... And many a woman child will say in her heart: 'I, too, will be fearless and chivalrous and brave.'[11]

Even strangers she had never met felt that her sacrifice and sufferings had been endured directly for them. In a letter of condolence written after her death one woman reminisced: 'I never saw her ... but, like many others, I feel today the same deep impulse of gratitude and love that we felt in the dark days when she lay in prison for us.'[12] By embracing anonymity through her Jane Warton disguise, Lytton was better equipped not only to identify with women across the class divide but also to draw attention to the ordeals endured by forgotten women. Ever ready to listen with compassion to the stories of such women, she was told by fellow-activist Mary Gawthorpe that 'these are women quite unknown – nobody knows or cares about them except their own friends. They go to prison again and again to be treated like this, until it kills them!'[13] The adopted persona of Jane Warton offered Constance Lytton the opportunity to go beyond empathy to an identification with such women, which enabled her not only to create but also to live out her own narrative of working-class resistance.

What seems on the surface to be an extraordinary transformation of Lady Constance into Jane Warton was really part of an ongoing identification with the poor and oppressed. It is likely that she was reacting against being a member of a family whose conspicuous display of wealth epitomised colonialism and aristocracy. Until the age of ten, she spent much of her childhood in India, where her father Robert presided as the first Viceroy. In 1877, he had proclaimed Queen Victoria to be Empress of India; she would later invite Constance's mother, Edith, to become her lady-in-waiting. Inculcated into young Con (as she was known in her family) was her parents' sense of duty, service and obedience. A natural reserve steered her away from embracing a public role as a daughter of the Viceroy. Her compassionate nature, love for animals and delicate health developed into an empathy with those who were powerless, exploited and marginalised. Her physical frailties did not prevent her on one occasion from carrying the bags of two women of the 'cottage class'[14] for seven miles. It was not unknown for her to take on some of the domestic servants' tasks at Knebworth House. While in Holloway Lytton indulged in her favourite hobby of cleaning which enabled her to contribute to the 'housecraft of prison' with which she was so fascinated.[15] Despite feeling helpless after being force-fed and vomiting over the floor of her cell, Lytton insisted that she, rather than a conscripted prisoner orderly, ought to be cleaning up the mess. This was more than an egalitarian gesture since she had been provoked by the way in which the warders had been mocking her fellow prisoner.

Lytton's consciousness of class and the ill-treatment of women also extended to animal welfare. While she was observing some men being cruel to a sheep that had escaped from the abattoir, it occurred to her that this was similar to the way in which women were used:

> held in contempt as beings outside the pale of human dignity, excluded or confined, laughed at and insulted because of conditions in themselves for which they are not responsible, but which are due to fundamental injustices with regard to them, and to the mistakes of a civilisation in the shaping of which they have had no free share.[16]

What she had witnessed marked a Pauline moment of 'conversion' in her support for the plight of women. Such a 'Road to Damascus' episode in suffragette autobiographies is virtually formulaic. In this case, the identification between women and animals is especially significant in view of the convergence between the women's movement and the anti-vivisectionists from the 1890s onwards.[17]

In 1908, Lytton had a chance meeting with Emmeline Pethick Lawrence and Annie Kenney, prominent members of the WSPU, who fired her interest in the cause of women's suffrage. The way in which the struggle for the vote had united women across barriers of class appealed to her egalitarianism. There was no better demonstration of this than the conversation that took place on that occasion between the daughter of an earl and Kenney, an ex-mill-worker from Lancashire. Lytton's great-grandmother, the socialist feminist Anna Wheeler, who wrote for Robert Owen's *The Crisis* and who co-wrote, with William Thompson, the *Appeal of one half the human race, women, against the pretensions of the other half, men* (1825),[18] would have approved of that meeting and its outcome. Even though Kenney proved to be particularly persuasive, she had not yet managed to convince Lytton of the imperative for militant action.

By 1909 Lytton was sufficiently won over and became a member of the WSPU. Around that time, she produced a pamphlet called 'No Votes for Women' where she refutes the arguments against enfranchising women on the same basis as men.[19] Her sisters Betty and Emily, who claimed to have been the first to have engaged her interest in women's suffrage, and Frances Balfour, Betty's sister-in-law, the leader of the Conservative and Unionist Women's Suffrage Association and President of the London Society for Women's Suffrage, favoured a constitutional route to reform. These tactics were in opposition to the militant methods adopted by the Pankhurst-led credo of the importance of deeds over words. The only other member of the family to support militancy was Constance's brother Victor, whose support she appreciated not only at home but also in the House of Lords, where he became its chief advocate. From this prominent position he was able to draw public attention to his sister's prison ordeals. Constance maintained that if other women of the leisured classes knew more about the lives of the majority of women, they too would 'burst through the gilded bars which hold their own lives in bondage'.[20]

By actively seeking imprisonment, Lytton was making a powerful statement that she was leaving a worse form of incarceration for one that would help bring about freedom for many women. Towards the end of her autobiography, she wrote: 'And why are these women imprisoned? Because they and many thousands, or rather several millions, of women with them, have asked for the vote, but the Government would not give it to them.'[21] The disenfranchisement of women, in the visible enactment of incarceration, provided the militants with powerful metaphors for their protest and policy of civil disobedience, which are deployed in the titles of Christabel Pankhurst's autobiography *Unshackled* (1959)[22] and Lytton's *Prisons and prisoners*.

WRITING THE BODY

Writing her autobiography would have been a reminder of the physical costs of refusing to capitulate during imprisonment. Because of the paralysis of her writing hand, Lytton was forced to write the book with her left hand.[23] It was not the first time that her body had become a signifier of protest and resistance. When first arrested for trying to enter the House of Commons as part of a fifth deputation of militant leaders on 12 October 1908, Lytton was sentenced to a term in Holloway Gaol. During her month's prison term, she decided to protest against her preferential treatment by carving the words 'Votes for Women' from her chest up to and on to her face. The last letter and full stop were intended to punctuate her cheek. Finding her skin tougher than she had anticipated, Lytton experimented with a sewing needle and then a darning needle before selecting a piece of sharpened enamel with which to carve out her injunction. After spending twenty minutes inscribing a 'V' on her breast more deeply than she had intended, and anxious in case she had given herself blood-poisoning, she deliberately aroused the suspicions of an officer. Her literal attempt to write the body was a political act that turned protest and protester into one. Such a spectacle of self-harm can be seen, at the same time, as a validation and a renunciation of traditional feminine values. A further contradiction emanating from these stigmata of suffragettism lies in the self-effacement and narcissistic display when Lytton revealed her 'wound' to the doctor and his ward superintendent. Basking in a sense of pride in her handiwork, she commented:

> I felt all a craftsman's satisfaction in my job. The V was very clearly and evenly printed in spite of the varying material of its background, a rib bone forming an awkward bump. As I pointed out to the doctor, it had been placed exactly over the heart, and visibly recorded the pulsation of that organ as clearly as a watch hand, so that he no longer need be put to the trouble of a stethoscope.[24]

By setting out to inscribe upon her body a political slogan and exposing her body to be read by others, Lytton had turned herself into an object of heroic resistance. Such extreme and presumably uncharacteristic exhibitionism must have been empowering by compensating her for past humiliations and rejections, which had impaired her sense of self-esteem. While living with her mother in the aftermath of her rejection by Ponsonby, Lytton despairs of how hopelessly ugly she believes she has grown. In politicising and objectifying this subjective negativity, she puts 'ugliness to the test'[25] first by threatening the prison officers at Holloway that she will disfigure herself by carving a political slogan on her face and second by disguising herself as Jane Warton. The nature of the experiment was to verify what she had already observed – that the least attractive prisoners were the worst treated. While locked into the prison-house of depression at Homewood, Lytton complains that her clothes are all hideous.[26] During her impersonation of a seamstress, she deliberately tried to make herself look unattractive. Getting her hair cut short, she wore it under a battered hat along with pince-nez and an old coat, bought for 8s 6d. Her appearance was so comic that the prison wardresses could not help laughing while undressing her. The prison clothes worn in the Third Division, of coarse brown serge, with cap and apron and with shoes that pinched her feet, were requisitioned for the purposes of protest. Refusing to wear her cap and apron in her cell, she pinned her skirt up around her neck in order to keep warm, much to the governor's disapproval. Even though it was the middle of January, she had made her prison conditions worse by opening the windows in her cell. This was a political action endorsed by her comrades who would, if necessary, 'open' a window by breaking it with their shoes. In her mother's house where there was no such political necessity to endure the cold which Lytton felt so keenly, she would sometimes keep herself warm by vigorously polishing her shoes rather than by lighting a fire.

Lytton's refusal to do the sewing which was the 'hard labour' part of her sentence is underscored by her seamstress disguise. The punishment she incurred was a bread and water diet for three days. Far exceeding this was the hardship she was about to inflict upon herself. Not only did she resolve to deny herself food but also drink. Hunger-striking for Emmeline Pankhurst turned out to be a 'mild experience' compared with the thirst-strike that was 'from beginning to end simple and unmitigated torture'.[27] Before she joined the WSPU while living in her mother's house, Lytton uses the imagery of hunger and thirst when feeling overwhelmed by the aridity of life following her rejection by Ponsonby: 'And I yearn and thirst, Oh! such thirst, for unattainable life fillers to be in my life.' Seized by the 'devils of old-time depression', she saw images of starvation rise up to be resisted, creating a bizarre dress-rehearsal for her performance as Jane Warton at Walton Gaol:

> But there remains something incongruous within me that doesn't grow old and experienced with the rest, that won't die quite for all the much-killing but turns round now and then on its starved bed and shrieks out for food and drink with a strength all useless and uncanny coming from I don't know where. And one can only hush it and hope it will die.[28]

The death throes of unrequited romantic love are seen in the metaphors of starvation which represent the insatiability of the ascetic denying herself the sustenance of the life of the emotions. Likewise the suffragette hunger-striker is consumed by an insatiable appetite for the rights of women. In the words of the Suffragette Song: 'Now in a cell / She sits and pines / And off thin skilly / Daily dines; / But still repeats, / As if by rote, / "I want – I want – I want a vote".'[29] What is empowering for Lytton is to deprive herself of primary needs as well as to embark voluntarily upon a regime of self-inflicted starvation. The control she is able to exert over her body contrasts with the powerlessness she had experienced in the past in connection with emotional wants. While needy for love, affection and mutual recognition from John Ponsonby, Lytton reveals the source of her greatest hunger. In a letter to her confidante and cousin Adela Villiers, she goes beyond constructing herself as a submissive woman, to cast herself in the role of victim saying:

> I think I'm by nature constructed more like an Eastern women [*sic*]
> than a European, with a thick proportion of slavish instincts in my
> blood. What I hunger for most is to be able to serve those I love. I
> don't want their respect, but that they should *need* me, whether as a
> servant, or a toy, or a wife.[30]

When this hunger is not satisfied, she can spiral into a death-like depression. Ponsonby's neglect makes her feel lifeless, able to be revived only with a word from him. Lying in prison emaciated through hunger-striking and half-dead as a result of force-feeding, Lytton recaptures this corpse-like state. Her affirmation of life is when she is able to sacrifice herself for others whether they be the leaders of the WSPU or Homer Lane, the furtherance of whose career was the final argument that swayed her to place herself in his hands. Paralysis may be seen as a metaphor as well as a gruesome enactment of her passive resistance to the prison doctor (perversely Lane was to claim that this was the result of a protest by her subconscious against her suffragette militancy). It is more reasonable to assume that the stroke was precipitated by the times when she turned her body into a site of passive resistance against the prison doctor and was force-fed on nine occasions.

HUNGER-STRIKING

While it was known by prison authorities that Lady Constance had a weak heart and therefore had to be prevented from going on hunger-strike and being force-fed, there was no such concern for the heart of Jane Warton, circumscribed as it was within the suffragette 'V' for 'Votes'. A junior doctor listened to only two beats of her heart, which he declared to be a 'ripping, splendid heart'.[31] Although such a peremptory examination was negligent, it ought to be pointed out that Lytton had resolved to withhold the information that she had valvular heart disease.[32] For Jane Warton this medical history was private while for Constance Lytton it was public knowledge.

Even before her real identity had been disclosed, the prison doctor had observed an extraordinary resilience in this otherwise undistinguished prisoner. Constance's sister, Emily Lutyens, was told by Dr Price that he had never observed such 'a bad case of forcible feeding', as 'She was practically asphyxiated every time.'[33] Describing herself as physically a coward, Jane Warton increased the agonising torture for herself by resisting the wooden gag which gave the prison doctor licence to force into her mouth a more severe metal equivalent. Her jaw was cranked open to an excessive degree, and an inordinately wide stomach tube about four feet long was thrust down her oesophagus. The burning and choking sensation increased as more and more food was pushed down the funnel. The transition from starvation to engorgement was so sudden that the prisoner patient regurgitated over the doctor and the wardresses. As Maud Ellmann has pointed out in relation to Sylvia Pankhurst:

> In this predicament, it is not by eating but by vomiting her food that Pankhurst restores her sense of self-identity. To '*pull myself together*,' she writes, 'I struggled till I had brought up what had been forced into me.' And what has been forced into her is not only the food but the ideology and even the identity of her oppressors. Under this torture, starvation rather than ingestion has become the last remaining recipe for authenticity.[34]

For Lytton it is not so much her sense of self-identity that is restored but rather her identification with her alter ego. Even in her autobiography, which at one level represents a manifesto of the self, she uses the third person when relating these events.

One way of dealing with trauma is to distance oneself from it and to use humour as a further distancing device. While being stripped by prison warders, Lytton recalls in her *Prisons and prisoners*: 'The look of Jane Warton was still comic in the extreme, the two wardresses laughed as they undressed her.'[35] In the negotiation of another humiliating moment, as when she is sick over the doctor and the wardresses, she again uses humour and objectifies herself as Jane Warton. In retaliation for this act of defiance, the doctor slaps her on the cheek 'to express his contemptuous disapproval':

> At first it seemed such an utterly contemptible thing to have done that I could only laugh in my mind. Then suddenly I saw Jane Warton lying before me, and it seemed as if I were outside of her. She was the most despised, ignorant and helpless prisoner that I had seen. When she had served her time and was out of the prison, no one would believe anything she said, and the doctor when he had fed her by force and tortured her body, struck her on the cheek to show how he despised her! That was Jane Warton, and I had come to help her.[36]

Seeing Lytton in Kafkaesque terms as a hunger artist, Maud Ellmann suggests that she is obeying an unconscious desire to be force-fed and thereby to bring about an inherent disintegration of subjectivity:

> Indeed, what makes these episodes particularly harrowing is that they reawaken a trauma familiar to us all. Our first experience of eating is force-feeding: as infants, we were fed by others and ravished by the food they thrust into our jaws. We eat, therefore, in order to avenge ourselves against this rape inflicted at the very dawn of life. The compulsive eater, who feels attacked by food, under-

stands the truth of eating better than the gourmand, who thinks that he is eating by his own volition, or the ascetic, who thinks he can resist the imperative of food. *All eating is force-feeding*: and it is through the wound of feeding that the other is instated at the very centre of the self.[37]

Lytton was not the first member of her family to have embarked upon a hunger-strike. Her grandmother, Rosina Bulwer Lytton, refused to eat when she was first confined in a private lunatic asylum by her husband Edward Bulwer Lytton in 1858 by way of insisting that she was sound of mind. On being told by the superintendent that this abstinence would be used as evidence of her insanity, she began to eat with gusto. Rosina's mother who visited asylums, and like her granddaughter, was an advocate of prison reform, worked with the poor and underfed. She had been forced to leave her home in Guernsey in 1816 owing to a deficit in the island's finances of £20,000, which she had channelled into poor relief. Both mother and daughter had been born and brought up in Ireland, where fasting, hunger and starvation have shaped much of the religious, political and social contours of the land.[38]

What is so well understood in Ireland is how hunger-striking can be used as a political weapon – from medieval Ireland, where a victim of injustice could fast against the person who had caused the injury, to the twentieth-century Republicans, held in British-run jails, who protested against being denied the status of political prisoners. The hunger-strike is also an internalisation and inversion of the way in which famine has been used by the British government to subjugate the rebellious Irish. Constance's grandmother and great-grandmother were sympathetic towards the Republican cause and friendly with leading Republicans like Daniel O'Connell. The first prisoners to go on hunger-strike for their political rights in Ireland were the Irish suffragettes in 1912, the first of whom was Hanna Sheehy-Skeffington. In her pamphlet 'Reminiscences of an Irish suffragette' (1941), she pointed out: 'Hunger-strike was then a new weapon – we were the first to try it out in Ireland – had we but known, we were the pioneers in a long line. At first, Sinn Fein and its allies regarded the hunger-strike as a womanish thing.'[39]

Through hunger-striking, men were feminised such as Irish hunger-striker Terence MacSwiney, Lord Mayor of Cork. Dying in Brixton Prison in 1920 after starving for seventy-four days for the Republican cause, his credo, derived from Thomas à Kempis's *Imitation of Christ* (1435), was: 'It is not those who can inflict the most, but those who can suffer the most who will conquer.'[40] This affirmation of martyrdom embodies Lytton's ideological position. While it cannot be denied that all the hunger-striking militants put their health and lives at risk, in her case the stakes were higher owing to heart disease. A doctor had already advised her that she risked paralysis or even death if she went on hunger-strike. Her decision to proceed was rationalised by objectifying herself as Jane Warton. Even though she had the same body, the fact that they had different names and belonged to different classes meant that one was treated very differently from the other.[41] The mistreatment of Jane Warton inexorably led to the partial paralysis and premature death of Constance Lytton.

Maud Ellmann finds it strange that Lytton can share the cause of women only by re-enacting 'the greatest trial' of their sex and argues: 'It is not enough to *know* about the wrongs of woman; one must *undergo* this lacerating *mise-en-scène*, in which the centuries of degradation that women have endured materialize in the spectacle of violation.'[42] The way in which Lytton felt that she could atone for the privileges of her class was to go beyond empathy to an identification with the poor and exploited, by levelling out the class differentials to challenge the way in which different social classes were treated in prison. The fission of self that this entailed is enacted through a psycho-drama of a poor woman denying food to her rich counterpart. What Jane Warton gave to Constance Lytton was the authorisation to hunger-strike and thereby the right to be treated like any other suffragette prisoner. It was as if Lytton was taking revenge on her own class through Warton. What her action represented was more than starving the aristocracy of its rights and privileges. A momentary equality through the communality of suffering for a cause that straddled the class divide had been achieved. Paradoxically this symbiotic relationship with the two sides of her personality and two identities provided a passport to another kind of privilege. With the radical elite of the militant movement, the hunger-strikers, Lytton was now standing shoulder to shoulder. Starvation is the great leveller and, as David Thomson has pointed out in regard to the Irish famines, 'when people of any nation starve they grow the same'.[43] Constance longed to be one of the many and part of the whole. At the same time, her desire to be singled out is an anomaly that cannot be explained entirely by the political expediency of ensuring that her case would be publicised. Her brother among others would draw public attention to her mistreatment at the hands of the doctor. Neither does pragmatism account for why *Prisons and prisoners* goes beyond functioning as a further exposé of political and social wrongs. Not only are the moments of derision and degradation laid bare in intimate detail, but also they are imbued with a fanatical exultation in suffering and a sense that Constance had made an unwritten resolution to 'suffer the most'.

HOLY ANOREXIA

To seek out extreme suffering by denial of food is behaviour associated with medieval holy anorectics such as St Catherine of Sienna.[44] As in their cases, Lytton's asceticism is not masochism or a dualism between the body and the spirit, but an effort to gain power and imbue with meaning the restrictions imposed upon women. Since food and the body are areas that fall within the control of women, these become symbols for the failure to exert control elsewhere. In a petition to the Home Secretary in which she complains of the preferential treatment she has received while in Holloway, Lytton identifies herself as a Liberal and 'as a believer in the teachings of Christ, and as a woman'.[45] In wearing the martyr's crown and inscribing herself with stigmata in the form of the 'V' above her heart, was she not following the example of Christ literally?

It is significant that a discourse of religiosity had permeated the militants. Joan of Arc was not out of place as their patron saint. The beatification of suffragette heroines, such as Emily Wilding Davison and Constance Lytton, and the enshrinement of the charismatic leaders, Emmeline and Christabel Pankhurst, contributed towards an iconography of woman worship and martyrdom. It was not uncommon for the discourse of religious revivalism to be applied to the militant movement. Annie Kenney voiced an unspoken truth when she compared the members of the WSPU to the sisterhood of a strict religious order:

> Nuns in a convent were not watched over and supervised more strictly than were the organisers and members of the Militant Movement during the first few years. It was an unwritten rule that there must be no concerts, no theatres, no smoking; work, and sleep to prepare us for more work, was the unwritten order of the day. These rules were good, and the more I look back on those early days the more clearly I see the necessity for such discipline. The changed life into which most of us entered was a revolution in itself.[46]

Constance's desire to be a suffragette prisoner is analogous to that of a postulant, particularly one that had entered a convent after being jilted. Not content with the trappings of a nun, such as discarding her clothes for poorer attire, having her hair cut off, and changing her name, Lytton aspired to suffragette canonisation through the martyrdom of being tortured for the faith. Determined to prove to the prison authorities that she could endure the hardship of the wooden bed in the punishment cell, she sleeps on the floor. No anchorite could have awaited more gladly enclosure within the walls of her cell which is a prospect she greets eagerly saying: 'At last the longed-for moment had arrived.'[47]

On entering solitary confinement, Constance was able to rediscover her hermit self in this place of self-abnegation. She is relieved that she does not have to share a cell. When asking herself what she wanted during her periods of depression in her mother's house, the answer was to be alone: 'The only wish I can define off-hand as being chronically there is to be alone, in fact, simply to be able to go my own way regardless of anyone else.'[48] Solitude in being the semblance of an independent life gave her an illusion of freedom.

THE CAGED DAUGHTER

At Homewood there were times when Lytton had felt as though she were a prisoner, whose every wish was accompanied by 'the certainty that it will be disapproved and worked against [which] acts like a cold wind'.[49] Frustrated at being thwarted by her mother Edith, Constance realises: 'She does it entirely for my good yet nothing could have been much further from what I like.' 'My wishes [she] studied only to oppose them, it being a kind of accepted thing that if I want a thing it's bad for me and therefore to be refused . . . it's the kind of attitude behind everything which gets on one's nerves at times.' After complaining to Maria Theresa Earle, known as Aunt T, of being treated like a 'semi-maniac'[50] by her mother, she experiences in prison the restraints and punishment associated with the way in which lunatics had been treated in the madhouses of the previous century.[51]

Desperately not wanting to hurt Edith, Constance insists that 'it would be impossible for me to do anything which would give her acute moral pain'.[52] Yet her militant activities contradict this assertion. One of her most painful moments in prison was when she was forced to choose between filial affection to her mother and solidarity with fellow prisoners when she refused to acquiesce with the bending of the prison rules to allow her to accept a letter from her mother. Just as her prison sentences had caused Edith much anguish, so too was she distressed and angry when Constance decided to leave home for the last time. The question of freedom was one that was a point of discussion with her favourite aunt. To Earle's enquiry what Lytton would do if she were 'quite free', the response is that she would probably be a vegetarian. Here was another area where she felt unable to exert control over the food she consumed both at home and in prison.[53]

By remaining unmarried, Constance escaped what her great-grandmother, Anna Wheeler, described as 'the eternal prison of the husband's house'.[54] Instead she was trapped in a role described by Earle as 'a caged daughter', being 'a thing of which I should have had the greatest horror if I had had daughters of my own. I think no parents have any right to trammel the lives of grown-up daughters. Why should women be more or less slaves because they do not happen to marry.'[55] The revolt of the daughters was topical and according to Constance had been christened in *The Times*, 'The Revolting Daughters'. In a letter to Victor, she takes up the discussion:

> Mothers who allow their daughters freedom have remarked 'How absurd it is to talk as if mothers tyrannised over their daughters like that.' And the mothers who look upon their daughters only as untrustworthy slavies have said – 'How can anyone make such a ridiculous proposal as that daughters should have any interests, occupations, or friends except those which their parents select for them.' It seems to me that the only cases in which it would be justi-

fiable for a daughter to 'revolt' (as it's called) i.e. make a stand in her own interests against her parents' wishes) are the cases when such a revolt would be utterly useless – impossible in fact . . . they have to conform themselves very often to the narrow life of – practically – an unpaid servant. This was consistent with the idea that marriage was their only goal.[56]

By now Constance had resigned herself to not marrying. When she wrote in a letter dated 23 May 1894 that it is 'not my wish to remain an old maid',[57] she was referring to her hopes of marrying John Ponsonby. Apart from her brother, Victor, the other man who had a major impact on her life (and death) was the notorious and ambivalent Homer Lane.

The founder in 1913 of a community for young delinquents of both sexes, called 'The Little Commonwealth', Lane professed to cure his 'citizens' by living with them.[58] His private practice consisted of treating patients through psychoanalysis, close observation and the force of his own personality. Eventually Lane was disgraced in a sexual scandal involving the alleged molestation of at least one young girl. Deported to America as an alien on a technical point, he died shortly after on 5 September 1925. Since he was particularly attractive to women, the question remains: was Lane an angelic liberator or a self-deluded charlatan? There is no doubt that Constance was obsessed by him. On 17 October 1922, she wrote to her brother Victor, who was another devotee: 'I can think of nothing but Laneisms from week to week, my mind and whole self are steeped in it.'[59] Admissions that he was the nearest thing to an angel that she had ever seen make it plausible that she was in love with him. Like John Ponsonby, who had the power of bringing her back to life, she states, 'He [Lane] has made me live again and content whether with life or death, paralysis or health.'[60]

Lane's methods were controversial. During his psychoanalytical sessions with Constance, he shifted the blame for her illness onto her and the WSPU. Trying to convince her that her stroke was a punishment for her suffragette activity, he argued that her subconscious was opposed to suffragettism and had taken revenge on her body through the stroke and ten years of illness. While his psychological interpretations and views on the fight for women's suffrage remain highly suspect, his medical knowledge was even more dubious. The likelihood is that he was a dangerous quack who misdiagnosed the early warning signs of Lytton's heart failure. She presented alarming symptoms: the veins in her paralysed right hand were becoming visible, her feet and legs were swelling and the distension of the stomach made it difficult to digest food. Lane's prognosis was that the circulation was returning to her paralysed side and that a cure was imminent. Reassuring her that these signs were not unexpected, by his authority and assurance, Lane assuaged her fears. According to Lane, Constance's health would improve if she stayed in London and left Homewood; otherwise she would undo all the good she had begun.

When matters got worse, Lane disregarded the medical opinions of Dr Mary Gordon, who opposed the move to London. Lytton reflected upon Dr Gordon's exhortion to her that 'it would be cruel, impossible to leave mother and I ought not to do it'.[61] Not surprisingly Edith endorsed this advice saying that Dr Gordon was indeed a wise woman. But the persuasive powers of her son Victor pulled her in a different direction. Victor insisted that she should see Lane to discover 'how intimately you are yourself connected with Con's illness and how much *you* can do to effect her cure'.[62] The driving force in support of Lane, Victor in his powerful position as head of the family was able to convince his sister Betty and his mother that Constance should follow Lane's treatment regime.[63]

In a letter dated 1 May 1923, Betty wrote to Constance that Homer Lane had accused her of 'playing' at recovery, insisting that if she wanted to recover her health, she must move to quarters that had been prepared for her and submit to Lane's treatment. Betty recommended that she put herself in his hands, reporting that Lane had exhorted her to swallow her pride. With its implication of refusing to eat and thereby disobeying the physician, this metaphor was a reminder that this time, unlike her resistance to the prison doctor, she must succumb to Lane's treatment. By calling her instincts for self-preservation 'pride', Lane sought to undermine her opposition. The most effective means of persuasion, however, was to appeal to her altruistic and self-sacrificing nature. Betty pleaded with her to agree not for her own sake but for the advancement of Lane's career, saying: 'you will be a mine of wealth to him.'[64] In a set of images that would have had resonance for Constance, Betty portrays her as a saviour of prisoners saying:

> every day you delay you are putting off his reward. I left him tread-ing on air. I felt as if I had seen held up a bright torch to prisoners in a pit, promising them light, freedom, safety. If you don't agree to put yourself into his hands it is as if you were snatching the torch and putting it out.[65]

The light that was to be put out was not, as a result of her decision, Lane's career but Lytton herself, who had been described as a 'kindly light'.[66] Unable to resist such an appeal, Constance agreed to put herself entirely in his hands. Twenty days later, on 22 May 1923, she was dead. She was only fifty-four.

Betty blamed her death on Lane, who privately blamed it on her mother. As Betty explains in a letter on 3 July to her devastated brother Victor:

> I feel fearfully disappointed and feel a glorious experiment has failed. Physiologically it is easy to explain her death . . . Lane so

completely ignored the D[r]'s view of the case that I think he thought the family surrounding her made her ill. The grim thing still to me is that I believe Lane in his heart thinks her family killed her and that he never had a chance of getting her free from all hampering love . . . It is much more true to say Lane killed her – but I don't regret it – for like you, better to make the attempt and fail than see her a hopeless prisoner.[67]

While domestic imprisonment had been killing her spirit, liberation had proved to be too much for her body or, rather, her heart.

By striding out on her own, was Lytton resisting her mother's wishes, obeying her brother and sister, succumbing to Lane's self-interest or following her own inclinations? What was to be a life-or-death decision turned out to be not such a gamble in that it was predicated on her belief that life at home was not worth living: 'My instinct is to do as mother wishes and give up living in London. At the same time I seem to know that my life here was in the grave and not vital or helpful to mother.'[68] It appears that her life was being measured in terms of its worth as a dutiful daughter. That Victor and Betty believed that she preferred death rather than living in captivity as the invalid spinster daughter is evident from Constance's reflections on the prospect of death:

I'm quite glad to live and there seems much to be done. But I shall always be, I think, quite glad to die. Living on the whole I have found a sad and painful thing and tho' with Lane . . . one could do many good and joy-making things still it will always remain a sad place, this world, through my spectacles, even if I myself am healthy and powerful.[69]

Heroism and martyrdom had been a means of self-empowerment but at the cost of causing Lytton even greater ill-health. Her melancholy sentiments above appear in a letter to her brother Victor in which she refuses to allow him to pay Lane's fees. Determined not to be a financial drain upon her relatives, she was never in a position to enjoy the independence that would have yielded her autonomy and self-sufficiency. Even when she did earn money she felt that she could not lay claim to it. Her earnings from journalism went towards presents for her mother and to pay her sister Emily's expenses to travel. The only time her earnings were spent on herself was the payment she received from Earle for her collaboration in her pot-pourri book. Alas Earle had made her feel so guilty for doing this that Lytton resolved to pay her back, sensing that the money had been given rather than earned. Yet she calculated that in the time during which she had been working on Earle's two pot-pourri books, she could have 'lawfully' earned the same amount of £75 from journalism.[70]

175

In the last year of her life, with her brother Victor, Constance had been involved in prison reform particularly in connection with women prisoners and supported the increased number of women standing for election to parliament. One such woman who was standing as the Labour candidate for Acton Division, was Mary Richardson, an ex-member of the WSPU, who had also been forcibly fed in prison and was an admirer of Lytton's work for women. But were her qualities of duty, loyalty and adulation misplaced in two key men in her life, John Ponsonby and Homer Lane who respectively accelerated her depressions and eventually the deterioration of her health? While each represented freedom – one from spinsterhood and the other from paralysis – significantly both opened up escape routes from her mother. The most resounding 'gaol-break', however, was achieved through her membership of the WSPU. As Judith Lytton pointed out to Constance's sister Betty after hearing her speak about her commitment to women's suffrage: 'She is lost to your mother for ever, just as a tamed hawk which has shaken off its hood and flown away into the sky.'[71]

CONCLUSION

To look at the life and writings of Constance Lytton as a series of contradictions breaks down the hagiographic approach, which simplifies her complexities and glosses over the deeper conflicts with which she struggled. While she defied authorities, such as the British government, in the fight for the vote, she was willing to entrust her well-being to a man like Homer Lane, who had a reputation for ensnaring impressionable women from wealthy families. While starving and punishing her body, she remained at her core a prominent member of the body politic as a member of the ruling class. Was it a masochistic impulse that caused her to redirect negative feelings about herself into politicised channels of self-inflicted injury and force-feeding? Or was she motivated by the highest political ideals in the sex war? There was no doubt in Annie Kenney's mind that Lytton was 'one of the finest, most unselfish, and most loyal of loyalists' who 'never demurred one moment from undertaking the most serious piece of militancy'.[72] This tribute does not suggest that the masochist (which for these purposes is being read as a glorified martyr) is in conflict with the militant activism of the WSPU. Although Lytton would have agreed with Emmeline Pankhurst that her decision to go to prison was in order to gain the rights of full citizenship, martyrdom was also a viable desideratum towards that end. Maybe Lytton felt that she had more to sacrifice in terms of family name and, by the same token, more for which to suffer or atone. Furthermore much of her suffering was centred on self. There is no doubt that she harboured an active desire to suffer for the cause through acts of self-deprivation and self-harm, which met with the self-gratification of self-sacrifice.

While her partial paralysis was brought about by acts of passive resistance against imprisonment, such as hunger-striking and being force-fed, her imprisonment helped liberate both herself and other women. With a characteristically genuine sense of humility, Lytton, whose story has inspired so many women, explains in the 'Dedication to Prisoners' in *Prisons and prisoners* how indispensable had been the inspiration given to her by fellow-prisoners:

> In my ignorance and impudence I went into prison hoping to help prisoners. So far as I know, I was unable to do anything for them. But the prisoners helped me ... Prisoners, I wish I could give to you, for your joy, something of the help you gave to me, and that in many ways I could follow your example.[73]

From prisoners Lytton gained insights into the other kinds of imprisonment, both public and private, that she had been enduring. These ranged from the limitations placed upon her as a spinster daughter and carer, through to her restricted female role as a member of the aristocracy, to the confinement of the body in her life as an invalid. More importantly, what prisoners and her own experience of prison gave Lytton was the courage to escape.

NOTES

I would like to thank Lord Cobbold for giving me exclusive access to the archives, the Knebworth archivist Clare Fleck for her assistance and Mary Links for sharing with me her reminiscences of Aunt Con. Much appreciated too have been the insights given to me by Marion Glastonbury, and the way in which John Charles Smith and Hilda Kean so diligently scrutinised my chapter.

1 See Marie Mulvey[-]Roberts and Tamae Mizuta (eds), Suffrage fallacies: Sir Almroth Wright, Militant hysteria. To the editor of *The Times*, in *The opponents: the anti-suffragists* in the series *Controversies in the history of British feminism* (London, Routledge/Thoemmes Press, 1995). For discussions relating to the nature of militancy see Sandra Stanley Holton, *Suffrage days: stories from the women's suffrage movement* (London, Routledge, 1996), J. Liddington, *The life and times of a respectable rebel: Selina Cooper, 1864–1946* (London, Virago, 1984), Marie Mulvey[-]Roberts and Tamae Mizuta (eds), *The militants in perspective in the history of British feminism* (London, Routledge/Thoemmes Press, 1994) which is an anthology of writings by Christabel Pankhurst, Constance Lytton and Kathleen Roberts, etc. . . . and Ann Stanley and Liz Morley, *The life and death of Emily Wilding Davison* (London, Women's Press, 1989).
2 See June Purvis, The prison experiences of the suffragettes in Edwardian Britain, *Women's History Review*, 4, 1, 1995, pp. 103–133.
3 I am writing the authorised biography of Constance Lytton and other members of her family. See Michelle Myall, 'Only be ye strong and very courageous': the

militant suffragism of Lady Constance Lytton, *Women's History Review*, 7, 1, 1998, pp. 61–84.

4 Emmeline Pankhurst, *My own story* (London, Eveleigh Nash, 1914), pp. 187–188.

5 The context for this remark was apparently after Judith Lytton witnessed a speech made by Constance on which she reported in a letter to Betty Balfour dated 28 March 1909. It survives as a copy made by Aunt T and was unearthed at Knebworth Archive from Box 125 by Clare Fleck. Constance's power of oratory is apparent from Judith's observations: 'I have never seen any thing like it. It had the quality which belongs to earthquakes, thunderstorms and volcanic eruptions, before which one can only tremble.'

6 Constance Lytton, *Prisons and prisoners: some personal experiences by Constance Lytton and Jane Warton, spinster* (London, William Heinemann, 1914), pp. 39–40.

7 Lytton, *Prisons and prisoners*, p. 264.

8 Marion Glastonbury pointed out to me that upper-class nurseries were kept deliberately austere with plain food. It is likely that Constance's mother Edith would not have encouraged pampering from nannies. Constance may have felt impelled to close the gap between her family's affluence and the surrounding poverty in India:

> The time is out of joint. O cursed spite,
> That ever I was born to put it right!
> (Shakespeare, *Hamlet, Prince of Denmark*, act 1, scene 5, ll. 189–190)

9 Mary Links, *Edward and Elizabeth: a Chancy marriage and its Outcome* (privately printed, 1996), p. 203.

10 Lytton, *Prisons and prisoners*, p. 63.

11 Katherine Roberts, *Pages from the diary of a militant suffragette* (Letchworth and London, Garden City Press, 1910), p. 137.

12 Hilda Kean, Searching for the past in present defeat: the construction of historical and political identity in British feminism in the 1920s and 1930s, *Women's History Review*, 3, 1, 1994, p. 69.

13 Lytton, *Prisons and prisoners*, p. 235.

14 Betty Balfour, *Letters of Constance Lytton* (London, William Heinemann, 1925), p. 52.

15 Lytton, *Prisons and prisoners*, p. 100.

16 Ibid., p. 13.

17 See Hilda Kean, 'The smooth cool men of science': the feminist and socialist response to vivisection, *History Workshop Journal*, 40, 1995, pp. 16–38.

18 For the first time Anna Wheeler's name has been included with William Thompson's on the title page for the editions of *Appeal of one half the human race, women, against the pretensions of the other half, men, to retain them in political, and thence in civil and domestic slavery; in reply to a paragraph of Mr. Mill's celebrated 'Article on government'*, which I co-edited with Michael Foot in the series *Subversive women* (1994) for Thoemmes Press in Bristol and with Tamae Mizuta in *Socialist feminists* in *Sources of British feminism* (London, Routledge/Thoemmes Press, 1995). See Dolores Dooley, *Equality in community: sexual equality in the writings of William Thompson and Anna Doyle Wheeler* (Cork, Cork University Press, 1996).

19 Constance Lytton, No votes for women: a reply to some recent anti-suffrage publications (1909), in Marie Mulvey[-]Roberts and Tamae Mizuta (eds), The militants, in *Perspectives in the history of British feminism* (London, Routledge/Thoemmes Press, 1994).

20 Lytton, *Prisons and prisoners*, p. 135.
21 Ibid., p. 336.
22 Frederick Pethick Lawrence gave this title to Christabel Pankhurst's autobiography which he prepared for publication after her death in 1958.
23 Mary Links points out that she got a typewriter in 1917 when friends clubbed together. See Links, *Edward and Elizabeth*, p. 204.
24 Lytton, *Prisons and prisoners*, p. 167.
25 Ibid., p. 239.
26 After Robert died the family had to let out Knebworth House as there were financial problems and move to a nearby smallish house known as The Danes. In June 1902 they moved to a recently built house called Homewood.
27 Pankhurst, *My own story*, p. 316.
28 K.A., transcript, 01274, p. 43. Letter from Constance Lytton to Adela Smith, 6 September 1907.
29 Reprinted in an illustration in Mulvey[-]Roberts and Mizuta (eds), *The militants*.
30 K.A., transcript, 01274, p. 25. Letter from Constance Lytton to Adela Villiers, 28 August, 1900.
31 Lytton, *Prisons and prisoners*, p. 275.
32 This is the terminology Pankhurst uses in describing Lytton's heart condition in *My own story*, p. 187. Infantile and girlhood chronic rheumatism had weakened her heart. See Lytton, *Prisons and prisoners*, p. 74.
33 Lytton, *Prisons and prisoners*, p. 298.
34 Maud Ellmann, *The hunger artists: starving, writing and imprisonment* (London, Virago Press, 1993), p. 34.
35 Lytton, *Prisons and prisoners*, p. 261.
36 Ibid., p. 270.
37 Ellmann, *The hunger artists*, pp. 35–36. Here Ellmann is over-stating the case unless she is referring specifically to spoon-feeding or maybe to the bottle-fed infant. Breast-feeding is a symbiosis of harmonious supply and demand whereby the milk spurting from a mother's teat is in direct response to the suction and stimulus regulated by the baby. Also on p. 35 in this otherwise excellent and important book, Ellmann states wrongly that Lytton's force-feeding ordeal when disguised as Jane Warton had taken place at Holloway Prison whereas it was while she was imprisoned at Walton Gaol.
38 See Cathal Póirtéir (ed.), *The great Irish famine* (Dublin, Mercier Press, 1995).
39 Hanna Sheehy-Skeffington, Reminiscences of an Irish suffragette (1941), in Rosemary Cullen Owens (ed.), *Votes for women: Irish women's struggle for the vote* (Dublin: c/o Trinity College Library, 1975), p. 23.
40 David Beresford, *Ten men dead: the story of the 1981 Irish hunger strike* (London, Grafton, 1987), p. 19.
41 For differentials in treatment according to class, with specific reference to Constance Lytton and her working-class compatriots, Selina Martin and Leslie Hall, see Purvis, The prison experiences of the suffragettes in Edwardian Britain, p. 118.
42 Ellmann, *The hunger artists*, p. 35.
43 David Thomson, *Woodbrook* (London, Vintage, 1974), p. 171.
44 See Rudolph M. Bell, *Holy anorexia* (London, University of Chicago Press, 1985) and Caroline Walker Bynum, *Holy feast and holy fast: the religious significance of food to medieval women* (London, University of California Press, 1987).
45 Lytton, *Prisons and prisoners*, p. 143.
46 Annie Kenney, *Memories of a militant* (London, Edward Arnold, 1924), p. 110.
47 Lytton, *Prisons and prisoners*, p. 263.

48 K.A., transcript, 01274, p. 28. Letter from Constance Lytton to Maria Theresa Earle, 25 August 1900.
49 Ibid.
50 Ibid.
51 Even though psychiatrists had been brought to Holloway Prison to examine the hunger-strikers, none was willing to certify them insane. This was verified by Reginald McKenna, the Home Secretary, who informed the House of Commons on 11 June 1914. See Elaine Showalter, *The female malady: women, madness, and English culture, 1830–1980* (London, Virago, 1987), p. 162. See Midge Mackenzie (ed.), *Shoulder to shoulder* (New York, Alfred A. Knopf, 1975), p. 277.
52 K.A., transcript, 01274, p. 27. Letter from Constance Lytton to Adela Villiers, 28 August 1900.
53 Lytton informed the prison doctor at Holloway Prison that she had cured her chronic rheumatism through vegetarianism and requested that she be provided with a vegetarian diet and flannel underclothing. See Lytton, *Prisons and prisoners*, p. 74.
54 Thompson and Wheeler, *Appeal*, p. 87.
55 Maria Theresa Earle with Ethel Case, *Pot-pourri mixed by two* (London, Smith, Elder, 1914), preface.
56 K.A., 41837. Letter from Constance Lytton to Victor Lytton, 29 April 1894.
57 K.A., in 4 April 1923 envelope. Letter from Constance Lytton to her sister Bets, 23 May 1894.
58 See E. T. Bazeley (1928) *Homer Lane and the Little Commonwealth* (London, Allen & Unwin, 1928). The introduction is written by Constance Lytton's brother Victor.
59 K.A., 01225. Letter from Constance Lytton to Victor Lytton, 17 October 1922.
60 Ibid., 18 September 1922.
61 Ibid., 6 January 1923.
62 See Lutyens, *Edward and Elizabeth*, p. 217.
63 Ibid., pp. 216–217.
64 Ibid.
65 Ibid.
66 Balfour, *Letters of Constance Lytton*, xiv.
67 Lutyens, *Edward and Elizabeth*, pp. 218–219.
68 K.A., 01225. Letter from Constance Lytton to Victor Lytton, 6 January 1923.
69 K.A., 01125. Letter from Constance Lytton to Victor Lytton, 31 October 1922.
70 K.A., 01274, transcription, p. 29. Letter from Constance Lytton to Maria Theresa Earle, 25 August 1900.
71 K.A., 125. Letter from Judith Lytton, who was married to Constance's brother Neville, to Betty Balfour, 28 March 1909.
72 Kenney, *Memories of a militant*, p. 88.
73 Lytton, *Prisons and prisoners*, p. x.

8

'DARE TO BE FREE!'

The Women's Freedom League and its legacy

Hilary Frances

INTRODUCTION

Among the Women's Freedom League's more distinctive claims was that of being a democratic, militant organisation. Other distinguishing features included socialist associations and the belief that women's emancipation involved more than enfranchisement: it entailed a fundamental questioning of the relationships between men and women.

While the Women's Freedom League (the League or WFL) began as a by-product of the maelstrom of the early Edwardian suffrage campaign, it can be seen as providing a link between the demands made by the nineteenth-century women's movement and late twentieth-century feminism. For example, besides continuing to support reforms in employment, education, marriage and divorce, it sought to transform gender relationships. Recognising that women could not achieve equality with men unless very basic tenets of gender relationships were changed, some leading members of the WFL extended the boundaries of public debate on sexual issues. Sometimes simultaneously with their suffrage work, sometimes subsequently, they sought to analyse sexual relationships to show how power imbalances in the social structure impacted on women's personal lives to maintain injustice and reinforce sexual oppression. These included issues explored by nineteenth-century campaigners for female emancipation and which are fundamental concerns of contemporary feminism: sexual harassment and abuse, incest, domestic violence and prostitution.

This chapter explores the construction of militancy within the WFL and then focuses on broader aspects of its campaigning in order to highlight the connections between earlier action to demand women's emancipation and twentieth-century feminist concerns.[1] Rather than reiterate the political aspects of the suffrage campaign I consider the ways in which members employed a variety of interpretations of militancy and so allowed the organisation to evolve. I argue that these strategies accommodated radical, independent suffragists, promoted more imaginative, wider-ranging programmes for reform and led to longer-term initiatives in the area of gender politics.[2]

THE LEAGUE'S FORMATION: 1907

Like other suffrage societies, the WFL based its claim for women's suffrage on the principle of equal rights for women as citizens and the belief that women had a particular contribution to make to society. Its principles and methods developed from several political groupings active in British politics: the socialist movement; the reformist, constitutional approach typified by conventional suffrage societies such as the National Union of Women's Suffrage Societies (NUWSS); the popular campaigning of the radical suffragists of northern England; the use of propaganda tactics derived from mass political movements and suffragette activism of the type developed by the Women's Social and Political Union (WSPU). As long as it remained tightly focused on the priority of women's suffrage, the League was able to combine these elements effectively. However, the diversities of political identity among WFL members contained seeds of dissension.[3]

Continuity of suffrage campaigning from the late nineteenth to the early twentieth century had been mainly sustained by working-class northern 'radical suffragists'.[4] Hostility from male trade unionists, who feared politicised women workers would weaken their bargaining power, made for an uneasy relationship with some socialist and union organisations. Effective cooperation between feminists and the nascent Labour Party in the first decade of the twentieth century was compromised by conflict over such basic objectives as complete adult or male suffrage without property qualifications or women's enfranchisement on the prevailing terms of a property qualification.

When the WSPU began its campaigning, from 1903, several of its leaders were members of the Independent Labour Party (ILP). Within five years the structure of the WSPU had become much less democratic, with some of its leaders moving further to the political right. Emmeline and Christabel Pankhurst in particular adopted very autocratic methods.[5] When WSPU members were forbidden to co-operate with the Labour Party, dissent was inevitable from such socialists as Mrs Cobden Sanderson, Richard Cobden's daughter, Charlotte Despard, a life-long socialist and pacifist, Teresa Billington-Greig, the first woman organiser for the ILP in 1904,[6] Irene Fenwick Miller and Edith How Martyn, a WSPU secretary.[7]

Matters came to a head in September 1907 when Mrs Pankhurst vetoed arrangements made for the annual conference in October. Dissenters hastily formed a provisional committee and went ahead with the conference. Representatives from thirty-one out of fifty-two WSPU branches attended.

Many agreed with Teresa Billington-Greig, who became the League's leading political theorist, that democratic procedures were essential. It was useless to demand democratic rights to participate in government if their own system was undemocratic.[8] Moreover, only through direct participation could many women develop expertise and a sense of agency. The principle was immediately put into practice by a referendum to decide the new organisation's name. In that and their motto, 'Dare to be Free', they signalled wider visions of freedom than mere enfranchisement. By November the two organisations were separate. The new society relinquished claims to existing WSPU funds, documents and other assets. Although initially funds were low, totalling just £2 2s 1d, within a few weeks an office was established in London. A strong commitment to provincial representation was promised, a pledge which at times became a source of tension between metropolitan leaders and provincial members.[9] The WFL aimed to be 'another militant body pledged to work heart and soul for Votes for Women'.[10] What else did it offer? There were two main thrusts: an insistent analysis of gender relationship; and affiliations with socialism.

From the start the League recognised that relationships between men and women needed to be transformed if real equality was to be achieved. This, according to the League's correspondent in *Women's Franchise* in 1908, was the major reason why women demanded political power:

> Only when women are valued equally with men, will it be possible to find a solution to the problems of modern life, without any kind of unequal law for the two sexes.[11]

The League kept its links with the ILP and maintained a focus on women's economic position in the workplace and in the home.[12] From the League's progressive political analysis sprang support for exploited industrial workers during strikes and lock-outs, wages for housework, and condemnation of cheap and sweated labour. The input of working-class members at local level particularly helped to shape League priorities. Some women also belonged to the Women's Co-operative Guild, the ILP and other left-wing organisations. They held joint meetings and sometimes campaigned together.[13]

In terms of class composition, most of the members were middle class. Nonetheless, working-class women made significant contributions. Among them were Emma Sproson, an executive committee member, who had begun work as a part-time factory hand at the age of nine, and Edith Watson, born in Hackney Workhouse, the illegitimate daughter of a domestic servant, who sustained the League's crusade to reform the judicial system. Class divisions were never completely eradicated, however. The leadership was comparable with that of the WSPU, rather than that of the NUWSS with its political connections.

The WFL was the smallest of the three main women's suffrage organisations. There has been some debate over its size. How Martyn's ebullient account of its founding published in *The Vote* on 9 December 1909 probably overestimates the swing away from the WSPU. In her short, celebratory history of the League (1957), Stella Newsome glosses over membership numbers and size.[14] Garner questions Rosen's estimate that only 20 per cent of the WSPU left to join the League, quoting Billington-Greig who thought that half the WSPU branches attended the break-away conference. By 1908 there were fifty-three branches in England, Scotland and Wales and by 1914 membership was estimated to be 4,000.[15]

The WFL retained its democratic structure, a formally elected national executive committee, honorary and paid officials. Its annual conferences provided an arena for delegates to raise issues about which branch members felt strongly. On occasion friction developed between the regions and the strongly London-centred national leadership. Because a successful local group was very much dependent on the skills and experience of its personnel, the establishment and running of some local branches proved problematic. Different systems were tried out with paid and voluntary speakers to stimulate activity in smaller branches; later district organisers were allocated to areas where WFL activity was strongest. This included the industrial north, Wales, parts of the eastern counties and the south coast. The WFL was particularly strong in Scotland, with very active branches in Glasgow and Edinburgh.

DEMOCRACY IN PRACTICE

It was not always easy to keep to the democratic ideal; on occasion the internal dynamics of the WFL paralleled the WSPU and the Pankhursts. Allegiance to Charlotte Despard, the WFL President from 1909 until 1918, provided cohesion. However, although she was a highly popular figure, her idiosyncratic style of leadership caused difficulties.[16] Her autocracy contributed to the resignation of seven members from the national executive committee in 1912.[17] As Alison Neilans pointed out, only through taking part in deliberations did 'the average woman of average parts' have an opportunity for self-development and self-government.[18] On the whole the League managed to prevent controversy turning into acrimonious confrontation on critical issues such as whether membership should preclude belonging to other political organisations, whether men should be admitted, or the nature of militancy. Annual conference verbatim minutes reveal Despard's obfuscatory addresses. For example, she accused Neilans of 'cowardliness' for not taking independent action during demonstrations following the Conciliation Bill's failure in 1912, without recognising that such spontaneous deeds contradicted democratic processes. It may have been casuistry when, calling for militant volunteers, Despard said:

> We have adopted militancy as a necessary weapon; it has an elastic quality. We can use it or we can refrain from using it.[19]

The policies which resulted from open debate were given wide interpretations which helped avoid further splits.

Initially the League contributed a page to the weekly journal *Women's Franchise*, produced by the Men's League for Women's Suffrage. Through the efforts of Marion Lawson, a national executive committee member, in 1909 the WFL launched its own weekly paper, *The Vote*.[20] Frequently in a financially precarious position, *The Vote*'s circulation peaked at over 13,000 in November 1913, slumping to 400 a week in 1919. Cicely Hamilton was proposed as one of the first editors, but did not take up the post, probably because the WFL was unable to offer a salary.[21] Consequently Marion Holmes and Mrs T. P. O'Connor were listed as the editors in the first issue. The League founded its own publishing company, the Minerva, whose shares were offered to members; Marion Lawson became the company's managing director. For many years *The Vote* was financially supported by Dr Elizabeth Knight.[22] Along with full reports of suffrage events, news from branches, and political commentaries, *The Vote* included short stories, plays, poetry, and book and theatre reviews.[23] It also gathered news from allied interest groups such as the National Society for the Prevention of Cruelty to Children, the Association for Moral and Social Hygiene (AMSH), the Ladies National Association for the Abolition of State Regulation of Vice (LNA), and the Criminal Law Amendment Committee.[24] This focus on issues which had long been priorities in the earlier women's movement demonstrates continuity from the nineteenth to the twentieth century. One of *The Vote*'s most notable and innovatory features was the column 'How Men Protect Women', a critique of a substantial pillar of prevailing ideologies of gender relationships. Before examining the League's initiatives here, I shall discuss its efforts to develop peaceable alternative strategies of resistance, its distinguishing contribution to the suffrage campaign.

HAMMERING OUT THE MEANINGS OF MILITANCY

While suffragette activities brought the movement to public prominence, especially after 1905, they also led to fragmentation of the women's movement, and to the deflection of attention from broader, substantive demands based on profound questioning of the relationships between men and women. To some extent the WFL was able to straddle that divide. Earlier I defined militancy as political dissent expressed through a range of tactics including direct action. As the suffrage campaign gathered momentum the League's interpretations of militancy evolved. In particular it developed the theory and practice of non-violent militancy, thus extending the repertoire of militant tactics. Allowing a degree of autonomy within a democratic framework enabled it to embrace diverse shades of opinion.

Initially both constitutional and militant societies worked together. Indeed, throughout the years of suffrage campaigning, some differences were not insurmountable. Throughout the period all wings of the suffrage movement united on occasion to demonstrate the strength of public feeling for their cause, for example, by massive popular demonstrations and joint deputations to government.

In 1906, a deputation on women's suffrage from all parliamentary supporters and representatives of twenty-five women's organisations met the Prime Minister, Campbell-Bannerman.[25] He recommended they practise 'the virtue of patience'. From that point NUWSS activity revived and WSPU militancy increased. By 1907 however, the question of militancy had become divisive. Mrs Cobden Sanderson probably expressed a common feeling of impatience with constitutional methods when she exclaimed, 'We have talked so much for the Cause; now let us suffer for it!' as she was arrested for the first time at a mass demonstration at the House of Commons in October in 1906.[26] On their release those who had been imprisoned were given a banquet of honour by the non-militant suffrage societies, despite some consternation among the leaders of the NUWSS.[27] By 1908 the NUWSS was protesting against the inclusion of WFL news in *Women's Franchise* and publicly severed its connections.[28] The prospect of women stepping so far outside their ascribed role as to participate in violent, noisy public demonstrations also alienated many radical suffragists, whose working-class sensibilities were vulnerable to charges of lack of respectability and who may have had more to lose than middle-class activists.[29]

The WFL had proclaimed itself a 'militant' society. What did that mean? In addition to conventional means of petitioning, lobbying government and seeking influence through the mass media, it took the protest onto the streets. Members spoke at street corners, outside factory gates and on propaganda tours with a WFL caravan. A team of speakers and organisers was gathered to campaign at elections and by-elections. Other activities included heckling and door-stepping politicians, picketing and demonstrations.

One way of developing non-violent militancy was to choose significant representational targets as a focus for action. Thus, the point at which the individual negotiates mechanisms of state, that is, legal, economic, bureaucratic and political institutions, was used to highlight the injustices suffered by women as citizens without the vote. Lawcourts, the tax system, the census count, the ballot box became sites for symbolic demonstrations which, being neither violent nor destructive, helped increase strategic possibilities.

In autumn 1907 members began a series of actions in police courts. When a militant activist appeared in court they would disrupt proceedings to object to voteless women being tried by man-made laws.

One form of WFL resistance which drew on historical precedent was tax resistance, which had been mooted early in the suffrage campaign. Dora Montefiore of the WSPU had successfully resisted taxation for two years from 1904, barricading her house against bailiffs for six weeks, an act perceived by some as the first act of 'constitutional militancy'. Billington-Greig, then a WSPU worker, had organised demonstrations in her support.[30] From 1907 the WFL leadership recommended tax resistance and some members were already refusing to pay taxes. These efforts to develop alternative strategies of resistance coincided with those suggested by Despard, a friend of Montefiore, who had discussed *satyagraha,* a form of spiritual resistance which might involve civil disobedience.

For some time WFL members debated the question of militancy and its various forms. Its legitimacy was argued by Billington-Greig who cited historical resistances such as the Non-Conformist Tax Resistance League, the Chartists and the Corn Law League as influences.[31] Opinions varied: activists, whose frequent experiences of hostility had inured them to caution, were in favour of provocative militant action; others thought any possibility of injury should define the limits. Besides differential class perspectives, there was dissonance between provincial rank-and-file members and urban enthusiasts.[32] Not least were the practicalities of co-ordinating militant acts when members were beset by the opposing pulls of spontaneity and democratic decision-making.[33]

As Christabel Pankhurst observed, aggression by women was far more threatening to the social fabric than men's violence; accordingly reactions to militancy could be extreme.[34] The associated risks, at a time when middle-class women received social opprobium merely for speaking at open-air meetings or parading with sandwich boards to sell newspapers, should not be discounted. Several times the windows of the WFL publicity caravan were smashed and the organisers and supporters harassed. Such hostility and the likelihood of physical abuse from police and public, arrest and imprisonment, might mean suffragettes would incur serious hardship and financial loss, particularly working women, mothers, women with dependants and provincial members operating within local communities.[35]

An attitude of 'passive resistance' towards all government business was proposed in November 1908 and the resolution that 'we do not set out to damage persons or property' was supported unanimously by the national executive committee.[36] In 1909 Edith How Martyn defined militancy as:

> the spirit of self-sacrifice which leads its members to protest against the exclusion of women from citizenship even when the result of that protest is the prison cell. [37]

Controversy about the value of active militancy flared up again in 1909 after the 'ballot box' protest by Alison Neilans and Margaret Chapin which was intended to be a symbolic action directly disrupting the voting process. They poured an inky substance into a ballot box at the Bermondsey by-election. Both were arrested, found guilty and imprisoned.[38] Both went on hunger-strike and were forcibly fed.[39] Much was learned from the experience.

The gender and class bias of the judicial system had been fully demonstrated. Whereas upper-class prisoners were sometimes released on the grounds of ill-health, poor health and a working-class background had not prevented Mrs Chapin's forcible feeding. Supporters of the protesters had been refused entry to the trials which added fuel to the WFL campaign of protest against such discrimination in the judicial system. New rules had been invented by the Home Office to prevent the prisoners receiving support.[40] Reactions in the League varied; some supported the protest but others were very disturbed, partly because they had read biased and ill-informed reports in the national press immediately following the incident on 28 October.[41] Initially newspapers reported that the by-election presiding officer, Mr Thorley, had been injured in the protest; Mrs Chapin was charged with throwing some noxious fluid over him causing grievous bodily harm. In fact the protesters had carefully consulted Edith How Martyn (whose husband was a scientist) about the fluid to ensure that it was not harmful. In the mêlée immediately following the incident, Thorley had been splashed with the inky fluid, some of it going in his eye, whereupon a colleague had applied ammonia mistakenly thinking it was an antidote. At the trial on 24 November, Thorley himself told the court the injury 'was caused accidentally'. Mrs Chapin's defence reiterated there had been no intention to cause any injury whatsoever and the judge directed the jury to convict her for common assault rather than the more serious grievous bodily harm.[42] Nevertheless, inaccurate reports in the national papers had by then exacerbated the situation throwing into sharper focus the differences within the League. In the suffrage papers, *The Vote* provided long and detailed accounts of the case and *Votes for Women*, the WSPU journal, reported it in a factual manner without a great deal of emotive material.

It was important, too, for the WFL to distance itself from the extremities of WSPU agitation. It needed to maintain the publicity value and shock tactics of militancy without provoking further anti-suffrage backlashes or counter-productive sentiments from the public. By 1912, when the WSPU was escalating attacks on government property, the WFL annual conference discussed the proposal that militancy was 'any kind of protest involving the risk of imprisonment'. Tax resistance was excluded but, as Despard argued, since women were being imprisoned for tax refusal, militancy should also include these forms of resistance.[43] Progressively the WFL's interpretation of militancy became much wider than that of the WSPU. There was a firm theoretical basis and in practice the League's flexibility meant that individuals could choose whether to participate or not.

Although there was strong support for its establishment as a WFL branch, the Women's Tax Resistance League (WTRL) was created (in October 1909) as a separate organisation. Hence it may be said that through the WFL the political principle of 'No Taxation without Representation' was developed to promote women's enfranchisement. Members of the WTRL were drawn from a number of suffrage societies including the NUWSS and the WSPU, evidence of co-operation and networking among all shades of opinion.

NON-VIOLENT MILITANCY

To maximise publicity, flair, imagination and efficient planning were necessary for non-violent militant actions, many of which, as I have said, were highly symbolic – and fun. Often they required considerable daring and panache. When Muriel Matters chained herself to the grille of the House of Commons Ladies Gallery in 1908, she provoked an awkward situation: should Commons' business be adjourned for the sake of a disenfranchised woman? To remove her, the grille had to be taken down and it was never replaced. In one night that year, 5,000 proclamations demanding votes for women were stuck up by League members. When permission to distribute handbills was refused in 1909, Muriel Matters took to a hot-air balloon to scatter leaflets over London. After the Prime Minister, Asquith, had refused to see a deputation, the League organised a massive picket of House of Commons sittings which lasted from 5 July to 28 October 1909, an aggregated total of 14,000 hours.[44] Members from all over Britain participated, an indication of effective organisation on a national scale. The pickets varied, one night there would be a group of working-class women, another a group of graduates. It was described by H.G. Wells as:

> extraordinarily impressive – infinitely more impressive than the feeble-forcible 'ragging' of the more militant section.[45]

In 1912 from a boat on the Thames Nina Boyle and Edith Watson harangued MPs taking tea on the terrace of the Houses of Parliament, an effective propaganda exercise, admired even by political opponents.[46] Nina Boyle, who rose to prominence in the League after 1911, gave fresh impetus to WFL agitation over male domination of the police and judiciary. In one instance she and five other League members chained themselves to the doors of Marylebone magistrates' court, giving fictitious names when arrested and imprisoned, despite court officials' full knowledge of their identity. The WFL initiated the boycott of the 1911 Census, which was taken up by both the WSPU and conventional suffrage societies, once they had realised that the form of the protest would appeal to many ordinary members. It gave a feeling of solidarity across the movement and was a rare instance of effective militant protest which did not result in confrontation, physical abuse from crowds or police, or imprisonment.[47] Thus the League initiated wide-ranging tactics of active and passive resistance to create its hall-mark of non-violent militancy.

GRASS-ROOTS DEMOCRACY

For those members who had little stomach for militant acts, yet who believed passionately in women's enfranchisement, the WFL offered alternatives at grass-roots level. Because democracy was a guiding principle, rank-and-file members had opportunities to develop initiatives of their own. Branches provided the facility to develop non-hierarchical ways of working and to debate issues of concern to many women. In its regular recording of news of branch activities, *The Vote* depicts the less glamorous but essential staple of political and democratic participation. Branches discussed a range of topics: the impact on women of government reform such as the National Insurance Act or old age pensions; women's employment, pay, working conditions and unionisation; education, health, marriage and divorce reform and sexual relationships. At local level the potential for collective action was realised through practical schemes to improve the quality of women's lives (for example, in demanding more lodging houses for working-class women), to give support to striking women workers, and to create schemes to improve the health and welfare of women and children.

Other suffrage societies were, of course, concerned with such issues but, as Eustance argues, the development of a 'broad based platform of reforming issues' alongside the League's commitment to non-violent militancy, generated a woman-centred political culture within the WFL.[48] Through engaging in such a culture many women gained the experience and expertise necessary to make substantial contributions to local government and welfare politics. With hindsight we can see how the crystallisation of feminist demands around women's enfranchisement tended to obscure former wider visions of social change. The nineteenth-century movement had demanded reform in many areas in the pursuit of women's emancipation. Previous campaigns to reform relationships between the sexes were extended by the WFL or individual League members. It is to these aspects of the wider programme that I now turn.

THE WOMEN'S FREEDOM LEAGUE AND SEXUAL POLITICS 1910–1914

Generally the turn of the century saw the breaking-up of very traditional attitudes towards sexual matters. Some of this was due to earlier successes of the women's movement; for example, the passing of the Married Women's Property Acts and the public debates of the late 1880s about marriage and a woman's right to control her own body. By the Edwardian era fears of a sexual revolution had helped create what was popularly designated the 'sex war'.

On the whole the WFL public stance on controversial topics tended to be similar to that of other suffrage organisations. It did, however, provide an arena for individuals to extend the frontiers of discussion and overall its awareness of and interest in gender politics were more sustained. There was a strong nucleus of radicalism on sexual questions which included some attempts to examine them in relation to class.[49] Some individuals continued to emphasise women's purity and sexual passivity, laying the burden of morality on women; others held notions of an active female sexuality, together with the view that men should exercise more self-control. Participation in the suffrage campaign itself had led to much more open discussion on sexual matters between women of all classes according to Neilans, an authority on public attitudes to sexual relationships.[50]

The founding of *The Freewoman* in 1911 by Dora Marsden illustrates something of members' desires and difficulties in establishing uninhibited debate.[51] Originally Marsden hoped the WFL would sponsor her plans to produce an independent journal to provide an intellectual, wide-ranging forum for the women's movement as a whole. Edith How Martyn responded enthusiastically:

> it would be a joy to me to work to make the WFL the intellectual leader of the Suffrage Societies.[52]

However, Marsden's request for complete editorial control and a salary proved impractical.[53] Additionally, the WFL was anxious to avoid public controversy which would reflect badly on its suffrage work. For a short time *The Freewoman* did provide space to debate political, economic and sexual issues, but its criticism of the suffrage movement and its advocacy of revolutionary moral as well as political systems had limited appeal.[54] Several WFL national executive members wrote for *The Freewoman*, including the then Treasurer, Constance Tite, and Katharine Vulliamy, Bessie Drysdale and Nina Boyle.[55]

By 1911, *The Vote* exemplified changing attitudes between generations. It expounded the post-Victorian belief that knowledge would protect girls and women better than a spurious 'innocence'. It criticised the social purity movement's obsession with 'rescue' of prostitutes, suggesting the major cause of prostitution, economic necessity, could be eliminated by decent wages for girls and women.[56] The rights of all women to have free access to public space had been an issue in the campaign to repeal the Contagious Diseases (CD) Acts of the 1880s. Proponents of women's emancipation and the social purity movement had worked together then. Despite co-operation on issues like this, they proposed very different solutions to a number of problems, particularly on prostitution and venereal disease.[57] Feminists deplored the curtailment of women's rights and freedoms perceived by many others as the best solution. These ideological differences continued to be marked in a constellation of issues in public discourses on sexuality, although feminist and social purity co-operation included working to secure the 1912 Criminal Law Amendment Act.[58]

When she resigned from the WFL in 1911 Billington-Greig expressed the view that women's emancipation from 'sex-servitude' and the creation of a new spirit were becoming obscured by the suffrage movement's obsession with the vote.[59] In 1913 she created further controversy and dismay in both camps by accusing the social purity and feminist alliance of engendering moral panic about what was popularly called the 'white slave trade'.[60]

In 1914 the WFL annual conference discussed birth control but was not prepared to endorse it publicly. Membership in the League of the prominent Malthusians Alice Drysdale Vickery and Bessie Drysdale, and of other women who were prepared to defy convention to practise their moral convictions, suggests acceptance and no great tension.[61] At an individual level they were prepared to subsume personal differences. While members privately supported greater sexual freedom for women, it seems their freedom to speak out was restricted by the need to be seen as impeccably respectable.

THE NINETEENTH-CENTURY INHERITANCE

The WFL carried forward some elements of nineteenth-century campaigns, particularly those concerning domestic violence, child abuse, sexual abuse and harassment, and women's right to control their own bodies. As lack of space prevents a full exploration, I shall focus on domestic violence and sexual abuse, touching on prostitution and birth control, before concluding with a few examples of the ways in which networks begun in the League were continued.

Reforms to protect children – for example, from incest and by raising the age of consent – had been demanded earlier.[62] Wife-beating had been identified in 1878 by Frances Power Cobbe as one consequence of women's economic and sexual subordination but nineteenth-century campaigns were not mobilised around family violence directly.[63] In the case of birth control, few reformists of any kind were prepared to advocate it publicly, although Alice Vickery had long been campaigning for this unpopular cause.

HOW MEN PROTECT WOMEN

In the early years of the twentieth century, domestic violence and sexual abuse were unmentionable topics. With a limited sexual lexicon and without access to information, women had little power to transform this situation. They were literally excluded from the arena for at that time women were expelled from court when criminal offences involving violence and sexual behaviour were being heard; witnesses and victims, including children, had to give evidence in an all-male law court.

On behalf of the WFL Nina Boyle and Edith Watson set out to change the situation. They wished to record the prevalence of many types of domestic violence and sexual abuse and aimed to bear witness to the injustices suffered by females through a biased judicial system.

To a large extent the initial impetus for demanding reform arose directly from the militants' own experiences of dealing with the police and courts. They were probably much more conscious of the realities of the legal underworld than women who had never been in trouble with the law.[64] Early in 1912, Edith Watson appealed in *The Vote* for WFL members to monitor court proceedings. Having spent some time in courts on behalf of arrested militants, she had been appalled at the number of cases of assault and indecency, the way victims and witnesses were treated and a value system which placed greater emphasis on property than on the physical and emotional well-being of females.[65] She compared Emily Wilding Davison's sentence of six months' imprisonment for attempting to burn letters with a four-month sentence for a man's repeated 'abominable and atrocious' assaults on a girl of seven.[66] She began the column:

> to show not only how women suffer from acts of violence, but how slight a penalty the law exacts for such violence in comparison with crimes against property.[67]

The idea and the ironic title of the feature, 'How Men Protect Women', intended to expose the flaws in mythologies about men's protection of women, were not original. A similar rhetorical response to refusing women's emancipation had been made years earlier.[68] For three years in nearly every issue of *The Vote* Boyle and Watson listed daily occurrences in the lawcourts. Four pages of *The Vote* were given over to child abuse in June 1913 and in September the same year a special issue was devoted to the judicial system. Correspondents from WFL branches all over the country monitored court proceedings locally and extracts from newspapers and periodicals were reprinted. Contingent as it was on volunteers, coverage tended to be inconsistent and patchy. Their methods and data would be judged inadequate by current standards, yet the work was an attempt to quantify and analyse intractable social problems.

Dissatisfaction with the judicial system crystallised in the WFL around two main issues: the injustices suffered by females in the whole system and women's exclusion from lawcourts when indecency cases were heard. As evidence mounted, a critique informed by feminism began to emerge. Boyle and Watson analysed many aspects of policing and the legal system and explored issues at the heart of gender politics. These included widely held conceptualisations about two kinds of women, the 'pure' and 'impure'; the impact of sexual double standards on the law and its administration; the lack of women's participation and effects of male control of the judicial system; the ways legal jargon neutralised the sufferings of women and girls; problems of corroborative evidence for cases of sexual abuse and the difficulties and traumas for women and children giving evidence; the lack of compassion for battered women, for unmarried mothers, for the ignorant and the very poor. Their stress on male violence as a cause of women's subordination suggests they were working towards a theory about incipient male power. The view that the female body is a site of oppression is a radical tenet; in the context of violence this is the case at a personal level. Women's bodies become the nexus for gender and power at a social level because the subjection of women and girls is reinforced by power structures within the social system. Hence Boyle and Watson's work can be seen as a forerunner to late twentieth-century radical feminism.

Partly through these efforts there was by 1914 more general public awareness of the value that women officials could bring to the system. The presence of a police matron to help female prisoners and witnesses was being gradually accepted. Following a series of appeals against banishment, the right for women to attend all court proceedings on the same basis as men was upheld.[69] Naturally, the WFL demanded that women should have entry to the legal profession.[70] Another solution was to found a women's police service which would act in the interests of all women. Within three weeks of the start of the First World War, Boyle and Watson turned their attention to this prospect.

A WOMEN'S POLICE SERVICE – FOR WOMEN

Prior to 1914 there had been spasmodic interest and discussion about the value of women serving at police stations. Some social purity and philanthropic societies had tried a few very small-scale experiments with female volunteers on patrol in public places to guard the moral welfare of girls, part of the crusade which led to the Criminal Amendment Act of 1912. When a call for Special Constables to help cope with the social upheavals of the war was made in August 1914 Nina Boyle responded quickly. Under WFL auspices she organised a volunteer force, the Women Police Volunteers (WPV). She designed the uniform and appealed in *The Vote* for money to help equip the group.[71] It was essential to have volunteers from all classes. They wanted a women's police service to reflect women's priorities, not to cushion middle-class uneasiness about the state of the streets, as was very much the case with another group formed under the leadership of Margaret Damer Dawson, a member of the repressive National Vigilance Association. Whereas Damer Dawson's group comprised mostly middle- and upper-class women who saw their patrols as a mission to prevent prostitutes soliciting in public and to control the sexual activity of working-class females, members of the WPV were drawn from all social classes. However, to avoid duplication the two groups amalgamated and worked together for a while.

As the war progressed, the police and the military were given sweeping powers; for example, to impose curfews on women in areas where there were military camps. Yet again many suffragists rallied to oppose attempts to reintroduce regulations similar to the Contagious Diseases Acts made under Defence of the Realm Acts (DoRA).[72] When the women's police service was asked to patrol a curfew made under DoRA in 1915, open conflict broke out between the two factions. Damer Dawson was prepared to collude with male-dominated authorities in order to obtain official acceptance of women police, whereas Boyle and Watson felt feminist principles should be paramount. But Damer Dawson won the support of most members; she renamed her new association the Women Police Service and placed it at the disposal of the state and the military. The remnants of the WFL-inspired police service continued for a little while but by 1916 they had disbanded. Official ambivalence about women as police continued. Moreover, the women's police patrols themselves were often unpopular with the young women they were supposedly protecting.[73]

CAMPAIGNING CONTINUED – AFTER 1914

When the First World War broke out the WFL sustained many aspects of its work at national and local levels. It organised the Women's Suffrage National Aid Corps which provided a varied programme of work to assist women and children whose lives had been overturned by the effects of the war. Although major militant action ceased, the League carried on campaigning and was prominent in protesting against the restrictions on women's freedom dictated, ostensibly, by military needs. Like other suffrage organisations it strove to contain the differences thrown up by members' allegiances to patriotism or pacifism.

In the 1918 election seventeen women stood as parliamentary candidates, among them WFL members Charlotte Despard, who resigned as president that year, Eunice Murray and Edith How Martyn.[74] Once the objective of securing women's enfranchisement had been partially achieved, the WFL expanded its programme to include the rights of women to sit as peers in the

House of Lords, to receive equal pay and to have access to all professions. It continued to pursue an equal moral standard and demand more women as magistrates, in the police force and throughout the prison service.

As the 1920s and 1930s progressed other political imperatives such as socialism, internationalism and the search for peace took their toll on membership. For some, class and party political affiliations proved stronger than the aim of women's equality. In order to retain a broad consensus the League focused on recording women's progress and achievements in all fields, celebrating when females broke through the barriers of male preserves. It continued its work for equal rights and to promote a feminist view; for example, bringing together twenty-one women's organisations in 1940 to ensure women's interests were recognised in wartime and in 1946 criticising the Beveridge proposals which saw married women as dependants and not entitled to benefits in their own right.[75] The League finally wound up in 1961.

Suffrage campaigning at every level had been a significant experience for many members whose politicisation underwrote subsequent work in their communities on behalf of women and children. Eustance points out how participation in the woman-centred political culture of the WFL contributed to feminism's post-war development.[76] The later trajectories of some WFL members also illustrate the ways in which political activism during the suffrage campaign underwrote work to reform sexual relationships.

'OUR JOB IS TO FREE WOMEN FROM THE CONTROL OF MEN'[77]

During the war Nina Boyle worked with the Scottish Women's Hospital Unit and after the Russian Revolution travelled in Russia with Lilian Lenton, another suffragette.[78] They helped establish what became the Save the Children Fund on whose committee Boyle was to serve for over twenty years. She became impatient with feminism's dilution with socialism and pacifism.[79] She was to develop her views on male violence, continuing to protest about female sexual subjugation. This included questioning customs in British colonies such as child-marriage in India and south-east Africa, the *Mui-Tsai* system in Hong King (where very young girls were sold into domestic slavery or concubinage) and the practice of female genital excision in Africa.[80] Her writing influenced Eleanor Rathbone and the Duchess of Atholl to seek reform of the latter customs in the 1930s; in the 1950s Edith Watson was writing to the national press about the issue in Kenya.

As already mentioned, women's equal right of access to public spaces had been part of nineteenth-century campaigns. Alison Neilans continued this work through her leadership of the Association for Moral and Social Hygiene. For thirty years she maintained the feminist case in public debate on such topics as prostitution, the international trade in women and the sexual abuse of children, becoming well known internationally for her work on behalf of prostitutes. In the 1920s, Boyle and Neilans co-ordinated campaigns to demand more women police and to expose the extent of child abuse; in the early 1930s Neilans published Boyle's work on women's sexual slavery.

Although birth control was not part of the programme of Victorian campaigners for women's emancipation, the question of reproductive control was inherent in, for example, demands for an equal moral standard and companionate marriage. To a few WFL members it was 'a struggle for freedom of peculiar interest to women'.[81] Initially Alice Vickery and Bessie Drysdale worked to promote birth control through the Malthusian League. Edith How Martyn joined them in 1910. Together they helped establish one of the first birth-control clinics in Britain in 1921. From 1915 How Martyn spent forty years aiming to provide information about reliable, safe methods of contraception in Britain and all over the world. She co-ordinated a national campaign initiated by Labour women in 1923 to allow contraceptive information to be given at local authority welfare clinics.[82] The group she founded in 1929, the Birth Control International Information Centre, was a forerunner of the Family Planning Association and the International Planned Parenthood Association.

With Lilian Lenton, How Martyn also founded the Suffragette Fellowship in 1928, the year when female suffrage on the same terms as male voters was gained. The fact that it was for *suffragettes* rather than suffrage campaigners suggests that the recollection of militancy and suffering was important, a common bond. It demonstrates their view of the importance of shared experience in shaping people's identities.[83]

Fragmentary and tenuous as the evidence is, I feel it represents a substantial amount of cross-fertilisation, of communication and support, which grew out of the common bond of feminist ideals and friendship in the WFL.

CONCLUSION

Membership of the WFL during the crucial seven years of the Edwardian suffrage campaign gave women opportunities to participate in a vigorous organisation run by women at a time when they were marginalised in mainstream politics. Alternative strategies of resistance were created through the development of non-violent militancy, a highly visible means of drawing attention to the cause. At the same time, adherence to democratic principles provided the framework for all members to have the chance to explore non-hierarchical methods of working which fostered their politicisation. Because they had laid a solid foundation of action to improve the lives of women, many members continued to campaign on several fronts for decades. Some of these issues, in health, welfare and sexual relationships, stemmed from earlier bids for emancipation. On this account the

Women's Freedom League may be seen to bridge nineteenth- and twentieth-century demands for women's freedom.

NOTES

1 Here, militancy is taken as political dissent expressed through a broad range of tactics including direct action which involved legal or illegal tactics and civil disobedience. For a discussion of the term feminism see N. F. Cott, *The grounding of modern feminism* (New Haven, Yale University Press, 1987), pp. 4–5.

2 As differences between suffragists and suffragettes were not clear-cut, I use the term suffragist to cover all campaigners for women's suffrage, both constitutional and militant. The term suffragette is used to denote militant activists.

3 Claire Eustance's study of the WFL examines the development of a specifically feminist critique of inequalities in gender relations and the ways in which competing claims of class, party and political priorities were played out after the vote was won. C. Eustance, *'Daring to be free': the evolution of women's political identities in the Women's Freedom League 1907–1930*, DPhil thesis, University of York, 1993. I am grateful to her for sharing aspects of her research with me. See also C. Eustance, Meanings of militancy: the ideas and practice of political resistance in the Women's Freedom League, 1907–14, in M. Joannou and J. Purvis (eds), *The women's suffrage movement: new feminist perspectives* (Manchester, Manchester University Press, 1998), pp. 51–76.

4 For accounts of the continuities in suffrage campaigning, see J. Liddington and J. Norris, *One hand tied behind us* (London, Virago, 1985) and S. S. Holton, *Suffrage days: stories from the women's suffrage movement* (London, Routledge, 1996).

5 L. Garner, *Stepping stones to women's liberty: feminist ideas in the women's suffrage movement 1900–1918* (London, Heinemann, 1984), pp. 28–29.

6 Garner, *Stepping stones*, p. 35.

7 S. Newsome, *The Women's Freedom League 1907–1957* (London, WFL pamphlet, n.d.), Fawcett Library, London, 324.62306041. See also T. Billington-Greig, The birth of the Women's Freedom League, in C. McPhee and A. Fitzgerald (eds), *The non-violent militant: selected writings of Teresa Billington-Greig* (London, Routledge & Kegan Paul, 1987), pp. 102–108 and E. How Martyn, *The Vote*, I, 7, 9 December 1909. Fenwick Miller was an ILP member and the first woman arrested for militancy in London.

8 T. Billington-Greig, *The militant suffrage movement: emancipation in a hurry* (London, Frank Palmer, 1911), pp. 87–88.

9 Eustance argues that tensions were felt particularly over militancy. Local branches evolved alternative strategies and activities which led to greater diversity. Eustance, *'Daring to be free'*, pp. 90–91.

10 How Martyn, *The Vote*, I, 7, 9 December 1909.

11 *Women's Franchise*, 10 September 1908. For example, the League campaigned on behalf of unmarried mothers. In 1908 it supported nineteen-year-old Daisy Lord, who had murdered her new-born baby. It organised demonstrations to secure her immediate release from prison. Provincial members established a local committee to protest at the treatment in 1911 of Daisy Turner, who had become pregnant as a result of rape. She killed the child at birth and within three weeks had been gaoled. The committee complained about the handling of the case, sending a memorial to the Home Secretary. *The Vote*, V, 105, 28 October 1911.

12 Garner, *Stepping stones*, pp. 34–35. Eustance, *'Daring to be free'*, pp. 56–60.

13 Garner, *Stepping stones*, pp. 34–38. For an examination of their political associations, see Eustance, *'Daring to be free'*, pp. 61–62.

14 Thirteen branches were started in London by November 1907, *Women's Franchise*, 14 November 1907. Newsome seems to have confused London with nationwide branches. Newsome, *The WFL*, p. 2. The precise numbers of former WSPU members are unknown, according to Eustance, *'Daring to be free'*, pp. 53–64.

15 Garner, *Stepping stones*, p. 29. Because of its small membership the WFL was not eligible for affiliation to the International Woman Suffrage Alliance in 1915, a great disappointment. Eustance, *'Daring to be free'*, p. 258.

16 There are two biographies of Despard. M. Mulvihill, *Charlotte Despard: a biography* (London, Pandora, Unwin Hyman, 1989) and A. Linklater, *An unhusbanded life: Charlotte Despard, suffragette, socialist and Sinn Feiner* (London, Hutchinson, 1980).

17 Verbatim minutes WFL special conference, 27–28 April 1912, pp. 19–22. Fawcett Library, London. Among those who resigned were How Martyn, Alison Neilans and Bessie Drysdale.

18 Special conference minutes, 27–28 April 1912, p. 19.

19 Newsome, *The WFL*, p. 8. The third Conciliation Bill had been one of the best prospects for non-party solutions to legislation on women's enfranchisement.

20 Newsome, *The WFL*, p. 15. Marion Lawson joined the Women's Tax Resistance League (WTRL) and had her household goods sold after she refused to pay income tax.

21 L. Whitelaw, *The life and rebellious times of Cicely Hamilton* (London, The Women's Press, 1990), p. 103.

22 Knight, of the Knight's Castile Soap family, who was WFL Treasurer from 1913 onwards, gave generously to the WFL until her death in a car accident in 1933.

23 A front-page statement said the Editor was responsible for unsigned articles, whereas a by-line indicated the writer's own opinion was being expressed.

24 The LNA was founded in 1869 to work for the repeal of the Contagious Diseases Acts (CD Acts) in which discrimination against women was enshrined in law through legislation to inspect and control prostitutes to prevent the spread of venereal diseases. The Acts were repealed in 1886. Members also supported reforms such as the raising of the age of consent and the criminalisation of incest, through a series of amendments to the criminal law.

25 These included the NUWSS, WSPU, the Women's Co-operative Guild, socialist, Liberal and temperance organisations, women 'wage-earners', the textile workers and radical suffragists.

26 Recorded by Edith How Martyn, 24 October 1937. Reel 1, Group C 57.116, Suffragette Fellowship Collection, London Museum.

27 McPhee and Fitzgerald (eds), *The non-violent militant*, p. 6.

28 S. S. Holton, *Feminism and democracy: women's suffrage and reform politics 1900–1918* (Cambridge, Cambridge University Press, 1987), p. 48.

29 Letter to Millicent Garrett Fawcett from Eva Gore-Booth and Esther Roper, 25 October 1906, M. G. Fawcett Collection, M50/2, Manchester Public Library archives.

30 McPhee and Fitzgerald (eds), *The non-violent militant*, p. 104.

31 T. Billington-Greig, Notes on women's suffrage, Billington-Greig Papers, Box 399; Fawcett Library, London.

32 For an account of the contributions and differences between WFL local branches and national leadership, see Eustance, *'Daring to be free'*, pp. 88–144.

33 Verbatim minutes WFL fifth annual conference, 29 January 1910, pp. 9–17; special conference minutes WFL, 27–28 April, pp. 19–22.

34 Dale Spender, *Women of ideas and what men have done to them* (London, Routledge & Kegan Paul, Arc Paperbacks, 1983), p. 589.

35 Analysing suffragette accounts of imprisonment, June Purvis points to the range of backgrounds and social differences of the imprisoned women, not all of whom were middle-class or single, as has often been supposed. J. Purvis, Prison experiences of suffragettes in Edwardian Britain, *Women's History Review*, 14, 1, 1995. pp. 103–132.

36 National executive minutes WFL, November 1908.

37 How Martyn, *The Vote*, I, 7, 9 December, 1909.

38 *The Vote*, I, 6, 2 December 1909.

39 Ibid.; *The Vote*, I, 10, 30 December 1909; *The Vote*, I, 16, 12 February 1910.

40 *The Vote*, I, 16, 12 February 1912; *The Vote*, I, 10, 30 December 1909. See also Purvis, Prison experiences of the suffragettes, pp. 103–132.

41 Verbatim minutes WFL fifth annual conference, 29 January 1910, pp. 9–12; *The Vote*, I, 16, 12 February 1910; *The Vote*, II, 54, 5 November 1910.

42 *The Vote*, I, 6, 2 December 1909, pp. 62–63, 70; *Votes for Women*, III (new series), 90, 26 November 1909, p. 138.

43 Executive minutes WFL, 19–20 April 1912; *Manifesto militant action,* WFL pamphlet, 9 March 1912, Fawcett Library, London.

44 L. Housman, *The unexpected years* (London, Jonathan Cape, 1937), p. 267.

45 H. G. Wells, *The new Machiavelli* (London, Odhams Press, n.d.), p. 251.

46 M. Richardson, *Laugh a defiance* (London, Weidenfeld & Nicolson, 1953), p. 66. Constance Antonina (Nina) Boyle (1865–1943) was a brilliant speaker on the WFL's behalf, later acting as Despard's deputy. Edith Mary Watson (1888–1966) joined the WFL after hearing speeches on suffrage at Speakers' Corner, Hyde Park. She campaigned for many causes, among them the Divorce Law Reform Union and trade unionism, writing for the *Daily Herald* occasionally. I am grateful to her son, the late Squadron Leader Bernard Watson, for his help and allowing me access to her unpublished autobiography and newspaper cuttings collection.

47 Housman, *The unexpected years*, pp. 286–290.

48 Eustance, *'Daring to be free'*, p. 91.

49 Examining the WFL debates about sexuality, Claire Eustance indicates the shifts and conflicts in their discussions, pointing to class distinctions which were not successfully overcome. Eustance, *'Daring to be free'*, pp. 232–240.

50 A. Neilans, Changes in sex morality, in R. Strachey (ed.), *Our freedom and its results* (London, Hogarth, 1936), pp. 175–230. From 1913 onwards, Neilans (1884–1942) worked for the Ladies National Association for the Abolition of State Regulation of Vice (LNA), an organisation which fought for the Repeal of the Contagious Diseases Acts and for the legal rights of prostitutes. It became the Association for Moral and Social Hygiene (AMSH) in 1915.

51 Olive Banks states that Marsden was a member of the WFL; see O. Banks, *The biographical dictionary of British feminists*, Vol. I, *1800–1930* (Brighton, Wheatsheaf, 1985), pp. 120–121; however, Garner implies she applied to join when considering writing for them; L.Garner, *A brave and beautiful spirit: Dora Marsden 1882–1960* (Aldershot, Avebury, 1990), p. 52.

52 Letter from How Martyn to Dora Marsden, 26 March 1911, quoted in Garner, *Dora Marsden*, p. 52. Edith How Martyn (1875–1954), a graduate, gave up teaching for full-time suffrage campaigning.

53 Garner, *Dora Marsden*, pp. 51–52.

54 Ibid., p. 24.

55 Constance Tite was a member of the Criminal Law Amendment Committee which contained feminists and social purity crusaders. She advocated women police after having travelled abroad investigating policewomen's work.

56 *The Vote*, III, 88, 17 June 1911.
57 In the late 1870s a crusade against immorality was launched by the social purity movement, an amalgam of religious and moral organisations with some socialist, liberal and trade union associates. For an account of the relationships between feminism and social purity, see L. Bland, *Banishing the beast: English feminism and sexual morality 1885–1914* (Harmondsworth, Penguin, 1995). See also F. Mort, *Dangerous sexualities: medico-moral politics in England since 1830* (London, Routledge & Kegan Paul, 1987), pp. 117–119 and 126–130. Jeffreys presents a more positive view than Mort: S. Jeffreys, *The spinster and her enemies* (London, Pandora, 1985), pp. 6–26, as does Margaret Jackson in *The real facts of life* (London, Taylor & Francis, 1994), pp. 6–33.
58 From 1909 feminists and social purity activists sought reform on a number of issues through a Criminal Law Amendment Bill. Demands included raising the age of consent for girls to eighteen, control of homosexual importuning and reducing prostitution through punishing pimps. Known as the 'White Slave Act' the much reduced Act was passed in 1912; predictably, it resulted in further control of working-class women.
59 Billington-Greig, Women and government, in *The Freewoman*, 21 December 1911.
60 *The Shield*, XIV (new style), 145, October 1913, p. 96; *The Vote*, III, 190, 13 June 1913. The editor described it as an 'extraordinary article' and took 'strong objection' to Billington-Greig's criticisms of the suffrage movement's support of the Act. Very critical of conventional morality, especially the insistence on monogamy, Billington-Greig advocated 'free love'. Her own marriage included a nuptial agreement neutralising marriage and property laws. She wrote a pamphlet for the Malthusian League, *Commonsense on the population question*, in 1915. See also Eustance, '*Daring to be free*', pp. 243–244. Despite its racist connotations, I have used the term 'white slave trade' because it was used at the time.
61 Edith Watson lived with her lover before marriage. The Bradlaugh–Besant trial for publication of information about contraception took place in 1877. That same year Vickery, her partner Charles Drysdale and his brother George, founded the Neo-Malthusian League to promote Malthusian doctrines on population. Bessie Drysdale was Alice Drysdale Vickery's daughter-in-law. How Martyn felt the WFL failed to appreciate Alice Vickery fully because of her unconventionality, thinking Vickery's '50 years spadework' for 'the women's side' of birth control issues went unrecognised by British feminists. How Martyn, note, Wellcome Institute, London, SA/FPA A23/58.7; and letters to Margaret Sanger during 1929, Sophia Smith Collection of Women's History Archive, Smith College, Northampton, Mass.
62 For girls the age of consent was raised from thirteen to sixteen by the 1885 Criminal Law Amendment Act. Incest was criminalised in 1908.
63 Lambertz argues that late-Victorian feminists' investment in the family prevented a concerted effort on the issue. J. Lambertz, Feminists and the politics of wife-beating, in H. Smith (ed.), *British feminists in the twentieth century* (Aldershot, Edward Elgar, 1990), pp. 25–43. See note 67.
64 *The Vote*, IX, 242, 12 June 1914.
65 *The Vote*, V, 120, 10 February 1912.
66 Ibid.
67 Ibid.
68 The title varied, often appearing as 'How (Some) Men Protect Women'. Earlier campaigns to reform married women's property law had pointed to the violence women suffered from their husbands. Cases where courts had treated brutal men leniently were listed by *The Englishwomen's Suffrage Journal* and the

Englishwoman's Review. See J. Rendall, Citizenship, culture and civilization: the languages of British suffragists 1866–1874, in C. Daley and M. Nolan (eds), *Suffrage and beyond: international feminist perspectives* (Auckland, Auckland University Press, 1994), pp. 127–150. I am grateful to Jane Rendall for this reference.

69 A decision by the Law Lords in 1913 confirmed that the banning of women from courts was illegal. *The Law Times Reports,* 9, September 1913–February 1914, pp. 1–22.

70 WFL member Helena Normanton later became the first woman King's Counsel. She registered as a student at the Middle Temple within twenty-four hours of the passing of the Sex Disqualification (Removal Act) in January 1920.

71 When Edith Watson wore her uniform for the first time at the Old Bailey she attracted some excellent publicity.

72 Like the CD Acts of the 1860s, these were measures to protect the military and to attempt to control the spread of venereal disease through compulsory medical examinations, directed principally at women.

73 For a general discussion of the early days of the women police see: J. Lock, *The British policewoman: her story* (London, Robert Hale, 1979).

74 Newsome, *The WFL,* p. 13. Eunice Murray was president of the Glasgow branch of the WFL; she wrote for *The Vote.*

75 For an account of feminist activity from 1914 onwards, see J. Alberti, *Beyond suffrage: feminists in war and peace 1914–28* (London, Macmillan, 1989), and M. Pugh, *Women and the women's movement in Britain 1914–1959* (London, Macmillan, 1992).

76 Eustance, *'Daring to be free',* pp. 198–251.

77 N. Boyle, letter, *Jus Suffragii,* June 1927.

78 Lilian Lenton was famous for outwitting the police during the 'Cat-and-Mouse' episodes. She was known as the 'tiny, wily, elusive Pimpernel'. *The Times,* obituary, 4 November 1972.

79 Boyle was disappointed that women were not effectively represented at the newly formed League of Nations.

80 I use the general term here to cover a range of practices.

81 How Martyn. Printed invitation, June 1915.

82 It was not until 1967 that public provision of contraception was made freely available to all women.

83 Nym Mayhall suggests Fellowship members created stylised narratives: L. E. Nym Mayhall, Creating the 'suffragette spirit': British feminism and the historical imagination, *Women's History Review,* 4, 3, 1995, pp. 319–344. Members of the Suffragette Fellowship recorded their experiences of activism for an archive which became a principle source of information about the suffrage campaign, now housed at the Museum of London.

9

WOMEN TEACHERS AND THE SUFFRAGE CAMPAIGN

Arguments for professional equality

Alison Oram

Women teachers in state elementary schools were major players in the suffrage cause. In cities throughout England and Wales, they contributed to each
of the key women's suffrage groups, and brought the question into their own
professional body, the National Union of Teachers (NUT). Women teachers
felt passionately about the links between their professional status, citizenship
and the vote. In arguing for the suffrage resolution in a debate at the NUT
conference in 1912, Miss Cleghorn, who had been elected first woman president of the union in 1911, stressed her elevated position in the union and her
contribution to the community:

> They thought her good enough to be their President. (Cheers) She
> had not a vote. ('Shame!') She was a householder; she paid rates;
> she paid income tax – ('Oh!') – not much – (laughter) – but she had
> no vote.

She went on to argue that in their professional work women teachers were
entrusted with the task of creating citizens, but for a state which did not
properly recognise the teachers themselves as citizens:

> They earned their own living. They had to teach the children citi-
> zenship, loyalty and patriotism, and all that was necessary to make
> them good citizens, but were thought not to have the qualifications
> for the vote.[1]

Miss Cleghorn was a moderate suffragist and part of the union establishment, and her strong support for women's suffrage reflected the feelings
of the majority of women in the union, many of whom were far more militant than she was. In this speech she was making the equal rights arguments

typically favoured by teacher suffragists, that women deserved the vote as citizens, as taxpayers, and as members of a significant profession.

Sandra Holton has argued that the movement for women's suffrage 'gave ever-increasing prominence to an essentialist case for women's political emancipation', based on women's valuable contribution to political life as a consequence of their sex-specific natures and experiences. Women's motherly voice was needed to shape questions of social reform, suffragists believed. She goes on to argue that suffragism exhibited a range of varying emphases and convictions. A humanistic or equal rights case for women's suffrage, based on women's and men's common attributes, was much less pronounced in the suffrage movement, but never completely abandoned.[2] What is interesting about women teachers is that, at the height of the suffrage movement in 1908–1914, they were part of this latter group and did make their arguments for the vote on the basis of equal rights. Why, and how, did they take such a distinctive position?

Some research on women teachers has assumed that their feminist politics was swept into the mainstream in this period. Discussing their support for the teaching of domestic subjects, Dina Copelman has argued that women teachers moved towards adopting the language of gender difference in the years before the First World War. But in their campaigning for the vote (and in their arguments for equal pay and promotion prospects), the evidence shows that they did just the opposite; that they shunned gender-specific arguments and favoured a rhetoric of equality, justice and professionalism.[3] Women teachers saw the suffrage struggle as deeply connected to their idea of themselves as professional teachers. When they made reference to their work, they did not present it (as they might easily have done) as womanly work with children, but as professional work of national importance, building their case on their strongly felt professional identity, their skills and rights as teachers and as women workers. At the same time feminist teachers formed an active part of the wider suffrage movement which was arguing for the vote predominantly on the grounds of women's special values and attributes.

This chapter will examine the ideas of professionalism and equality used by suffragist teachers and their origins. Women teachers argued their case in contrasting political forums: the large mixed elementary teachers' union, the NUT, of which they were members; and both militant and non-militant organisations within the women's suffrage movement in the years leading up to the First World War. Their subjectivity – the way they saw themselves – affected the types of political activity they undertook in these organisations. The *effects* of their political aims and arguments were considerable, especially within the NUT, where their challenge disrupted male assumptions about the meaning of professionalism and profoundly split the union along gender lines.

WOMEN TEACHERS' PROFESSIONAL IDENTITY

The political rhetoric used by women teachers in arguing for their right to the vote had an important relationship to their identity as teachers. Women teachers' sense of themselves as professional women – which many developed into a feminist political language of equality – stemmed from their choices and perceptions when entering the occupation, their position as an academic elite, and was further enhanced by the financial investment in their training, and their relationship with their professional association, the NUT.

While elementary school teaching was a respectable and feminine occupation for women which was relatively easy to enter, it was also represented as a profession, offering a rewarding life-long career after higher education and training. It was work with children, but it was also intellectual work, public service, and it offered some approximation to professional material rewards. By female standards it provided a good, secure income for the working-class and lower middle-class girls who joined the occupation. The process of competing for teacher-training places enhanced women teachers' sense of themselves as an academic elite, while state and familial financial support for their education and training confirmed their professional worth. Many women teachers forged a strong professional identity and an attachment to and a pride in their work.[4]

Professionalism proved a congenial identity for women teachers and provided one route to assert their interests as feminists. The general language of professionalism was one of liberalism, individualism and merit.[5] While these concepts were gendered in the nineteenth century and later as the attributes of the gentleman (and indeed the formal routes to a liberal classical education were closed to women), nevertheless they could also be utilised by women to argue for participation in the professions and the public sphere generally.[6] Nineteenth- and early twentieth-century feminist activity often used the rhetoric of liberal individualism and equal rights, for example, as well as making gender-specific claims.[7] Women teachers, accepted into a professionalising occupation, found the meritocratic notions contained within the idea of the 'profession' appealing.

Joining a teachers' association itself enhanced a sense of professional identity. The NUT, set up in 1870, aimed to recruit all qualified (certificated) teachers in elementary schools and improve their employment position. Professionalisation is a gendered process and has been associated with masculinity and the exclusion of women from an occupation, the higher professions of medicine and law being obvious examples in this period. But rather than engaging in processes of exclusion, the teachers' associations offered women teachers validation of their professional identity (since membership was open only to qualified teachers) and the possibility of obtaining further benefits by upgrading the occupation as a whole and their place in it. The professional values and benefits offered *could* be read as ungendered, and though mixed, the NUT did not make distinctions of sex in entry or office-holding. Women teachers, in a similar way to their male colleagues, joined their association for instrumental reasons to gain material and professional benefits, for the insurance and welfare schemes they were offered, for legal advice and employment protection.[8] Members of the NUT could feel that their interests were represented by a body that had national authority and recognition. The union aimed to improve the salaries and working conditions of elementary school teachers; it also offered members a forum for the dis-cussion of educational and professional classroom matters. Women teachers could see it as a vehicle for their own professional and later their feminist aspirations. Feeling themselves to be professional teachers alongside their male colleagues, the women argued for equal access to professional benefits of pay, conditions and prospects, and increasingly developed this as a rhetorical strategy in their political activities. Since the discourse of profes-sionalism was being used by all groups of teachers to try to improve their status and conditions, this approach carried a great deal of weight.

It might be suggested that women teachers were naïve in their reading of professionalism as ungendered and equally open to women. But they were encouraged in this by the NUT itself. Not only did the union actively try to recruit women from the mid-1890s onwards; it officially treated them on equal terms with men, and at times congratulated itself on this. In 1911 the NUT republished as a recruitment leaflet a leading article which had appeared in the *Schoolmaster* (the journal of the NUT). Entitled *Miss Chairman*, it welcomed women teachers as equal professional colleagues:

> The Union treats alike, enrols, protects, defends, and honours men and women, wives, widows and spinsters; each is a member of the profession and of the Union; each has an equal claim ... Every woman who is a member of the Union has just the same right, power and privilege in voting as any man has ... absolute equality between Adam and Eve is the rule.

It pointed out that although the union did not enter into the suffrage debate, its General Secretary supported women's suffrage in a personal capacity in the House of Commons, and that women's involvement would bring equal pay and pensions, suggesting that NUT men would give sympathy and sup-port to their professional colleagues.[9] The *Schoolmaster* supported the women teachers' campaigns on a number of occasions.[10]

But while some NUT men agreed with the feminist claims for professional equality, others believed that women teachers had a gender-specific role in the profession and union distinct from that of men. Their professional inter-ests were seen as including the teaching of domestic subjects and child wel-fare issues, while the NUT's charities were identified as a particularly appropriate activity for women members.[11] At the 1910 conference, the newly elected vice-president, Miss Cleghorn, speaking to a women teachers' meeting, said 'she felt sure of support and sympathy, not only from the women, but from the men also'. Following her, however, a male executive member emphasised the gendered nature of women's professional expertise: 'Work was waiting for them in connection with the education of infants and the medical inspection of children, in respect of which their knowledge and experience were greatly superior to those of men.'[12] The women, too, held a range of views on what professionalism meant but many endorsed the idea of a different sphere for women's efforts *at the same time* as asserting equal rights with men. Their interest in the domestic subjects curriculum, emphasised by Dina Copelman,[13] did not preclude NUT women from also supporting professional equality of pay and conditions. It was, perhaps, easier for women teachers to reach out and claim equal rights and masculine privileges partly *because* they were at the same time safely rooted in the feminine tasks of teaching children.

But in their fight for suffrage (and also over equal pay and promotion opportunities), feminist teachers' demands laid bare the varying and conflicting meanings of teacher professionalism. In the NUT, women teachers discovered that apparently gender-neutral concepts were profoundly gendered, and professionalism was largely defined on men's terms. Because women teachers' reading of the concept of professionalism within a mixed trade union context was in conflict with that of many of the men, this led to acute gender antagonism.

However, this was not anticipated by feminist teachers at the beginning. In the early 1900s, women teachers did believe that they shared common professional interests with male colleagues and could pursue their claims within a mixed organisation. The NUT Executive encouraged female membership, and the number and proportion of women members rose rapidly in the early 1900s. Between 1905 and 1915 women's membership grew from 52 per cent to 60 per cent of the total membership of the NUT, while membership density among certificated women teachers was 75 per cent in 1914.[14] Optimistic feminists assumed they could build up a power base within the union hierarchy by using their numerical strength.[15] This strategy began to show some success as more women were sent as delegates to NUT conferences and female membership of the Executive increased, though the proportion of women on this body reached only around 10 per cent before the First World War. The election in 1910 of the first woman president, Miss Cleghorn, was greeted with enthusiasm by women members.[16]

Some women teachers within the NUT had raised issues of professional equality well before the development of the mass suffrage movement. From the 1880s the threat of a marriage bar was countered vigorously by London teachers; from the 1890s there was a vocal debate over promotion prospects for women teachers; and before 1900 an active lobby campaigned for equal pay in the NUT.[17] A victory in equalising discriminatory NUT welfare benefits stimulated the formation of an Equal Pay League within the NUT in 1903. In 1906 this pressure group changed its name to the National Federation of Women Teachers (NFWT). The rapid development of the suffrage movement after 1906 provided a feminist context for women teachers to make sense of their already existing concerns about equal pay and promotion, and supplied them with a broader political framework for their campaigns. It also gave feminist teachers an independent political base outside the teachers' associations, and the experience of an alternative single-sex method of campaigning.

WOMEN TEACHERS AND THE SUFFRAGE MOVEMENT

Traditional histories of women in teaching often assumed that they were not greatly involved in the suffrage movement.[18] But more recent work by feminist historians, notably Hilda Kean, on the huge amount of evidence available shows that these assertions are completely wrong.[19] The rapid growth of the NFWT, the setting-up in 1912 of the single-issue Women Teachers' Franchise Union (WTFU; see p. 210), and the massively contentious debates over the issue at NUT conferences, show that women teachers were centrally involved with suffrage. They provided substantial contingents on suffrage processions, were platform speakers at the Hyde Park demonstration in 1908 and were also involved in more militant activities such as setting fire to post offices, leading to arrest and imprisonment.[20] For example, Dorothy Evans, a prominent feminist from the 1920s to the 1940s, began her career as a teacher, was imprisoned nine times as a young woman in the suffrage movement and was forcibly fed.[21] Certainly contemporaries were aware that both elementary and secondary school teachers were often suffragists. In 1910 the *Journal of Education* noted that 'women teachers through their various associations have pronounced themselves almost unanimously in favour of Woman Suffrage'.[22] The anti-suffragist Mrs Humphry Ward, in a debate in *The Times* in 1912, wrote of 'the almost exclusive staffing of our higher schools and colleges for girls, at the present moment, by women holding suffragist opinions'.[23] *The Woman Teacher's Magazine*, a short-lived commercial paper for teachers, was forced to shift its position after making anti-suffragist comments in the first 1909 issue, to reflect the growing feeling among women teachers for political and professional equality.[24] Many teachers and former teachers were in fact among the leaders and organisers of the suffrage movement, including suffragettes Emily Wilding Davison, Teresa Billington-Greig, Margaret Nevinson and Dorothy Evans.[25]

Women teachers became actively involved in suffrage in a number of ways. Individual recruitment via friends or teacher colleagues was of great importance for drawing women teachers into the movement. Mary Harris, a

Swansea teacher, joined the NFWT after coming into contact with 'the magnetic influence of Miss Phipps, the pioneer of the women teachers' movement in Swansea'.[26] A family commitment to women's equal rights may have precipitated some teachers into support for suffrage. Miss Rosser's mother, who was a headmistress in Pontypridd and worked both before and after marriage, was a co-opted member of the local education authority, and 'a big suffragette' with strong views.[27] Feminist enthusiasm was also lit by the drama and sacrifice of the militant suffrage campaign. One teacher 'went from Leeds to join the great Suffrage Procession in London in 1908, [and] joined the National Federation of Women Teachers when a branch was formed in Leeds'.[28] Miss Phipps, who was president of the NFWT in 1917, and continued to be a prominent activist in the interwar years, described how she was converted to militant feminism by her disgust at witnessing the brutal treatment of suffragettes at a meeting in Swansea in 1908 where Lloyd George was speaking.[29]

It has been suggested that teachers' need for respectability within their local communities and their vulnerability to social pressure may have led them to shun the militant suffrage organisations.[30] Indeed many women teachers were members of the moderate National Union of Women's Suffrage Societies (NUWSS). For others, however, anger and frustration at their voteless position led them into active involvement in the militant wing of the movement. Hilda Kean has demonstrated that many serving teachers were local branch officers for the Women's Social and Political Union (WSPU) and for the less well-known but politically important Women's Freedom League (WFL), both militant suffrage groups.[31] The links between the women teachers and the WFL are worth exploring further.

The Women's Freedom League, which broke away from the WSPU in 1907 to form a democratic militant suffrage organisation, rejected the traditional idea of women's sphere in the family (unlike the NUWSS) and concerned itself with women's economic equality, an approach attractive to women teachers. Hilda Kean suggests that their position as state employees is also an important factor in women teachers' involvement in the WFL. The League addressed the relationship between women and the state, attacking the role of the state in taxing women, in passing legislation which affected women, in discriminating against women in the courts of law; all without women's representation.[32] This had particular meaning for women teachers who, like their male colleagues, were employed by the state, but were barred, on the basis of their sex, from the political processes which determined the discriminatory conditions of their employment.[33] Kean also suggests that they drew on the WFL's practice of democratic procedures to inform their criticism of the NUT structure.[34] Women teachers enthusiastically supported the WFL's militant strategies such as resisting taxation and the Census. Some London women teachers were among the crowd which spent enumeration day at the Aldwych skating rink, while Emily Phipps and the Swansea WFL group spent Census night 1911 in a cave on the Gower peninsula.[35] Miss Phipps later described this action and its purpose:

> Many women had determined that since they could not be citizens for the purpose of voting, they would not be citizens for the purpose of helping the Government to compile statistics: they would not be included in the Census returns. Different methods of evasion were followed. She and Miss Neal, together with two Training College lecturers and a business-woman, spent the night on the coast of Gower in a sea-cave, which they had previously located. Only one of their number obtained any sleep, since sitting or lying on sharp rocks was not conducive to repose. Their purpose accomplished, they returned the next morning to school, college, and shop, and the secret was well kept.[36]

Many women teachers, including Ethel Froud, who was to become the first general secretary of the NUWT, remained active members of the WSPU, and were involved in activities such as open-air speaking, chalking pavements and poster parades. In 1910 *The Times* reported that a woman teacher at a school in Deptford, south London, was reprimanded for absenteeism in order to attend a suffrage demonstration, and was later obliged to resign because she had been sent to prison.[37]

The fact that many teacher feminists were *militant* suffragettes shows how deeply they felt the injustice of their voteless position and how this jarred with their status as professionals. However, the constitutional NUWSS also held meetings at NUT conferences before the war, indicating that it, too, had a following among women teachers.[38] Agnes Dawson, a prominent NFWT member, later recalled that she had been 'twitted' by her comrades for being a constitutional suffragist. Interestingly, she also 'confessed' that the only time that she 'strayed from the path of virtue', was to take part in the 1911 Census boycott.[39] Clearly this was a political action resonant with meaning for women teachers. Although these teachers were profoundly divided by the type of tactics they were prepared to pursue to achieve suffrage, they were nevertheless ready to sink these differences in their active membership of the NFWT and the WTFU, to focus on their professional association.[40]

The strong links for women teachers between their professional identity as teachers and their suffrage politics are also shown by the formation of a professionally specific interest group, the Women Teachers' Franchise Union, set up in 1912, which can be compared with other occupational groups within the women's suffrage movement organised by women writers, actresses and artists. The skills these groups had to offer were utilised in the cause of suffrage by designing banners, writing propaganda plays and organising dramatic set-piece processions.[41] The image of the woman teacher – unenfranchised but highly educated (sometimes even a university graduate) –

when contrasted with the criminal and lunatic men who did enjoy the vote, was of immense symbolic value to the suffrage movement. Women teachers drew attention to their professional status in suffrage demonstrations and attempted, albeit unsuccessfully, to bring the weight of the NUT behind the demand for the vote.[42]

SUFFRAGE, PROFESSIONALISM AND GENDER IN THE NUT

The debate over women's suffrage in the NUT illustrates how understandings of professionalism were deeply gendered. Women teachers passionately believed that their suffrage claim was proper, relevant union business, but they failed to win much support from the men. The suffrage issue dominated British feminist politics after about 1907, being seen as the key to all the other equality demands by women. Feminists in the NUT tried to get their union to back the principle of suffrage for its women members, believing that this would aid the suffrage cause by influencing public opinion and the government.[43] As the fifth largest national union in 1910 and the major white-collar union, the NUT had considerable political weight.[44] Each year between 1911 and 1914, the annual conference of the NUT was asked to support the motion:

> That this conference expresses its sympathy with those members of the NUT who desire to possess and exercise the parliamentary franchise, but because they are women, and for that reason alone, are by law debarred from it.[45]

The following discussion of these debates at Conference, which was the union's main decision-making forum, will trace the main arguments put forward for and against making this expression of sympathy.

In 1911, the motion was put forward by the Executive, after representations from women teachers. In subsequent years, despite local antagonism and opposition, women teachers got motions of sympathy passed by many NUT associations and sent up to the national conference. The women's business meetings at conferences between 1910 and 1914 each discussed the issue and the tactics to be used in bringing it up in the main debate, and were almost unanimously in favour of it. Suffragist teachers also gained the support of the NUT Ladies Committee (the official voice of NUT women), and in 1911 Miss Cleghorn used her power as president to ensure that the suffrage resolution was introduced at conference. She made forceful speeches in favour at every debate in later years, too, where her status as past president at least ensured a fairly courteous hearing.

Right from the beginning, the suffrage issue produced vociferous opposition from the rank-and-file male NUT members, and from male conference delegates. In 1911, on the first occasion that it was debated, with Miss Cleghorn in the chair as president, the Executive proposed to suspend standing orders, to make space for suffrage on the conference agenda. Amid chaotic expressions of hostility, the Executive member who introduced this proposal was shouted down:

> Then broke out the wildest scenes of disorder . . . Hundreds of men, massed at the back of the hall, prevented Mr Croft from obtaining a hearing. They stamped, howled, hurling insults at the speaker and at suffragists, and utterly refused to allow Mr Croft's speech to proceed. This continued without intermission for thirty minutes . . . During the whole time the women suffragists had sat, calm and dignified, in the seats at the front of the hall; they were subsequently congratulated by Miss Cleghorn on their restraint.[46]

The motion was formally objected to on the grounds that the question of women's suffrage was not part of the union's business and that it had been introduced by the Executive, and not in the conventional way from the local associations. It was soundly defeated.[47] A second attempt the following day to get standing orders suspended in order to discuss suffrage, this time proposed by two women teachers from the floor of the conference after collecting the necessary signatures of support, was also defeated.[48]

In subsequent years, when the motion was sent up by local associations, it was debated but always defeated. Men teachers who opposed the motion represented the suffrage issue as one which was 'too political', was not a legitimate union objective and therefore not proper union business. Although one of the objects of the NUT was 'To secure the effective representation of educational interests in Parliament', it was argued by a perennial opponent, Mr Cook, at the 1912 conference, that:

> this was not an educational question. (Cheers.) It was absolutely a political question. (Cheers and counter-cheers.) If they were going to introduce this, and allow it to be introduced as part of the policy of their Union, they could assure them that they knew not where they were going to be led to in years to come. ('Hear, hear.') He also opposed it on the grounds that it would create disunity among teachers. Furthermore: 'There were members in that room, he believed, who had been associated with methods that had been adopted recently to obtain the vote. ("Shame.") . . . He was prepared to say to them that they were lowering the dignity of the profession. (Cheers.)'[49]

These arguments, including the denunciation of militant actions by women teachers, continued at later conferences, when the controversy over suffrage grew even more intense.

WOMEN TEACHERS' CASE

Suffragist teachers bitterly contested their opponents. In arguing for the support of the NUT they repeatedly made a number of points concerning women teachers' responsibility and status in the wider world, and their place in their own professional association. This discourse of equality united suffrage feminists across the union, from moderate suffragists like Miss Cleghorn (who was firmly committed to union goals as much as to women's issues) to the militant activists in the NFWT.

The central strand of their argument was the humanist principle of women's equal rights. This rhetoric of equality, stemming from liberal political philosophy, emphasised women's rights as citizens, property-owners and taxpayers. Teacher suffragists felt that they were intelligent, educated and skilled, and, like men, worked in the public sphere in which they should have a say. The argument that women teachers were 'every one . . . admirably qualified by education, by training and by natural capacity to make the most admirable use of the Parliamentary franchise' was first made in 1911.[50] In her speech to the 1913 NUT conference Miss Cleghorn argued that the claim for the vote was a logical outcome of women's improved education. Moreover, to cheers from the conference floor she argued: 'They had to go out and work for their living, and surely they had the right to think of the great things of the world.'[51]

This sense of themselves as independent women contributed to their strength of conviction in claiming the householder franchise on the same grounds as men. Miss Cleghorn had gained a strong response from Conference when making this argument in 1912, as quoted at the beginning of this chapter.[52] This point was similarly made in a letter from a woman teacher to the *Schoolmaster*:

> It is an accepted axiom of democratic government that taxation implies representation. The vote is due to women taxpayers. They have an urgent and pressing use for it – the amelioration of the hard conditions under which many of them live; but this urgency is not put forward here as adding anything to the abstract right.[53]

Teachers also strongly resented the fact that their status in the community was not reflected in their political rights. 'Besides that [the householder franchise case], they had to teach citizenship. They had to enter into the social problems of the day, and were they to teach the little child citizenship and then to have a little boy able to look up and say, "Yes, but you have not your-self the right to vote"?'[54]

A second element of women teachers' equal rights case was their sense that their professional position as teachers should be equal to men's. The claim for the suffrage was linked to the fight for equal salaries and promotion prospects (which predated it) which was argued for on the grounds of pro-fessional equality. The connection between these demands was made more explicit as the campaigns progressed. In an equal pay debate in 1913, women teachers argued that their training, expenses and professional responsibilities were the same as men teachers', and that one factor in the level of salaries was the status of the worker: 'At the present time the status of the women in England was low. They were not recognised as citizens, and they had no Parliamentary power.'[55] One woman teacher spoke in support of equal pay in a debate in the following year, 'on the grounds of sex equality and justice, and as one who had helped to bring the franchise question into the Union'.[56]

It is clear that women teachers favoured arguments based on their similar worth and contribution as citizens, and their equal professional value as teach-ers, to make a case for the NUT's supporting suffrage. Only occasionally was the argument for women's gender-specific contribution to the nation heard in the union. In 1912, Mr Dakers, the vice-president, supported the suffrage reso-lution, arguing that women had a special interest in the home, and therefore should not be denied a voice in making the laws on education; they were likely to make a better job of it than men had done.[57] In 1914, a male supporter on the Executive suggested that if women had the vote it was their interest in the wel-fare of the child which would appeal to them rather than Imperial politics.[58] But this approach was simply not in evidence from the women suffragists at Conference. Once, in 1913, Miss Cleghorn did refer to this argument, not in her main speech, but in response to an anti-suffrage speaker:

> Mrs. Burgwin told them that she did not believe in women's suf-frage because of the sanctity of home life. That was just the reason why others believed in it. (Cheers.) We lived in a democratic age, and our legislation touched the home life, the social conditions of the people, and the children in the schools. They wanted the vote because they wanted to help in framing such legislation. (Cheers.)[59]

Women's contribution to the nation on the basis of their sexual difference was an argument largely ignored by women teachers, who preferred to stress professional sameness and the human responsibilities of citizenship. The argument citing women's particular interest in laws concerning home life and children was made by supportive male teachers on occasion (perhaps to soften the challenge of the equality argument), but strikingly rarely by the women speakers in NUT debates.

As outlined above, one of the central issues of debate throughout these years was whether women's suffrage was proper union business. This strongly agitated and exercised both supporters and opponents. Indeed it begged the whole question of women teachers' voice and influence in their professional association, the NUT. The NUT women strongly contested the suggestion that suffrage was too political in the sense that it was outside the scope of the union's business, and a third strand in their equal rights case was that their demands were legitimate within their own professional association.

A cry of 'No politics' was raised as Mr Croft, the first speaker to raise suffrage in an NUT conference, rose to speak in 1911. In return he maintained that over the last ten or fifteen years at NUT conferences 'they had been continually discussing questions far more political than this'. During the uproar, the president intervened to ask the conference: 'What would be the power of the NUT if the men lost the vote? Answer that. ("None," and cheers.) Your answer was "None," and what is twice nought? ("Bravo!").'[60] The 'political' issue was addressed at length in the first proper suffrage debate in 1912: 'the Parliamentary influence of their Union was one of the greatest assets – (hear, hear) – and . . . they were continually in their Association meetings and in Conference discussing politics.'[61] At later conferences suffrage supporters stressed that the NUT was not being asked to do more than express sympathy with its unenfranchised members, and produced evidence that the union had tangled with equally political issues in the past. Miss Cleghorn again:

Such a resolution would give suffrage supporters 'something to cheer them on their way, to help them work on patiently, forbearingly ("Oh!") – and constitutionally – (cheers) – for what they considered justice and fairness for their sex . . . The NUT had never been backward in expressing sympathy to any of its members who desired sympathy. Years ago did they not give a grant to the Penrhyn miners? They expressed sympathy then with something rather political. She had not sat on the Executive for eighteen years without finding out that they would express sympathy with any member of the Union be he ever so weak.[62]

The NUT was a potent force in the settlement of educational questions, suffragists pointed out, because nearly all the men in the union were voters. Women argued that the NUT had spent union money to obtain the franchise for male members; for example, if they lived in school houses. Claims by individual men teachers to be entitled to a vote were dealt with on many occasions by the union's Law Committee and action taken, including an appeal to the High Court in one case. 'So that they had not only discussed the question of the franchise, but they had actually expended Union money in obtaining it.'[63] Feminist teachers argued that the NUT was within its powers in discussing suffrage, since its fifth object was 'to secure effective representation of educational interests in parliament. How were they to secure that if not by the right of franchise?'[64] Miss Cleghorn and others also pointed out that women members contributed to the NUT's parliamentary activities and to the salaries of the union's MPs, though they themselves were excluded from the parliamentary process.[65]

> Last year the Union spent between £6,000 or £7,000 on parliamentary expenses. She did not grudge a single penny of it. It was the best asset they had. Women paid, and paid willingly, their 2s. towards those expenses. Surely if they paid equally with the men, and did not grudge the expenses, they ought to be willing to grant the women their sympathy. There were no arguments against it.[66]

An external commentator, Beatrice Webb, considered all these arguments in her comprehensive 1915 *New Statesman* article on teachers' associations and pronounced in favour of the suffragist teachers; their case was 'not only plausible but just'.[67]

Alongside the political argument that women's suffrage was a legitimate consideration and would strengthen the power of the union, another point was very strongly made. The suffrage motion should be discussed – and passed – for reasons of fair play and justice to women members. Women were the majority of members in the union; this was an issue that most of them supported, and their voice should be heard. This argument was made right from the beginning of the 1911 conference. 'The President appealed for order. She said that if they did not hear Mr. Croft the women present would not consider they were fairly treated.'[68]

'Fair play' was not much in evidence over the years, however, as the suffrage claim was repeatedly denied and rejected by Conference. In 1913, Miss Cleghorn made a powerful speech asking for fairness for women teachers, on the grounds that the union had worked for men teachers' votes in the past, and that all the delegates there had been sent to Conference by the votes of women NUT members, and should in turn help them. She stressed that women had equal voting rights within the NUT and the union should support that principle outside:

> the Union, besides standing for sympathy, stood for fair play. Years ago they gave not only the Union strength but money and influence to secure the franchise for the men . . . The NUT believed in the equality of the sexes. (Cries of 'No.') . . . They believed in votes for women, for they were all sent there by the help of votes from women. Did they think those women had voted wrong in sending them there? Women had voted for the Executive. Did they find any unfairness there? . . . The women had been exceedingly good to them. Let them carry outside the Union what the Union believed inside.[69]

This sense of fairness and women's equal part in the profession and the NUT was similarly expressed by the 1912 NFWT president, Miss Thomas, who 'hoped that ... their co-workers would realise they did not as suffragettes wish to capture the NUT. The vote was a sign of equality, and they wished their menfolk to recognise their equality and joint rulership.'[70]

WOMEN'S PLACE IN THE UNION

For the women, there was no conflict between professional status, NUT aims and the suffrage question – possession of the franchise would strengthen their profession and the union. But the definition of women's franchise as too political, while men's vote was a legitimate cause for concern, indicates that the balance of power to control the meaning and direction of NUT politics still lay in men's hands, and that many men were not prepared to acknowledge that their women colleagues had the same rights and responsibilities in the profession and in the union.

An important minority of NUT men did support women's suffrage as a legitimate union concern, including almost all of the male Executive members. Male speakers spoke in favour of the suffrage resolution at each of the conference debates.[71] In 1911 the *Schoolmaster* condemned the intolerant reception of the suffrage resolution at that year's conference, and supported a proper discussion of the issue, on the grounds of 'fair play' and other considerations:

> There are the 38,374 women in the Union, there is the question of voting strength and electoral influence of the Union, there is the Osborne Judgement, there is the (foolish but earnest) refusal of suffragist women teachers to remain in the union.[72]

But for most men teachers, the contentious issue of women's suffrage did not fit easily into traditional trade union and professional goals. Many were active anti-suffragists, and the Anti-Suffrage League organised extensively against the feminists within the union throughout this period.[73] The suffrage motion was backed by the NUT Executive, by the majority of local associations, and by most women members. However, despite their majority among the membership as a whole, women made up only one-third or less of conference delegates. This enabled male anti-suffragists to maintain control, even when they were mandated by their associations to support the suffrage resolution.

This blocking of the democratic process infuriated the women teachers, and debates over supporting the principle of women's suffrage developed into arguments about union democracy, and whether it was worth remaining members if their views were stifled. At each conference between 1912 and 1914, Miss Cleghorn stressed the weight of feeling and the grass-roots support behind the demand for NUT support for suffrage. This increasingly highlighted the actions of the male-dominated conference delegates who opposed the resolution (often against the expressed wishes of their associations) and blocked it. In 1914:

> She asked them to pass it because of the principle in it, and because the Associations desired it should be discussed. They knew that . . . this had been going on for three years. Not only that, but the resolution came up with 22,000 backers . . . She asked the Conference to pass the resolution because most of the members believed in the principle of women's suffrage.[74]

At the end of the debate she again emphasised the obligation of the conference not to obstruct the wishes of the membership.

> Miss Cleghorn . . . mentioned that in the votes of the Associations as to the order in which subjects should come before Conference, women's suffrage on the first occasion had second place, and on the second and third sixth place . . . The trouble was that the Associations, having voted upon the order, did not instruct their delegates to stand by their Association.[75]

The hostility and obstruction aroused by the suffrage issue caused dismay and cynicism, and served to politicise the activist feminist teachers more deeply. Many began to weigh the cost of working within a mixed-sex organisation. The first woman president of the Birmingham NUT, Miss Byett, wrote:

> The Aberystwyth Conference [of 1911] first revealed the bitter antagonism of Union men towards the aspirations of their women colleagues. No woman who faced that 'howling mob' (as the newspapers described it), in the attempt to ask, not for money, not even for help, but merely for an expression of sympathy, will ever forget it.[76]

The anger felt by suffragette teachers also increased as a consequence of government actions, including the betrayal of suffrage Bills and the force-feeding of suffragettes.[77] Looking back, the NFWT activist Miss Froud linked the treatment of teacher suffragettes outside the NUT with that which they received inside the union, in paying tribute to 'those members who were ruthlessly flung out of Cabinet Ministers' meetings, or as ruthlessly gagged in teachers' meetings'.[78]

By 1913 and 1914, the NUT conference had become a major arena for national suffragist and anti-suffragist organisations, which set up offices and held meetings on the fringes of the conference.[79] The issue had become so explosive and divisive that in these latter years women delegates often had difficulty in gaining admission to conference sessions. In 1913 the guest speaker, the cabinet minister Lord Haldane, was interrupted by suffragette teachers, including one who protested against the forcible feeding of women teachers. A woman who asked him a question about girls' education was thrown out of the meeting.[80] By 1914, male anxiety and hostility to the suffrage question in the NUT had grown to the point that women teachers were almost prohibited from speaking. Indeed, the fact that women teachers had lost the battle over suffrage being seen as a legitimate professional issue was symbolised not only by the increasingly hostile rejection of feminist topics, but also by the controlling and silencing of the professional voices of women members of the NUT. At the 1914 NUT conference:

> The promoters of the conference were 'nervy'; they feared awkward questions – nothing worse – from suffragist teachers; every woman delegate was closely scrutinised before admission, and sometimes roughly handled . . .
>
> Soon after 10 o'clock, Miss Byett rose, and said, 'Mr President, may I ask a question?' Now, Miss Byett was known to be a believer in Women's Suffrage, and questions on that topic were not welcomed. Pandemonium ensued, with shouts of 'No!' 'Sit down!' 'Turn her out!' all of which Miss Byett took with characteristic calmness. At last, the President managed to secure order, and Miss Byett propounded her question: 'Would it be contrary to the regulations, Mr President, to ask if a window might be opened?'[81]

In a subsequent debate on salaries, a male delegate evoked applause by the remark that the word 'woman' had not once been mentioned in the debate.[82] During the actual suffrage debate, Miss Hewitt protested at an attempt to prohibit future discussion of suffrage within the NUT:

> She said that, as the President of a large London Association, she did not wish to go back and tell her people that the Conference had decided that the burning question of woman suffrage was no more to be discussed. She could not answer for the effect on the women of her Association . . . 'Do not let it go forward,' she added, 'to the civilised world that this great Union decides that the enfranchisement of two-thirds of its members is a subject not worthy of its discussion. I wish to convince you that I stand here an enthusiastic member of the Union, who desires the solidarity of the Union. But a great many women members are willing to come out at a sign.[83]

The process of women teachers voicing their feminist demands created immense conflict and antagonism with the men. It laid bare the power that men teachers exercised through their association. Most men teachers turned out not to be the benign professional equivalents of women teachers, and their supportive colleagues. Instead they were concerned to defend their gender interests and power in the teaching profession and their control of the NUT. Women teachers were denied a fully shared professionalism in the NUT; rather they were supposed to keep to the sidelines and concern themselves only with gender-specific topics. Suffragist teachers were particularly enraged at the manipulation of the union's machinery by male opponents.

> Women now were beginning to understand how it was the men won every time, even when they were beaten in debate; it was 'Heads we win and tails you lose' with them. Look at the Election results, look at the Suffrage debates, examine the results locally and then at Conferences, examine too the Salary debates, and those on Equal Pay; they, the men, were in possession of the machinery, and knew its cranks, every one.[84]

Feminist teachers' experience of challenging the gendered structure and control of their union is an important source for understanding the limitations women face in acting as an interest group to change supposedly open and democratic organisations. It is not surprising that the most committed feminist teachers began to see the women's movement as a more attractive campaigning vehicle than the mixed NUT. From 1916 the NFWT began preparations to separate from the main union, and in 1919 feminist teachers formally decided to leave the NUT, creating the National Union of Women Teachers in 1920.

CONCLUSIONS

Taking the fight direct to anti-suffragist men in a mixed-sex organisation, as women teachers did, was a very unusual activity in pre-First World War Britain, where it was still quite a novelty for women to speak in a mixed public forum. Suffrage was not a single issue for women teachers. Also important were equal pay, equal promotion prospects and their place in the union. But suffrage came to symbolise the struggle of women teachers in getting their views heard and fairly represented in the male-dominated NUT. It led to a furious debate about the meaning of professionalism, especially in terms of the objectives of their professional association. Were the political interests of women teachers to be allowed equivalent weight with those of the men? The answer was no, and the strength of feeling aroused inside the union mirrored the concurrent suffrage battles on the streets and in the courtrooms of the nation.

Their professional identity fired women teachers' sense of unfairness and the kinds of arguments they used. In their educational background, in their experience in the workplace and in their professional body, they received mixed messages about gender equality, but had learnt to value their work and their opinions. Suffragist teachers preferred to assert their equality with men. They formed an important, if minority, strand of the wider suffrage movement in pursuing liberal humanist arguments, stressing their parity of responsibility as householders and taxpayers, their educational and intellectual attributes, and their similar contribution as professional workers recognised by the whole of society. This equal rights case was a powerful one both inside and outside the NUT. In terms of favoured tactics, feminist women teachers covered the whole spectrum. A high proportion of activists supported and took part in militant suffrage organisations, while many followed the constitutionalist path. But their shared professional identity and sense of injustice meant they worked together, across tactical allegiances, on the suffrage issue as women teachers.

NOTES

I would like to thank the Editors and Annmarie Turnbull for their helpful comments on this chapter.

1 *Schoolmaster*, 13 April 1912, p. 719.
2 S. Holton, *Feminism and democracy: women's suffrage and reform politics in Britain 1900–1918* (Cambridge, Cambridge University Press, 1986), p. 17 and Chapter 1.
3 D. Copelman, *London's women teachers: gender, class and feminism 1870–1930* (London, Routledge, 1996), pp. 220–224. I do not discuss women teachers' campaigns for equal pay and promotion here; see A. Oram, *Women teachers and feminist politics 1900–1939* (Manchester, Manchester University Press, 1996).
4 For further discussion see Oram, *Women teachers and feminist politics*, Chapter 2.
5 Entry to the professions was based, in theory, on individual merit and the possession of the required education and training. W. J. Reader, *Professional men: the rise of the professional classes in nineteenth-century England* (London, Weidenfeld & Nicolson, 1966), pp. 9–10, 43. H. Perkin, *The rise of professional society: England since 1880* (London, Routledge, 1989), pp. xii–xiv, 4. H. Bradley, *Men's work, women's work: a sociological history of the sexual division of labour in employment* (Cambridge, Polity Press, 1989), p. 173.
6 Perkin, *The rise of professional society*, pp. 430–431. A. Witz, *Professions and patriarchy* (London, Routledge, 1992), pp. 92–93.
7 J. Lewis, *Women in England 1870–1940* (Brighton, Wheatsheaf, 1984), pp. 95–97. P. Levine, *Victorian feminism 1850–1900* (London, Hutchinson, 1987), pp. 61–63, 71. J. Rendall, Introduction, in *Equal or different: women's politics 1800–1914*, ed. J. Rendall (Oxford, Basil Blackwell, 1987).
8 B. Webb, English teachers and their professional organisation, Special Supplement to *New Statesman*, V, 129, 25 September 1915, p. 17.
9 *Schoolmaster*, 10 December 1910, p. 997. NUT propaganda leaflet, *Miss Chairman* (1911).

10 See, for example, *Schoolmaster*, 9 April 1910, p. 661; 29 April 1911, p. 869.

11 NUT circulars, *Union Membership – Women Teachers* (1896), C1.167, 169. The most common officer post held by women in local associations was Secretary to the Benevolent and Orphan Fund.

12 *Schoolmaster*, 2 April 1910, p. 628.

13 Copelman, *London's women teachers*, pp. 221–223.

14 These figures are calculated from the *Annual Reports* of the NUT.

15 See, for example, letter to the *Schoolmaster*, 25 May 1907, p. 1020. I am indebted to Hilda Kean for this reference.

16 NUT, *Annual Report* (1911), p. lviii; *Annual Report* (1912), p. lxi; and other years. *Schoolmaster*, 2 April 1910, pp. 583–584.

17 H. Corr, Sexual politics in the National Union of Teachers 1870–1920, in P. Summerfield (ed.), *Women, education and the professions* (Leicester, History of Education Society, 1987), pp. 55–56. Also see H. Corr, Politics of the sexes in English and Scottish teachers' unions 1870–1914, in H. Corr and L. Jamieson (eds), *Politics of Everyday Life* (London, Macmillan, 1990), p. 192. Webb, 'English teachers', p. 8.

18 G. Partington, *Women teachers in the twentieth century* (Slough, NFER Publishing, 1976), pp. 10–11.

19 H. Kean, *Deeds not words: the lives of suffragette teachers* (London, Pluto Press, 1990), especially Chapters 1 and 2. H. Kean, State education policy 1900–1930: the nature of the socialist and teacher trade unionist response, PhD thesis, University of London, King's College, 1988, pp. 206–230. Corr, Sexual politics in the NUT.

20 *Journal of Education*, December 1908, p. 808. *The Times*, 21 April 1910, p. 9. *Schoolmaster*, 13 April 1912, p. 720. Kean, *Deeds not words*, pp. 13, 21–22, 24–25.

21 *International Women's News*, 39, 1, October 1944, pp. 5–6 (her obituary).

22 *Journal of Education*, August 1910, p. 516. Also see *Schoolmaster*, 10 December 1910, p. 907.

23 *The Times*, 12 April 1912, p. 15; also see 9 April 1912, p. 8.

24 It began as a supposedly apolitical paper, but shifted its line after complaints from readers. *Woman Teacher's Magazine*, 1, 1, December 1909; 1, 3, February 1910. By 1911 the paper came out wholly in support of feminist teachers' demands. *Woman Teacher's Magazine*, 2, 21, August 1911. Also see Copelman, *London's women teachers*, p. 215.

25 A. Stanley with L. Morley, *The life and death of Emily Wilding Davison* (London, Women's Press, 1988), p. 15. Teresa Billington-Greig never lost her links with her former profession and advertised her stationery business in *The Woman Teacher* in the 1930s. Banks's survey of feminists' backgrounds shows that teaching was by far the largest occupational category for her cohort of prominent feminists of the suffrage generation, for both middle-class and working-class women. O. Banks, *Becoming a feminist: the social origins of first wave feminism* (Brighton, Wheatsheaf, 1986), pp. 11–12. Kean, *Deeds not words*, pp. 12–13.

26 *Woman Teacher*, 3 February 1933, p. 84 (obituary of Miss Harris). Women teachers also became involved through attending women's or suffrage meetings at NUT conferences. See *Woman Teacher*, 15 January 1937, p. 127 for an example of the latter.

27 University of Essex Oral History Archives, 'Family life and work before 1914'. Miss Mary Rosser, no. 371, pp. 4, 53. (Born 1890.) A family history of feminism had also inspired Miss Jackson, later a president of the NFWT: see *Woman Teacher*, 5 October 1928, p. 4.

28 *Woman Teacher*, 26 October 1934, p. 26. For the interconnections of teachers

with suffrage also see Amy Barlow, *Seventh child* (London, Duckworth, 1969), p. 64.

29 *Woman Teacher*, 5 October 1928, pp. 2–3.

30 Partington, *Women Teachers*, p. 10.

31 Kean, State education policy, pp. 218–219, and Appendix. Kean, *Deeds not words*, Chapter 2.

32 For discussion of the Women's Freedom League, see C. Eustance, Meanings of militancy: the ideas and practice of political resistance in the Women's Freedom League, 1907–14, in M. Joannou and J. Purvis (eds), *The women's suffrage movement: new feminist perspectives* (Manchester, Manchester University Press, 1998). L. Garner, *Stepping stones to women's liberty: feminist ideas in the women's suffrage movement 1900–1918* (London, Heinemann, 1984), Chapter 3. C. McPhee and A. Fitzgerald (eds), *The non-violent militant: selected writings of Teresa Billington-Greig* (London, Routledge & Kegan Paul, 1987).

33 Kean, State education policy, pp. 207–208, 213. H. Kean, *Challenging the state? The socialist and feminist educational experience 1900–1930* (London, Falmer Press, 1990), pp. 132–133. For further discussion on the relationship between women teachers, the state and their allegiance to the WFL see H. Kean and A. Oram, 'Men must be educated and women must do it': the National Federation (later Union) of Women Teachers and contemporary feminism 1910–39, *Gender and Education*, 2, 2, 1990, pp. 149–151.

34 Kean, State education policy, pp. 219–220. Kean, *Challenging the state?*, pp. 133–134.

35 NUWT Archive, Box 124. File on Miss Phipps. *Woman Teacher*, 5 October 1928, p. 3; 15 January 1937, p. 127.

36 She told this story at the 1928 NUWT dinner to celebrate full women's franchise. *Woman Teacher*, 5 October 1928, p. 3. The close relationship between Miss Phipps and Miss Neal was typical of many romantic friendships between women who were politically active in the suffrage movement.

37 *The Times*, 21 April 1910, p. 9. She was subsequently re-appointed as a supply teacher. For Miss Froud's activities see *Woman Teacher*, 5 October 1928, p. 4.

38 Kean, *Challenging the state?*, p. 99.

39 *Woman Teacher*, 5 October 1928, p. 3. Miss Crosby, another leading NUWT figure, had also been a suffragist: ibid., p. 4.

40 Similarly, Sandra Holton and Liz Stanley have shown that many women held overlapping membership of both militant and non-militant suffrage societies, and often co-operated in campaigns at a local level. Holton, *Feminism and democracy*, pp. 38–39. Morley with Stanley, *Emily Wilding Davison*, p. 152 and *passim*.

41 K. Cockin, Women's suffrage drama, in Joannou and Purvis (eds), *The women's suffrage movement*. J. Holledge, *Innocent flowers: women in the Edwardian theatre* (London, Virago, 1981). D. Spender and C. Hayman (eds), *How the Vote was Won and other suffragette plays* (London, Methuen, 1985). L. Tickner, *The spectacle of women: imagery of the suffrage campaign 1907–14* (London, Chatto & Windus, 1987).

42 Tickner, *Spectacle of women*, pp. 102, 119, 220. D. Atkinson (ed.), *Mrs Broom's suffragette photographs* (London, Nishen, n.d.). NUWT Archive: photographic evidence of women teachers' suffrage activities. Kean, *Deeds not words*, p. 22.

43 E. Phipps, *A history of the National Union of Women Teachers (London, NUWT, 1928)*, pp. 6–8.

44 H. A. Clegg, *A history of British trade unions since 1889*, Volume 2, *1911–1933* (Oxford, Clarendon, 1985), p. 3.

45 *Schoolmaster*, 13 May 1911, p. 974; 13 April 1912, p. 718.

46 A. M. Pierotti, *The story of the National Union of Women Teachers* (London,

NUWT, 1963), p. 5. Also see *Journal of Education*, May 1911, p. 32 and *Schoolmaster*, 22 April 1911, pp. 795, 822.

47 NUT, Ladies Committee minutes, 20 May 1911. *Schoolmaster*, 22 April 1911, p. 822. This procedure was not without precedent. On the same morning it was agreed that a motion on child labour and continuation schools could be added to the conference agenda. *Schoolmaster*, 22 April 1911, pp. 795, 822.

48 *Schoolmaster*, 22 April 1911, p. 796; 29 April 1911, p. 876.

49 *Schoolmaster*, 13 April 1912, p. 719.

50 *Schoolmaster*, 22 April 1911, p. 822.

51 *Schoolmaster*, 5 April 1913, p. 714.

52 She repeated the point in the 1913 debate; ibid. This was also the single argument cited in an Executive discussion on the suffrage resolution, after the 1911 conference. Report of the meeting of the Executive, *Schoolmaster*, 13 May 1911, pp. 974–975.

53 Letter from Jane Dinning, Northumberland, *Schoolmaster*, 15 April 1911, p. 774.

54 *Schoolmaster*, 5 April 1913, p. 714.

55 *Schoolmaster*, 29 March 1913, p. 654.

56 *Schoolmaster*, 18 April 1914, p. 816. Also see pp. 812, 814.

57 *Schoolmaster*, 13 April 1912, p. 720.

58 *Schoolmaster*, 18 April 1914, p. 824.

59 *Schoolmaster*, 5 April 1913, p. 715. Mrs Burgwin was an important figure in the union, and President of the Benevolent and Orphan Fund. A member of the Anti-Suffrage League, she spoke against the women's suffrage resolution in 1912 and 1913. Kean, *Deeds not words*, pp. 40, 42. Copelman, *London's women teachers*, p. 201. She was an anomalous figure among the women, however; the evidence suggests overwhelming support for the resolution among the women teachers who attended conference.

60 *Schoolmaster*, 22 April 1911, p. 822.

61 *Schoolmaster*, 13 April 1912, pp. 718–719.

62 *Schoolmaster*, 5 April 1913, p. 714.

63 *Schoolmaster*, 13 April 1912, pp. 719–720. Also see *Schoolmaster*, 5 April 1913, pp. 714–715.

64 *Schoolmaster*, 5 April 1913, p. 714. Also see: 13 April 1912, p. 719; 18 April 1914, p. 824.

65 Corr, English and Scottish teachers' unions, p. 202.

66 *Schoolmaster*, 5 April 1913, p. 714.

67 Webb, English teachers, pp. 8–9.

68 *Schoolmaster*, 22 April 1911, p. 822.

69 *Schoolmaster*, 5 April 1913, p. 714; also see 13 April 1912, p. 719.

70 *The Times*, 8 April 1912, p. 8. NFWT conference.

71 *Schoolmaster*, 18 April 1914, p. 794. At the same time as arguing that women's suffrage was too political, an editorial in the *Schoolmaster* noted (approvingly) that the 'General Secretary has voted a dozen times in the House of Commons in favour of woman suffrage'. *Schoolmaster*, 10 December 1910, p. 997.

72 *Schoolmaster*, 29 April 1911, p. 869.

73 Kean, *Deeds not words*, pp. 40–41.

74 *Schoolmaster*, 18 April 1914, pp. 822–824; also see 13 April 1912, p. 718; 5 April 1913, p. 715.

75 *Schoolmaster*, 18 April 1914, p. 826.

76 NUWT Pamphlets, *Why I left the NUT* (n.d.: early 1920s), p. 8.

77 In 1914 the NFWT passed a resolution at their conference protesting against the revival of forcible feeding and drugging. *The Times*, 13 April 1914, p. 13.

78 *Woman Teacher*, 5 October 1928, p. 4.

79 Kean, *Deeds not words*, pp. 35–36.
80 In his speech he had concentrated on boys' education. Phipps, *History of the NUWT*, pp. 11–12. *Schoolmaster*, 29 March 1913, p. 626.
81 *Woman Teacher*, 5 October 1928, p. 4. *Schoolmaster*, 18 April 1914, p. 790.
82 *Schoolmaster*, 18 April 1914, p. 792.
83 *Schoolmaster*, 25 April 1914, p. 890.
84 Agnes Dawson in NUWT Pamphlets, *Why I left the NUT*, p. 4.

10

'I HAD NOT BEEN TO LONDON'[1]

Women's suffrage – a view from the regions

June Hannam

INTRODUCTION

In June 1908 the National Union of Women's Suffrage Societies (NUWSS) organised a procession of 15,000 men and women in London. Among the marchers were members of the Portsmouth branch who carried a banner inscribed with Nelson's signal 'Engage the enemy more closely'. Their leader, Miss Nora O'Shea, described as 'the red-haired rebel', informed the Hampshire Telegraph that it was one of their proudest moments:

> Our banner was the first one unfurled. We met at Northumberland-avenue, and with the assistance of civilians and helpers, we raised our banners first . . . Of course we had a lot of good-natured chaff, but the sympathy of the men in the street was admirable . . . 'Good old Pompey', 'Well done, Portsmouth'. Such were the exclamations heard on all sides, and one Marine even saluted the banner.[2]

This combination of pride in a sense of local identity and exhilaration at being part of a national campaign was a crucial feature of the early twentieth-century suffrage movement. Although women demanded the right to have access to parliament and to take part in national politics, it was their local group which provided the key site for most of their suffrage activity and it was locally that they gained their political experience.

Until recently, however, histories of the suffrage movement have tended to be London-centred. The development of national suffrage organisations after 1897, with their headquarters in London, encouraged historians to focus their attention on the capital. Their studies concentrated on detailing the aims, ideas and activities of one of the suffrage organisations, with most attention being directed towards the Women's Social and Political Union (WSPU) and the development of militancy. The WSPU, with its flamboyant tactics, is depicted as responsible for reviving the suffrage movement, but then as becoming increasingly authoritarian, isolated from other movements and extreme in its methods.[3] When the NUWSS was finally recognised as having also played a key role in the pre-war suffrage movement its democratic structure, constitutional methods and growing links with the labour movement were seen as providing a complete contrast with the WSPU.[4] In the last decade there has been an extensive re-interpretation of the suffrage movement.[5] The characteristics of the main suffrage groups, their relationship with each other and with broader political organisations and the nature and meaning of militancy have all been re-assessed. Attention has been drawn to the importance of exploring these issues through in-depth local studies which in turn have then helped to shape the new historiography.

We are now in a position to know a great deal more about local suffrage politics.[6] Recent biographies of women who were active at different levels of the movement have yielded valuable insights into local suffrage activities.[7] There have also been a growing number of studies, often arising from postgraduate dissertations, which focus on particular towns and regions.[8] Nonetheless, the importance of local studies is not always recognised, either because they are not easily available or because they are not drawn together and considered comparatively. It is the aim of this chapter, therefore, to suggest ways in which local studies can shed new light on the suffrage movement, in particular for the period 1890–1914, and to draw attention to the varied studies which have been undertaken. Examples will also be drawn from Scotland and Wales where branches of all the main suffrage groups were established. Although Scotland and Wales are separate countries with their own political traditions, rather than local areas, a study of developments there is in keeping with the emphasis of this chapter on examining the suffrage movement from the perspective of grass-roots activism outside London and away from formal parliamentary politics.

DEVELOPING A POLITICAL IDENTITY IN THE BRANCHES

An examination of the suffrage movement at a local level is not only important because it helps to modify or challenge existing interpretations, but also because it was here that the majority of suffrage activists engaged in campaign work and developed a political identity. On a purely practical level, many women had neither the resources nor the time to travel to London for large demonstrations or to lobby MPs and therefore had to take action in their own local area. For example, when the NUWSS wrote to the Glasgow and West of Scotland Association hoping that 75 members would go to a demonstration in London in June 1908, Leah Leneman claims that this was 'an impossible number for the Association to contemplate in view of the cost of travel. The Association also decided not to display posters for the event "as we are at too great a distance from London for such an advertisement to be effective".'[9] Some women were too sensitive to the needs of other family members to move outside their own region. Mabel Barton, president of the Carnforth and District Women's Suffrage Society, had an elderly father who supported the local Unionist MP. He did write to the latter to urge support for a limited franchise, but he had 'a great horror of much publicity' and therefore while he lived Mabel would not head any deputation which went to London.[10]

More crucially, it was the local branch which provided the focus for feminist political development.[11] Labour historians have long recognised the importance of local political activity and allegiances in building up national movements. In his study of the Independent Labour Party (ILP) David Howell argues that the 'analysis of a political organisation's growth cannot begin with a study of its formal structure. It must start from an examination of the possible bases of support.' These bases were often ambiguous, uneven, but essentially creative responses to an array of local social, political and economic forces. Local particularities were then transformed into a wider identity 'built around a commitment to an organisation'.[12]

Indeed, it is difficult to understand the growth of the suffrage campaign into a mass movement in the Edwardian period without recognising how much of this was due to the liveliness, enthusiasm and sheer hard work of the provincial branches. In Keswick, for example, a local branch of the NUWSS was formed when Catherine Marshall moved into the area in 1908. Only a few 'ladies' attended the first meeting at Catherine's home, but by the end of the year there were 250 members, 50 of whom were men. This growth can largely be explained by the very active publicity campaign conducted by the branch, which involved open-air meetings, the distribution of handbills and the sale of literature. A great deal of effort was put into preparing the ground for the visit of the suffrage caravan, organised by Newnham students, and for Millicent Fawcett's speaking tour of the Lake District late in 1908. Keswick members, who were now more experienced as speakers and organisers, used the occasion of Millicent Fawcett's tour to help to establish other branches in the region. In nearly all provincial areas members from strong suffrage centres made great efforts to reach out and take their message to other towns and villages. The intention was not simply to pay a flying visit but to encourage those who lived in the area to establish permanent organisations.[13]

Local branches not only carried out directives from the centre but also took a more active role, often initiating new developments. The campaign of women textile workers in Lancashire, for example, played an important part in reviving interest in women's suffrage before the WSPU had even been formed.[14] Within the NUWSS tactics were often developed in the regions first and then were adopted nationally. Catherine Marshall's suffrage stall, which she set up at Keswick market, and the caravan tour by Newnham students, which was based on the socialist Clarion vans of the 1890s, were both taken up more widely. Policy initiatives could also come from the regions; at the 1909 NUWSS conference Keswick and Birmingham suggested that structures should be set up to encourage co-operation between branches. This led to the establishment of regional federations which had financial autonomy and could become alternative centres of power, challenging the leadership over policy.[15]

There was also a complex relationship between the branch and the national leadership within the WSPU which has traditionally been viewed as far more autocratic and tightly controlled than the other groups. Krista Cowman's study of Merseyside suggests that WSPU members developed their own ways of working which suited local conditions. There was already a thriving branch before paid organisers were sent to the area and therefore conflict arose when they tried to introduce changes: Ada Flatman's attempt to appeal to a more middle-class membership by holding drawing-room meetings was opposed by local members and therefore she left. The next organiser, 1911–1912, tried to drop open-air meetings but recruitment and growth suffered. The Wirral branches remained most active because they were furthest away from her influence. Cowman concludes that local workers tried to follow their own tactics but would put the branch first, above conflicts with the organiser. There was therefore a subtle interplay between branch, organiser and the nation WSPU which was sustained by the rank and file and not just Clement's Inn.[16] Rank-and-file members, as the case of Emily Wilding Davison shows, frequently took militant action on their own initiative which was then sanctioned, albeit reluctantly, by the national leadership.[17]

The significance of studying women's involvement in the suffrage movement at a local level goes deeper, however, than a re-evaluation of the importance of the branch in terms of the organisation of the movement. It is crucial for understanding the process by which women became politicised and the meaning of political activity in their lives. In their study of Emily Wilding Davison, Stanley and Morley suggest that it was not just the formal organisations which were important, but the 'informal connections between people made on the basis of friendship, political analysis, social interests and emotional and sexual involvements'.[18] Friendships could bring women into suffrage organisations and the loyalties they developed there could sustain political activism in an often hostile environment.

In some instances women built on existing friendship links which had developed through involvement in other social and political causes. In Liverpool a Women's Suffrage Society was formed in 1894 by Mrs Alfred Booth, Mrs Allan Bright and Nessie Egerton Stewart Brown. They were from wealthy shipowning families, were active in Liberal politics and had long been involved in organisations that promoted the welfare of working women. Their class and political backgrounds were very similar to those of the national leaders of the NUWSS and the local group 'followed closely the style and tactics of campaigning' of the national organisation.[19] For other women, such as Emily and Mary Blathwayt, the wife and 27-year-old daughter of a retired colonel from Batheaston, near Bath, the suffrage movement provided their first experience of political activity.[20] After reading the extensive press coverage of the movement in 1906 they began to subscribe to suffrage newspapers and carried out propaganda among a network of local friends. They exchanged newspapers when they made social calls, and held meetings in each other's homes. The Blathwayts were members of both the Bath Women's Suffrage Society and the WSPU, but were increasingly drawn to the latter because its members were willing to take action and it had 'inspiring leaders'.[21] One of these was Annie Kenney who was instrumental in persuading Mary to join her in Bristol and to give a full-time commitment to suffrage work. Two of Mary's closest friends, Grace and Aethel Tollemache, the daughters of a clergyman, were also committed to the WSPU, whereas others remained in the Bath Society.

Mary and Emily Blathwayt both wrote diaries which provide a daily record of their suffrage activities. Sources such as these can be valuable in shifting attention away from well-known leaders and in providing detailed accounts which enable historians to explore the complex choices made by rank-and-file campaigners.[22] Mary Blathwayt's introduction to suffrage politics was affected by her own personal circumstances, including her age and her circle of friends and family, and also by the local context in which she lived. The socioeconomic structure of a local area coupled with existing political traditions and the personalities of local leaders could all help to explain which groups predominated, who was involved in the suffrage movement and why they chose particular groups.

SOCIAL BACKGROUND OF LOCAL SUFFRAGE CAMPAIGNERS

As the campaign gathered momentum after 1900, suffrage supporters were increasingly drawn from a variety of social backgrounds; Liddington and Norris were the first to draw attention to the widespread support for women's suffrage amongst Lancashire textile workers who debated the subject in their trade unions and Women's Co-operative Guild branches.[23] Esther Roper and Eva Gore Booth, leaders of the North of England Women's Suffrage Society, tried to build on this interest and worked closely with local working women, including Sarah Reddish, Sarah Dickenson and Selina Cooper, to gather thousands of signatures for suffrage petitions.

Liddington and Norris describe the textile workers as radical suffragists because they demanded the vote for all women over the age of twenty-one and aimed to build a mass movement of working women. They began to work independently of the more staid North of England Society, holding 'factory gate meetings, pushing suffrage motions through union branches, organising through trades councils'.[24] When the movement lost momentum after 1906 Liddington and Norris claim that radical suffragists were alienated by the militancy of the WSPU and its hostility to the labour movement, but were able to continue their work from within the decentralised, democratic and non-party political NUWSS.

In many respects the position of the well-organised Lancashire working woman was a unique one. It is difficult to find such active and widespread support for the suffrage movement from working-class women in other regions, and certainly not within the NUWSS. In Leicester, for example, where female members of the Boot and Shoe Workers' Union did take an interest in women's suffrage, they became involved in the WSPU.[25] In most districts, including some areas of Lancashire, the membership of the NUWSS was drawn from well-educated, wealthy, middle-class women who, at a local level, were often seen as closely allied to the Liberal Party. In Oldham a Suffrage Society was formed in 1902 at the height of radical suffragist campaigning and its members were drawn from the Women's Co-operative Guild and local labour groups. It was disbanded in 1906, however, and when a new society was formed in 1910 it had very different leaders; they were all middle-class women with a record of involvement in voluntary organisations. Marjorie Lees, the president, came from a wealthy Oldham family. She was a Poor Law Guardian and active in the Charity Organisation Society and the National Union of Women Workers. Her sister-in-law, Sarah Anne Lees, had an interest in progressive causes such as the National Union of Women Workers and the Oldham Nursing Association as well as women's suffrage. In 1907 she became a Liberal councillor and between 1910 and 1911 was installed as Mayor of Oldham. Two other leading members of the Oldham Society were Rachel Helen Bridge, a former headmistress, wife of a JP and a member of the executive of the Oldham Women's Liberal Association, and Mrs Mary Siddall, a workhouse visitor and the wife of a brush manufacturer. The membership of the Oldham Suffrage Society increased from 130 in 1910 to 857 in 1913, but most were recruited from the 'progressive liberal thinking middle and upper classes, including several clerics'.[26] Terry Jane Berry claims that both its propaganda and its activities were aimed at the middle class; members' meetings, for example, were usually held in the home of the president and included cultural lectures.

Studies of Portsmouth, South Wales and the major towns in Scotland reveal a similar pattern. The Portsmouth NUWSS drew its members from the relatives of gentlemen of independent means or the professional classes. Others, as might be expected in a naval town, were from service families. Peacock suggests that the WSPU was less genteel. Its members included a dealer, who did well out of the rummage sales, a sanitary inspector and a 'stout red-faced woman' who was in the movement to help her husband's business. He was a money-lender.[27] In Wales, where working-class women were not employed extensively outside the home and had no organised base, the most active support for both the NUWSS and the WSPU came from middle-class women. Cook and Evans note that speakers and organisers tended to come into Wales from more active English districts and that the movement was slow to develop.[28] Although the WSPU eventually had five branches the main support in the country was for the NUWSS, whose members had mostly cut their political teeth in the Women's Liberal Associations and who remained loyal to liberalism throughout the period.

In Scotland too it was the NUWSS which had most support. The movement was far stronger here than in Wales and could draw on many years of suffrage activity; Edinburgh, for example, had been one of the first towns to form a Women's Suffrage Society in the late 1860s. Events in Lancashire inspired the formation of new branches in Scotland after the turn of the century. The Glasgow and West of Scotland Association was formed in 1902, with delegates attending from various women's liberal groups and from the Women's Co-Operative Guild; it affiliated to the NUWSS in 1903. The Association had strong links with other reform groups but was not interested in the organisation of working-class support.[29] A group was also formed in Aberdeen with approximately 60 members but it did not join the NUWSS until 1905. After 1909 more effort was made to set up branches throughout Scotland and in November a Scottish Federation was formed. Leneman claims that by this point most Scottish activists were in the NUWSS or the Women's Freedom League, but she found little evidence of working-class involvement in the NUWSS.[30]

Contrary to assumptions made in many mainstream texts, it appears that working-class women were more likely to be involved in the suffrage movement as members of the WSPU, rather than the NUWSS, in particular in towns such as Glasgow and Liverpool where there was a close association between the National Union and the Liberal Party and where campaigning methods were 'decorous'. In Liverpool the WSPU was the largest organisation in the city and drew its membership from across all social classes, including a substantial number of working-class women. Cowman suggests that they were attracted by the links between the WSPU and the ILP and by the tactics used which were familiar to socialists, such as street meetings and chalking pavements. The local WSPU branch was formed by Mrs Morissey, a socialist, who was helped by Patricia Woodlock, the daughter of a painter, and Mrs Emma Hillier who had had a variety of occupations, including missionary and dressmaker.[31] Cowman argues that working-class women were not put off by militancy since they could choose whether or not to engage in actions which would lead to arrest. There were plenty of other things they could do such as organising meetings, selling newspapers or running the suffrage shop.

Detailed local research may yet reveal a greater participation of working-class women than appears on the surface. In an interview many years later

Jessie Stephen, who joined the WSPU in 1909 at the age of sixteen, claimed that there were a 'tremendous number' of working-class women involved in Scotland. Leneman traced working-class members of the Scottish WSPU through newspaper advertisements and concluded that 'not one of these women's names can be found in any suffrage literature of the period, and it is only historical accident that has rescued them from obscurity'.[32] A variety of local studies suggest, therefore, that Liddington and Norris's argument about the close links between working-class radical suffragists and the NUWSS did not necessarily apply outside of Lancashire.

PARTY POLITICS AND THE LABOUR/SUFFRAGE ALLIANCE

At a national level the main suffrage groups declared themselves to be independent of party politics. The WSPU opposed Liberal candidates and were critical of the Labour Party, whereas the WFL, while sympathetic to socialism, maintained independence. The NUWSS, on the other hand, gave support to individual candidates who declared themselves to be in favour of a limited franchise for women. Locally, however, women retained a far greater commitment to party politics. It was common for women from labour and socialist backgrounds, whether middle-class or working-class, to be drawn to the WSPU where they continued to link socialism and feminism as they pursued the goal of women's suffrage within a single-sex organisation. There are numerous examples of socialist women who were active in the WSPU in 1906–1908; Isabella Bream Pearce, who had written a women's column in the ILP newspaper *Labour Leader* in the 1890s, became joint secretary of the Scottish WSPU in 1907. Both she and Mary Phillips, another member of the WSPU, wrote regular columns in the Glasgow *Forward*, an ILP paper which gave sympathetic coverage to the suffragettes.[33] Mary Gawthorpe of the Leeds ILP was an organiser and speaker for the WSPU until 1912, while several ILP members were among the eleven Yorkshire working women arrested in a WSPU raid on the House of Commons in 1907.[34] In Woolwich, the Labour Party, which was dominated by the ILP, actively supported the WSPU, at least up to 1908.[35]

It was not easy for socialist women to channel their energies from a broader party agenda to a single-issue campaign[36] or to retain a commitment to socialist politics alongside the women's cause. It became harder to maintain a friendly working relationship, even in areas such as East Leeds, Preston and Glasgow where co-operation had been strong, once the WSPU declared war on the Labour Party in October 1912 because of its continued support for the Liberal government.[37] In these circumstances, socialist members of the WSPU, who valued their autonomy, followed the strategy of the national leadership. In Leeds, for example, members of the East Leeds

Women's Labour League and the ILP, who were also members of the WSPU, joined their suffrage colleagues in heckling the Labour MP Philip Snowden when he visited the city in 1913. They were criticised by the secretary of the Leeds Central Women's Labour League who argued that League members were expected to support Labour candidates and that this was incompatible with membership of the WSPU. Mrs Dightam, secretary of the East Leeds Women's Labour League, disagreed and defended her actions on the grounds that the Labour Party had fallen away from its ideals in refusing to support sex equality.[38] Similarly, many local leaders of the NUWSS remained close to the Liberal party and they too faced difficulties at election times if all three candidates were to be supported.

There was no simple relationship, however, between political allegiances and membership of particular suffrage groups. In the north-east the NUWSS had a broad membership base after 1905 and three of its leaders had strong labour links: Dr Ethel Bentham, who later became a Labour MP; Florence Bell, a teacher married to a trade union official; and Lisbeth Simm, the wife of an ILP organiser. They were joined by Dr Ethel Williams, a leading member of the Women's Liberal Association, who was radical in her outlook.[39] Lisbeth Simm was very critical of the WSPU and felt that the organisers 'had little idea of the poverty of the region or the hardship their fund-raising would produce'. She disliked the style of the leaders, commenting: 'how very theatrical they are.'[40]

A branch of the WSPU was formed in the north-east in 1908 after an argument about the refusal of the NUWSS to oppose government candidates. Mona Taylor, a Liberal and wife of a Northumbrian landowner, led a group of thirteen dissidents to join the WSPU. Taylor had been active in the suffrage campaign both locally and nationally since the 1890s. At an early stage she showed an interest in moving away from sedate drawing-room meetings and tried to attract working-class members by holding meetings at factory gates and distributing literature as widely as possible. It would not have been an easy decision, however, to join a group which was antagonistic to the party she had supported for so long. The Newcastle WSPU drew its support mainly from upper-class and middle-class women, and professional women such as teachers, although there were some working-class members in the Jarrow WSPU.[41]

In Scotland too Leah Leneman questions any simple analogy between political outlook and the type of organisation which women joined. She disputes Les Garner's assertion that the split within the WSPU which led to the formation of the Women's Freedom League (WFL) in 1907 reflected the growing conservatism of Christabel and her mother and that the crisis was a left/right division. Instead she found that there were socialist women in the Women's Freedom League, such as Bessie Stewart Semple in Glasgow, Agnes Hubbard in Dundee and Anna Munro, but that many of the most active socialists such as Mary Phillips, Janie Allan, Jessie Stephen and Helen

Crawfurd were members of the WSPU.[42] The WFL became the predominant 'militant' group in Scotland. This may have been because one of its founders, Teresa Billington-Greig, had been sent to Scotland as a WSPU organiser and had built up a personal following and links with the labour movement. She also remained in the country after the split.

The relationship between the suffrage movement and party politics was transformed at a national level in 1912 when the NUWSS entered into an alliance with the Labour Party for electoral purposes and organised support for Labour candidates through an Election Fighting Fund. Resistance to the alliance, and an unwillingness to work actively for it, was far greater in branches with Liberal sympathies such as Liverpool, Wales, Oldham and Portsmouth.[43] In some NUWSS branches the main links were with the labour and socialist movement and it was from these, in particular Manchester, Edinburgh and Newcastle, that arguments were put long before 1912 that the NUWSS and the Labour Party should form an alliance.[44] Indeed, it has been suggested that the alliance would never have worked if there had not been enough support for it from the grass roots. In the north-east, Labour women managed to persuade the local Women's Suffrage Society to support the Labour candidate, Pete Curran, who was standing in a by-election in Jarrow in 1907, although the NUWSS executive had declared that both the Liberal and the Labour candidates should have support. Curran won and this inspired Ethel Bentham to put a resolution to the provincial council calling on the NUWSS to change its election policy in favour of the Labour Party, a stand that was not yet acceptable to the executive.[45]

The alliance did not just come about, therefore, because of national policy decisions. It must be seen as the result of hard work by Labour and socialist women at a national and at a local level who built up support by speaking to trade union branches, trades councils, local socialist groups and women's suffrage meetings. With the formation of the Election Fighting Fund committee propaganda work was intensified among labour groups and it became easier for labour women's organisations to join in support of the suffrage. In Bristol, for example, when the ILP member Walter Ayles, a keen supporter of women's suffrage, stood as a candidate in the East Bristol by-election of 1913, support was co-ordinated by the ILP member Mrs Townley and the East Bristol Women's Suffrage Society. East Bristol was a very poor area of the city and it was claimed that working women had up until then been unable to give time or money to women's suffrage, but those already organised in the Women's Co-operative Guild, the Railway Women's Guild and the Women's Labour League 'are rallying with enthusiasm to the fight'.[46] The local autonomy enjoyed by branches of the Women's Labour League and the Women's Co-operative Guild, however, meant that in some local areas these groups had been involved in the suffrage campaign for a number of years.[47]

The Labour/suffrage alliance not only helped to draw more working-class women and their organisations into suffrage politics, it also helped to build support for women's suffrage more generally within Labour Party branches. The extent to which women were able to influence the agenda of political parties has often been overlooked and yet their local involvement could have a crucial role. Pat Thane has suggested that the democratisation of local politics, which enabled men and women to take part in elections for local government bodies, played a key part in influencing the agendas and politics of national political parties. She argues that women played an important role in building the Labour Party from this local base and ensuring that women's suffrage and women's rights 'became firmly established on the radical agenda. By 1914 "democracy" could no longer be discussed in isolation from the question of women's suffrage, and democracy was central to progressive politics.'[48]

Such a relationship was not, however, straightforward. As women's suffrage became more associated with democratic politics, so the arguments for full adult suffrage became more attractive to some labour women who had taken a limited suffrage position beforehand. Although Florence Bell and Lisbeth Simm had helped to lead the North East Women's Suffrage Society from c. 1906, Lisbeth Simm increasingly gave more of her energies to the Women's Labour League and both women became involved in the People's Suffrage Federation. In 1909, therefore, Bell resigned as secretary of the North East Society. During the South Shields by-election of 1910 friction was obvious between Simm and Bell and other socialist women in the North East Women's Suffrage Society. In the absence of a Labour candidate there was no question of Simm or Bell giving support to a Unionist pro-suffrage candidate now that they were distancing themselves from tactics related largely to women's suffrage. What is interesting is that neither they nor the Women's Labour League gave help to the Election Fighting Fund committee when it campaigned in by-elections in the north-east despite the fact that the goals of both organisations and their tactics were now much closer. Neville uses this to support his argument that personality clashes and personal histories could be as important in explaining the actions of individual suffragists as class or formal political perspectives.[49]

MILITANCY

In any discussions of why women joined particular suffrage organisations and the extent to which they were able to link suffrage and party politics, the character of the tactics used by suffrage groups is invariably seen as a crucially important factor. In standard accounts of the suffrage movement a distinction is drawn between the militant WSPU and the non-militant NUWSS. The WSPU is characterised as bringing new life to the Cause through its disruptive tactics which led to women's imprisonment, and the impression is given that the NUWSS played a more passive role. It is suggested that as the scale of militancy increased, in particular after 1912, individual acts of violence replaced collective mass protests and alienated many members of the WSPU which became more isolated as an organisation.

This interpretation has been questioned in more recent studies which draw attention to the need to define militancy more broadly. If, for example, it is taken to mean actions which took women out of the drawing room and into the public realm of the street, or 'forceful activism', then the NUWSS must also be seen as militant, in particular after 1907. Thus Sandra Holton suggests that the term constitutionalist should be used rather than non-militant. She also cautions against seeing the militant and constitutionalist wings as unchanging, or as too coherent, since 'both wings of the movement experienced internal tensions, and sometimes divisions'.[50]

Again it is local studies which have helped to contribute towards this reinterpretation of militancy by revealing the wide range of activities undertaken by women from all the suffrage organisations and the complex choices which faced individual suffragists at different periods. Krista Cowman argues that militancy should be seen as encompassing a 'breadth of actions' which were about challenging views of feminine behaviour and not just about breaking the law.[51] Women could be involved in poster parades, paper-selling, chalking pavements for meetings and making protests at places of entertainment, and these activities continued alongside the more violent forms of militancy.

In some local areas the NUWSS provided a complete contrast to the tactics of the WSPU. In Liverpool Cowman argues that the experience of members of the NUWSS was a passive one; the branch was led by Eleanor Rathbone, the daughter of the MP and philanthropist William Rathbone. She was elected to the Liverpool City Council and helped raise the profile of the Liverpool Society, but was opposed to mass campaigning and, according to Cowman, it was unthinkable for a woman of her position to sell a newspaper such as the *Common Cause* on the street.[52] In many other areas, however, the NUWSS engaged in a wide range of activities in the public arena and these also changed over time. When Helen Fraser resigned from the WSPU in Scotland in 1908, because she could not approve of stone-throwing, she joined the NUWSS and borrowed a horse-drawn caravan to make a suffrage tour of the Borders which would never have been thought of before the 'advent' of the WSPU.[53]

In the north-east David Neville suggests that there was very little difference in the tactics of the NUWSS and the WSPU until 1912, when the latter began to attack private property and the NUWSS moved closer to the Labour Party. They both held weekly meetings where speakers addressed a wide range of topics, they held processions and public meetings and used similar fund-raising tactics, including the opening of suffrage shops.[54] This may have been because of the early relationship between the labour movement and the North East Women's Suffrage Society, although there is a similar picture in Portsmouth and south-east Hampshire where there were no such links and where the NUWSS predominated. In Portsmouth members of the branch held public meetings, lobbied MPs, spoke on street corners, sold suffrage literature, marched through the town and carried out extensive fundraising. In 1913 NUWSS members took part in the Pilgrimage, a national event in which women marched in procession from all parts of England, Scotland and Wales to converge in London for a mass demonstration, an action which would have been considered militant several years before. Harriet Blessley, the daughter of a Portsmouth businessman, recorded the hostility that the marchers met from local crowds who were incensed by the growth of militancy. But she also showed that NUWSS women could be inspired by a crusading spirit which was akin to that experienced by WSPU members. She recalled that the marchers left the Portsmouth Town Hall at 5 p.m. on 17 July 1913:

> Marched off round back of Town Hall to front, and up the road. Hot and smelly. Hemmed in with back streeters and boys running in between police. Band played march to suit masculine strides; had hard job to keep up . . . a cheer or two and one tomatoe [sic] on my hat. Reach boundary. Police leave us. March some distance unescorted. Cosham police (three) take charge outside Cosham. Inhabitants excited and displeased. ('Go home and mend your stockings!' 'Where's Mrs Pankhurst?') . . . reach field adjoining Miss O'Shea's house. Blessed green grass and rest! Labour Party strong. Revd Thompson spoke to crowd outside hedge. Sang! Three cheers for Cause, Labour Party and Pilgrims.[55]

Local studies do reveal continuing connections between suffrage groups which are often seen as separate in standard accounts. Numerous examples can be found of women who were members of more than one group, in particular in the period 1906–1910. When the Edinburgh WSPU was formed in 1908 many members still belonged to the NUWSS, although in Glasgow the difference in tactics placed more strain on women's loyalties. In 1910 when the Women's Freedom League directed that committee members should not belong to any other militant organisation, some activists in Scotland continued with dual membership.[56] In Bath, despite her long years of association with the NUWSS and leadership of the Bath Women's Suffrage Society, Lilias Ashworth Hallett was sympathetic to the WSPU; she wore a Votes for Women badge, maintained a close relationship with the Blathwayt family and attended the first Women's Parliament in London in 1907.[57] She became critical of militancy after 1909, however, when it began to involve personal violence. Lilias Ashworth Hallett's cousins, the Priestman sisters, who were in their seventies, had also been involved in suffrage campaigning in the

Bristol area since the 1860s. They had always taken an independent stance, refusing to pay their rates in the 1870s and trying to link suffrage and liberal politics through the Bristol Women's Liberal Association. After the turn of the century they established the Women's Reform Union which sought a wide range of reforms as well as women's suffrage, but in 1910 this amalgamated with the Bristol Women's Suffrage Society. Nonetheless, the Priestmans also gave financial and moral support to Annie Kenney when she worked as an organiser in the south-west.[58]

Suffrage organisations could work together at a local level even at times when relationships were strained nationally. In Portsmouth the NUWSS disassociated itself from the militancy of the WSPU after 1908 but was still willing to hold joint meetings until 1912. In the north-east the NUWSS and the WSPU continued to have a close relationship up until the First World War, although this was put under greater strain after 1912. Joint demonstrations and other activities were frequently held. During the truce in 1910 the squabbles at a national level about the organisation of a joint march were not mirrored locally since a demonstration involving the NUWSS, the WSPU and other suffrage groups was held in advance of any national initiatives. Neville suggests that this close working relationship grew out of the friendship links between members of the different groups. They continued to meet in the same building and took part in common ventures such as the suffrage choir where the green sash of the Internationale was worn.[59]

Women were also able to join together in a range of smaller organisations which are usually neglected in standard accounts of the movement; they included the Conservative Women's Franchise Association, the Church League for Women's Suffrage and the Catholic Women's Suffrage Society as well as groups based on particular occupations. When she resigned from the Bath WSPU Emily Blathwayt joined the Conservative Women's Franchise Association because at least the group did not support Liberal candidates.[60] Cowman argues that these societies could create alternative identities for suffrage activists rather than representing rival organisations. They provided a space where militants and non-militants could get together, in particular as militancy escalated. The Church League for Women's Suffrage, for example, could unite existing suffrage activists who were Anglican, while others could use it to proclaim their suffragism without belonging to a separate suffrage body. Cowman suggests that the existence of numerous small groups provides more proof of the adaptability of Edwardian feminism in a period when the leadership is often viewed as rigid.[61]

Nonetheless, contemporaries did see real differences between groups – in particular between the WSPU and the NUWSS – and these should not be underestimated. The willingness to take disruptive action which went way beyond the bounds of acceptable feminine behaviour and the sense of excitement this generated, as well as the belief that something positive was actually happening, attracted women to the WSPU. When Lilias Mitchell, who belonged to a prosperous Edinburgh family, heard Mrs Pankhurst and Mrs Pethick Lawrence speak, she wrote:

> Never shall I forget the blazing warmth of that meeting; we felt completely lifted out of ourselves, joined the society there and then and went home walking it seemed on air. I was twenty three at the time and was more than ready for an opening for work of this kind. In fact, after that meeting, the hockey, reading, music clubs, violin lessons, even dances, seemed sheer nonsense when the Vote had yet to be won.[62]

A sense that they were doing something was all-important for WSPU members. The son of Blanche Surry, a Portsmouth WSPU member, recalled that she soon tired of the 'mildly constitutional methods' of the NUWSS and joined the WSPU instead.[63]

Women's allegiances to particular groups did not remain fixed and they often moved between organisations as political strategies and tactics changed. Suffrage campaigners themselves also 'changed a good deal as a consequence of things they did and things that happened to them'.[64] There is no one discernible pattern in the choices that women made. The escalation of militancy did cause many women to leave the WSPU, but they differed in the timing of this. Emily Blathwayt resigned from the WSPU in 1909 when two young friends of hers attacked Asquith, because she could not tolerate personal violence.[65] Her daughter Mary, who had never taken part in active service herself and who felt uncomfortable about breaking the law, did not resign until 1913 when the destruction of personal property was at its height. As already noted, Helen Fraser left the Scottish WSPU as early as 1908 when stone-throwing began, but Mona Taylor did not leave the Newcastle branch until 1912 when the Pethick Lawrences and the Pankhursts parted company. She had welcomed earlier forms of militancy, but found the escalating violence unacceptable.[66]

Not all women were put off by the escalation of militancy; in Liverpool, Glasgow and Leeds there was an increase in membership of local WSPU branches after 1912. In Bath Mary Blathwayt's friends, Grace and Aethel Tollemache, remained in the WSPU after 1912, took part in actions such as pouring tar into post-boxes, and suffered imprisonment. Dr Alice Ker, a member of the Birkenhead Women's Suffrage Society, became more interested in the WSPU after 1910 and by 1912 had switched her allegiance to the militant group. She was arrested in 1912 for breaking shop windows in London and remained committed to militancy until the outbreak of war.[67]

The loyalties and friendship ties between women who had taken action together made it very difficult for them to leave their local groups. Dr Elizabeth Baxendale recalled that her mother disapproved of later militant attacks but remained in the Edinburgh WSPU because of loyalty to her friends. Others did resign on principle from particular organisations, but suffered greatly in personal terms. Helen Fraser found it very painful to leave the Scottish WSPU and wrote to a friend, Caroline Phillips, that: 'I had a worrying time before I resigned and felt very tired and ill when I did . . . it doesn't seem true, even yet, that I am no longer connected with you all – I feel sure somehow we shall still work together for suffrage.'[68]

Relationships between the main suffrage groups did get more strained as the National Union began to criticise the WSPU and its methods in public. Although she was friends with many members of the Bath Women's Suffrage Society, and had resigned from the WSPU in 1909, Emily Blathwayt was still supportive of friends such as Annie Kenney and Mrs Pankhurst and could be scathing about the NUWSS for its timidity. Referring to a friend who had complained that militancy had put back the cause she recorded: 'Men used to think women would be so quiet and Conservative and now! these women!! . . . Well whether they have put it back or not, it certainly would not have come from the respectable party, so we have lost nothing.'[69] Alice Ker from Liverpool maintained two circles of friends in the period 1910 and 1911 as she gradually moved from membership of the NUWSS to a commitment to the WSPU. She became more bitter about her old colleagues in the NUWSS in 1912 when she suffered imprisonment and found that the National Union was joining in the chorus of public criticism of the WSPU:

> When I come out I think I am going to let the Nationals know what I think of them, as well as the men. One sees clearly in this atmosphere, and, what makes even more difference, one has nothing left to be afraid of in speaking one's mind. Why should they not only not support us, the advance guard, as the rear guard should, but even fire into us from behind. No, I am associating with heroines here, and I don't feel inclined to suffer cowards so gladly as I have hitherto done.[70]

Local studies suggest, therefore, that historians need to exercise caution in making generalisations about the nature of militancy and its effects on women's political choices. There could be co-operation and a fluid membership between groups at a local level, but also loyalties to a particular organisation could grow stronger if it appeared that the group, and women's right to take autonomous action, was under attack from all sides. Friendship ties and loyalties were important, and could override concerns about changes in tactics and political strategies, but they did not necessarily stop women from following their principles and resigning from a group if they could no longer give approval to the overall methods adopted.

CONCLUSION

The preceding pages of this chapter have attempted to argue that local suffrage politics was not just about building support for a national movement – at particular times the local branches *were* the movement. An understanding of grass-roots activism therefore does not just add interesting details to an existing national picture, it also transforms our view of the nature and meaning of suffragism for the participants. What emerges from local studies is a very complex picture in which individual women made a variety of choices about which groups to join and which tactics to pursue; these choices are not easy to classify or to categorise under neat labels such as 'militant', 'non-militant', 'radical suffragist' or 'democratic suffragist'. The main suffrage organisations display less clear-cut characteristics when viewed from the branches, which could have their own particular 'flavour', rather than from a national perspective.

Local groups were an important site for direct action, for fund-raising, for retaining and building loyalties and for giving women a sense of political identity. This identity could be a complex one, however, and involve negotiations which took a different form over time and in specific localities. While the choices made by individual women did not follow any clear pattern, they were nonetheless affected by the socioeconomic structure of a region and its existing political traditions. Although some women relished the opportunity to engage in a woman-centred politics and to challenge contemporary notions of appropriate feminine political behaviour, it caused tensions for others who continued to relate their suffragism to class loyalties and party politics. These difficulties lay behind the very complex discussions over the form that the demand for women's suffrage should take and the shifts made by individuals between an adult and a limited suffrage position. They also surfaced during the First World War when the pacifist and labour loyalties of many WSPU members proved far greater than their loyalties to the Pankhursts, and again in 1918 when women had to decide how best to use their new status as voters to achieve more change for their sex. It is to be hoped that an increasing emphasis on local studies will enable the historian to trace the negotiations women made between class, sex and party political loyalties beyond the watershed of the First World War into the very different context of the inter-war years.

NOTES

1 M. Gawthorpe, *Up hill to Holloway* (Penobscot, ME, Traversity Press, 1962), p. 216.
2 *Hampshire Telegraph*, 15 June 1908, quoted in S. Peacock, *Votes for women: the women's fight in Portsmouth* (Portsmouth, Portsmouth City Council, the Portsmouth papers no. 39, December 1983), p. 12.

3 See, for example, C. Rover, *Women's suffrage and party politics in Britain, 1866–1914* (London, Routledge & Kegan Paul, 1967); A. Rosen, *Rise up women! The militant campaign of the Women's Social and Political Union, 1903–14* (London, Routledge & Kegan Paul, 1974); D. Mitchell, *The fighting Pankhursts: a study in tenacity* (London, Macmillan, 1967).

4 L. P. Hume, *The National Union of Women's Suffrage Societies, 1897–1914* (New York, Garland, 1982).

5 In particular, see S. S. Holton, *Feminism and democracy: women's suffrage and reform politics in Britain, 1900–1918* (Cambridge, Cambridge University Press, 1986) and most recently *Suffrage days: stories from the women's suffrage movement* (London, Routledge, 1996)

6 For an overview, see L. Leneman, A truly national movement: the view from outside London, in M. Joannou and J. Purvis (eds), *The women's suffrage movement: new feminist perspectives* (Manchester, Manchester University Press, 1998).

7 See, for example, A. Morley with L. Stanley, *The life and death of Emily Wilding Davison* (London, Women's Press, 1988); G. Lewis, *Eva Gore Booth and Esther Roper: a biography* (London, Pandora, 1989); J. Hannam, *Isabella Ford, 1855––1924* (Oxford, Blackwell, 1989); J. Liddington, *The life and times of a respectable rebel: Selina Cooper, 1864–1946* (London, Virago, 1984); J. Vellacott, *From liberal to labour with women's suffrage: the story of Catherine Marshall* (Montreal, McGill Queen's University Press, 1993).

8 K. Cowman, Engendering citizenship: the political involvement of women on Merseyside, 1890–1920, unpublished PhD thesis, University of York, 1994; D. Neville, The women's suffrage movement in the north east of England, 1900–1914, unpublished MPhil thesis, Newcastle upon Tyne Polytechnic, 1991; T. J. Berry, The female suffrage movement in South Lancashire with particular reference to Oldham, 1890–1914, unpublished MA thesis, Huddersfield Polytechnic, 1986; M. Shoebridge, The women's suffrage movement in Birmingham and district, 1903–1918, unpublished MA thesis, Wolverhampton Polytechnic, 1983; G. Barnsby, *Votes for women: the struggle for the vote in the Black Country* (Wolverhampton, Integrated Publishing Services, nd).

9 L. Leneman, *A guid cause: the women's suffrage movement in Scotland* (Edinburgh, Mercat Press, 1995 revised edn), p. 63.

10 Vellacott, *From liberal to labour*, p. 159.

11 Cowman, Engendering citizenship, p. 29; Morley with Stanley, *Life and death of Emily Wilding Davison.*

12 D. Howell, *British workers and the Independent Labour Party, 1886–1906* (Manchester, Manchester University Press, 1983), pp. vii–viii.

13 Vellacott, *From liberal to labour*, pp. 38, 42–46.

14 J. Liddington and J. Norris, *One hand tied behind us: the rise of the women's suffrage movement* (London, Virago, 1978).

15 Vellacott, *From liberal to labour*, pp. 44, 65–66. See also Holton, *Feminism and democracy.*

16 Cowman, Engendering citizenship, Chapter 6.

17 Morley with Stanley, *Life and death of Emily Wilding Davison.*

18 Morley with Stanley, *Life and death of Emily Wilding Davison*, p. 175. See also, Holton, *Suffrage days*, p. 243.

19 M. Van Helmond, *Votes for women: the events on Merseyside, 1870–1928* (Liverpool, National Museums & Galleries on Merseyside, 1992), p. 21.

20 The following paragraph is based on the diaries of Mary and Emily Blathwayt. These are kept at Dyrham park, near Bath. I am grateful to the National Trust for giving me permission to consult them.

21 Emily Blathwayt, *Diary*, 30 April 1908.

22 For example, see T. Thompson (ed.), *Dear girl: the diaries and letters of two working women 1897–1917* (London, Women's Press, 1987).

23 Liddington and Norris, *One hand tied behind us*.

24 Liddington and Norris, *One hand tied behind us*, p. 26.

25 R. Whitmore, Radical traditions and working women in the Leicester WSPU, paper presented at Seeing Through Suffrage conference, Greenwich University, 1996.

26 Berry, The female suffrage movement in South Lancashire, p. 28.

27 Peacock, *Votes for women*, p. 9.

28 K. Cook and N. Evans, The petty antics of the bell-ringing boisterous band; the women's suffrage movement in Wales, in A. V. John (ed.), *Our mothers' land: chapters in Welsh women's history, 1830–1939* (Cardiff, University of Wales Press, 1991).

29 Holton, *Feminism and democracy*.

30 Leneman, *A guid cause*, pp. 38–41, 93.

31 K. Cowman, 'The stone-throwing has been forced upon us': the function of militancy within the Liverpool W.S.P.U., 1906–14, *Transactions of the Historic Society of Lancashire and Cheshire*, 145, 1995, p. 177. A contingent of working women from South London attended the WSPU Hyde Park demonstration in June 1908. I. Dove, Women, suffrage and Woolwich Labour Party: 1908, *South London Record*, 1, 1985.

32 Leneman, *A guid cause*, p. 94.

33 There were numerous articles and reports on the suffragette movement, in particular between 1906 and 1909, in the Glasgow *Forward*.

34 J. Hannam, 'In the comradeship of the sexes lies the hope of progress and social regeneration': women in the West Riding ILP, *c.* 1890-1914, in J. Rendall (ed.), *Equal or different? Women's politics, 1800-1914* (Oxford, Blackwell, 1987), p. 232.

35 Dove, Women, suffrage and Woolwich Labour Party. See also I. Dove, *Yours in the cause: suffragettes in Lewisham, Greenwich and Woolwich* (Lewisham Library Services and Greenwich Libraries, 1988).

36 C. Eustance, *'Daring to be free': the evolution of women's political identities in the Women's Freedom League, 1907–1930*, unpublished DPhil thesis, University of York, 1993.

37 C. Collins, Women and Labour politics in Britain, 1893–1932, unpublished PhD thesis, LSE, 1991, p. 121.

38 Hannam, 'In the comradeship of the sexes', p. 234.

39 Neville, The women's suffrage movement in the north east of England.

40 C. Collette, *For Labour and for women: the Women's Labour League, 1900–1918* (Manchester, Manchester University Press, 1989), p. 73.

41 Neville, The women's suffrage movement in the north east of England.

42 Leneman, *A guid cause*, p. 52.

43 Cowman, Engendering citizenship; Cook and Evans, The petty antics of the bell-ringing boisterous band; Peacock, *Votes for women*; Berry, The female suffrage movement in South Lancashire.

44 Holton, *Feminism and democracy*.

45 Neville, The women's suffrage movement in the north east of England, pp. 39–42.

46 *Common Cause*, 3 October 1913.

47 Collette, *For Labour and for women*.

48 P. Thane, Labour and local politics: radicalism, democracy and social reform, 1880–1914, in F. Biagini and A. Reid (eds), *Currents of radicalism* (Cambridge,

Cambridge University Press, 1991), pp. 259–260. See also Holton, *Feminism and democracy.*

49 Neville, The women's suffrage movement in the north east of England, Chap. 8.

50 S. S. Holton, Women and the vote, in J. Purvis (ed.), *Women's history: Britain, 1850-1950* (London, UCL, 1995), pp. 290–292. See also S. S. Holton, The suffragist and the 'average' woman, *Women's History Review,* 1, 1, 1992, pp. 9-24.

51 Cowman, Engendering citizenship, p. 238.

52 Cowman, Engendering citizenship. See also the different tactics at elections described in Van Helmond, *Votes for women.* The Glasgow Association also did not involve itself in public demonstrations and held sedate meetings: Holton, *Feminism and democracy.*

53 Leneman, *A guid cause,* p. 66.

54 Neville, The women's suffrage movement in the north east of England, pp. 50–56.

55 Peacock, *Votes for women,* p. 18.

56 Leneman, *A guid cause,* pp. 63, 91.

57 I am grateful to Sandra Holton for this information. See also the diaries of Emily and Mary Blathwayt.

58 J. Hannam, 'An enlarged sphere of usefulness': the Bristol women's movement, *c.* 1860–1914, in M. Dresser and P. Ollerenshaw (eds), *The Making of modern Bristol* (Tiverton, Redcliffe Press, 1996).

59 Peacock, *Votes for women*; Neville, The women's suffrage movement in the north east of England.

60 Emily Blathwayt, *Diary,* 4–6 October 1909.

61 Cowman, Engendering citizenship, Chap. 7.

62 Leneman, *A guid cause,* p. 73.

63 Peacock, *Votes for women,* p. 7.

64 Morley with Stanley, *Life and death of Emily Wilding Davison,* p. 175.

65 Emily Blathwayt, *Diary,* 8 September 1909.

66 Neville, The women's movement in the north east of England.

67 Van Helmond, *Votes for women,* Chap. 5.

68 Leneman, *A guid cause,* p. 64.

69 3 July 1910, quoted in B. M. Wilmott Dobbie, *A nest of suffragettes in Somerset* (Batheaston, Batheaston Society, 1979), p. 43.

70 Letter to Alice Ker's daughters, 16 March 1912, quoted in Van Helmond, *Votes for women,* p. 62.

11

JENNIE BAINES

Suffrage and an Australian connection

Judith Smart

In March 1943, the popular Australian women's magazine, *Pix*, featured a two-page spread on 77-year-old Jennie Baines – 'Was Famous Suffragette: Fought for Women's Right to Vote' – in which Mrs Baines proudly displayed her most treasured possession, the medal presented to her by the Women's Social and Political Union (WSPU) before she left Britain in 1913. Inscribed 'For Valor', it had originally had five bars, one for each time she used the hunger-strike, though two were now missing. With some understandable exaggeration after the passage of three decades, she described her position in the WSPU as 'Chief Organiser of the Militant Section' and also displayed photos of herself with Mrs Drummond and Mrs Pethick Lawrence. Another prized relic was her window-smashing bag, a small reticule with long ribands, filled with stones and swung against shop windows with a quick practised flick of the wrist.[1] It was as if she were remembering a brilliant stage career, or recalling the heroic achievements and comradeship of war. And, indeed, between 1905 and 1913, the WSPU had assumed characteristics of both the theatre and the armed forces. On the one hand, there was the carefully planned ritual, the staging and sets, the scripts and costumes, and, not least, the performance and high drama orchestrated by the leadership;[2] on the other hand, the movement was hierarchical and autocratic, demanding unquestioning loyalty and obedience, and military precision in execution of orders and conduct of campaigns. It needed actors, chorus and audience, generals, officers and foot-soldiers, and it needed courage, commitment and self-sacrifice. It is not surprising then that Jennie Baines, forced from the campaign at its most dramatic point by her failing health and constant re-arrests under the 'Cat and Mouse' Act 1913, remembered the suffragette years as her peak experience, a time of unparalleled excitement, when life seemed to take on shape and meaning and an enduring exalted significance, when ordinary women perceived themselves to be acting out unique roles for an imminent transformation of society.

Jennie Baines was an ideal soldier and chorister but one with initiative as well as dedication, a rebel with an independent cast of mind but not an individualist, junior officer material or useful supporting actor. Does this mean that she saw her life and work in Australia as exile, cut off from the command centre, and hence an inevitable anticlimax? Did the suffrage years provide the singular template upon which she built her identity? Certainly that is not the way she explained her personal history to others. Moreover, Jennie Baines' Australian career does not exhibit the insatiable hunger for new sources of enthusiasm that led another, more famous, expatriate suffragette, Adela Pankhurst, to move feverishly from cause to cause.[3] Like Adela, she continued to call on the militant and melodramatic tactics of the WSPU, and both were accused of introducing these methods into Australian political protest during the Great War, 1914–1918. But Jennie was solidly rooted in working-class politics and in an evangelical imperative to justice. The last two decades of her life were spent, in a nicely symmetrical echo of her pre-suffrage years in Lancashire, working as a special magistrate in the children's court at South Melbourne and organising locally for the Labor Party.

In the prewar period, Baines was inevitably caught up in the contemporary vitalist impulse, similar in its stress on heroic action to the 'romantic feminism' Sandra Holton has identified in Emmeline and Christabel Pankhurst.[4] Vitalists manifested a Sorrelian urge to glorify violence and the will to power. But there are signs that, like other working-class members of the WSPU, Baines was beginning to have misgivings during 1913, and it is unlikely that she would have turned her passion for 'the Cause' to patriotism in August 1914, had she stayed in Britain.[5] In this chapter, I will argue that Jennie Baines' sense of self arose from a primary class identification – a necessarily gendered one – and that she understood her suffrage years, however exciting and pivotal, as the strategic and temporary culmination of her political endeavours, not as a separate and idealised episode. Further, recognising the similarities in working-class life and culture between her native Midlands and the industrial inner suburbs of Melbourne, both in a sense provincial, she and her family quickly settled and integrated into the local community. Among prominent suffragists with international political experience and repute, Jennie Baines' perspective was thus unusual – working-class rather than middle-class; local, provincial and, paradoxically, international more than national; action-oriented rather than theoretical; collective more than individual; migrant and resident rather than transient participant.

SUFFRAGETTE SOLDIER AND WORKER

Like so many English suffragists of all affiliations, Jennie Baines grew up in the Midlands. The daughter of a gunmaker, James Hunt, and his wife, Sarah, she was born on 30 November 1866 in Birmingham, and started work in the Birmingham small-arms factory at the age of eleven.[6] This early familiarity with guns and explosives may have contributed to her value as an arsonist in the later stages of the WSPU campaigns, though commitment to social justice and to practical methods of achieving it were what first directed her into full-time work for 'the Cause'. At least that's what one can read into the limited evidence we have of her pre-WSPU days, and it is also what she intended we should read. Writing about Baines' early life is like reciting a catechism – a neatly packaged received wisdom strung together from her own practised accounts. We know what she thought was relevant and we only know that from what she told others; the very little she wrote was functional and practical, rhetorical not reflective. There are few other sources to draw on beyond those that establish a socio-cultural context and the few personal comments gleaned from extant correspondence. It is a familiar problem, especially in researching working-class lives, one that Liz Stanley and Ann Morley ran up against in their search for Emily Wilding Davison's network of friends, and Jill Liddington and Jill Norris also acknowledged in trying to recover the lives and hopes of the radical suffragists among the textile workers of Lancashire.[7] In any case, self-reflection was for most such women an expensive luxury and the emphasis Jennie Baines gave to the material and the practical accurately reflected their priorities. The earliest account from Baines herself occurred at her trial at Leeds Assizes in 1908 for unlawful assembly, riot, inciting to riot, and sedition. It is worth repeating in full both to see at a glance the shape she gave her own story and to note the unvarnished mode of its telling:

> I am the daughter of a working man, and at the early age of eleven I helped to support myself. Between the age of 14 and 15 my father became an officer in the Salvation Army. We were in the Salvation Army for a number of years. After a few years' time my father was unable to carry on the work as an officer in the Army, and my mother and I assisted him as lieutenants. At the age of 20 I was appointed as an evangelist to an independent working men's mission in the town of Bolton. I went to the Court each morning to look after and take an interest in the women who were charged with various offences. Two years I held that position, and then I was married, and for a few years I led a quiet life. During that time I gave birth to five children, of which there are three alive. My eldest daughter is 20. After a time I took a great interest in the Temperance movement. I spoke on public platforms. I have been a speaker on public platforms since I was 14 years of age. My husband is a boot and shoe maker by trade. His average wage was 25s per week, and I had to work to help support my family. One part of my time I worked as a sewing machinist in the City of Manchester. I felt that the wages

were not sufficient to get for my children, my husband and myself the necessary food, and during that time I was compelled to refrain from public work because my duties were so heavy. I was a candidate for the Board of Guardians in the town of Stockport, and I lost by two votes. I have been on the Unemployed Committee for two years and I was also on the Feeding of School Children Committee. Three years this last October I read in the newspapers of the arrest of Miss Christabel Pankhurst and Miss Annie Kenney . . . For two years I worked as a voluntary worker, having my out-of-pocket expenses paid by the Union. I have been paid as an official organiser for nine months.[8]

Other snippets of information reveal she had belonged to the Independent Labour Party and husband George was a staunch trade unionist and socialist.[9] Unlike middle-class women activists, Jennie Baines could not depend on servants but she did have 'a daughter capable of managing the home' and there is evidence that she was only too glad to escape household chores: a granddaughter recollected that 'she was a rotten cook & housekeeper'.[10] Recurrent attacks of chorea, commonly called St Vitus' Dance, saved her from being force-fed while in prison. An affliction that causes involuntary and irregular muscular movement, especially of the face and limbs, chorea is usually associated with emotional stress. Probably a consequence of childhood rheumatic fever, it may have been complicated by pregnancy. Whatever the cause, it necessitated long periods of total rest after extended organising trips and stints of imprisonment.[11]

The most significant elements of these accounts are, in my view, the experiences of work and motherhood (including the deaths of two children), and the discipline, inurement to persecution and ridicule, and the single-minded evangelical imperative to reform engendered by Salvation Army mission and rescue activities. Salvationism and a specific focus on temperance prepared her well for the later dedication to socialism and an initial singular focus on votes for women. A uniform, playing the cornet in public and speaking at open-air gatherings to frequently hostile audiences provided good theatrical training, and, though slightly built, she was apparently blessed with a 'deep, rich and powerful voice'.[12] The intermingling of class and gender identity with moral outrage is evident in the outline she gave the magistrate of her address to the crowds on the occasion that led to her 1908 Leeds trial:

One of the things I told the public was that that afternoon Mr. Asquith would be in the Coliseum dealing with the Licensing question. I said that it was more a woman's question than it was a man's, because it was the women who suffered most through intemperance, and no temperance reform would ever be brought about until women had a voice in the matter. I said that the unemployed question was also more a woman's question than it was a man's . . . If a working man had a small wage, sufficient, perhaps, to keep himself and his family, but unable to save anything, it was the woman who suffered the most, especially I said, when the landlord had to be faced . . . I said that when the children came home from school and there was no food in the house, and the cupboard was bare, it was the women, who loved the children better than their lives, who heard them crying for bread, who suffered most . . . Mr. Asquith had never known what it was, as I had done, to go without food, or to go to school hungry . . . I said that all the questions before the country at the present time were questions which concerned women . . . yet they had no voice in making the laws which they were called on to obey.[13]

Baines was convicted of taking part in an unlawful assembly in which she 'agreed with certain persons to use force and violence'. She and her co-accused, the leader of the Unemployed Committee, denied collusion but, as defending lawyer, Frederick Pethick Lawrence, said, 'she had the right to hope that some of the unemployed would be there'. For Baines, class and gender issues were, though not one and the same, at least based on a common concern about justice, especially justice for working-class women. Because she refused to be bound over to refrain from force or incitement to violence, she was sentenced by a noticeably reluctant judge to six weeks' imprisonment in the Second Division. As Pethick Lawrence explained, 'My client has no intention of using violence or inciting to violence, but in view of the present political position she cannot consent to being bound over'. Mrs Baines stated her reasons in explicitly feminist terms: 'I do not recognise the laws of this Court administered by men'.[14]

Leeds was not the first time that Jennie Baines had been arrested and imprisoned but it was the first time that a WSPU member was tried by jury and, for that reason, an event the organisation marked with appropriate celebration and ritual. On being released from Armley Gaol, 'our brave soldier on outpost duty', as Mrs Pankhurst called her,[15] was met by WSPU representatives from London ('General' Drummond and Miss Crocker) and by Adela Pankhurst, as well as 'a large crowd of the general public'. What followed was pure theatre, a carnivalesque display of women's claims to a share of political power. Mrs Baines was taken in a carriage drawn by 'women attired in the clogs and shawls of the Yorkshire mill-hand', preceded by a band playing 'The Cock o' th' North', to a special breakfast. The next day, the celebrations continued in London, where Mrs Baines and Mrs Drummond were met at King's Cross Station by 'two bands and a carriage drawn by a pair of white horses'. After Mrs Pethick Lawrence presented Jennie with a purple, white and green bouquet, the procession made its way to Trafalgar Square to the strains of 'See, the conquering hero comes'. The bands played the 'Marseillaise' as Mrs Baines was escorted to the platform. It was all very heady stuff – the only moment in which Jennie Baines occupied centre stage alone during her years in the Union – and the photos taken on this occasion were those reproduced in *Pix* thirty-five years later. But her speech still reflected the same basic concerns – the needs of working-class women. Beginning with the value of the vote to temperance reform, she turned to the conditions under which vast numbers of women lived and laboured: 'Women were considered too delicate to vote but they were not too delicate to work 60 or 70 hours a week, or to live lives of misery and shame.'[16] About this time, too, according to her own record, she helped expose the infamous 'live-in' system, with its starvation wages and encouragement to prostitution, operated by some of the large drapery stores.[17] Baines' value to the Pankhursts, as with Annie Kenney, lay in her working-class background and her specific ability to communicate with working-class women. As Christabel Pankhurst wrote about organising in Bristol in 1907, 'We want you, if you will, to go there too & rouse the workers by means of open air meetings. Your Birmingham experience will be very useful'.[18]

According to Mary Leigh's account, Jennie Baines was one of the five women who met 'in a little back room in Manchester' in 1905, and, on deciding 'that a woman outside the Constitution could not fight with constitutional means', began to devise the strategies of WSPU militancy.[19] Her dedication to militancy earned her a reputation as one of the most effective regional organisers in the union; by the end of 1909, Christabel was acknowledging that 'All the organisers of the protests have got an eye on your fighting women' and 'You are such an expert in militant work that your help and presence in any protest centre must be an advantage, even if another organiser is on the spot.'[20] For £2 per week, she travelled the Midlands and the north by train and bicycle (staying in temperance or Salvation Army hostels), organising tickets and tactics of disruption for cabinet ministers' meetings, holding open-air rallies (frequently with Adela Pankhurst as the main speaker), visiting door-to-door and at hospitals, schools and co-operative societies, and establishing new branches. Judging from the letters from head-quarters in London, some of this was done on Baines' initiative but most on regular orders. Yet, in her loyalty to the Midlands and north, as well as in her retention of links with working women, she shared many of the characteristics of the radical suffragists whose history Liddington and Norris have uncovered.[21] The difference was a single-minded preparedness to focus on the franchise and to forsake formal links with the ILP and the Labour Party – at least for the time being.

The letters from London cease in December 1909 but Baines spoke at the Great Hyde Park Demonstration of 23 July 1910 and was described then as organising in Hull. By this stage, she had been imprisoned again and refused food, a weapon first used by Marion Wallace Dunlop in July

1909.[22] She reappeared on centre stage, using the pseudonym Lizzie Baker, in July 1912, when, along with Mary Leigh and Gladys Evans, she was tried for conspiracy to burn down the Theatre Royal in Dublin the night before Prime Minister Asquith was scheduled to speak there. The decision to set light to the curtains and the cinematograph box during the interval, when very few people were in the theatre, was consistent with WSPU policy of attacking property not persons. It was, moreover, an arson attack with a specific objective – the prevention of Asquith's meeting the following night. Leigh and Evans were cast in the principal roles; Jennie Baines was a supporting actor. She was not at the theatre, but in the handbag she had left at rented rooms in Lower Mount Street were rubber gloves and an envelope of gunpowder, together with a medicine bottle containing petrol. She pleaded guilty to a minor offence under the Malicious Damage to Property Act and was given seven months' hard labour in Mountjoy Prison. The other two received five years. Baines and a group of Irish suffragists, then also in gaol, were granted the privileges of political prisoners but, on discovering that Leigh and Evans were not, they joined them on hunger-strike. Released after five days without food, Jennie was admitted to a Dublin nursing home where she remained some weeks. In characteristically melodramatic prose, *Votes for Women* referred to her as a 'woman whose soul is filled with passionate desire to rescue the oppressed, who hates compromise, who is a stranger to fear ... The front fighting line is the place that she loves, and therefore it was no surprise to her friends to hear that she was concerned in the Dublin protest'.[23]

They probably *would* have been surprised to read of the last occasion on which she attracted notoriety in Britain – an alleged attempt, with her husband and their seventeen-year-old son, to bomb two railway carriages in a siding at Newton Heath on the Lancashire and Yorkshire Railway. The blast, late on 8 July 1913, destroyed a first-class carriage. As the *Manchester Guardian* reported, there was 'evidence of the agency to which the explosion was due. Suffragette literature had been left about, and ... a message was found' – it read 'Kind Regards to Mr. Asquith. Votes for women'.[24] The Baines family, who lived nearby, were obvious suspects and another local WSPU activist, Kate Wallwork, of Withington, was also arrested. At the time, Jennie Baines' licence under the 'Cat and Mouse Act' had expired and she was in disguise as an elderly lady.[25] Given the precariousness of her situation and health, she was unlikely to have wished to attract further police attention. Further, she had not previously supported purposeless militancy; nor had she ever directly involved members of her family. When the case was finally heard, she stated explicitly that she was 'not near the railway sidings and had had nothing to do with the explosion'. 'If she had done it, she said, she would have unflinchingly said so. She had been in prison on nine previous occasions, and on every occasion had pleaded guilty.' Nevertheless, all three members of the Baines family were committed for trial, though

Wallwork was discharged.[26] Further evidence against Mrs Baines' involvement emerged in the trial itself: only one witness had seen her in Monsall Road near the sidings, and his description was of a 26- to 29-year-old woman with a 'fresh complexion'. Jennie Baines was forty-six at the time and, as the defence lawyer delicately put it, 'she did not answer that description. She had been "hunger-striking," and instead of being fresh complexioned was very sallow'.[27]

It is difficult to believe that Jennie Baines had committed this unfocused act of arson. She made no attempt to argue the case for suffrage at the committal hearings. Her main concern was to protect her husband and son. On leaving the dock, she was rearrested and consigned once more to Holloway where she resorted again to a hunger- and thirst-strike. Released 'in a very serious condition . . . her life for several days being despaired of', she agreed to being spirited out of the country, leaving her husband and son to stand trial alone. Her granddaughter's version is that Jennie, her daughter and other son, and one of her daughter's two children were hidden in Wales before boarding the *Ballarat* for Australia in November under the name of Evans.[28]

The trial at Manchester Assizes took place on 27 and 28 November. The evidence consisted of conflicting eye-witnesses' accounts and incriminating materials found in the Baineses' home and workshop, which were explained by the requirements of bootmaking and George Baines' involvement in competitive athletics. All had convincing alibis and the judge even expressed the view to the jury that Mrs Baines' absence should not sway them, since, under the circumstances of the 'Cat and Mouse' Act, 'it might be said it was not fair to expect her to come back and run any further risk'. The jury took only fifteen minutes to return a verdict of not guilty.[29] George and Wilfred Baines left the country soon after. With daughter Annie's second son, they arrived in Melbourne, capital of Victoria and of the Commonwealth of Australia, early in 1914.[30]

THE MELBOURNE SCENE IN 1914

Victoria conceded the franchise to women in 1908, the last state to do so, six years after the vote was won for the national parliament.[31] The most industrially advanced of the Australian states, it was also the most politically diverse. The organised women's movement was the oldest, the most disparate and, certainly by 1913–1914, the largest in Australia. Though Victoria was the ideological home of political liberalism in Australia, the seat of the national employers' organisation, and also boasted the largest conservative women's association, the Australian Women's National League, it was a centre of radicalism too. The Political Labor Council (PLC), or Labor Party, had always been in opposition and, having broken with the 'lib-lab' tradition after a cataclysmic railway strike in 1903, was more open to socialist ideas than its counterparts in the other states. A mass party like the PLC was of necessity an umbrella organisation, a compromise among many radicalisms. But pacifists, feminists, socialists and most others in the labour movement found common cause there, sharing an understanding of terms like 'freedom' and 'justice' that distinguished them sharply from Liberals and conservatives.

The Victorian Socialist Party (VSP), founded by Tom Mann, had operated as a radical conscience within the PLC since 1905,[32] providing a forum for discussion within the framework of ideas of the Second International. Its methods were propagandist and its influence on the Labor Party out of proportion to its size.[33] The VSP debated and experimented with different brands of socialism from co-operative enterprises to syndicalism but did not advocate violent revolution. The battles it did fight in the streets were over civil liberties issues.[34] It developed a communal atmosphere among its members, influenced by contemporary English guild socialism, and was unusual for the number of positions its women members held at executive level. They formed their own independent Women's Socialist League but were not averse to occasionally organising relief committees and providing refreshments at VSP functions.[35] Some of the more avowedly feminist amongst them also belonged to the Women's Political Association (WPA). Formed in Melbourne by Vida Goldstein in 1903, the WPA had quickly pronounced itself non-party but, by 1914, its position was identifiably pacifist and socialist, though its major concern was to increase women's political participation.[36] Membership was probably no greater than 400–500 when war broke out.

Jennie Baines presented her credentials and joined all three organisations soon after her arrival in Melbourne, and George carried a letter of recommendation to the VSP.[37] No one knows for certain why Australia was chosen as their destination: possibly Tom Mann, whom the Baineses had known from presuffrage free speech fights in Bolton, was influential; or it may be that Jennie had met Vida Goldstein in England in 1911; or there may have been contact with other WPA visitors such as Mrs Singleton.[38] Certainly Mrs Baines knew Australian expatriate Muriel Matters and former New South Wales activist Nellie Martel, who had become a leading WSPU organiser.[39] The most likely explanation, however, is that Australian women had the vote. This released Jennie Baines from the stresses of militant campaigning (and especially from the cycle of hunger-striking) and rewarded her in the most appropriate way for her suffering. For the rest of her life, she prided herself on being the first to vote in her electoral subdivision on polling days – 'a suffrage so hardly won, is not to be lightly regarded'.[40]

Mrs Baines found that, at least until the arrival of Adela Pankhurst, she was a celebrity in Melbourne, a fact that reflected the ambiguous feelings of Australian feminists towards England. On the one hand, they took great pride in their use of the vote to achieve Australia's much vaunted social reforms. In England in 1911, Goldstein had spoken constantly of Australia's progressiveness and, in the National Union of Women's Suffrage Societies' procession of 1908, Australian women carried a banner that reversed the conventional colonial–metropolitan relationship. On it, the daughter figure, Australia, advised the maternal figure, Britannia: 'Trust the Women, Mother, as I have done'. On the other hand, Australian suffragists were caught up in the excitement of the campaign in Britain and argued the pros and cons of WSPU militancy with great vehemence. They travelled to England not just to advertise the advantages of the vote but also to be at what they still regarded as the centre. And, as was the case for Goldstein, the experience deepened their understanding of the many aspects of women's oppression – sexual as well as political and economic.[41] Thus, when Jennie Baines entered Melbourne's socialist and feminist circles, she was greeted as 'one of the most prominent of militant Suffragettes' and was in great demand as a speaker.[42]

Migration to Australia released Baines from her WSPU pledge 'to undertake not to support the candidature of any political party at parliamentary elections until women had obtained the parliamentary vote'.[43] As a 1912 profile in *Votes for Women* pointed out, she had taken the pledge because she realised that, while 'it is by political power alone that society can be re-organised to a saner and fairer plan . . . for women to depend for aid upon parties managed by men is futile'.[44] With equal voting rights in Australia, membership of the Labor Party and the VSP now became possible. But, in the first months of her Australian years, the WPA and Goldstein's candidature for the federal parliament occupied most of her time. As she told the *Socialist*, now that women had the vote they must fight to take their rightful place in parliament not only to look after the interests of the workers but, 'above all . . . to look after the women and children'.[45]

After living in one of the poorest industrial suburbs, Fitzroy, for some months, Jennie was seeing parallels with the injustices suffered under capitalism by women and the working classes in the Old World. In addition to speaking on 'Experiences as a Suffragette and as a Hunger Striker', she was soon addressing meetings on 'The White Slave Traffic' and 'Slums, Sweating and Starvation'.[46] It was disgraceful, she said, that in a new country like Australia, she could still 'hear the cries in her ears of little children denied the right to live like human beings'.[47] Women, too, were 'living in misery and shame', with prostitution the only means to 'secure the bare necessities of life', just as she had discovered among the workers in some of the large drapery stores in England in 1908.[48]

THE WOMEN'S WAR IN AUSTRALIA

The outbreak of war in August 1914 provoked a crisis within the WPA, Vida Goldstein arguing that the organisation's platform should be explicitly antiwar and anticonscription. War roused no patriotic and imperial fervour in Jennie Baines' breast either. She voted with Goldstein to strengthen the association's antiwar policy and was one of the founding members of the paradoxically named Women's Peace Army, formed in July 1915 to accommodate Labor Party women recently ordered to resign from the WPA.[49] It is possible that Baines' and Adela Pankhurst's experiences of the military-style organisation of the WSPU were influential in its naming.[50] Adela had arrived in Melbourne in March 1914 and was offered the position of secretary to the WPA early in 1915; she now coupled this with organising the Peace Army.[51] Baines and Pankhurst easily resumed the working relationship they had had in England, Adela again playing the dominant role. The two frequently appeared on the same platform in 1916 during the first conscription referendum campaign and both addressed the United Women's No Conscription procession of 10,000 that filled the city's streets with music, tableaux and singing in October.[52]

In the wake of conscription's defeat, Jennie Baines spoke to many resolutions asserting 'the principle of international brotherhood and the federation of the workers of the whole world', in support of a declaration of peace terms, and appealing for an Australian People's Peace Conference.[53] In December 1916, she joined the new Labor Women's Political, Social and Industrial Council and addressed lunchtime factory assemblies, suburban street-corner gatherings and Labor Party meetings not only on conscription but also on the need for a government labour bureau for women and girls, and hostel accommodation for penniless women. But, when the Labor Party disbanded the organisation early in 1917, Baines turned her energies back to the Peace Army and the VSP. Elected an officer of the former in February, she was appointed to the Open-Air Meetings Committee of the latter in June, and then to its executive in September.[54]

But it was the artificial shortage of foodstuffs and further restrictions on free speech and assembly during 1917 that re-ignited Baines' passion for justice. Throughout August and September, she and Adela took to the public stage once more, Jennie in a supporting role as they led thousands of Melbourne's working-class women in street protests against the soaring cost of living. There was plenty of evidence of a general decline in living standards. Since the outbreak of war, retail prices of food and groceries in Melbourne had risen 28.2 per cent. Wages had not kept pace – for Victoria as a whole they increased only 15.4 per cent.[55] The problem of food prices was complicated by a wartime agreement whereby the wheat harvest for 1916–1917 had been bought up by the imperial authorities, and, from 1915, all frozen meat available for export was guaranteed to Britain. But a shipping shortage in 1917 resulted in a build-up of meat in Australian stores and left the grain not in silos to the depredations of weevils and mice.[56] Flour mills closed down and farmers stopped selling animals for slaughter, causing local unemployment in both industries as well as closure of many retail outlets and hence shortages and higher prices for consumers.

On the afternoon of 15 August, Adela Pankhurst led a crowd of 2,000–3,000, mostly women, to the steps of Parliament House, in defiance of a War Precautions Act regulation prohibiting such gatherings. Heedless of police warnings, she began to speak and was promptly arrested. The angry women followed her to the city watchhouse and then marched back toward Parliament House, reassembling in the nearby Treasury Gardens where they were encouraged to attack the cool stores and forcibly seize the meat.[57] A second demonstration in the Treasury Gardens on 22 August was addressed by Pankhurst, Baines and another VSP activist, Lizzie Wallace. After denouncing food profiteers and government inaction, they led a crowd of 7,000–8,000 up to Parliament House and along the city's main thoroughfares chanting 'We want food and fair play'. Outside the Athenaeum Hall in Collins Street, where the National Service Bureau was enrolling strike-breakers in an attempt to defeat the general strike that had paralysed much of Sydney and Melbourne, they shook umbrellas decorated with red ribbons and jeered the scabs before returning to the gardens, singing 'The Red Flag'. Five of the demonstrators, including Pankhurst, were arrested but Jennie Baines urged the crowd to reassemble at 2 p.m. the next day.[58] On 3 September, Jennie and Adela were arrested in another major clash and charged under the War Precautions Act,[59] Pankhurst calling on the women to 'break into Parliament House, if necessary, to see Billy Hughes to know what he will do to give food for the starving children'. Jennie Baines tried to address the meeting before being pushed off her chair in the crush but she and Adela linked arms and moved off towards Parliament House, followed by the crowd. The leaders were quickly arrested. Pankhurst and Baines were sentenced to three months' gaol for taking part in a meeting exceeding twenty people in a proclaimed place 'on a pretext of making known their grievances'. Their refusal to enter into a recognisance of £100 earned them an extra six months but they were released on 11 September pending an appeal to the High Court, which they won on technical grounds.[60]

The pinnacle of the demonstrations was a 'torchlight procession' on 19 September attended by 10,000. Beginning at the Yarra Bank, where Pankhurst and Baines spoke, the initial crowd of about 2,000 moved along the riverside and into the city, growing bolder all the while as thousands more joined in. Two women carrying the red flag at the head of the procession were quickly arrested and before long the protest turned into a mêlée. Demonstrators hurled road metal at police but, after an hour and a half, the crowd was broken up by baton-wielding constables. Some who had escaped into the city centre began smashing shop and office front windows on a trail of destruction later estimated at £5,000–£6,000. Particular premises were singled out by demonstrators. At Sennitt's Ice Works, they smashed windows, before barricading themselves with rabbit crates against the mounted police. At the Dunlop Rubber Factory, more windows were broken in protest against the dismissal of 1,250 rubber workers for refusing to handle black goods.[61] Only the firing of shots into the air by policemen finally dispersed the crowd. The riots and strikes were put down at the end of September after the prohibition of meetings at the Yarra Bank, Flinders Park and other well-known venues, the invocation of the Riot Act, and the enrolment of over 400 special constables.[62]

In a previous discussion of Melbourne's cost-of-living riots, I stressed the persisting elements of pre-industrial moral economy and the evidence they provide of resistance by working-class women to middle-class efforts to turn them into compliant modern citizens.[63] The food riot was very much a female protest. As Jennie Baines had pointed out at her Leeds trial, it was women who noticed the first pangs of hunger in their families, who had to deprive themselves, and, as Olwen Hufton has reminded us, thieve, lie, prostitute their bodies and spill over into riot.[64] Consumption and, hence, the stability of prices was still of greater concern to ordinary women in 1917 than wage levels. As 'workmen's wives' and the providers of food, their interest was less in earning the money than in spending it wisely.[65]

My primary purpose here is to highlight the actions of Pankhurst and Baines as a suffragette performance. In taking charge of the protest, they called on the scripts they had spoken and the roles they had played before. The police officers who provided information about the protests were adamant that the two former suffragettes were responsible for this outburst of militancy. Constable Kiernan and Sergeant Grange believed that the whole campaign, including the strategic destruction of property, had been pre-arranged. Kiernan remarked specifically that it was 'highly probable that the window smashing idea originated with the two leaders Pankhurst and Baines who are evidently introducing similar tactics to those adopted in England when on the suffragette campaign'.[66] The orchestration of some of the street processions – the planning of routes to pass strategic sites, the decoration of umbrellas with red ribbons and the singing, for example – were indeed reminiscent of the suffrage marches when middle-class as well as working-class women demanded their right to public space.[67] Processions of worker organisations were not new in Melbourne but the dominance of women in them, as occurred in the women's anticonscription demonstration in 1916 and now in the cost-of-living protests, was a deliberate assertion of their right to public visibility and audibility. The decision to attack specified property but not people was also consistent with WSPU militant tactics. As Adela Pankhurst told a VSP meeting she and Jennie Baines addressed on 3 September: 'I am not afraid to fight even if it does come to the destruction of property'. To an audience in Yarraville the night after the torchlight procession, she explained 'glass windows have got no feelings whatever', and, even if the authorities did 'send some of us to gaol, there will be others to take their places, and it will take a year or two to build gaols to hold us'. She concluded with the most characteristic of WSPU refrains: 'I believe in action not words'.[68] Their women supporters also followed the suffragette practice of demonstrating outside the prison where the soldiers of the cause were held – on the evening Baines and Pankhurst were gaoled, a hundred women went to Pentridge and 'rendered socialist songs and hearty salvos of appreciation to those within the terrible walls'.[69]

Members of the Peace Army and the WPA spent the rest of 1917 assisting the victims of the great strike and supporting the second anticonscription campaign. The WPA established the Guild Hall Commune, which became a sort of self-sufficient village, providing groceries, meals, a boot repair shop and a barber's salon, and also arranging for the billeting of children where necessary. The boot repair shop was run by Jennie's son, Wilfred, and husband George provided the equipment and helped set it up.[70] The commune was only wound up when wharf labourers finally returned to work.

In 1918, Jennie Baines campaigned against a new regulation enabling boys over eighteen to enlist without parental consent, asserting that, 'if women had been in the Australian Parliament they would have voted against the war. The wrong done to boys by war was shown by the facts in regard to venereal disease and drink'.[71] She also helped to organise and was elected president of the Labor Women's Welcome Home Committee, a group formed in June 1918 without the approval of the Labor Party, many members of which saw it as patriotic 'flag-wagging'. But, as the secretary of the committee pointed out: 'we consider that we are in no way offending against the laws and precepts of our great movement, rather we are upholding them, by showing our returning soldiers that, while we strongly oppose the politics of some of them, we sympathise with their sufferings'.[72] This was a grass-roots position that Baines clearly shared, the actual needs and anxieties of working-class families superseding more abstract, hardline, antiwar principles.

It was 'flag-wagging', albeit of a different kind, that brought Mrs Baines back into the limelight towards the end of the year. During 1918, antiwar feeling was encouraged by the Bolshevik victory and exacerbated by continuing assaults on civil liberties at home. Jennie Baines, like many other Australian labour activists, now linked all the manifestations of economic and social injustice, local and international, together. In a two-hour address to Maryborough socialists on 'The Political and War Situation', for example, she ranged across the capitalist system, Ireland, the cost-of-living demonstrations, conscription, censorship, the immorality of war and secret treaties.[73] And, when the display of the international symbol of socialism, the red flag, was banned under a War Precautions Act regulation in September,[74] she was one of the first to be arrested for defying the prohibition. Baines and VSP colleague Jane Aarons were given a fourteen–day sentence in December, with seven days' grace 'to think it over' when they refused to enter into a bond not to offend again.[75] Though the Trades Hall and the Labor Party had decided not to make an issue of the flag, the VSP represented the ban as a symbol of the arbitrary restriction of civil liberties – and it was in defence of civil liberties, specifically free speech and assembly, that Jennie Baines had first been arrested in her Salvation Army days and later with Tom Mann on Bolton Hill Square.[76]

The VSP, somewhat provocatively, organised Sunday 26 January 1919 – founders' day – as Red Flag Day at the Yarra Bank, and Jennie Baines was one of a number of speakers who, on raising the red flag at the end of each address, were charged under the War Precautions Act and sentenced to a month's gaol. Though she refused to be bound over, she was again given seven days' grace during which she continued both to speak in favour of socialism and the Russian Revolution and to display the red flag. Finally, on 18 March, she and Dick Long – the VSP's poet – were gaoled for six months for flying the flag at Flinders Park on 23 February. Both refused to enter into bonds.[77] Baines' suffragette experience was again evident in her court performance and the press particularly remarked the theatrical character of her leave-taking. After the magistrate pronounced sentence, she turned to the audience of socialists assembled and began to hold forth on the injustices to which Victoria's citizens were being subjected. Dragged from the dock, 'she cried out in sepulchral tones, into which she infused a wealth of feeling, "If I do not obtain a speedy release, my death will lie at your door!"'[78] In the face of a long gaol term, she resorted once again to the hunger-strike, reputedly the first person in Australia to do so.[79]

George Baines was alarmed. Jennie had always been ill after hunger-striking and had been warned before she left England that another bout would kill her. Besides, she was now in her mid-fifties and less robust. While she refused food and drink, George Baines spoke to the press of his fears and sent a circular to selected members of parliament. The Acting Prime Minister, W. A. Watt, called a special cabinet meeting and, on the advice of the Attorney-General, ordered Mrs Baines' release – four days after she had begun the strike.[80] Although she faced three more summonses for flying the red flag and one for calling Senior Constable Scanlon 'an Irish renegade', her health did not permit another period in prison and the fines were paid, mostly by the Fitzroy branch of the Labor Party and the VSP.[81] Each time she appeared in court, she was accompanied by a socialist chorus applauding her performances and singing 'The Red Flag'. Sent to the country to recuperate, she wrote that the authorities had not weakened her determination to fight for social and industrial freedom. The language resonates with suffragist theatrical melodrama and the hellfire and brimstone of her evangelical training:

> I will not, nor will I allow the workers if I can prevent it, to be cowed and driven by the miserable curs and creatures of political superstition and treachery, supported by their equally depraved hirelings and tools, who will commit any atrocity against the intelligence and

physique of humanity in the name of 'law and order' and for pay and position. I have lived for many years now in the fight of men and women against the despotism and robbery of those of their kind, who class themselves as deities and rulers on earth; and the years which I have yet to live will be devoted to the same cause.[82]

FOR A 'BETTER AND NOBLER' WORLD

By the end of 1919, the WPA and the Peace Army had collapsed in the absence of Vida Goldstein, who was travelling in Europe and the United Kingdom. And, during late 1919 and 1920, the VSP suffered an internal struggle between supporters of the 'old show' reformist socialism like R. S. Ross and those who favoured the Bolshevik line. Jennie Baines supported the revolutionaries and, in 1920, became a founding member of the Melbourne branch of the Communist Party.[83] She had, in any case, recently threatened to resign from the VSP after a falling out with Ross over distribution of the Seamen's Relief Committee funds, which, as secretary, she had allocated almost solely to the wives of the strikers.[84] But her Communist Party career did not prosper either. In late 1924, Baines was elected to the executive but was expelled in February 1925 after she refused to support the party's preferred candidate in a by-election.[85] Perhaps, as she aged, she found that she could no longer be the loyal unquestioning soldier and chorister, or it may be that her WSPU work had been far enough away from London headquarters to allow for the exercise of individual judgement where membership of the Communist Party did not.

Returning to the mainstream Labor Party and local issues concerning women and children, Mrs Baines became vice-president of the Fitzroy branch in 1926 and a member of the state Labor Women's Organising Committee. The family moved to the inner-bayside, working-class suburb of Port Melbourne later that year and she stood (unsuccessfully) for election to the local council in 1927, arguing that 'woman was as necessary in the Council as in the home'. In 1928, the newly elected state Labor government appointed her, first, a probation officer and, then, a special magistrate to the South Melbourne Children's Court, a position she held for twenty years.[86] During the Depression years, she arranged for the Myer Emporium to deliver leftover cakes and pastries to Port Melbourne for distribution among local children on Saturday afternoons, and once a year she organised a free theatre afternoon at the local 'picture palace'. But she did not lose her fire or her sense of the dramatic. Labor Party and Communist Party veterans remember her performances on the hustings during the 1930s and 1940s, and, at the end of 1928, she was one of a party of angry women armed with umbrellas, who shouted abuse at the state Labor government from the visitors' gallery in parliament for its failure to protect striking waterside workers against scab labour and police gunfire.[87] As her grandson remarked many years later, she was 'a firebrand, a real firebrand'.[88] Only months before her death in February 1951, she was still speaking from the public platform.

Jennie Baines' life was not an ordinary one, nor was it easy. But it is interesting because it shows a continuity in militant activism across decades and hemispheres. It was a life driven by a practical working-class feminist consciousness and experience, not the abstract internationalist and universalising discourses of Vida Goldstein and Adela Pankhurst. And, where these two moved from the material to the spiritual, Jennie Baines' original Christian conviction – not a spiritual one in any case – gave way to a profoundly humanist and materialist faith. Though drawn by the theatre and ritual of the suffrage struggle, Jennie Baines chose to act out her life in the tradition of social realism. She gave it meaning through the military and religious metaphors of practical service and devotion to a cause; as she wrote in the conclusion to her letter to VSP members in 1919: 'To fight for that which is better and nobler in this world is to live in the highest sense, but to submit and tolerate the evils which exist is to merely vegetate in the sewers of iniquity.'[89]

NOTES

1 *Pix*, 13 March 1943, pp. 28–29. 'Valor' was the spelling used in the article, rather than the more usual contemporary English spelling 'valour'.

2 See also L. Tickner, *The spectacle of women: imagery of the suffrage campaign 1907–14* (London, Chatto & Windus, 1987).

3 V. Coleman, *Adela Pankhurst: the wayward suffragette 1885–1961* (Melbourne, Melbourne University Press, 1996), p. 175.

4 S. Stanley Holton, 'In sorrowful wrath': suffrage militancy and the romantic feminism of Emmeline Pankhurst, in H. L. Smith (ed.), *British feminism in the twentieth century* (Aldershot, Edward Elgar, 1990), pp. 7–24. On Sorrelian influence, see R. Wohl, *The generation of 1914* (Cambridge, Mass., Harvard University Press, 1979).

5 See A. Morley with L. Stanley, *The life and death of Emily Wilding Davison: a biographical detective story* (London, the Women's Press, 1988), Chapter 6, for growing dissent in 1913.

6 *Australian dictionary of biography*, Vol. 7, ed. B. Nairn and G. Serle (Melbourne, Melbourne University Press, 1979), pp. 145–146; E. G. Meyer, Jennie Baines: a life of commitment, BA Hons thesis, Monash University, 1989, Chapter 1.

7 Morley with Stanley, *The life and death of Emily Wilding Davison*, Chapters 4 and 6; J. Liddington and J. Norris, *One hand tied behind us: the rise of the women's suffrage movement* (London, Virago, 1978).

8 *Votes for Women*, 26 November 1908, p. 143.

9 Ibid., 18 June 1908, p. 254.

10 E. Hill and O. Fenton Shafer (eds), *Great suffragists – and why: modern makers of history* (London, Henry J. Drane, 1909), p. 218; Letter, Muriel Stevenson to Judith Smart, undated (*c.* 1977), in author's possession.

11 Letter to George Baines about his wife's illness (Teresa Billington to Mr Baines,

18 [month unclear] 1906). Baines Papers, Fryer Library, University of Queensland. Other letters in this collection refer to Mrs Baines' ill-health. See also *Herald* (Melbourne), 20 March 1919, p. 6.

12 Muriel Stevenson to Judith Smart. Jennie Baines was 5 feet 1 inch tall, weighing 8 stone, 4 lb.

13 *Votes for Women*, 26 November 1908, pp. 143–144.

14 Ibid., pp. 143–147.

15 E. Pankhurst to Mrs Baines, 11 October 1908. Baines Papers.

16 *Votes for Women*, 17 December 1908, p. 202.

17 Muriel Stevenson to Judith Smart; *Herald*, 20 March 1919, p. 6.

18 C. H. Pankhurst to Mrs Baines, 28 August 1907. Baines Papers.

19 *Votes for Women*, 16 August 1912, p. 744.

20 Emmeline Pethick Lawrence to Mrs Baines, 7 April 1908; C. H. Pankhurst to Mrs Baines, 3 December 1909; Christabel Pankhurst to Mrs Baines, 4 December 1909. Baines Papers. Baines was ahead of Christabel in the move to more militant tactics. On 2 March 1909, Christabel wrote: 'As to what you say about strong action, the time is not yet ripe for that; I hope it never may be'.

21 Liddington and Norris, *One hand tied behind us*, pp. 227–228.

22 *Votes for Women*, 22 July 1910, p. 714; J. Purvis, 'Deeds not words': the daily lives of militant suffragettes in Edwardian Britain, *Women's Studies International Forum*, 18, 2, 1995, p. 97. The hunger strike was also employed by women arrested at the Birmingham demonstration Baines organised in September. C. H. Pankhurst to Mrs Baines, 23 September 1909. Baines Papers.

23 *Votes for Women*, 26 July 1912, p. 696; 9 August 1912, pp. 729–730; 16 August 1912, p. 741; 23 August 1912, pp. 757, 763, 765; 30 August 1912, p. 772; 6 September 1912, p. 784.

24 *Manchester Guardian*, 9 July 1913, cited in *Suffragette*, 18 July 1913, p. 674; *Manchester Guardian*, 28 November 1913, p. 12.

25 *Suffragette*, 18 July 1913, p. 674; 8 August 1913, p. 747; *Manchester Guardian*, 29 November 1913, p. 12.

26 *Suffragette*, 15 August 1913, p. 766.

27 *Manchester Guardian*, 28 November 1913, p. 12.

28 *Suffragette*, 15 August 1913, p. 755; Muriel Stevenson to Judith Smart. It was WSPU policy to exile persistent 'mice' – of the twenty-five wanted in 1913, ten had left the country. *Suffragette*, 1 August 1913, p. 724, cited in Meyer, Jennie Baines, p. 36.

29 *Manchester Guardian*, 28 November 1913, p. 12; 29 November 1913, p. 12.

30 Muriel Stevenson to Judith Smart. Melbourne was the capital of the Commonwealth of Australia until 1927.

31 A. Oldfield, *Woman suffrage in Australia: a gift or a struggle?* (Cambridge, Cambridge University Press, 1992).

32 G. C. Hewitt, A history of the Victorian Socialist Party, 1906–1932, MA thesis, LaTrobe University, 1974, Chapter II; H. McQueen, Victoria, in D. J. Murphy (ed.), *Labour in politics* (Brisbane, University of Queensland Press, 1975); I. A. H. Turner, Socialist political tactics 1900–1920, *Labour History*, 2, May 1962, pp. 10–11.

33 It reached from 1,500 to 2,000 in 1907, but dropped to 430 by 1909, rising again during the war. McQueen, Victoria, p. 314; Turner, Socialist political tactics, p. 11; Half-yearly meeting, 29 September 1915, Victorian Socialist Party Minutes, MS 564, National Library of Australia (NLA); J. Damousi, Socialist women in Australia *c*. 1890–*c*. 1918, PhD thesis, Australian National University, 1987, p. 293.

34 Hewitt, A history of the Victorian Socialist Party, pp. 45–51; Damousi, Socialist women, pp. 106–109.
35 *Socialist*, 1913–1915, *passim*; Hewitt, A history of the Victorian Socialist Party, Chapter IV; Damousi, Socialist women, Chapter 6; Victorian Socialist Party Minutes, 1914–1921.
36 First called the Women's Federal Political Association. J. Bomford, *That dangerous and persuasive woman: Vida Goldstein* (Melbourne, Melbourne University Press, 1993); *Australian dictionary of biography*, Vol. 9, ed. Nairn and Serle, pp. 43–45; F. Kelly, Vida Goldstein: political woman, in M. Lake and F. Kelly (eds), *Double time: women in Victoria – 150 years* (Melbourne, Penguin, 1985), pp. 167–178.
37 Mrs Baines' membership of the WPA was arranged from England and she had a letter of introduction to J. P. Jones of the PLC and VSP from Keir Hardie. She and George also had letters from John Scurr of the Dock Workers' Union. Meyer, Jennie Baines, p. 37.
38 A Mrs Singleton was mentioned by George Baines at his trial as an alibi for Jennie's whereabouts. The WPA's Mrs Singleton was in England at this time. *Woman Voter*, 10 June 1912; 26 August 1913.
39 She reported to Martel's lodgings on reaching London for the demonstration outside the Strangers' Entrance to the House of Commons where she was arrested alongside Muriel Matters. Christabel Pankhurst to Mrs Baines, 10 December 1906. Baines Papers.
40 *Pix*, 13 March 1943, p. 29.
41 B. Caine, Vida Goldstein and the English militant campaign, *Women's History Review*, 2, 3, 1993, pp. 363–376. On the 1908 banner, see Tickner, *The spectacle of women*, pp. 82, 255. On arguments between Goldstein and Sydney's Rose Scott, see J. A. Allen, *Rose Scott: vision and revision in feminism* (Melbourne, Oxford University Press, 1994).
42 *Woman Voter*, 3 February 1914; *Labor Call*, 19 February 1914.
43 Purvis, 'Deeds not words', p. 96.
44 *Votes for Women*, 23 August 1912, p. 763.
45 *Socialist*, 26 June 1914.
46 *Labor Call*, 19 February 1914; 18 June 1914; 6 August 1914; *Woman Voter*, 3 March 1914.
47 *Socialist*, 26 June 1914, cited in Meyer, Jennie Baines, p. 39.
48 *Argus* (Melbourne), 10 February 1914, p. 7; *Socialist*, 20 February 1914. Both cited in Meyer, Jennie Baines, pp. 42–43.
49 *Woman Voter*, 1 July 1915; 15 July 1915. The PLC proscribed the WPA in November 1914 because Goldstein stood for parliament.
50 The pledge army members signed does have some echoes of the WSPU pledge. See Australian Women's Peace Army file, Merrifield Collection, LaTrobe Library, State Library of Victoria.
51 Coleman, *Adela Pankhurst*, p. 64; *Woman Voter*, 23 December 1915.
52 The Defence Act permitted compulsory military service within Australia but not conscription for overseas service. Two plebiscites during the First World War (28 October 1916 and 20 December 1917) attempted to gain popular consent for this to be changed. On both occasions, conscription was rejected. On Pankhurst and Baines' appearance together, see *Woman Voter*, 21 September 1916; 28 September 1916; 12 October 1916.
53 Ibid., 26 October 1916; 16 November 1916; 21 December 1916. In 1918, she was the Socialist Party's delegate to the Australian Peace Alliance. Victorian Socialist Party Minutes, 26 June 1918.
54 *Labor Call*, 8 February 1917; 1 March 1917; Meyer, Jennie Baines, p. 57; Half-

yearly meeting, 28 February 1917, and annual meeting, 5 September 1917, Victorian Socialist Party Minutes; *Socialist*, 13 September 1917.

55 *Victorian year book*, 1917–1918, pp. 1158–1159, 1088.

56 E. Scott, *Australia during the war*, Vol. XI of *Official history of Australia in the war of 1914–18*, ed. C. E. W. Bean (Sydney, Angus & Robertson, 1938), pp. 529–542.

57 *Argus*, 16 August 1917.

58 *Age* (Melbourne), 23 August 1917; *Argus*, 23 August 1917.

59 Passed in October 1914, this Act followed the British Defence of the Realm Act.

60 Porter vs Adela Pankhurst *et al.*, CL164, Crown Solicitor's File (including notes of the hearing before the Full Court of the High Court, 2 October 1917), Australian Archives (AA); *Argus*, 5 September 1917.

61 Kiernan vs Walsh, CL760, Crown Solicitor's File, AA; *Argus*, 20, 21 September 1917; *Age*, 21 September 1917.

62 *Argus*, 24, 26, 27 September 1917.

63 J. Smart, Feminists, food and the fair price: the cost of living demonstrations in Melbourne, August–September 1917, *Labour History*, 50, May 1986, pp. 113–131.

64 O. Hufton, Women in revolution, *Past and Present*, 53, November 1971, pp. 94–95.

65 Deputation to Sir Alexander Peacock, 17 August 1917, *Argus*, 18 August 1917. See also R. Pringle, Women and consumer capitalism, in C. N. Baldock and B. Cass (eds), *Women, social welfare and the state* (Sydney, Allen & Unwin, 1983), p. 92; E. P. Thompson, The moral economy of the English crowd in the eighteenth century, *Past and Present*, 50, February 1971, p. 79.

66 Kiernan vs Walsh.

67 Tickner, *The spectacle of women*, pp. 75, 78.

68 Kiernan vs Walsh.

69 *Socialist*, 14 September 1917.

70 *Woman Voter*, 30 August, 6 September, 13 September, 27 September, 4 October, 8 November 1917.

71 Meyer, Jennie Baines, p. 74; *Labor Call*, 30 May 1918.

72 *Labor Call*, 13 June 1918; 19 September 1918.

73 *Maryborough and Dunolly Advertiser*, 3 June 1918. Cited in Meyer, Jennie Baines, p. 74. Baines is recorded in the *Socialist* as speaking at a number of country venues on 1918 and 1919.

74 Like the Sinn Fein flag, which had been banned in March, the red flag was represented as the emblem of 'an enemy country'. On the red flag controversies in Australia, especially Queensland, see R. Evans, *The red flag riots: a study of intolerance* (Brisbane, University of Queensland Press, 1988).

75 *Woman Voter*, 18 December 1918; Damousi, Socialist women.

76 Letter, Jennie Baines to Les Barnes, 6 November 1946. Cited in Meyer, Jennie Baines, p. 10.

77 *Socialist*, 31 January, 7 March, 21 March 1919.

78 *Herald*, 18 March 1919.

79 *Socialist*, 28 March 1918; *Woman Voter*, 10 April 1919.

80 *Herald*, 20, 21, 22 March 1919.

81 *Socialist*, 4 April 1919.

82 Ibid., 11 April 1919.

83 Minutes of the Victorian Socialist Party, 24 September 1919, 29 September, 22 November and 2 December 1920; J. Damousi, *Women come rally: socialism, communism and gender in Australia 1890–1955* (Melbourne, Oxford University Press, 1994), p. 110.

84 *Socialist*, 25 July 1919; Meyer, Jennie Baines, p. 86.
85 Meyer, Jennie Baines, p. 87.
86 *Pix*, 13 March 1943, pp. 28–29.
87 Meyer, Jennie Baines, pp. 90–91, 92.
88 Harvie Baines. Cited in ibid., p. 93.
89 *Socialist*, 11 April 1919.

12

'A SYMBOL AND A KEY'

The suffrage movement in Britain, 1918–1928

Johanna Alberti

When we strove with most passion for the vote, we sought it not for itself only, but as a symbol and a key.[1]

INTRODUCTION

In February 1920, the first issue of a journal *The Woman's Leader* was published. The paper was the successor to *The Common Cause* although it was not the official organ of the National Union of Societies for Equal Citizenship (NUSEC), the renamed and reconstructed National Union of Women's Suffrage Societies (NUWSS). The leader in this first issue, under the title 'The Woman's Leader and the Task before It', looked back at the years 1900–1914 when the whole of the women's movement was concerned with the 'breaking down of one especial barrier', a barrier so powerful that the movement became 'a strong and at moments a torrential stream' which had in the end loosened that barrier. The concentrated effort required to break down the barrier against the women's parliamentary vote meant that the movement had flowed in those years in a single channel, but, the leader asserted: 'Now, again, the women's movement is a double stream.' The first of these two main streams, 'which sometimes flow separately and often intermingle', was 'an effort to break down barriers, the other an effort to expand into fresh life'. The first stream included 'the struggle for the vote' and 'the struggle for equal opportunities in the professions and in industry'; to the second belonged the 'development of women's education, of women's citizenship, and of women's work'. The challenge now was to ensure that women working in different ways 'did not lose sight of one another'. The writer of the article also identified a new generation of young women with a different perspective whom the paper intended to help, not only in 'making their own lives, but in doing good service to their country and to humanity'.[2]

Contained within this article were the principal strands of thought and

267

activity in the continued suffrage movement in the 1920s: the pressure for equality in a male-dominated world of work, and a redefinition of the public sphere now that women were officially recognised as part of that world. (These two strands would be referred to as 'New' and 'Old' Feminism later in the decade.) There was no sense that the struggle was over, but a distinct perception that the nature of the struggle would change.

Suffragists were fully aware of the way that the struggle for the vote, suffragism, had eclipsed the other aspirations of the women's movement before 1918. They were also aware of the problems that might occur once this central focus had been at least partially removed. Articles in *The Freewoman* just before the war had criticised the suffrage movement for its emphasis on the vote which, it was argued, had restricted the scope of analysis of the oppression of women and prescriptions for change.[3] Yet if we read the words of suffragists it is apparent that for them the vote was so profoundly associated with the oppression of women that it was impossible to speak of one without the other. As Sandra Holton has cogently expressed it: 'votes for women carried a psychological, ideological and cultural significance that went well beyond its formal political meaning, or practical utility.'[4] The achievement of enfranchisement in principle had momentous symbolic meaning; it also released the energies of women in other directions. In a reflective and discerning article in March 1920, *The Woman's Leader* took a long-term view of the history of women on a world scale, concluding that the oppression of women had been 'modified very little' since 'the dawn of history'. Turning to 'this particular country', the writer asserted: 'the possession of the vote . . . is a finer weapon than we have ever possessed; even before we actually held it in our hands we were made to feel its power, and at the moment our consciousness of that power is almost overwhelming.' Yet she also maintained that the 'tremendous and outstanding victory' of the suffrage 'carries with it a peculiar danger of its own . . . It compelled us to concentrate all our force, all our hope, all our enthusiasm, upon a single, narrow front. *It immensely simplified the women's movement.*' Suffragists during this intense period, she argued, had not had to make any 'effort of thought beyond that which was necessary to secure the best possible straightforward campaign'. As a result it seemed to such women – and she reckoned they would be the younger ones who had known no other period of suffrage activity – 'it seemed the battle had been won. It hadn't, of course, it was only the immediate objective that had been won; a brilliant strategic position.' Now suffragists had to make choices as to where to put their energies, and two dangers loomed. The first was that 'the fighting forces of the women's movement may fail, owing to the vastness and diversity of their front, to see that front as a whole: the danger that a section may become isolated and in its isolation make a separate peace'. The second danger was greater: 'that this precious weapon of the franchise, upon whose organisation so many years of concentrated force may have been spent, may lose its significance'.[5]

Did the suffrage movement in the 1920s fall victim to these perils? Some historians have described the interwar women's movement in terms which would suggest that it did. Susan Kingsley Kent has contended that while the 'legal barriers excluding women from public life were being dismantled, the institutional practices enforcing separate spheres came to be replaced by psychological ones'.[6] Hilda Kean has described 'feminist groups' in the 1920s as 'small and completely separate from each other',[7] and Martin Pugh has taken a lofty view, cautioning against making judgements concerning the impact of women's enfranchisement too soon, but using terms such as 'stagnation', 'loss of momentum' and 'organisational diaspora'.[8] In contrast, Cheryl Law, Clare Eustance and Maggie Morgan have studied the 'diaspora' and have found women's organisations to be both thriving and collaborative.[9]

Each of these historians offers a different perspective on the women's movement of the 1920s: their words echo those of contemporary voices which will be heard in this chapter. We can hear Susan Kingsley Kent in Cicely Hamilton; Cheryl Law in Winifred Holtby; Martin Pugh in Ray Strachey; Maggie Morgan in Margery Corbett Ashby. Here I will tell another story of postwar suffrage. I will place the viewpoints of a number of active feminists in the context of the landscape drawn by these historians. These are the women whose voices you will hear. Ray Strachey, who was born in 1887, was primarily committed after the war to the achievement of equality in employment for women, and was active in the NUSEC and the London Society for Women's Service. (She was probably the author of *The Woman's Leader* article quoted above, judging from her review of Millicent Garrett Fawcett's history of the suffrage movement from 1911–1918 published by the paper a week later.) Helena Swanwick (born 1869) was the first editor of *The Common Cause*: during and after the war she devoted her time to organisations concerned with peace. Eleanor Rathbone (born 1872) had also been a leading member of the NUWSS before the war and was to become President of the NUSEC when Millicent Garrett Fawcett retired from that post in 1919. She worked closely in the twenties with Eva Hubback (born 1886), NUSEC's parliamentary secretary. Cicely Hamilton (born 1872) had been a suffragette and active in the Women's Freedom League: after the war she was a widely published writer and journalist. She and Margaret Rhondda (born 1883) had also been active members of the Women's Social and Political Union (WSPU) and after the war were founder members of the Six Point Group. Rhondda financed *Time & Tide*, which was launched in March 1920. Margery Corbett Ashby (born 1882) had like Ray Strachey combined political activism with motherhood, and was President of the International Woman Suffrage Alliance in the 1920s. The voices of a new generation of feminists will also be heard: Vera Brittain (born 1896), Winifred Holtby (born 1898) and Naomi Mitchison (born 1897), all three of them politically active novelists and journalists. Naomi Mitchison's voice will be heard in correspondence with her aunt, Elizabeth Haldane (born 1862), who was also

269

a writer and had been active before and during the war in a variety of voluntary projects, including suffrage.

THE IMPACT OF WAR

The First World War did not destroy the suffrage movement. The general expectation that the war would be short led to a pause in suffrage activities in the last months of 1914 and in 1915, but 1916 saw a resurgence of activity and the establishment of a consultative committee of twenty-three suffrage societies in March of that year. The inclusion of women in the Representation of the People Act which was passed in February 1918 was, Cheryl Law has argued convincingly, the result of the 'continuation of suffrage and women's rights activities throughout the Great War'.[10] Nevertheless, the widespread movement involving thousands of women did to some extent disperse, and for many activists the war replaced the suffrage as the central focus of their thought and effort. This was especially the case for women who brought the women's peace movement into existence, and for those who worked as volunteers, civil servants, doctors, nurses, on the land and in the armed services. For many suffragists the peace movement became the central focus of their activities. For one of these, Helena Swanwick, the drive to dedicate herself to peace was as compelling as her sense when she joined the suffrage movement that 'I could do no other', but whereas in suffrage there had been 'unquenchable hope and buoyant comradeship, there was now a rending pity, a horror of black darkness, and in my brain, almost physically audible at times and never ceasing, something like a monotonous bell for ever tolling: "Wicked! Wicked! Wickedly silly! Cruel! Silly! Silly! Silly!"' When the war ended she was unable to celebrate: 'I seemed to be crying all the time inside, and I had to hold myself tight.' Enfranchisement did not lift this pall for her: 'though, of course, I used my vote, it was with no hope and no rejoicing.'[11] In 1918, Cicely Hamilton was working in a hospital near the Western Front: 'At the moment of official enfranchisement . . . I didn't care a button for my vote; and, rightly or wrongly, I have always imagined that the government gave it me in much the same mood as I received it.'[12]

Given the destructiveness of war, and the changes in the structure of women's lives during wartime, it is not surprising that there followed a period of conservatism in the literal meaning of that word. The threat that war posed to the lives of men and women and to the social structures led to an intensification of pronatalist anxieties, and a widespread determination to 'reconstruct' society after the war. Although the ideology of reconstruction was to some extent informed by a desire to return to an ideal of prewar stability informed by nostalgia, it was also and at the same time an aspiration for change. As Margaret Rhondda wrote in her autobiography of the postwar period:

> We found ourselves in an utterly changed world ... We could not, even had we wished, join this new, comparatively sane world on the jagged edges of the one that had broken off five years before – this new one was quite a different place. The war had broken down the barriers and customs and conventions. It had left us curiously free.[13]

There was uncertainty about what the changes could and should be. Naomi Mitchison, who was twenty-one when the war ended, wrote to her aunt, Elizabeth Haldane:

> You have still a balance for your life: all that incredible pre-war period when things seemed in the main still settled, just moving solidly and calmly like a glacier towards all sorts of progress. But we have had the bottom of things knocked out completely, we have been sent reeling into chaos.[14]

The sense Mitchison expresses of the war creating a lacuna between generations of women may well be significant in the dispersal of feminists in the period after the war. All women experienced the war, but there appears in the writings of the younger generation an assumption that their own experience was categorically different. Mitchison's correspondence with Elizabeth Haldane, that between Margaret Rhondda and Winifred Holtby, that between Ray Strachey and her daughter Barbara, bear witness to different generations of women struggling to understand each other. There is an awareness of different experiences, a sense of separation which often seemed to be rooted in the war. An acute awareness of the legacy of the older generation is captured in a letter from Vera Brittain to Evelyn Sharp:

> You have always fought so bravely for all the things I care for most, that at times I felt almost moved to tears by the thought of how much my generation owed to the fighters of yours, and how little gratitude we generally show for it.[15]

The younger generation of feminists recognised the valour of those who had campaigned for the vote over so many years, but they also asserted their own desires, their own responsibilities which could be different in a different historical context. Naomi Mitchison wrote to her aunt:

> we have to learn to try and make a world for ourselves, basing it as far as possible on love and awareness, mental and bodily because it seems to us that all the repression and formulae, all the cutting off of part of experience, which perhaps looked sensible and even right in those calm years, have not worked.[16]

There is a hint in these words of the influence of the ideas of psycho-analysis, or those sexologists whose ideology has been seen as so destructive of feminism by Sheila Jeffreys and Susan Kingsley Kent. Jeffreys has argued that 'feminist theory was undermined by the creation of a new prescription of correct female and male sexual behaviour with all the authority of science'.[17] Kingsley Kent focuses specifically on the part played by the First World War:

> War became, in many accounts, a metaphor for gender and sexual relations. The resolution of conflict through mutual, pleasurable sexual experiences within marriage was regarded by many sexologists and sex reformers as a means of reducing the threat of war by removing the sexual repressions and tensions that, as they often implied and sometimes asserted outright, helped to bring it about.[18]

This is a seductive story. Many women's lives in the interwar period bear witness to the desire for peaceful, productive lives which included a satisfying sexual relationship with a man. The losses associated with war contributed to the intensity of this desire. The increasing emphasis on sexuality and the use of the concept of frigidity in such a way as to undermine the confidence of the spinster is well documented. But this process was not dependent on the war: sexology, as Jeffreys attests, was developing before the war. Moreover, it is only one story. The lives and writings of other women demonstrate resistance to pressures on them to conform. I will argue later in this chapter that the desire for independence was for feminists in the twenties as significant as and more durable than the desire to appease.

A STRIP OF PAVEMENT OVER THE ABYSS

Kent's argument about the impact of war is based on the presumption that the demand for the vote as expressed in the pre-war movement represented a radical critique of the gender system. This is only one way of looking at an immensely varied and complex movement. The complexity and the extent of the suffragist demands became more apparent after partial enfranchisement. Kent's depiction of the feminist movement of the twenties as 'circumscribed', and characterised by an obsession with 'maternity and motherhood' and a 'nervous hesitation between "equality" and "difference"', so that it lacked the ability to 'exist and operate effectively'[19] fails to recognise both the way the demand for the vote had simplified an intricate web of feminist demands, and the particular political context in which suffragists were living and campaigning in the 1920s.

In her autobiography Cicely Hamilton was to describe the postwar years as 'years of reaction, often savage and insensate, against the discipline and over-close union that the period of war had imposed on us; the years of disillusion and hope falsified'.[20] Hamilton's sense of disillusionment is one that was not, of course, peculiar to feminists. The First World War undermined the confidence in Western civilisation of people throughout Europe: the image of life as a 'strip of pavement over the abyss'[21] which Virginia Woolf used in her diary at the end of 1920, catches the sense of precariousness which is apparent in the thinking and writing of many at the time. It seemed that women had achieved a foothold in parliamentary politics just when that structure was ceasing to inspire confidence. On 25 June 1920 a leading article in *The Woman's Leader* was entitled: 'Is the End of Parliamentary Government at Hand?'

The sombre tone of articles in *The Woman's Leader* in 1920 reflects the sobering experience of the suffrage movement in the two years which had passed since the Representation of the People Act had granted limited female suffrage. The Act had rapidly been followed by an election in which only one woman candidate, Constance Markiewicz, was successful: she had gained a seat for Sinn Fein that she had never had any intention of taking. The 1919 Restoration of Pre-War Practices Act led to the rapid expulsion of women from jobs and, in the Civil Service, the demotion of women in order to reserve the better-paid posts for men. Lady Rhondda, President of the Women's Industrial League, who led a deputation to the Prime Minister in protest, pointed out that the women civil servants were better trained and more efficient than the men who were replacing them, and that many were widows with families to support.[22] Unsatisfied with the efforts of existing feminist organisations, Rhondda joined with others to form the Six Point Group in February 1921. The manifesto of the new group referred to 'a period of stagnation' which had followed partial enfranchisement, and urged women 'to use their newly won power with energy and vigour to achieve a set of overdue reforms.'[23]

There was a crucial enmeshing of anxieties over the postwar economic instability with the uneasiness about women's newly established place in the political world. Billie Melman's study of the discourse on women in the Rothermere Press provides an astute analysis of this process. The terms in which the *Daily Mail* had welcomed the prospect of women's partial enfranchisement on 26 November 1918 are revealing:

> The need for association of women in the deliberation and government of the national affairs was never greater than now ... The protective instinct of women is equally at enmity with all those disruptive and destructive tendencies which may seek to introduce a new social order.[24]

Women were thus expected to prevent disruption and destruction: it is not surprising then, that when political instability occurred, this was also seen as the responsibility of women. It was young women who bore the political brunt of the resulting hostility in the paper's opposition to the enfranchisement of the 'flapper', but the source of the anxiety which emerges most forcefully in the early 1920s, is the numerical imbalance between the sexes. As the demobilisation of four million men took place, so women active in the public economic sphere were seen by the *Daily Mail* as a threat to men:

> The human race is going through an evolutionary process which some hundred years ago or more was taken by that highly organised society of hive-bees. Mankind is going to move towards a state in which there will be a small proportion of mother-women to maintain the race, and a host of male drones. They will be supported by the labour of an immense number of sterile female workers. Men will be utterly ousted.[25]

The reference to 'sterile women' was part of the particular hostility to the spinster which was such a visible feature of the interwar years. This hostility was intensified by the disquiet arising from knowledge of the way war had physically mutilated and psychologically damaged many men. In contrast to the deformed male, young women were described as fit, muscular, verging on the androgynous and threateningly confident. The 'unnatural' appearance of such women was seen to be the cause of infertility: 'this change to a more neutral type . . . can be accomplished only at the expense of the integrity of her sexual organs'.[26] Young women were described as refusing to 'undertake the proper and natural employment' that was awaiting them.[27] Their unnatural employment was seen to be threatening men's employment and their masculinity.

In the mid-1920s, the conflict which came to a head in the General Strike of 1926 shifted the focus of the right-wing press from gender to class. The hostility to younger women again surfaced in the period from April 1927 to the autumn of 1928 as the threat of woman's full enfranchisement and thus her numerical supremacy in the electorate became a reality. The headlines of the *Daily Mail* on 16 June 1928 read:

Flapper Issue Resumed
Election Swamped by Women
Conservative Alarm at Flapper Vote Results
Men Outnumbered Everywhere[28]

The potential threat from women was enmeshed with the threat of socialism. The two threats to the status quo were brought together by Marion Phillips in her editorial for the May 1929 issue of *Labour Woman* in a powerful extension of the discourse of women as conservers of the race. She wrote of the new woman voter in the election of 1929:

You can, as I say, call her a flapper if you want to be petty and stupid. I should prefer to call her the ruler of our destinies, for that is what she is today. In her small, strong hands rests the future of us all. She is, this new citizen of ours, the arbiter of fate in the coming General Election.[29]

LOSING SIGHT OF ONE ANOTHER

The increasing diversity of images of women to be found in this period provides an antidote to the tendency in the nineteenth century to place women in one category under the umbrella title 'the woman question'. Sandra Holton has argued persuasively that within an agreed framework, prewar suffragists put forward largely unexamined claims for the vote ranging from those based on essentialist views of women, to those which were deliberately humanist.[30] I will argue here that the different bases for claims were to become crucial when women were choosing where to put their energies, or advocating priorities in public policy.

After 1918 women did indeed, as Cheryl Law puts it, seek 'to improve their lives, as wives and mothers, as workers, and by extending their scope of involvement throughout society'.[31] But, as they knew, the interests of the paid woman worker did not necessarily coincide with those of wives and mothers, and extending their scope was neither simple nor easy. The two most crucial divergences of interest revolved around the issues of protective legislation and equal pay. Legislation which gave women shorter hours of work, and prevented women from doing night work and from working, for example, underground in mines or in contact with toxic paints, was seen by equalitarians as treating women as lesser beings, and in the same category as children. As one contributor to a debate in NUSEC put it, 'the moment a woman engages in a "gainful occupation" she becomes as fragile as a humming bird's egg'.[32] Defenders of such legislation were to be found particularly among women in the labour movement who saw it as recognising women's particular needs, but also defended it on the grounds that protection should be given to all workers, and it was better to make a start with women if that was what was politically possible.[33]

No suffragist argued against equal pay, but for Eleanor Rathbone, one of the most articulate of those whose views would in the mid-1920s be termed 'New' feminist, demands for equal pay ignored the needs of wives and mothers, and she pressed for the prior introduction of what was then known as family endowment. The campaign for the introduction of family endowment assumed that many, even most, women were dependent during the years in which they brought up children on a man's wages. But it also challenged the idea of the family wage, the assumption that a man's pay should include sufficient for the support of his family. The removal of this aspect of pay would make the demand for equal pay feasible and fair.[34]

275

Susan Pedersen has demonstrated what happened to such 'difference-based' arguments when they were 'pitted against the male-breadwinner norm as an organizing vision for social policy'. The social policy initiative Pedersen examines is the introduction of the Widows', Orphans' and Old Age Contributory Pensions in 1925. The pressure groups had wanted pensions for all widows, but the Act which emerged was based on the premise that a woman's access to benefit was mediated through her husband's insurance benefit. Pedersen describes the resistance of the government and the Civil Service to any idea of a 'separate but equal' status for women, and hence the continued growth of a welfare state system which was 'profoundly gendered'.[35] Contemporary suffragists were aware of the limitations of the Act, but, as with suffrage, they hoped it would be a first step. Moreover, they did not have our awareness of the way social reform could militate against women's wider interests. Perhaps, as Susan Pedersen has said of Eleanor Rathbone, their perception of the state was naive.[36] Rathbone tended to conflate the concepts 'community' and 'society' with 'the state'.[37] Certainly suffragists had an optimistic faith that the gaining of political power by women would bring with it remedies to social evils. One of the roots of nineteenth-century suffrage was women's recognition of their duty and responsibility to others, especially the disadvantaged, but this did not mean that they were unable to make the distinction between social reform and feminism.[38] Mary Stocks, who was a 'New feminist', acknowledged later that the measure for Widows' Pensions was part of a 'tide of social reform'. But the other measures achieved in the first half of the twenties were, in her view, feminist reform.[39]

The most significant of these measures were the Married Women's (Maintenance) Act which gave women a legal claim to maintenance under a separation order; the Law of Property Act which placed husband and wife on equal footing in the inheritance of property from each other; the Matrimonial Causes Amendment Act of 1923, which allowed a wife grounds for divorce equal to those of a husband; and the Guardianship of Infants Act of 1925, which provided for equal rights between male and female guardians. These measures can be seen as social reform, but they were also concerned with equality: suffragists at the time were happy to take credit for them. Martin Pugh concludes of this 'record of legislation' that it was 'formidable', and that 'it is difficult to escape the conclusion that it is attributable to the effect of women's enfranchisement in altering the priorities of the politicians'. Pugh reckons that the range of topics covered by the legislation is partly explained by the 'redeployment of efforts that had previously been focussed almost exclusively on the franchise question'.[40] However, it is also the case that the achievement of these reforms was unopposed by all three political parties precisely because they did not challenge the prevailing and arguably strengthening ideology which saw women as primarily if not exclusively wives and mothers. Legislation for which feminists pressed which did not get on the statute book concerned women as workers, as members of the House of Lords, as taxpayers. It was awareness of the continued resistance to equal status which led to the resignation of the majority of the executive committee of the NUSEC in 1927. Anxiety that social responsibility would become the predominant concern of the NUSEC was expressed by those who resigned. One of them – Dorothy Balfour – went further and accused her opponents of accepting the 'theory of Equality only in so far as it will help towards the achievement of the particular Social Reforms advocated by its supporters'.[41]

Eleanor Rathbone had been arguing since the achievement of partial enfranchisement that feminism was not limited to demands for equality, where equality meant 'identity'.[42] Accusations of not being properly feminist have been levelled against her by historians: she has been described as furthering 'those discourses which insisted upon motherhood as women's primary and even exclusive function in life',[43] and accused of promoting family endowment in order 'to ensure women did not work in certain industries'.[44] I see Rathbone's position differently. Differences in wages, she believed, were the result of 'the arrangement' which led the 'male parent' to bear 'the cost of raising future generations'.[45] Only if that perspective was shifted by the introduction of family endowment would it be possible to argue successfully for equal pay. She was also aware of the strength and depth of resistance to any move which would make women no longer economically dependent on their husbands, which for her was the main motive behind the introduction of family endowment.[46] It was indeed partly the feminist challenge inherent in family endowment which meant that it was accepted wholeheartedly by no political party, despite the efforts of many women who were politically active between the wars.

THE POLITICAL FEVER

Cheryl Law has argued convincingly that 'in 1919 there was an impressive network of organizations marshalled to promote and protect women's rights during the years of reconstruction'.[47] She and Clare Eustance have also demonstrated that these organisations co-operated with each other. Nevertheless, they were not, unlike the prewar suffrage societies, agreed on a single goal. Unsurprisingly, given the broad front of the demands of the women's movement, the number of members active in the successor bodies to the old suffrage societies dropped after 1918. One of the reasons for this was that women who were intensely interested in the practice of politics were more inclined to concentrate their activities in the political parties than the suffrage organisations after 1918. Before 1918, women's lack of the vote, together with the distinctive appeal of the suffrage movement, gave those organisations the edge over political parties. There had been links between

⌐ists and the political parties; perhaps most notably a bond had devel-
⌐ed just before the war between the NUWSS and the Labour Party through
the Election Fighting Fund (EFF) established by the former body. Although
in 1920 there was an initiative by Jim Middleton, secretary of the Labour Party,
to persuade suffragists who had been heavily involved in the EFF before
1914 to work for the Labour Party after the war, this was within the context
of an increasingly antagonistic situation.[48] The links between suffragists and
the political parties had always been tense and in the postwar situation this
tension was exacerbated by the new political potential of women as voters.

Women were vitally important to the main political parties as voters and as
workers, but this did not, of course, mean that they were able to achieve
power within the parties or easily become MPs. The Labour Party constitution which was drawn up in 1918 allowed for individual membership and
constituency parties which gave women considerable scope for active participation. At the same time, a separate organisation for women within the
party, with its own separate hierarchy, was instituted. By 1929 over 1,800
women's sections had been created with over a quarter of a million members.
The women's sections and the separate Women's Conference constituted
both a space for women to develop their own political agenda, and a way of
marginalising women within the party. Pat Thane has described the struggle
that went on within the Labour Party between men and women, making it
clear that there was a fundamental division between their views, and that the
reason why 'the male vision usually won' was that women's views were
'blocked by the crude exercise of male power'.[49] By the late 1920s the
Conservative Party claimed to have 4,000 women's branches with a million
members: it both encouraged women's membership and controlled them in
much the same way.

When it came to selecting parliamentary candidates, women were rarely
chosen, the largest number before 1928 being forty-one (less than 3 per cent
of the total). Even then four out of five selected stood in constituencies where
there was no prospect of their being elected. There were strongly held views
among women as to how this situation could be improved. Marion Phillips
believed that the most effective way for women to use their vote was through
existing political structures and that this implied working exclusively in
those structures and alongside men. As Labour Party Women's Officer, she
discouraged party members from joining suffrage societies.[50] Women, in her
view, had to be patient. The prevailing view expressed in *Time & Tide* was
opposed to this, with increasing force as the decade progressed. In 1923 the
paper had forecast that it was the 'strength of non-party women's organisations which is likely to decide the amount of interest taken by the parties in
women's questions'.[51] In 1927, the paper asserted:

One subject of vital importance to women is almost completely
ignored by all parties – equal pay and equal opportunities for

women. Next to equal franchise it is, in fact, the most important question affecting women, and yet the party-woman seems hardly aware of its existence.[52]

This judgement demonstrated ignorance of the debates within the Labour Party but does reflect the failure of Labour women to get their demands on to the party's agenda.

Individual women struggled throughout the decade to represent women's interests within the political parties. Women such as Margery Corbett Ashby, who was active both in the NUSEC and the Liberal Party, were often stretched to the point of exhaustion. Corbett Ashby stood for parliament and was one among many women who experienced at first hand the difficulty women had in becoming MPs. Experience of this frustrating process was not such as to encourage many women to become politically active. Ray Strachey, however, revelled in political activities, unable to 'shake off' the 'political fever' as she put it, and was an enthusiastic candidate in 1918, 1922 and 1923. She stood as an Independent, unable to take on board the tenets of any of the political parties, and her candidature was doomed in the increasingly polarised politics of the postwar period. Another of Ray Strachey's handicaps was that she was the mother of small children. She was accused of neglecting her children in the 1922 election campaign, and in 1924 expressed relief not to be in parliament because her hands were so full with the children. Her letters to her mother bear witness to the push and pull she experienced between the pleasures of motherhood and of political activism and writing. In 1916 she pondered in a letter to her mother whether she would 'retire from public life when we get the vote. I hope so I'm sure, & yet, its extraordinarily interesting, & chockful of wickedness which is such fun.' Later she wondered: 'if I didn't have to attend to children & house & all the other distractions, I should enjoy the snatched moments of work so much? It is obvious I could have more of them; but would they be so precious? Its impossible to tell!'[53]

Strachey had the means to pay other women to look after her children, and later to send them away to school, leaving her with the freedom to be a political activist and writer. It was generally true that the division of labour between the sexes in the care of children was rarely challenged during this period and there is some justice in Dyhouse's judgement that this was at least partly because the middle classes could rely on paid labour to 'black their stoves for them'.[54] Certainly the responsibility of women for the domestic space, whether that meant working there or organising the work that took place, remained unchallenged as women continued to move into public spaces.

INDEPENDENT CITIZENS

The drive behind middle-class women's determination to combine mother-hood with work was fuelled by a combination of a desire for economic inde-pendence and a related sense that they could not fulfil their potential in the home. Eva Hubback's daughter reckoned that her mother worked because, as a widow, she had a family to support, but implies that her earnings were used to pay for 'things which made life significant for her, such as holidays and buying books'. She then adds that Eva 'needed to get outside her own home' because she disliked domestic tasks.[55] Margery Corbett Ashby wrote to her husband and son from the USA:

> I think of you both the whole time and miss you dreadfully. It seems wrong somehow to leave all the wealth of love you both shower on me and which makes me the happiest woman in the world. Yet on the other hand interesting work comes along and I am reluctant to lose the chance of seeing and learning new things from new people. I suppose like all of us I want to eat my cake and have it too.[56]

Liberal ideals such as economic independence and personal fulfilment crucially informed the thinking of Eleanor Rathbone. She had seen in the separation allowances paid to wives of serving men during the war the vital economic independence which women needed in order to be full human beings:

> There can be no real independence, whether for men or for women, without economic independence. Few of us can realise how con-stantly and subtly this half-conscious, but ever-present sense of the economic dependence of the woman upon the man corrodes her per-sonality, checks her development, and stunts her mind.[57]

Economic independence, Rathbone argued, conferred 'status'.[58] But there was more to the concept of independence than economic self-sufficiency. The first step to this independence of public action was the vote, *Time & Tide* argued, since for suffragists 'every kind of status both social and economic rests at bottom upon the political status'.[59] The autonomy which the eco-nomically dependent woman lacked could also be conferred on her by the vote. The rallying cry for the 1926 campaign for equal franchise was inde-pendence, and a leader in *Time & Tide*, considering the gaining of the vote in 1928, used the term parasite to describe all those who were unable to make unpopular decisions, something 'which neither men nor women find easy, but until people can do that they are not complete human beings'.[60] Ten years earlier, Rathbone had asserted that the vote would lead married women to 'recognise they have become persons – wholly, and not fractionally, as before. It will matter what they think, and it will matter enormously what they should think.'[61]

In a pamphlet published in 1924 the NUSEC referred to the vote as 'the key to citizenship' and demanded full franchise to enable women to enter 'into their rightful inheritance of responsible citizenship'.[62] Although the nature of women's claim to citizenship was contested, it was central to the demand for the right of women to vote. The concept of citizenship carried with it a freight of meanings at the centre of which was a relationship to the wider society: this relationship was powerfully significant for the women who supported the struggle for the vote. For some women active in philanthropy in the nineteenth century, it seemed possible fully to satisfy their desire to act as dutiful citizens in such endeavour. Philanthropy linked women's role as guardians of the family, the heart of the social order, to the public domain. Those who became suffragists felt that the lack of the vote curtailed the opportunities and the responsibilities of women as citizens. Once women had been partially enfranchised, the demands of their responsibilities as citizens could be considerable, especially where they were combined with bringing up children and with paid work.

In Eleanor Rathbone's view citizenship required effort and commitment. Her speeches as President of NUSEC are full of exhortations to women to be politically active.[63] Rathbone was responsible for the setting up of the first Women's Citizen's Association (WCA) in Liverpool in 1913. The express intention of this and subsequent associations was the fostering of a sense of citizenship in women. In 1917 it was decided to establish the WCA as a national body with local branches. Some local suffrage societies in the following year transformed themselves into WCAs, and leading suffragists expressed concern that the National Union would lose its identity or its members to the newer organisation. In 1924 the two bodies merged: it is clear that they catered for very much the same constituency of middle-class activists. Eleanor Rathbone had hoped that the WCAs would be popular places for working-class women to learn about the responsibilities and possibilities of their citizenship.[64] Working-class women, however, were in much larger numbers exercising their citizenship and developing their political consciousness in other organisations than the NUSEC, the WFL and the Six Point Group.

INCLUSIVE FEMINISM

The largest women's organisation in the twenties was the National Federation of Women's Institutes (NWFI) which reached a quarter of a million members by 1925 and did not drop below that level. The establishment of the first institute in 1915 was a radical move, both because it involved rural women, who had arguably never been organised before, and because of the development of a democratic and stable structure which has lasted to this day. Maggie Morgan has argued convincingly that the WIs successfully challenged the perception of many women that the political process was alien to their lives, and turned this recognition into political activity. She offers persuasive evidence that the women in the NFWI 'struggled in national political terms and locally to improve the material circumstances of women's lives', and that they 'provided a space for women to fight the internalization of male domination and to adopt an alternative value system'.[65] The NUSEC recognised both the appeal to women and the political potential of the institutes when discussing the future of their own organisation after the final achievement of the vote. In 1928 members of NUSEC were encouraged to form 'guilds' in small towns on the same lines as the institutes which were all based on villages.[66] The Women's Co-operative Guild was smaller – numbering some 67,000 by 1930 – but even more obviously political and feminist in its demands and its outlook. The guilds spoke for the consumer, and aimed to translate the needs and demands of married women into political programmes and campaigns. As in the nineteenth century, many suffragists embraced such developments, taking an inclusive perspective, seeking to 'address the needs of as wide a body of women as possible'.[67] Naomi Mitchison expresses this inclusive perspective vividly in a letter to Elizabeth Haldane. Politics, she wrote:

is dealing with people and groups of people in relation to one another and their material environment. What is wrong with that as a living occupation? The moral basis of politics goes down to our deepest roots, politics means danger and beauty, conversion and rebirth. It also means a lot of small, ordinary things – more dustbins and bathrooms for people who haven't got them, more leisure and more education for people who need them desperately.[68]

The one demand for which women from a wide variety of organisations worked together conspicuously was equal franchise. Efforts to achieve equal franchise were made throughout the period between the 1918 and 1928 Acts. By 1925, repeated rebuffs had led some suffragists to be exceedingly cautious in their estimates of likely success. Eva Hubback warned that 'Equal Franchise' was the reform advocated by the NUSEC which was least likely to be achieved. She noted that although Prime Minister Baldwin had committed himself to support for 'equal political rights' during the election campaign at the end of 1924, he was leading a party of which a third at least was opposed to equal franchise.[69] In the following year, however, equal franchise was the most urgent demand on the agenda of the NUSEC, the Women's Freedom League, the Six Point Group and the Women's International League for Peace and Freedom. Eva Hubback and Elizabeth Macadam, secretaries to the NUSEC, wrote a pamphlet protesting against the 'absurd anomalies which at present prevent three million women under the age of thirty, just because they are women, and two million above that age, because they are poor in this world's goods, from entering into their rightful inheritance of responsible citizenship'. They urged women with the vote not to become so absorbed in their own work as to forget the unenfranchised, and to campaign 'with some of the zeal and enthusiasm which characterized the long pre-war struggle for the vote'.[70]

Some of the prewar atmosphere of the suffrage movement was re-created in the years from 1926 to 1928. On 2 July 1926, 3,500 women from over forty societies marched from the Embankment to Hyde Park while Mrs Elliot Lyn flew over the marchers in an aeroplane. Speakers addressed the crowds from fifteen platforms, demanding equal franchise. An Equal Political Rights Campaign Committee with Margaret Rhondda in the chair was set up to co-ordinate the activities of the women's organisations. On 8 March of the following year, the Prime Minister at last agreed to see a deputation from the committee. Baldwin pleaded pressure of business from more urgent matters, so the lobbying by societies intensified. A letter from Eleanor Rathbone to Eva Hubback gives a taste of the pressure that was maintained on the government and MPs by women's organisations:

Dr. Jane Walker told us she had had a letter from Major Hill (most confidential) saying he knew *for certain* that the Government had decided on votes at twenty-one and that we had better do nothing ... Lady A. is worried because we are pressing for twenty-one: I reassured her that it was only on the tactical point. I surmise that possibly the government has switched round to twenty-five and is going to push that through, giving as their excuse that the Labour Party have refused the Conference, so that they are free to drop the idea of an agreed measure. The tremendous barrage in the Press in favour of twenty-five makes this probable. If it should turn out to be true, what shall we do about it? My idea is not to protest at the age, but make it perfectly clear that the one thing which concerns us is equal rights and that provided we are satisfied that the Government means business about that, the age on its merits does not concern us. If that happens, send an immediate wire saying if you have any suggestions differing from this; or telephone if you have detailed suggestions. I should get on to Rhondda at once if that happened and try to make her take the same line.[71]

On 13 April 1927, Baldwin announced that a Bill giving votes to women at the age of 21 would be introduced in the next session. The final debate in the House of Commons a year later was something of a celebration: there were just ten votes against the Bill which became law on 2 July 1928. *Time & Tide* acknowledged that it marked 'the end of an epoch', but added:

What about the exclusion of women from the House of Lords? What about the barring of women from the diplomatic service? What about the dismissal of women on marriage, and equal pay for equal work in the Civil Service? What about the whole body of restrictive legislation? We are a long way from equality of treatment between men and women even so far as actual legal enactments go.[72]

THE POWER OF WOMEN

It is perhaps too easy to forget that women did achieve a measure of power in the 1920s. And here women's experience during the war, as well as the winning of partial enfranchisement, is significant. Clare Eustance's exploration of the activities of the WFL during the war, leads her to conclude that they 'created an environment where women were able to take effective power particularly in community affairs and local government. Many of the initial moves in this direction had already been made prior to August 1914, and the war had served as a catalyst, rather than a cause, of these developments.'[73] Leading suffragists from all strands of the movement achieved positions at least of influence and sometimes of power during the war: for example, women volunteers involved in the Soldiers' and Sailors' Family Association, notably Eleanor Rathbone, administered the separation allowances granted to the families of serving men as agents of the War Office. Marion Phillips and Mary Macarthur were leading members of the Central Committee for Women's Employment and it was her experience on that committee which converted Violet Markham to suffrage. The Women's Services and the newly instituted Women's Police were run by women.

After the war, these women continued to be active in public life and some became, in the words of Mary Stocks, 'statutory' women who constituted 'a kind of stage army appearing on one government assignment after another'. Stocks wrote: 'The country as a whole teemed with able and public-spirited women, those who sojourned in the "corridors of power" did not know who or where they were and took little trouble to find out.'[74] This was undoubtedly the case, but it is fair to acknowledge that women did enter those corridors, albeit in small numbers. The Sex Disqualification (Removal) Act of 1919 granted general legislative freedom from disqualification by gender and, although it was later severely restricted by the continued power of local authorities to dismiss married women and by protective legislation which actually increased the limitations on women's employment opportunities, did make it possible for women to become JPs. Most of those appointed were middle-class, and the job was a voluntary one, but twelve of the original appointments were of members of the Women's Co-operative Guild. Again, the numbers of women involved were small and by 1930 women represented only 9 per cent of existing magistrates.

The percentage of members of parliament who were women was, of course, even smaller, not even reaching 1 per cent before 1928. Cheryl Law has pointed out that not enough attention has been paid to the activities of women in Parliament in the 1920s. What is already apparent is that they made a distinctive – and varied – mark on parliamentary life. Nancy Astor, the first woman to take her seat, after a by-election in 1919, was cautiously welcomed by suffragists who had assumed that the first woman MP would be 'one of ourselves ... a woman of tried political experience, knowledge and wisdom', but by 1923 was commended in the pages of *The Woman's Leader* as 'doing all the work that we had dreamed that our first woman in parliament would do'.[75] She was followed by Margaret Wintringham who also proved to be a supporter of women's interests. In 1923, eight women were elected, including the first four Labour women MPs. Ellen Wilkinson, who had been a suffragist, was to prove a staunch feminist in and out of parliament, but the careers of Margaret Bondfield and Susan Lawrence, who became the first women ministers, demonstrate the desire of some women to act in parliament exactly as men did.

The suffrage movement was concerned centrally to get women into Parliament. Its motives for doing so were feminist. However, not all feminist aims could be achieved through the gaining of the suffrage, although some prewar suffragists wrote and perhaps believed that they could; postwar suffragists were more realistic, whether, like Elizabeth Robins and Dora Russell, they wrote in terms of a sex war, or, like Eleanor Rathbone, concentrated on small battles. The article which opens this chapter demonstrates the knowing of the women of the period.

CONCLUSION

The activities of the interwar suffragists and feminists have been censured by historians from different angles. Susan Kingsley Kent believes that '"New Feminism", by accepting the terms of the larger culture, by putting forward a politics of sexual difference, found itself severely constrained in its ability to advocate equality and justice for women.'[76] She mourns what she sees as the weakening in the interwar period of the prewar challenge to separate spheres of ideology.[77] Martin Pugh, on the other hand, sees the roots of the failures of postwar feminism in the ideology of prewar feminists:

> Women had capitalised effectively on the differences rather than the similarities between the sexes. Domesticity had been used as a Trojan Horse; but once inside the citadel it proved difficult to escape from the successful stratagem.[78]

Claire Eustance and Cheryl Law give much more recognition both to the difficulties facing interwar suffragists and to their achievements. They draw

285

attention to the way the sheer number of new women's groups campaigning on specific issues which emerged in the twenties threatened the membership levels of the earlier women's suffrage organisations. Eustance has also noted the 'range and diversity' of questions discussed in the WFL before the war, and looks at 'the ways in which an environment was created which was firmly enmeshed in their understanding of the political process'.[79] Her study crosses what has tended to be a boundary in studies of women's suffrage: where other historians stop or begin in 1914 or 1918, she covers the period 1880–1930. She sees the period as a whole, and does not distinguish any marked change in strategy or ideology. From this perspective the twenties saw the continuation of a process which had begun before the war: women were continuing to move outwards from the suffrage issue to other campaigns, as indeed they had done since the 1860s. As Eustance points out: 'It was a necessary process that in campaigning for their right to vote they also identified their interests and concerns in women and inequality. For many such interests did not only come out of the suffrage campaign, but had been present long before.'[80] She also identifies the cost of this diversity: 'the development of a plethora of political identities among women who had seemed so united in their demands for women's suffrage.'[81] Moreover, her analysis leads her to conclude that:

> suffragists and feminists in the 1910s and 1920s called for and acted on perceptions of women's unity, while at the same time acknowledging women's diversity. Thus their attempts to change gender relations in political, economic and social life were fraught with contradictions. It is this process which provides a key to understanding how women developed their political identities in the enfranchised world.[82]

At the beginning of this chapter I demonstrated that suffragists were well aware of the problems facing them after the partial achievement of the vote in 1918: the danger that the 'vastness and diversity' of the women's movement would lead to a failure to see it as a whole. This is, perhaps, another way of describing what Eustance has identified as 'the development of a plethora of political identities'. Certainly, the women's movement was less circumscribed, and the dispersal of suffragists which resulted from the extension of their ability to choose the nature of their involvement in the public world makes it more difficult to write of a single movement. Whether diversity can be equated with a weakening of 'the cause' or its expansion is a moot point.

The second danger, that the vote 'might lose its significance', may also have loomed over the twenties in two senses. Women's experience of politics in the ten years between the two Acts, while it did not necessarily lead to any lack of energy in total, took the edge off the optimism as to what could be achieved by the vote. The hope that women's right to equal pay and financial independence would be recognised was not realised, and the struggles to achieve equal pay and even equal franchise were frustrating and slow. Yet there is a ring of confidence, despite setbacks and continuing misogyny, and much agreement between feminists. Moreover, the nature of the changes demanded by feminists and suffragists contained within it what Carole Pateman has termed 'Wollstonecraft's dilemma'.[83] They demanded full citizenship and its concomitant equality before the law, using the language of liberalism which asserted the need for independence and autonomy. But they also sought recognition of women's difference, in particular their primary responsibility for children. In the interwar period more women came to feel that they must make a choice – at least of where they put their main efforts – between these two paths to citizenship. Pateman's solution to the dilemma, to take as the starting point of democratic citizenship the assumption that the 'primary task of all citizens is to ensure the welfare of each living generation of citizens is secured',[84] was, I would suggest, the position taken by the advocates of family endowment. The problems of developing such a proposal in practice are as intractable now as they were in the 1920s.

Suffragists in the twenties were well aware of the profoundly complex issues of gender and power which faced them and still face us. They were on the one hand determined that 'women's contribution to national life' should be 'a very distinctive contribution' and should 'make a very great difference'.[85] And they were aware of the pressures which the struggle to attain this placed on the women's movement. A member of the NUSEC wrote in 1927, when the executive was divided, of her recommendation for 'securing unity in diversity'. The 'various sides' should 'affirm . . . their own position', but 'refrain from denying the modicum of truth in their opponents' positions. *But do let us hold to our affirmitives* [sic], and let us all be neither old nor new feminists, but just present day feminists with a glorious tradition to follow, to add to, and to hand on.'[86]

NOTES

1 *The Woman's Leader*, 6 February 1920, p. 4.
2 Ibid.
3 L. Garner, *Stepping stones to women's liberty* (London, Heinemann, 1984), pp. 62–63.
4 S. Holton, The suffragist and the 'average woman', *Women's History Review*, 1, 1, 1992, p. 13.
5 *The Woman's Leader*, 12 March 1920, p. 125.
6 S. Kingsley Kent, *Making peace: the reconstruction of gender in interwar Britain* (Princeton, Princeton University Press, 1993), p. 139.
7 H. Kean, Searching for the past in present defeat: the construction of historical and political identity in British feminism in the 1920s and 1930s, *Women's History Review*, 3, 1, 1994, p. 64.

8 M. Pugh, *Women and the women's movement in Britain 1914–1959* (Basingstoke, Macmillan, 1992), p. 312; The impact of women's enfranchisement in Britain, in C. Daley and M. Nolan (eds), *Suffrage and beyond: international feminist perspectives* (Auckland, Auckland University Press, 1994), pp. 313, 324, 326.

9 V. C. Law, The women's cause is won, PhD thesis, University of London, 1992; C. Eustance, 'Daring to be free': the evolution of women's political identities in the Women's Freedom League, PhD thesis, University of York, 1994; M. Morgan, The Women's Institute movement – the acceptable face of feminism?, in S. Oldfield (ed.), *This working-day world: women's lives and culture(s) in Britain 1914–1945* (London, Taylor & Francis, 1994).

10 Law, The women's cause is won, p. 433.

11 H. Swanwick, *I have been young* (London, Gollancz, 1935), pp. 307–308.

12 C. Hamilton, *Life errant* (London, Dent, 1935), p. 67.

13 M. Rhondda, *This was my world* (Basingstoke, Macmillan, 1933), p. 294.

14 no date (Haldane Papers, National Library of Scotland, Acc. 9186(1)).

15 16 June 1933 (Nevinson Papers, Bodleian Library).

16 (Haldane Papers, 6033 f. 295.)

17 S. Jeffreys, *The spinster and her enemies* (London, Pandora, 1985), p. 4.

18 Kent, *Making peace*, p. 140.

19 Ibid., pp. 140–141.

20 Hamilton, *Life errant*, p. 186.

21 Virginia Woolf, *A writer's diary* (London, Hogarth Press, 1953), 25 October 1920.

22 Pugh, *Women and the women's movement*, p. 60.

23 *Time & Tide*, 25 February 1921, p. 215.

24 Cited in B. Melman, *Women in the popular imagination in the twenties* (Basingstoke, Macmillan, 1988), p. 17.

25 8 August 1921, ibid., p. 19.

26 *Daily Express*, 12 November 1924, ibid., p. 23.

27 *Daily Mail*, 19 November 1924, ibid., p. 26.

28 *Daily Mail*, 16 June 1928.

29 *Labour Woman*, March 1929, p. 34.

30 S. Holton, *Feminism and democracy: women's suffrage and reform politics, 1900–1918* (Cambridge, Cambridge University Press, 1986), p. 28.

31 Law, The women's cause is won, p. 434.

32 *The Woman's Leader*, 3 September 1926, p. 279.

33 J. Alberti, *Beyond suffrage: feminists in war and peace, 1914–1928* (Basingstoke, Macmillan, 1989), pp. 174–180.

34 E. Rathbone, The remuneration of women's services, in V. Gollancz (ed.), *The making of women: Oxford essays in feminism* (London, Allen & Unwin, 1917); *The disinherited family* (Bristol, Falling Wall Press, 1986). The Family Endowment Committee, *Equal pay and the family* (London, Headley Bros, 1918).

35 S. Pedersen, The failure of feminism in the making of the British welfare state, *Radical History Review*, 3, 1989, p. 87.

36 S. Pedersen, Gender, welfare and citizenship in Britain during the Great War, *American Historical Review*, 95, 4, 1990, p. 1004.

37 J. Alberti, *Eleanor Rathbone* (London, Sage, 1996), pp. 44–45.

38 Holton, *Feminism and democracy*, pp. 14–15.

39 M. Stocks, *Eleanor Rathbone* (London, Victor Gollancz, 1949), p. 112.

40 Pugh, *Women and the women's movement*, p. 110.

41 *The Woman's Leader*, 25 February 1927, p. 493.

42 *Common Cause*, 15 February 1918, p. 373.

43 Kent, *Making Peace*, p. 120.
44 Kean, Searching for the past in present defeat, p. 63.
45 E. Rathbone, *The problem of women's wages* (Liverpool, Northern Publishing, 1912), p. 23.
46 Family Endowment Committee, *Equal pay and the family*, p. 10.
47 Law, The women's victory is won, p. 140.
48 Alberti, *Beyond suffrage*, pp. 94–96.
49 P. Thane, The women of the British Labour party and feminism 1906–45, in H. Smith (ed.), *British feminism in the twentieth century* (Aldershot, Edward Elgar, 1990).
50 *The Woman's Leader*, 2 March 1923, p. 33.
51 *Time & Tide*, 15 June 1923, p. 607.
52 *Time & Tide*, 13 May 1927, p. 445.
53 Ray Strachey to Mary Berenson, 13 November 1924 (Smith Papers, Indiana University, Bloomington, Indiana); Ray Strachey to Pippa Strachey, 10 August 1924 (Fawcett Library Autograph Collection, 6c/276); Ray Strachey to Mary Berenson, 22 August 1916; 8 May 1931 (Smith Papers).
54 C. Dyhouse, *Feminism and the family in England* 1880–1939 (Oxford, Blackwell, 1989), p. 144.
55 D. Hopkinson, *Family inheritance: a life of Eva Hubback* (London, Staples Press, 1954), p. 84.
56 Margery Corbett Ashby to Brian Ashby (Corbett Ashby Papers, Fawcett Library, 13), 23 March 1925.
57 Family Endowment Committee, *Equal pay and the family*, p. 10.
58 *Common Cause*, 25 October 1918, p. 322.
59 *Time & Tide*, 29 January 1926, p. 123.
60 *Time & Tide*, 6 July 1928, p. 653.
61 *Common Cause*, 25 October 1918, p. 322.
62 Hopkinson, *Family inheritance*, p. 91.
63 E. Rathbone, *Milestones: presidential addresses* (Liverpool, National Union of Societies for Equal Citizenship, 1929).
64 *Common Cause*, 30 June 1916, p. 155.
65 Morgan, The Women's Institute movement, p. 38.
66 Proposed lines of expansion for the NUSEC (Fawcett Library, Box 341), December 1928.
67 Sandra Stanley Holton, *Suffrage days: stories from the women's suffrage movement* (London, Routledge, 1996), p. 18.
68 no date (Haldane Papers, Acc. 9186).
69 *The Woman's Leader*, 21 November 1924, p. 343.
70 Hopkinson, *Family inheritance*, p. 91.
71 Ibid., p. 93.
72 *Time & Tide*, 6 April 1928, p. 328.
73 Eustance, 'Daring to be free', p. 297.
74 M. Stocks, *My commonplace book* (London, Peter Davies, 1970), p. 165.
75 *The Woman's Leader*, 14 December 1923, p. 368.
76 Kent, *Making peace*, p. 141.
77 Ibid., p. 5.
78 Pugh, *Women and the women's movement*, p. 312.
79 Eustance, 'Daring to be free', p. 24.
80 Ibid., p. 30.
81 Ibid., pp. 24–25.
82 Ibid., p. 2.
83 C. Pateman, *The disorder of women* (Cambridge, Polity, 1989).

ιe, 'Equal citizenship', *The Woman's Leader*, 12 February 1920,

he Woman's Leader, 25 February 1927, p. 493.

INDEX

27322293R00173

Printed in Great Britain
by Amazon